DESERT STORM

DESERT STORM

A Forgotten War

*Alberto Bin, Richard Hill,
and Archer Jones*

PRAEGER

Westport, Connecticut
London

Library of Congress Cataloging-in-Publication Data

Bin, Alberto, 1957–
    Desert Storm : a forgotten war / Alberto Bin, Richard Hill, Archer
Jones.
      p.   cm.
    Includes bibliographical references (p.) and index.
    ISBN 0–275–96319–5 (alk. paper).—ISBN 0–275–96320–9 (pbk. :
alk. paper)
    1. Persian Gulf War, 1991. I. Hill, Richard, 1949– .
II. Jones, Archer, 1926– . III. Title.
DS79.72.B496   1998
956.7044'2—dc21   98–24040

British Library Cataloguing in Publication Data is available.

Library of Congress Catalog Card Number: 98–24040
ISBN: 0–275–96319–5
    0–275–96320–9 (pbk.)

First published in 1998

Praeger Publishers, 88 Post Road West, Westport, CT 06881
An imprint of Greenwood Publishing Group, Inc.

Printed in the United States of America

The paper used in this book complies with the
Permanent Paper Standard issued by the National
Information Standards Organization (Z39.48–1984).

10 9 8 7 6 5 4 3 2 1

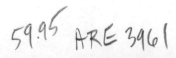

Copyright Acknowledgments

The authors and publisher gratefully acknowledge permission for use of the following material:

Excerpts from Military History Magazine, *Desert Storm* (Empire Press, 1991). Reprinted by permission of Cowles History Group.

Excerpts from Stan Morse, ed., *Gulf Air War Debrief* (London: Aerospace Publishing, 1991). Reprinted by permission of Aerospace Publishing.

Excerpt from letter in *Science*, January 24, 1992. Reprinted by permission of Robert A. Skelly, Raytheon Company, Lexington, Mass.

Every reasonable effort has been made to trace the owners of copyright materials in this book, but in some instances this has proven impossible. The authors and publisher will be glad to receive information leading to more complete acknowledgments in subsequent printings of the book and in the meantime extend their apologies for any omissions.

When, without stratagems
But in plain shock and even play of battle
Was ever known so great and little loss
On one part and on the other?

William Shakespeare, *Henry V*, Act IV, Scene 8

For Haney W. Hill, CWO-4.

*To the civilians who suffered on
both sides, victims of humanity's
narrow-mindedness, cruelty,
and viciousness.*

*To the courageous soldiers of both
sides, who fought and died for what
they believed in, exemplifying
humanity's idealism, fortitude,
and adaptability.*

Contents

Illustrations

FIGURES

TABLES

MAPS

Preface

Work on this book started the day after hostilities commenced on 17 January 1991. However, it was never our intention to publish our work immediately after the conflict ended. Much information on the war was made available only long after the end of hostilities. Our main drive has been to collect reliable information from primary sources and eyewitnesses, and to use well-accepted political and military theories to organize and present this material. The contents of this book are based entirely on official documents available to the public and on interviews that either were published or conducted by us on the phone and in person with people in the United States and Europe. Given the paucity of unclassified sources, most of our data come from official military accounts, in particular the comprehensive *Gulf War Air Power Survey* by Eliot Cohen et al., which, despite their shortcomings, are invaluable sources.

This book builds on the literature available to date and tries to go beyond it by covering Arab, European and U.S. participation in the events; by relying mainly on official primary sources; and by offering new, and in some cases controversial, interpretations of well-known events. We have included many firsthand accounts from soldiers in an attempt to show the "face of war" and to dispel the image that Desert Storm was a collection of "aseptic surgical strikes." We have attempted to place these accounts into context by providing connecting summary narratives of events and economic, military, and statistical analyses.

We hope that we have succeeded in producing the first comprehensive history addressed to the general public that does not, paraphrasing Col.

Richard Swain,[1] depend on journalistic instant narratives for its sources.

We have assumed that the reader either is familiar with the functions and capabilities of modern weapon systems or does not have much interest in this subject. Thus, we have attempted to provide in the text sufficient detail to allow anyone to understand what were the main uses and effects of weapon systems, while not burdening the reader with detailed explanations that he or she may already know, or not care about. The first section of Chapter 9 and the Glossary contain information about the principal weapon systems used in the Gulf War; readers who wish to brush up on this topic may consult these sections as they read the main text.

It is always difficult to know whether political decisions reflect the consensual will of a nation or the individual will of the leader of the nation. This is particularly true of nations that do not have a democratic political system. Thus we do not know to what extent Iraqi actions reflect the will of President Saddam Hussein alone, or the will of the ruling Baath party, or the will of the Iraqi people. In the text, we often use expressions such as "Iraqi actions" or "Iraqi statements"; we do not mean to imply by such terms that we believe that the Iraqi people approved of the actions or statements; however, we feel that attributing decisions to the collectivity known as "Iraq" is more neutral and less emotionally charged than attributing them to one man, Saddam Hussein, who may or may not have reflected the consensus thinking of other Iraqis.

While all of us are Westerners by birth and education, we have striven to overcome our backgrounds and personal biases and to present a balanced view of the conflict.

Nearly 100 people directly assisted us, and hundreds more indirectly contributed by compiling information and anonymously preparing official reports. Most of the 50 or so soldiers we interviewed are named in the text.

We wish to thank everyone who contributed, directly or indirectly: this book would not have been possible without you. But most especially we would like to thank the public relations departments of the various defense establishments, especially that of the United States of America, for making this project possible, and John M. Pickering for valuable editorial assistance.

The design of the figures is based on the principles given in *The Visual Design of Quantitative Information* by Edward R. Tufte (Graphics Press, 1983). This book has been composed, edited and camera-ready masters printed using Hewlett-Packard hardware, Microsoft Word 5.0, and the Micrografx Charisma graphical package.

Collecting and verifying data was not the primary mission of the military forces involved in the conflict; thus certain data are unavailable and some reported numbers are undoubtedly in error. Considering that data collected by full-time experienced professionals in normal circumstances (for example, a

---

1. Col. Richard Swain, *"Lucky War": Third Army in Desert Storm* (U.S. Army Command and General Staff College Press, 1994), p. 365.

national census) can be in error by several percent, we would be highly surprised if any data reported here are subject to less than 20% error.

We have put considerable effort into trying to report only verified facts and data. However, official reports from different sources are at times inconsistent, so some minor errors may be found in the text. We would appreciate being informed of them.

NOTES TO THE READER

Descriptions of specific military actions involving individuals are interspersed throughout the text. In order to avoid confusion, a smaller font (9 point) has been used for these. Thus a paragraph in smaller font contains what might be called a microscopic description of a specific military action.

Numbers are shown in U.S. format: thousands are separated by a comma; the decimal separator is a period. Thus 1,500.2 indicates one thousand five hundred and two tenths.

Times are shown in military format; thus 1500 hours is 3 o'clock P.M. Dates are shown in the format day-month-year: 1 January 1991.

There are numerous ways to spell Arabic words and names in English. The most sophisticated systems utilize special characters, such as the apostrophe. We have preferred to use whatever spelling is commonly found in the readily available literature, even at the risk of being slightly inconsistent.

Introduction

I am sick and tired of war. Its glory is all moonshine. . . . War is hell.[1]

—Gen. William T. Sherman

Why did a Coalition of over 30 nations[2] feel it necessary to go to war to liberate Kuwait after it was invaded by Iraq? Why wasn't it possible to prevent the war? The causes of the Gulf War reflected a profile of the world's geopolitical and economic features at the time. On the one side, there was what U.S. President Bush called "a New World Order." On the other side, there was Iraqi President Saddam Hussein's mixture of nationalism and pan-Arabism. In addition, both leaders had objectives of a personal nature.

Bush's New World Order affirmed the principles of the United Nations. First among these is the sovereignty of all nation-states, with the major powers as guarantors of that sovereignty. The collapse of the Communist systems and the end of the Cold War ended open rivalry among the major powers with respect to economic and foreign policy issues. The economic crisis within the USSR cast the United States as the undisputed major world power. Unrestricted access to the world's natural resources—oil being the critical

---

1. This quotation and many other quotations in chapter headings are from Justin Wintle, *The Dictionary of War Quotations* (Free Press, 1989).

2. We use the capitalized term *Coalition* to refer to the multinational alliance that took economic and military measures against Iraq. The number of nations was given as 28 by U.S. President Bush in several speeches. However, Eliot Cohen et al., *Gulf War Air Power Survey: Statistical Compendium* (U.S. Department of the Air Force, 1993), table 12, p. 45 (as well as several other official sources) lists more than 30. Fifteen nations participated in offensive military operations.

one—was another key principle. That such access should be based on free-market principles was accepted by all the major nations, excepting perhaps China, which still clung to Communist ideology. Iraq's apparently formidable military machine (including a potential future nuclear capability) seemed to threaten both the sovereignty of its neighbors and Western access to the world's largest known oil reserves.

The United States' long-standing special interest in the stability of the Middle East was formalized in 1980 as the Carter Doctrine and has been reiterated by the succeeding administrations. It stems from historical factors, notably protection of Mediterranean seaways and support of Israel, as well as the increasing dependence of the United States on imported oil. It seems safe to assume that Bush and his advisers remembered that high oil prices were a prime cause of the Carter administration's problems in the 1970s. A major threat to the oil supply was thus politically intolerable. The economic considerations also applied to a great degree to all Western members of the Coalition.

Finally, on the U.S. side there was the memory of Vietnam. This acted as a two-edged sword for both the administration and the Democratic opposition. On the one hand, the repetition of a costly stalemate would clearly have been political suicide. On the other hand, a quick victory at minimal cost would have been a master stroke.

Saddam Hussein accurately equated his personal popularity (or at least invulnerability to coup attempts) with Iraqi nationalism. On the other hand, he greatly misjudged his stature as a symbol of Arab unity. Although he undoubtedly had sympathizers throughout the Arab world, only the Palestine Liberation Organization (PLO) formally supported him, and no Arab country provided military aid. Nine Arab nations, including Egypt, Saudi Arabia, and Syria, joined the Coalition. Finally, Saddam Hussein over-estimated his standing among the "have-not" or "developing" nations. When the U.N. Security Council authorized the use of "all means" to force Iraqi withdrawal from Kuwait, China abstained and only Cuba voted against.

Arab members of the Coalition were largely motivated by their fear that a victorious Saddam Hussein would continue his expansion, thereby threatening their position in the Arab world.

1

Why Did Iraq
Invade Kuwait?

War seldom enters but where wealth allures.

—John Dryden

In the dead of night, at 0100 on 2 August 1990, three Iraqi mechanized and armored divisions crossed the border separating Iraq from Kuwait. Almost simultaneously, Iraqi special forces conducted heliborne and amphibious assaults against government and other key facilities inside Kuwait City. By early afternoon, 3 August, Iraqi troops had taken up positions on the Kuwaiti-Saudi border and threatened to cross into Saudi Arabia.[1]

These events appeared in the West[2] to have followed largely from the positions taken by Iraqi President Saddam Hussein. These positions—a mixture of nationalistic and pan-Arab elements—are not easily defined in Western terms. At their heart lies the notion of a unified Arab world with Baghdad at its center. The modern Arab nation-states, according to this view, are recent artificial creations of Western colonialism. Iraq reestablished its leadership, according to its president, by defending the Arab world's eastern flank against Iran—an Islamic but not an Arab nation. And the boundaries imposed by Western powers after the collapse of the Ottoman Empire resulted in an unfair distribution of wealth by allocating oil reserves to sparsely populated nations—artificial nations created by the West, in Saddam Hussein's view.

---

1. U.S. Department of Defense, *Conduct of the Persian Gulf War: Final Report to Congress* (April 1992), pp. 1-3.

2. Throughout the text, we shall use the terms "West" and "Western" to refer to the United States and its close allies. They include western Europe and Japan.

Beyond Saddam Hussein's long-term ambitions in the Gulf and the Arab world, however, there were two additional factors that influenced Iraq's immediate attitude toward Kuwait. First, successive regimes in Baghdad have argued that the oil-rich emirate is part of Iraq. The second factor has to do with Iraq's financial difficulties resulting from Baghdad's ill-fated decision to invade Iran in 1980. Thus, on the domestic level the Iraqi regime may have felt that its very survival depended on increasing its oil revenues by grabbing a vulnerable, oil-rich neighbor.[3]

THE CONSEQUENCES OF THE IRAN-IRAQ WAR

Ten years separate Iraq's premeditated attack against Iran from its brutal invasion of Kuwait. The country that had entered the decade with an economic level close to that of the least-developed regions of the West[4] left it heavily in debt, an economy close to collapse, and its leaders convinced that the invasion of the small and seemingly defenseless emirate was the only feasible way out of Iraq's deep economic and political crisis—a crisis created by the unsuccessful war with Iran.

The Iran-Iraq War ended in 1988 without either side achieving a clear victory, although it can be argued that Iraq lost, since it did not achieve the objectives for which it had started the conflict in 1980. After eight years of intermittently furious fighting, and something like three-quarters of a million casualties—of which perhaps one-third were Iraqis—the borders remained essentially unchanged.[5] Iraq, whose leaders claimed victory, came out of the war with a heavy debt due to purchases of weapons abroad; in addition, its plans for economic and social development were badly shaken.

From an economic point of view, the war had catastrophic consequences for Iraq, as shown in Figure 1.1. Note in particular the brutal drop in real (that is, inflation-adjusted) gross national product (GNP) from 1980 to 1981, which resulted in more than a 30% reduction in per capita GNP measured in dollars. Such drops in GNP characterized the Great Depression of the 1930s in

---

3. A fascinating (albeit somewhat speculative) in-depth analysis and explanation of the Iraqi president's motivations and behavior is provided by Efraim Karsh and Inari Rautsi, *Saddam Hussein: A Political Biography* (Futura, 1991). Their analysis is based on the assumption that Saddam Hussein acted primarily to safeguard his own position and that of the ruling Baath party. See also Efraim Karsh and Inari Rautsi, "Why Saddam Hussein Invaded Kuwait," *Survival*, 33, no. 1 (January-February 1992): 18-30. For an interpretation of Saddam Hussein's behavior stressing his dilemmas and threat perception, rather than ambitions for hegemony, as causes for the invasion of Kuwait, see Lawrence Freedman and Efraim Karsh, *The Gulf Conflict 1990-1992: Diplomacy and War in the New World Order* (Princeton University Press, 1993).

4. See United Nations, *National Account Statistics* (1988).

5. On the Iran-Iraq War, see Shahram Chubin and Charles Tripp, *Iran and Iraq at War* (I. B. Tauris, 1988); Efraim Karsh, ed., *The Iran-Iraq War: Impact and Implications* (St. Martin's Press, 1989).

Western economies. Much of the reduction in GNP was due to the disruption in oil production caused by the war: it went from 2.7 million barrels per day (MBPD) in 1980 to 1.1 in 1981, stayed at that level until 1983, then climbed slowly to 1.3 in 1984 and 1.6 in 1985.[6] Accompanying the drop in GNP, and aggravating its effects, government expenditures increased from 15% of GNP to over 40%, reflecting the huge resources required to fight the war. Thus during the 10 years from 1981 to 1990, the Iraqi population experienced a very significant reduction in standard of living that reversed the positive trend of the years 1968-1980; at the end of the war, the Iraqi economy as a whole was at a lower level than it had been in 1979 or 1980.

Figure 1.1
Iraq's economy during the Iran-Iraq War

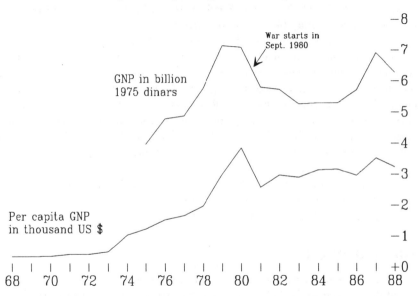

Oil revenues, which accounted for essentially all of the country's export revenues, reached $15 billion in 1989, while imports were $16 billion, of which $5 billion was spent on military items. Oil revenues, which were barely sufficient to cover imports, did not increase in 1990, mostly because the international oil market was steadily becoming less favorable for producing countries. When the war ended, Iraq faced reconstruction costs estimated as high as $60 billion and a foreign debt on the order of $70 billion; the debt was due to military equipment acquired abroad and to large loans made by the Gulf states (including Kuwait), which were worried by a potential spread of Khomeinist Islamist thinking and were thus ready to support Iraq in its war

---

6. Data are from Iraq, *Annual Abstract of Statistics* (1988).

against Iran. In fact, although it benefited from a considerable economic potential in both the medium and the long term, Iraq soon found itself in a very delicate financial situation: on the one hand, it was unable to ensure the repayment of its foreign debts; on the other hand, it was penalized by the changed attitude of Western nations, which, although they had supported Iraq during the war with Iran, now were increasingly less willing to grant the loans needed to rebuild the country.

Daily life was characterized by shortages of many foodstuffs and by inflation that reached 45% in 1989, which put all non essential goods out of reach of most people. The reduced buying power of government salaries was an especially serious threat to the regime's stability: something like 30% of the civilian population was employed by the state (50% of the total population, if the armed services are included).[7] Many of these people held their jobs thanks to their support for the ruling Baath party, which had only 25,000 full members but something like 1.5 million peripheral supporters.[8]

The Baath, or Rebirth, party had dominated the Iraqi political scene since 1968, using totalitarian methods to control the country. The erosion in the standard of living of public-sector employees reduced support for the party and threatened the very survival of the regime. As Efraim Karsh and Inari Rautsi put it: "By 1990 Hussein had probably begun to suspect that, as far as his personal position was concerned, the termination of the war might not have been the light at the end of the tunnel, but rather the tunnel at the end of the light. . . . An immediate economic breakthrough had thus become, literally, a matter of life and death."[9]

The only way to ensure that the economic crisis didn't turn into a political crisis was to find money; and the only readily available source of money was oil: either Iraq's oil sold at high prices, or Kuwait's oil.

THE LURE OF OIL

The importance of natural resources to international politics is as old as the world itself. The Trojan War may well have been fought to gain control over rich deposits of tin, an essential strategic metal at the time, since it was needed for the manufacture of bronze weapons. Many wars in the nineteenth and twentieth centuries were waged because of issues linked to resources. One of the most typical cases occurred in 1941, when the U.S. embargo of iron, steel scrap, and oil supplies to Japan played an important role in the process of escalation that finally resulted in open war. Most instances of international conflict and war are, of course, much more complex than just a struggle for

---

7. Samir al-Khalil, *Republic of Fear: Saddam's Iraq* (Hutchinson Radius, 1991), p. 40.

8. Christine M. Helms, *Iraq: Eastern Flank of the Arab World* (Brookings Institution, 1984), p. 87.

9. Karsh and Rautsi, *Saddam Hussein*, p. 204.

resources. On the other hand, the foregoing examples illustrate that natural resources have long been associated with tension and have been important causes of war between nations.[10] The 1990-1991 Gulf crisis is another good example.

Oil was indeed the key factor in the crisis, the one responsible for sparking it.[11] For the West, it was the extraction of oil and its unrestricted exportation that made the Gulf a vital zone. At the outbreak of the crisis, Kuwait was producing 1.7 million barrels of oil per day (MBPD); Saudi Arabia, 5.3; Iraq, 2.6; and Iran, about the same. Had the annexation of Kuwait been passed over in silence by the world community, Iraq would have been able to produce about 4.3 MBPD—almost as much as Saudi Arabia. The annexation would have given Iraq control over 22% of the world's identified oil reserves and hoisted it into second position, right behind Saudi Arabia's 28%. Occupying such a position would have allowed Iraq to play a major role in OPEC and to influence its policies.

Ever since World War II, as far as the Western world is concerned, the primary natural resource issue has been oil production, and specifically Middle Eastern oil production. This issue received dramatic attention during the so-called oil crises of the 1970s.[12] The first oil crisis, in 1973-1974, occurred when a group of Arab oil producers used the "oil weapon" against the West in conjunction with the October 1973 Arab-Israeli War (the Yom Kippur or Ramadan War). These nations, united through the Organization of Petroleum Exporting Countries (OPEC), implemented an embargo on shipments to certain Western countries (notably the United States), thus dramatically increasing the price of oil (from about $3.60 per barrel just before the war to over $11 at the end of 1973). The second crisis, in 1979, resulted from the political instability in Iran, a key producing country, following the Khomeinist revolution, and resulted in an increase from about $14 per barrel in 1978 to nearly $29 in 1981. The economic losses caused by the second oil shock were calculated at about 5% of GNP in 1980 by the Organization of Economic Cooperation and Development (OECD), and at about 8% in 1981, a total for the two years of about $1,000 billion, the equivalent of about twice the entire annual GNP of France or the United Kingdom at the time. During the same years, unemployment in the OECD rose from 19 million in 1979 to 29 million in 1982. Those negative effects were the result of drastic price increases rather than of physical shortages. Oil prices thus became a key concern for Western countries in the early 1980s.

Later in the decade this concern—which reflected the vulnerability of industrialized countries to energy prices—receded somewhat. At the same

---

10. Hanns W. Maull, "Energy and Resources: The Strategic Dimension," *Adelphi Papers*, no. 244 (Autumn 1989): 500-518.

11. Pierre M. Gallois, "Rivalry in the Gulf or the Birth of a Crisis," *Geopolitique*, no. 32 (Winter 1990-1991): 58-61.

12. Maull, "Energy and Resources," 500-509.

time, many oil-exporting developing countries experienced acute economic problems as a result of shrinking export markets and falling prices. The Iran-Iraq War of 1980-1988 caused substantial disruptions in supplies from both countries but failed to have a major impact on prices; indeed, oil prices fell substantially in spite of the war. This drop was the cumulative result of the profound changes in the patterns of oil demand and supply that emerged in response to the price increases of the 1970s. Figure 1.2 shows how inflation-adjusted prices increased significantly in 1973 and 1980, then dropped steadily. It also shows production volumes in MBPD by OPEC and non-OPEC countries.[13]

Figure 1.2
Oil prices and production, 1970-1988

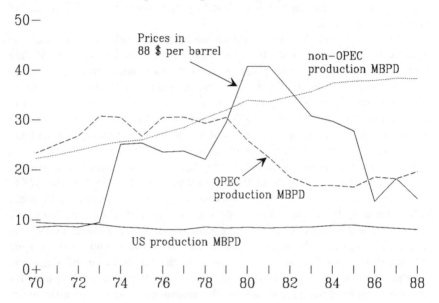

On the demand side, OECD oil consumption started to fall after 1979, as industrialized countries implemented oil conservation and substitution measures (for example, favoring alternative energy sources such as natural gas,

---

13. There are many different prices for oil: spot prices, average contract prices, and so on. Spot prices vary considerably according to the quality of the oil. The data in this section are from C. D. Masters, D. H. Root, and E. D. Attanasi, "Resource Constraints in Petroleum Production Potential," *Science*, 253 (12 July 1991): 146. Prices in Figure 1.2 and elsewhere are average U.S. import prices. As an example of the variability in prices, consider the following: in 1980 the spot price for Iranian light crude, as reported in United Nations, *Energy Statistics Yearbook*, was $30 per barrel; the U.S. import price was $29; the OECD import price, as reported in OECD, *Economic Outlook* (July 1991), was $33.

coal, and nuclear fission). On the supply side, the higher prices stimulated the search for new oil fields and enhanced recovery of oil from existing fields. As a result, OPEC's share of world oil supplies fell from 53% in 1976 to 31% in 1985. (OPEC includes some non-Arab, non-Middle Eastern suppliers, such as Indonesia, Nigeria, and Venezuela, but about 73% of OPEC production in 1988 came from Arab countries and Iran.)

As a consequence of market forces, oil prices peaked in 1981 and started to drop significantly after 1985. However, OPEC's share of world oil production increased after 1985, reaching 34% by the end of the Iran-Iraq War (1988); it was forecast to reach 50% by 2000. OPEC's production had risen from its 1985 low of about 17 MBPD to about 20 MBPD in 1988, and was thought likely to rise to about 30 MBPD by 2000.[14]

Most of the increase in OPEC production was absorbed by Western countries, which thus once again became more dependent on the natural resources of the Middle East. The principal reason for this increase in Western dependence was lower oil prices, which resulted in increased demand and reduced investment in further oil prospecting and research programs for alternative energy sources. For example, U.S. oil imports had risen from a low of 4.5 MBPD in 1985 to 6.7 MBPD in 1988. This represented close to half of U.S. oil consumption and about a third of total OECD oil imports. And in 1990 U.S. imports were forecast to increase further: by 2000, they might reach 13 MBPD; European and Japanese oil imports were also thought likely to increase. Since OPEC accounted for some 68% of identified world oil reserves, and the Middle East for 63%, most of this additional import demand would have to be met by these countries.

This potential dependence loomed despite important differences between the situation in the 1970s and that in the 1990s. By the end of the 1980s an increase in proven worldwide oil reserves had, at least temporarily, diminished the importance of Middle Eastern reserves. In addition, Western countries had created considerable stockpiles that would have allowed them to survive a short-term embargo with far fewer difficulties than in 1973 (for example, the U.S. strategic oil reserve held enough to replace imports for well over two months). Another key difference was the fact that in the 1990s the international oil industry was primarily driven by market mechanisms, unlike the situation in 1973, when the industry was controlled by the oligopolistic actions of the major oil companies (the so-called Seven Sisters: British Petroleum, Exxon, Gulf, Mobil, Shell, Standard Oil, and Texaco). And, finally, Arab countries realized that the use of oil as a weapon had ultimately been a failure. Yet despite these differences in the world oil market, Western policy makers seemed unable to quench their thirst for Middle Eastern oil.

In fact, the Kuwaiti crisis came at a crucial time for the West. As we can see in Figure 1.3, between 1985 and 1988, net oil imports rose from 4.5 to 6.7

---

14. Taiwo Idemudia, "OPEC and the International Oil Markets," *OPEC Review* (Summer 1989).

MBPD for the United States and from 15.7 to 18.7 for the OECD.[15] U.S. oil production declined from 9 to 8 MBPD. Net oil imports thus rose from 29% of U.S. consumption to 49%. In the first half of 1990, imports rose to over 7.6 MBPD—more than half of total U.S. oil consumption. At a conference held in London on 19 October 1990, U.S. Assistant Energy Secretary Henson Moore stated that U.S. oil might account for 80% of American oil consumption by 2030.[16]

Figure 1.3
Oil imports and consumption

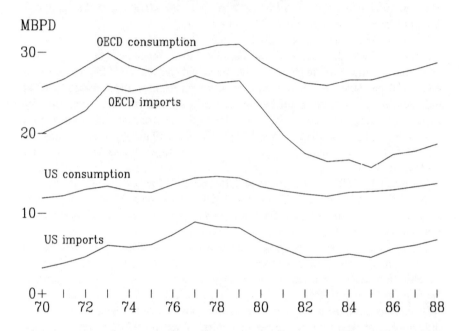

For the United States in particular, and the Western world in general, the control of the Gulf, a region that contains nearly two-thirds of the world's known oil reserves, became a "must": an imperative for economic well-being. Table 1.1 shows the world's main oil-producing countries and their reserves, listed in order of 1988 production.

In 1988, Kuwait and Iraq had roughly 100 billion barrels each of identified crude oil reserves, together accounting for 22% of the world's total. Each country's known reserves were nearly 60% larger than those of Iran, 25% larger than those of the USSR, about twice as large as those of the United

---

15. These data and those in Figure 1.3 are from OECD, *Energy Statistics* (1987-1988).

16. Pierre Terzian, "The Gulf Crisis from the Point of View of Oil," *Geopolitique*, no. 32 (Winter 1990-1991): 56-57.

States or the UAE, and 60% smaller than those of Saudi Arabia. However, while Iraq had a population of about 18 million, Kuwait had only 2 million. Demography gave rise to an obvious disparity: Kuwait had a per capita reserve nine times that of Iraq. Kuwait's extraordinary oil wealth did not mean, however, that Iraq could be described as poor. Not only did Iraq possess one of the world's biggest oil potentials (its reserves were exceeded only by Saudi Arabia's, and its reserves-to-population ratio was among the top five in the world), but in the long run it could hope to be agriculturally self-sufficient and to develop something of an industrial base. The Iraq-Iran War added short-term differences to the long-term differences already existing between Iraq and Kuwait. The economics of natural resources prompted Iraqi leaders to covet Kuwait.

Table 1.1
Principal oil producing nations

Country	1988 production (MBPD)	Identified reserves (billion barrels)	Ultimate reserves (billion barrels)[17]
USSR	12.3	80	181
USA	8.1	48	98
Saudi Arabia	4.9	255	296
Iraq	2.7	99	144
China	2.7	22	70
Mexico	2.5	27	64
Venezuela	2.2	34	54
UK	2.2	14	25
Iran	1.6	63	85
UAE	1.6	56	63
Nigeria	1.6	16	25
Kuwait	1.4	96	99
Canada	1.4	7	40
Indonesia	1.4	8	18
Libya	1.1	22	30
Norway	1.1	11	24
Algeria	1.1	8	11
World total	58	922	1469

Iraq needed to double its oil earnings to resolve its economic problems, whereas Kuwait could do without oil and, in a worst-case scenario, live

---

17. As estimated by Masters, Root, and Attanasi, "Resource Constraints in Petroleum Production Potential." The line "World total" is greater than the total of the other lines because minor oil producing nations are not listed individually.

comfortably without the revenue oil brought in.[18] In addition, Iraq owed part
of its debt to Kuwait itself which, like Saudi Arabia and, to a lesser extent, the
UAE and Qatar, had given it financial assistance—in the form of
loans—during its eight-year war with Iran.

Iraq's economic problems would have been manageable on two conditions:
first, it had to be able to export at full production rates (somewhere around 3
MBPD); and second, the price of crude could not drop too low.[19] At a price
of $25 a barrel, Iraq could have hoped to earn $27 billion a year from oil,
which would have allowed it to meet its military expenditures (estimated on
the order of $9 billion per year), pay off its debt service charges (roughly $4
billion per year), continue importing food and other civilian items (roughly
$12 billion per year), and still have adequate funds to reactivate an economy
battered by the war. But of these two conditions, only the first could be
fulfilled.

A few months after the end of the Iran-Iraq War, OPEC granted Iraq a
production quota equal to that of Iran, which amounted both to a political
maximum (a higher quota would not have been acceptable to Tehran) and an
economic minimum (Baghdad could now export as much as possible). But the
second of Iraq's key economic conditions (a high price for oil) was at the
mercy of two Gulf countries—the UAE and Kuwait—whose leaders couldn't
resign themselves, it seemed, to the discipline required by OPEC for balancing
supply and demand and stabilizing the price of crude. Kuwait, in particular,
represented a major source of concern. In 1988, the emirate exceeded its
OPEC quota by 0.2 MBPD; in 1989, by 0.3; and in the winter of 1990, by
0.45. Nothing, it seemed, could control Kuwait's oil production, although, of
all the OPEC members, it alone was capable of maintaining a high standard of
living without the earnings from oil exports.

Moreover, as increasing supplies were driving oil prices down, other OPEC
members were tempted to exceed their own production quotas in an attempt to
balance the losses caused by the fall in prices. In short, OPEC was trapped in
a vicious cycle: increased production led to lower prices, which led to a loss of
revenue that could be compensated only by increasing production, which
resulted in still lower prices. As the result of constant overproduction, the
price of crude collapsed in the spring of 1990, falling from an average of
around $19 per barrel in the first quarter, to $17 in April, to $16 in May, then
to below $15 in June. This meant that Iraq's oil earnings fell from a rate of
$17 billion per year in January to $13 billion per year in June, not even
enough to cover its military expenditures and the service charges on its foreign
debt. Figure 1.4 illustrates the situation.[20]

---

18. Indeed, Kuwaiti investments abroad, amounting to almost $100 billion, brought
in more revenue to the emirate than did sales of oil.

19. Terzian, "The Gulf Crisis from the Point of View of Oil," pp. 53-55.

20. Data are OECD import prices from OECD, *Economic Outlook* (July 1991).

Fearing the threat of economic strangulation, the Iraqi regime took an important political initiative in preparation for the summit of the Arab League at Baghdad in May 1990. In April, President Saddam Hussein sent a letter to his Iranian counterpart, Ali Akhbar Hashemi Rafsanjani, with a view to normalizing relations with Tehran. The consequence, as far as the politics of oil is concerned, was official support from Iran when Iraq called on Kuwait and the UAE to abide by the OPEC quotas. Had Iran and Iraq still been at war, Iran might have been tempted to exploit the divisions that had appeared among the Arab countries of the Gulf or, at the very least, have refused to support an Iraqi move quite so openly (even one that was in Iran's own economic interests). However, this time Iran publicly declared its agreement with Iraq on the oil question.

Figure 1.4
Oil prices and production, early 1990

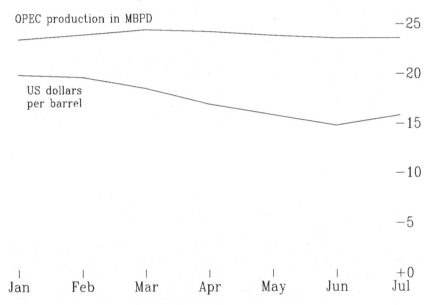

Iraq first signaled its displeasure regarding the oil production issue in February 1990, at a meeting of the Arab Cooperation Council. Forceful statements were made by Iraq in May, at the OPEC meeting in Geneva and at an Arab summit in Baghdad. Badghdad Radio subsequently reported that Saddam Hussein had said that continuing over production of oil, and its consequent effect on prices, was "a kind of war against Iraq. . . . we have reached a point where we can no longer withstand pressure."[21]

---

21. Baghdad Radio, 18 July 1990. For a well-researched detailed account of these events, see Freedman and Karsh, *The Gulf Conflict*, pp. 45-46.

In June, following up on the support obtained from Iran for reducing OPEC production, the Iraqis demanded that OPEC's existing quotas be respected so long as prices did not reach at least $25 per barrel. The price at the time was around $14 per barrel. Iraq's request was openly supported by Iran.

Reinforcing Iraq's previous actions, its minister of foreign affairs, Tarik Aziz, sent a formal note to the general secretary of the Arab League on 16 July 1990. The note clearly spells out the causes of the conflict, and at times sounds like a declaration of war. In particular, it stresses that, since Kuwaiti (and UAE, for that matter) policies had caused oil prices to drop, Iraq had experienced an important loss of revenue at a time when its economy was suffering from financial difficulties due to the military expenditures of the Iran-Iraq War.[22]

Although Iraq had strongly requested that the minimum reference price be set to $25 per barrel, on 27 July 1990 OPEC agreed to $21 per barrel for its oil and froze production quotas, reducing them from 23.5 to 22.5 MBPD until this price was reached. In its final statement, OPEC took the unusual step of pointing out that "all member governments at the highest level" had made a "total commitment to ensuring strict respect" of the OPEC decisions, "including the quotas fixed herein, and not to allow any member country to exceed its quota for any reason whatsoever."[23] The conference set up two quota watchdog groups to enforce these decisions, one chaired by Iraq and the other by Iran. It was assumed that the Iraqi-Kuwaiti dispute had momentarily been shelved when both the UAE and Kuwait agreed to reduce their production by about 0.5 MBPD, to 1.5 MBPD each.

GEOGRAPHICAL CLAIMS

But there was another factor of disagreement between Iraq and Kuwait: long-standing disputes over their boundary and, in fact, over Kuwait's very right to exist as an independent state.[24]

Leaders in Baghdad had long argued that Kuwait's territory should be part of Iraq. This claim was essentially based on the fact that Kuwait formally became part of the Ottoman province of Basra in 1871, and that Iraq was created in 1921 by joining the Ottoman provinces of Mosul (in the north), Baghdad (in the center), and Basra (in the south).

However, the claim ignored several key events. In 1899 the UK acquired a protectorate over Kuwait, in effect detaching it from the Ottoman Empire. While the Ottomans did not formally agree to this state of affairs, several

---

22. Radio Baghdad, 18 July 1990. Extensive extracts from Aziz's note are found in Freedman and Karsh, *The Gulf Conflict*, pp. 47-48.

23. Quoted in Terzian, "The Gulf Crisis from the Point of View of Oil," p. 56.

24. For an extensive analysis of Iraq's historical dispute with Kuwait, see Richard Schofield, *Kuwait and Iraq: Historical Claims and Territorial Disputes* (Royal Institute of International Affairs, 1991).

international treaties signed after the collapse of the Ottoman Empire during the years 1919 to 1923 recognized the existence of a distinct Kuwaiti state and the U.K.'s protectorate of this state. In 1932 Iraq itself legitimized the existence of Kuwait when its representatives signed an international treaty related to their common borders.[25]

In 1961 the UK granted independence to Kuwait, which was recognized as a sovereign country by both the United Nations and the Arab League. Although Iraq refused to accept Kuwait's status in 1961—withdrawing from the Arab League in protest and threatening to invade the newly independent state—the Iraqi regime that came to power in 1963 did formally recognize Kuwait's independence.[26]

Thus, without entering into the detailed technicalities of international law, one must conclude that Kuwait had as much right to be considered an independent sovereign state as did Iraq. Furthermore, the principle of self-determination is today considered far more important than borders based on ancient empires.

In fact, Kuwait had a long history of relative autonomy within the Ottoman and British empires, and it had been traditionally ruled as a hereditary monarchy, like many other countries. There can be no doubt that the people of Kuwait did not wish to be annexed to Iraq and that the principle of self-determination would negate any Iraqi claims to the whole of Kuwait.

However, the situation is less clear-cut with respect to territorial disputes, particularly those concerning Iraq's access to the sea and the islands of Warba and Bubiyan. The Uqair agreements of 1922-1923 specified Kuwait's northern borders with Iraq, following the lines of those defined in the U.K.-Ottoman convention of 1913—a convention that had never been ratified. The 1923 borders were favorable to Kuwait, since they gave it the islands of Bubiyan and Warba. The emirate's northwestern and western borders were specified in the Iraqi-Kuwaiti convention of 1932, after Iraq had become an independent state. Despite its formal recognition of Kuwait in 1963, Iraq continued to request modifications of the borders, particularly with respect to the islands.[27]

Iraq's only maritime outlet is the Persian Gulf; whatever government is in power in Baghdad, direct access to the Gulf will always be an Iraqi goal. Geography hides nothing about the long-term designs of any Iraqi government. Ever since its creation, the modern state's access to the sea had been blocked on every side: by Iran, Turkey, Syria, Jordan, Saudi Arabia and, of course, Kuwait. Since Iraq has only a narrow outlet to the sea, at the rear of a Gulf controlled by other powers, its oil pipelines have to cross other countries and reach their terminals on foreign shores—this cost Iraq dearly when Syria cut

25. United Nations, *The United Nations and the Iraq-Kuwaiti Conflict 1990-1996* (1996), p. 165.
26. Ibid., p. 166.
27. Habib Ishow, "The Reasons Behind the Invasion of Kuwait," *Geopolitique*, no. 32 (Winter 1990-1991): 22-25.

off the flow of Iraqi exports through its territory during the Iran-Iraq War. Faw and Umm Qasr, Iraq's coastal areas, were negligible outlets for a state rich in oil, water, and human resources.

Iraq has no natural site on the Gulf that would lend itself to the construction of a modern port. The port of Basra is situated 50 kilometers upstream on the shallow Shatt al-Arab, and it silts up every year with millions of tons of alluvial mud brought down by the Tigris and Euphrates. The one site on which Iraq could construct a deep-water port happens to be on the Kuwaiti coast. The Iraqi seacoast, moreover, is a mere 19 kilometers in length and is hemmed in by the two Kuwaiti islands of Warba and Bubiyan and their territorial waters. In October 1963, Baghdad sought to have the border readjusted, claiming the islands which would have given it access to the roadstead off Kuwait City. The emirate rejected the idea of amputating its territory in this way, and in 1984 refused to lease the islands to the Iraqis.[28]

SADDAM HUSSEIN'S VISION OF HIS ROLE

Every international event is the result, intended or unintended, of decisions made by individuals. Individual decisions in turn reflect the values and beliefs of the decision maker. This seems to be especially true in the case of Saddam Hussein.[29]

The Iraqi leader was born in 1937 near Tikrit; most of the members of the ruling Baath party's inner circle come from this same area. Saddam Hussein's family were peasants, and he did not attend school until he was nine years old. He joined the Baath party in 1956 and was forced to leave Iraq after the failed 1959 coup attempt against President Qassim. He returned to Iraq in 1963, after living in Egypt, Syria, and Lebanon. The years 1964-1979 saw his irresistible rise to the summit of political power: first as a member of the Baath Regional (Iraqi) Directorate; next as the right-hand man of President Bakr; finally as president of the Republic, president of the Revolutionary Command Council, and secretary general—that is, head—of the Baath party. Feared by all, worshiped by his supporters, hated by old and new enemies, Saddam Hussein nevertheless managed to obtain the popular support of the majority of Iraqis thanks to his tireless energy. Tall, athletic, often elegant, sporting a thick black mustache, self-assured but always cautious, he seemed to possess two distinguishing characteristics: first, a determination to be remembered in history; second, a certain vision of the future—albeit not always a clear vision, as the events of 1991 showed. He speaks no foreign languages and has visited the West only once (France in 1976). He reportedly has little grasp of the realities of the Western world. It has been conjectured that, as with most dictators in history, his decisions are based on less than complete information, since his advisers are wary of contradicting him in any way.

---

28. Gallois, "Rivalry in the Gulf," pp. 59-60.
29. For an in-depth analysis, see Karsh and Rautsi, *Saddam Hussein*.

Saddam Hussein firmly believed that Iraq was the source of Arab glory. Many of his speeches had made reference to the ancient splendor of his country. This can be understood as an attempt to create a mythical continuity in Iraq's greatness, running from Hammurabi (the great legislator and king of Babylon) through the Abbassid caliphate and Saladin (a Kurdish warrior who fought the Crusaders and became the quintessential hero of modern Arabs), to the modern state and its ruler. The same sentiments were expressed on 10 August 1991 by Iraqi Foreign Minister Tarik Aziz: "Iraq is one of the oldest nations in the world . . . and the Iraq of today is the same as the Iraq of the last 5000 years."[30]

Throughout history the rulers of Baghdad, Cairo, and Damascus, the traditional centers of Arab power, each aspired to assume the leadership of the Arab world. During the 1980s the old pattern of competition for leadership and hegemony, coupled with ambitious military buildup, reasserted itself, with Iraq leading the way.[31] Saddam Hussein's vision of his role as pan-Arab leader was probably reinforced by the Iran-Iraq War, which took on racial connotations (Persians versus Arabs) and which official propaganda described as a heroic defense of Arab interests and of the Arab world's eastern flank. In retrospect, it appears that Saddam Hussein has aspired to a much more central role for Iraq in the Arab world ever since his seizure of power. However, his involvement in the war with Iran forced him to postpone his broader schemes. Once the war was over, and Iraq could be presented as a winner, his ambitions were redirected to the Arab world.[32]

A successful annexation of Kuwait would have provided Saddam Hussein with an opportunity for enhancing his prestige among fellow Iraqis and supporters of the pan-Arab movement, perhaps even allowed him to assume the mantle of Nasser, the charismatic Egyptian president of the 1950s and 1960s.

Iraq had made several attempts before 1990 to assume leadership of the Arab world, including the attack on Iran, which was partly justified as an attempt to "liberate" the Arab peoples who form the majority of the inhabitants of the part of Iran called Khuzestan by Persians and Arabistan by Arabs. This attack took place after Egypt—which many considered the true leader of the Arab world—had been excluded from the Arab League because it made peace with Israel in 1979. The world's reaction to Iraq's aggression against Iran may have seemed to confirm Saddam Hussein's dreams. The West in

---

30. No specific reference will be given for unsurprising quotations from public statements made by public figures, since they can be found in a number of places, notably the *New York Times*. Saddam Hussein's speeches were published by Radio Baghdad and the Iraqi News Agency (INA). Many can also be found in Ofra Bengio, *Saddam Speaks on the Gulf Crisis* (Dayan Center for Middle Eastern and African Studies, Tel Aviv University, 1992).

31. Yair Evron, "Gulf Crisis and War: Regional Rules of the Game and Policy and Theoretical Implications," *Security Studies*, 4, no. 1 (Autumn 1994): 131.

32. Ibid., pp. 131-132.

particular, fearing an Iranian victory more than an Iraqi one, did more to help Iraq than Iran (in spite of the bumbling attempts by some advisors of U.S. president Reagan secretly to trade weapons for Iranian good-will—an episode named Irangate by Western media). But as soon as the war ended, the West did not expand its economic support for Iraq and did not treat it as a victorious ally. Western ambivalence may have been seen as duplicity or indifference to the sacrifices that Iraq had, according to its propaganda, made in order to preserve the status quo in the Gulf—a status quo that favored Western countries. Hostility to the West, and a desire to redress supposed wrongs, would flow easily from such a line of thinking.

SUMMARY

All wars have many causes, some remote, some immediate. There can be no doubt that the proximate cause of the Gulf War was the desire to control oil. Oil was responsible both for originating Iraq's invasion of Kuwait and for the Coalition's subsequent military effort to liberate the emirate.

Among the underlying causes, we single out three: the domestic economic crisis that Iraq endured as a consequence of its long war with Iran and that menaced the stability of the Baathist regime; Iraq's long-standing claims on at least part of Kuwait's territory; and President Saddam Hussein's vision of his role as pan-Arab leader and his ambitions for hegemony and influence in the Gulf area and the Arab world. On the Coalition side, the sovereignty of states—as defined by the U.N. Charter and the fundamental principles of international law—transcended all national and regional sentiments. Yet the Coalition's legal position, as the next chapter demonstrates, was colored by its members' geopolitical perceptions and domestic policies. Thus geographic, strategic, legal, political, and domestic factors were involved in addition to economic interests. As General Khaled bin Sultan put the matter: "To see the war only in terms of Western interest in the defense of oil . . . obscures the true nature of the crisis by overlooking the impact of Saddam's move on regional politics and on the interests of regional players. Saddam's folly was to threaten the interests of all the neighboring states, as well as of several further afield."[33]

---

33. HRH Gen. Khaled bin Sultan, *Desert Warrior: A Personal View of the Gulf War by the Joint Forces Commander* (HarperCollins, 1995), p. 27.

2

The Path to War

The Korean War began in a way in which wars often begin. A potential aggressor miscalculated.

—John Foster Dulles, 1953

At the time, it seemed as if the world had been taken by surprise and that events had taken a totally unexpected turn. Yet many of the reasons that had prompted the Iraqi invasion of Kuwait were plain for all to see. What is surprising, then, is the idea that the invasion had caught the world, particularly the West, by surprise.[34] Are we to believe that the invasion of Kuwait really, as Fred Harris put it, "came as a complete surprise to Mr. Bush's government, to the CIA and to the members of the President's National Security Council?"[35] Even though "military indicators of a potential invasion were first detected in mid-July when Iraqi artillery and armor units were reported moving south?"[36] Even though both the U.S. Central Command and the Defense Intelligence Agency issued warnings in late July of possible Iraqi military action against Kuwait?[37] Even though in the fall of 1989, the U.S. Department of Defense had shifted its focus in the Persian Gulf away from a perceived Soviet threat because "the growing military capability and ambitions of Iraq—with its forces toughened by its war with Iran—and the sharp

34. Gallois, "Rivalry in the Gulf," p. 58.
35. *International Herald Tribune,* 3 August 1990.
36. U.S. Central Command, briefing, Riyadh, Saudi Arabia, 26 December 1990; and Eliot A. Cohen, et al., *Gulf War Air Power Survey: Chronology* (U.S. Department of the Air Force, 1993). Hereafter *GWAPS*.
37. Cohen, *GWAPS: Chronology*, p. 4.

disparity between its forces and those of the wealthy oil-producing nations of the Arabian Peninsula pointed to the growing possibility of conflict between these regional powers?"[38] Even though several serious causes of war existed? In his autobiography, General Schwarzkopf gives the following account of a visit to Kuwait in October 1989: "I couldn't help noticing that all of Kuwait's guns were pointed north, towards Iraq. Major General Mizyad al-Sanii, the Kuwaiti chief of staff, told me point-blank that Iraq was the number-one threat to Kuwait. He explained that Saddam Hussein had failed to achieve one of the major objectives of his war with Iran: regaining Iraq's access to the Persian Gulf. Now, he said, . . . Saddam Hussein would very likely try to seize Kuwait's Bubiyan Island."[39]

THE EVENTS LEADING TO THE INVASION OF KUWAIT

In January 1990, Iraq reportedly proposed to lease Bubiyan and Warba islands, which it had long coveted in order to improve its access to the Gulf. Although Kuwait initially agreed in principle, the two sides were unable to find mutually acceptable terms, and talks were suspended in March. At a summit meeting of the Arab Cooperation Council (Egypt, Iraq, Jordan, Yemen) in Jordan in February, Iraqi President Saddam Hussein reportedly asked other Arab leaders to convey to the Gulf states the message that Iraq needed financial assistance and was determined to obtain it.[40] In the Spring of 1990, Baghdad forcefully raised the oil production issue by violently criticizing Kuwait for consistently exceeding OPEC production quotas (see Chapter 1).

In parallel with these events, the image of Saddam Hussein's regime began to degrade in the eyes of Western public opinion because of a series of incidents. On 15 March 1990, Baghdad announced the execution—in spite of Western pleas for clemency—of a British journalist of Iranian origin, Farzad Bazoft, who had been arrested in September 1989 and condemned to death for spying for Israel and Great Britain (the charge of espionage was probably justifiable, even if the punishment was extreme, since Bazoft had attempted to visit a missile plant). On 28 March, five arms merchants were arrested in London as they attempted to export electronic circuits that allegedly could be used to build triggers for nuclear weapons. (Iraq stated that the circuits were intended for civilian use; however, repeated Iraqi statements that it was fully complying with the Treaty on the Non-Proliferation of Nuclear Weapons were proved false in July 1991 when inspectors from the International Atomic

---

38. U.S. Department of Defense, *Conduct of the Persian Gulf War*, Appendix D, p. 5.

39. Norman Schwarzkopf, *It Doesn't Take a Hero* (Bantam Books, 1992), p. 282.

40. Bruce M. Weitzman, "The Inter-Arab System and the Gulf War: Continuity and Change," Occasional Papers, Series 2, no. 1 (Carter Center of Emory University, 1992).

Energy Agency visited Iraq's nuclear facilities and found that "the large uranium enrichment program in Iraq was clandestine, it was not placed under safeguards and no confidence can arise it had peaceful purposes." The agency officially declared that Iraq had violated the treaty—the first country to have done so.) On 2 April, Iraqi President Saddam Hussein claimed that Iraq was able to produce nerve gas and explicitly threatened to use it against Israel: "By God, we will make fire eat up half of Israel if it tries anything against Iraq. Yet everyone must know his limits. Thanks to God, we know our limits and will not attack anyone." On 11 April, U.K. customs inspectors discovered eight huge steel cylinders that were suspected to be intended for the construction of a supercannon whose range would allow the shelling of Israel. (Characteristically, Iraq stated that the cylinders were part of an oil pipeline, but in this case we know that the Iraqi statement was false: after the end of the Gulf War, in July 1991, Iraq admitted that the cylinders were going to be used to build a supercannon designed by Gerald Bull, an arms expert assassinated in Brussels in March 1990, perhaps by Israeli agents.)[41]

Meanwhile, Saddam Hussein continued to state Iraq's displeasure regarding the oil production issue. In mid-June he declared: "War . . . is also conducted by economic means. . . . [The current oil price situation] is in fact a kind of war against Iraq. . . . We have reached a point where we can no longer withstand pressure." On 17 July, Saddam Hussein escalated the verbal debate by threatening to use force against *certain Arab countries* [italics ours]" if they did not cut back their oil production: *"As God is my witness, we have warned them! If words fail to protect us, we will have no choice but to engage in an action that will reestablish the correct order of things and ensure the restoration of our rights."*

When Kuwait rejected the Iraqi accusations and demands on 19 July, the Arab League and Saudi Arabia agreed to serve as mediators. Iraq started concentrating troops on its border with Kuwait on 21 July, even as Arab leaders such as Egyptian President Hosni Mubarak and Jordanian King Hussein attempted to reach a compromise solution. Mubarak later stated that Saddam Hussein had told him that the troop concentration was only an intimidation measure, and that no invasion would take place (however, according to Tarik Aziz, Iraq had only stated that it would not invade as long as talks were taking place).[42]

King Hussein later stated that he had the impression that the Kuwaitis did not feel concerned with any of this. On 25 July, Mubarak announced that

---

41. For more details on Bazoft, the electronic circuits, and the supergun, see Kenneth R. Timmermann, *The Death Lobby: How the West Armed Iraq* (Houghton Mifflin, 1991).

42. Mubarak quoted in U.S. News & World Report, *Triumph Without Victory: The Unreported History of the Persian Gulf War* (Times Books, 1992), p. 22; Aziz quoted by the Iraqi News Agency (INA) 9-13 January 1990. See also the discussion in Freedman and Karsh, *The Gulf Conflict*, p. 50, and p. 446 note 20.

direct Iraqi-Kuwaiti talks would take place in Jeddah, Saudi Arabia, at the end of July. But Iraq continued to match actions to words, concentrating significant numbers of troops on the Kuwaiti border: building the 30,000 troops present on 21 July up to something like 100,000 men and 300 tanks by 31 July. These concentrations were reported through official U.S. military and intelligence channels, and the reports were leaked to the press.[43] Yet the only U.S. military reaction was to send two tanker aircraft and six combat ships (*not* including an aircraft carrier) for exercises in the United Arab Emirates.[44]

On 19 July, U.S. Secretary of State James Baker issued the following circular: "The United States takes no position on the substance of the bilateral issues concerning Iraq and Kuwait. . . . We remain committed to ensuring the free flow of oil from the Gulf and supporting the sovereignty and the integrity of the Gulf states. . . . We also remain committed to supporting the individual and collective self-defense of our friends in the Gulf, with whom we have deep and long-standing ties."[45] On 24 July, further qualifying its position, U.S. State Department spokesperson Margaret Tutwiler pointed out that "we do not have any defense treaties with Kuwait, and there are no special defense or security commitments to Kuwait."[46]

In the aftermath of the 1991 Gulf War, questions were raised about the Bush administration's ambiguous policy toward Iraq prior to 2 August 1990. U.S. policy toward Baghdad was developed in the context of the Iran-Iraq War. The Reagan administration, with its antipathy toward the Khomeinist regime, began to tilt toward Iraq after 1982, when it appeared that Iran might be winning. With the end of the Iran-Iraq War in the spring of 1988, the United States was confronted with a new strategic balance in the Persian Gulf. Iraq had replaced Iran as the military power in the region, thanks in no small measure to U.S. support. As President Reagan's final term drew to a close, the U.S. government was still undecided how it would deal with Saddam Hussein's Iraq. By the spring of 1989, President George Bush's administration decided on a policy of constructive engagement with Iraq in the hopes that such a policy would lead to Saddam Hussein's moderation. On 2 October 1989, the National Security Council (NSC) issued National Security Directive (NSD) 26, which summarized U.S. policy toward the Persian Gulf and Iraq in the following manner:

Access to Persian Gulf oil and the security of key friendly states in the area are vital to U.S. national security. The United States remains committed to defending its vital interests in the region, if necessary and appropriate, through the use of U.S. military force. Normal relations between the United States and Iraq would serve our longer-term interests and promote stability in both the Gulf and the Middle East. The United

---

43. See, e.g., the *New York Times* and the *Washington Post* of 24 July 1990.

44. Cohen et al., *GWAPS: Chronology*, p. 4.

45. Quoted in Zachary Karabell, "Backfire: U.S. Policy Toward Iraq, 1988-2 August 1990," *Middle East Journal,* vol. 49, no. 1 (Winter 1995): 44.

States should propose economic and political incentives for Iraq to moderate its behavior and to increase our influence with Iraq.[47]

Until the very day of Iraq's invasion of Kuwait, the Bush administration pursued a policy of constructive engagement toward Iraq, aiming at moderating Saddam Hussein. It pursued this policy in the face of evidence that Iraq was violating human rights, producing and using chemical weapons,[48] producing biological weapons, violating nuclear nonproliferation agreements, evading U.S. export controls, obtaining illegal loans for weapons procurement (through the Atlanta branch of the Banca Nazionale del Lavoro), and mismanaging and misusing U.S. development credits. The Bush administration reluctantly pulled back from tightening relations with Iraq, primarily because of domestic pressure to do so emanating from both Congress and the public. Only when continued support for Iraq became a domestic liability were steps taken to send strong signals of displeasure. Diplomatic correspondence took on a more anti-Iraq tone and development credits—the cornerstone of constructive engagement—were suspended. Yet until the invasion of Kuwait on 2 August, the policy enunciated in NSD 26 remained in effect. In short, until Saddam Hussein invaded Kuwait, the Bush administration was committed to Iraq as a vital link in U.S. strategy in the Middle East.[49]

The one action that the Bush administration took to show its concern about developments in the Gulf was to instruct the U.S. ambassador in Baghdad, April Glaspie, to seek clarification of Iraqi intentions. There has been speculation concerning what Glaspie said to Saddam Hussein during a meeting with him on 25 July 1990.[50] The transcript of the meeting released by the Iraqis in the fall of 1990 was not markedly different from Glaspie's account of the meeting.[51] In fact, this meeting is probably less important than the overall posture of the U.S. administration, and what was actually said is perhaps less important than what Iraq thought was said. The fact remains, however, that Glaspie did no more than repeat the policy line that had been established by Baker on 19 July.[52]

On 28 July, following up on the 25 July meeting with Ambassador Glaspie, Bush sent a cable to Saddam Hussein stating that any use of force would be unacceptable, and reiterating the administration's desire to improve relations with Iraq. But the key statements were perhaps those made on 31 July 1990 by Assistant Secretary of State for Near Eastern and South Asian Affairs John H.

46. Quoted in U.S. News & World Report, *Triumph Without Victory*, p. 24.

47. Karabell, "Backfire," pp. 28-33.

48. United Nations, *Iraq-Kuwait Conflict*, p. 395.

49. Karabell, "Backfire," pp. 45-46.

50. For example, see the *New York Times*, 23 September 1990.

51. For the Iraqi transcript of this meeting, see Micah L. Sifry and Christofer Cerf, *The Gulf War Reader* (Times Books, 1991), pp. 122-133.

52. See, e.g., Karabell, "Backfire," pp. 44-45.

Kelly to a congressional subcommittee.   The question/answer session is
partially reported below:

Q: Do we have a commitment to our friends in the Gulf in the event that they are
engaged in oil or territorial disputes with their neighbors?
Kelly: We have no defense-treaty relationships with any of the [Gulf] countries. We
have historically avoided taking a position on border disputes or on internal OPEC
deliberations, but we have certainly, as have all administrations, resoundingly called
for the peaceful settlement of disputes and differences in the area.
Q: If Iraq, for example, charged across the border into Kuwait, for whatever
reason, what would be our position with regard to the use of U.S. forces?
Kelly: "That . . . is a hypothetical or a contingency, the kind of which I can't get
into. Suffice it to say we would be extremely concerned, but I cannot get into the
realm of "what if" answers.
Q: In that circumstance, it is correct to say, however, that we do not have a treaty
commitment which would obligate us to engage U.S. forces?
Kelly: That is correct.

We don't know if the Iraqi leadership was aware of this exchange; however,
it is indicative of the Bush administration's hands-off approach to the crisis,
and this approach may have been taken into account in Baghdad. There can be
no doubt today that the Iraqi leadership, in particular President Saddam
Hussein, misjudged U.S. willingness to go to war if Kuwait was invaded.
Public U.S. statements prior to the invasion are not unequivocally clear
statements of U.S. intentions.   Indeed, one might have concluded that the
United States would not intervene militarily to protect Kuwait. A more acute
observer might have drawn a different conclusion by recalling the record of
U.S. military interventions and the fact that, while the United States may
profess peace, it will—as will any country—go to war energetically when it
feels that its vital interests (real or perceived) are in danger.
    Future historians who will have access to currently classified archives will
be able to address the question of the extent to which U.S. policy toward Iraq
was formed as a compromise among agencies with differing mandates, or
instead was deliberately directed in order to attain specific goals.[53]
    Contemporaneously with Kelly's testimony, direct Kuwaiti-Iraqi talks had
started in Jeddah on 31 July, but collapsed on the same day. They were
officially suspended on 1 August. On that very night, spurred on by its
economic crisis, by Kuwait's intransigence, by misplaced confidence in its
armed forces, by the erroneous conviction that Western powers would not

---

53. For example, Pierre Salinger has recently argued that the United States made
no effort to stop the Iraqi invasion of Kuwait before it took place, and did not negotiate
directly with Iraq in the aftermath of the invasion. Furthermore, he contends that the
United Nations was not informed of the Iraqi threat to Kuwait before August 1990, and
was never asked to act as a mediator between the parties concerned. See Pierre
Salinger, "The United States, the United Nations, and the Gulf War," *Middle East
Journal*, 49, no. 4 (Autumn 1995): 595-613.

react and that the Arab world would support its actions, Iraq ordered its troops to invade the emirate.[54]

THE INVASION OF KUWAIT

Elements of the approximately 80,000[55] Iraqi troops, mostly Republican Guards equipped with 350 tanks, who had been concentrated along the Iraq-Kuwait border during July crossed into Kuwait in the early morning of 2 August 1990. About 30,000 men, including armored brigades equipped with T-72 tanks, sped across the desert towards Kuwait City. Even though greatly outnumbered, the Kuwaiti army (about 20,000 men), had it been prepared, could have offered some resistance and slowed the Iraqi invasion. But the Kuwaitis were taken by surprise: according to Gen. Khaled bin Sultan, no one in the Arab world had envisaged that Iraq could actually intend to occupy Kuwait City.[56]

This seems confirmed by the Kuwaiti leadership's easygoing attitude toward the mounting Iraqi threat. Saudi sources quote an account by Kuwaiti Emir Jaber of the May 1990 Arab League summit in Baghdad: "I invited Saddam to visit Kuwait, since he had not done so for a long time. His answer was that he would visit Kuwait next month. I asked him for the date, so that we could prepare a big reception. His answer was that his visit would be a surprise. Saddam went on to say that he would resolve our border disputes in a surprising way within the following month. *I took his words in a brotherly logic, meaning that there were no problems between us and Iraq, except for the border disputes* [italics ours]."[57] On 21 July 1990, at the height of the crisis, the Kuwaiti crown prince publicly expressed his conviction that this "was a summer cloud which would pass away."

Although the Kuwaiti army had gone on full alert after Saddam Hussein's 17 July speech, the alert level was reduced one week later, and Kuwaiti forces were unable to reassemble in time to resist the very rapid Iraqi advance effectively. One Kuwaiti brigade and the Kuwaiti air force offered some

---

54. An interesting interpretation of the events leading to the invasion of Kuwait is found in William H. Kincade, "On the Brink in the Gulf. Part 1: Onset of the 'Classic' 1990 Crisis," *Security Studies*, 2, no. 2 (Winter 1992). In the author's view, examination of mind-set, character, crisis context, political culture, and deterrence theory helps demonstrate that the invasion of Kuwait stemmed from flawed images and related miscalculations in Washington, Baghdad, and the other Arab capitals during the precrisis and crisis-onset phases in the first seven months of 1990.

55. Official reports vary, some going as high as 140,000 troops organized into 8 divisions with 1,500 tanks and armored personnel carriers.

56. bin Sultan, *Desert Warrior*, p. 175.

57. Saudi Press Agency, *Asdah al-Moukef al-Saudi Khilal Ahadath al-Kalij al-Arabi* (The Saudi Position During the Events in the Arabian Gulf) (1991).

resistance, but were overwhelmed by the mass and speed of the Iraqi invasion.[58]

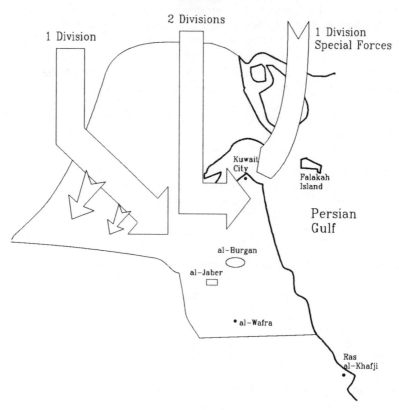

Map 2.1
The invasion of Kuwait

The Iraqis crossed the border in three places at 0100 hours and were met by some artillery fire. A mechanized infantry division and an armored division conducted the main attack while another armored division conducted a supporting attack farther west. Around 0130 hours, Iraqi special operations forces launched a helicopter attack against key government facilities in Kuwait City. Helicopters also landed troops on the uninhabited islands of Warba and Bubiyan—long a bone of contention. Ports and military airfields were damaged by artillery and air bombardment, and army bases at al-Jarah, west of the capital, were overrun. As the advance was taking place, a unit broke away

---

58. In December 1990, the Kuwaiti government claimed that 4,200 Kuwaiti soldiers had been killed during the invasion. It is not clear if this number includes those killed during the subsequent occupation.

and occupied Abdaly, 80 kilometers north of Kuwait City. Reportedly to the surprise of most Kuwaitis, the Iraqis did not stop after they had occupied the disputed border zones and oil fields, but advanced into Kuwait City itself at 0530, taking the airport and destroying the emir's palace. Sheikh Fahd al-Ahmad al-Sabah, one of the emir's brothers, organized resistance at Dasman Palace and was killed. Some of the Kuwaiti air force ran bombing missions, cratering a runway in the northern airfield and attacking some of the advancing Iraqi columns. As the Iraqi troops approached and it became clear that no one was going to stop them, many Kuwaiti pilots wisely flew their planes to Saudi Arabia. A few months later, these pilots would join the Coalition air forces that conducted the air campaign against Iraq and liberated Kuwait.

Kuwait City was secured by 1900 hours, and the occupation of Kuwait was largely completed in twelve hours. By the afternoon of 3 August, strong forces were concentrated on the border with Saudi Arabia, and Kuwait's crown prince, who was observing the concentration, abandoned all hopes of remaining in Kuwaiti territory. The emir had left his country the previous day, driving over the border just ahead of the advancing Iraqi columns.[59]

From the beginning Iraqi actions played into the hand of interventionist tendencies in the West, and especially the United States. As the *New York Times* put it on 3 August: "Without warrant or warning, Iraq has struck brutally at a tiny Kuwait, a brazen challenge to world law . . . 'Naked Aggression!' is the correct term for President Saddam Hussein's grab at a vulnerable, oil-rich neighbor." Indeed, the attack was sudden and unprovoked; a transparently fabricated call by Kuwaitis for Iraqi intervention was given as the motive of the attack; it took place while intra-Arab efforts to resolve the Iraqi-Kuwaiti disputes were still taking place; Iraqi troops advanced up to the border of Saudi Arabia; and there were widespread reports of looting, rape, and other atrocities.

There can be little doubt that Iraq underestimated the effect on Western public opinion of two key points that later became the mainstays of anti-Iraq propaganda in the West: first, the fact that Westerners could not accept any justification for the invasion and saw it merely as an attempt to grab oil fields; second, the fact that reports of brutality against civilians increased hostility toward Iraq.

Iraq made many public statements about its position in the crisis, its grievances, and the justification for taking action against Kuwait. However, most of these statements were addressed to Arab nations, and Iraq did little to explain its position carefully to Western public opinion (believing, perhaps, that Western opinion was irrelevant, since the West would lack the will to intervene militarily). Even if Iraq had explained its position, it would have been unable to justify to Western public opinion the massive and total invasion that took place.

---

59. U.S. Department of Defense, *Conduct of the Persian Gulf War*, pp. 1-3.

Initial reports of Iraqi brutality were shocking to Westerners: surrendering Kuwaiti soldiers shot en masse; severely sick people thrown out of hospitals; a nurse's dormitory turned into a brothel for rape; babies removed from incubators and left to die; suspected resistance fighters tortured to death; research equipment, computers, and libraries carted off to Iraq wholesale. While some of these early reports have been subsequently disproved, there is no doubt that significant looting and brutality took place during the invasion.[60]

In any case, Western public opinion believed that the Iraqi invasion had been brutal and that Iraqi troops had not acted in accordance with the high-minded modern principles of war enshrined in the Geneva Convention. It is possible that Western political leaders would have had to work harder to justify Western intervention if Iraqi troops had behaved less brutally.

As a consequence of the harsh conditions during the occupation, most Kuwaitis fled abroad. Reportedly, relatively few Kuwaiti citizens were left in the city when it was liberated. However, the citizens of the emirate were not the only people who suffered during the invasion. Well over 2 million Egyptian, Palestinian, and other foreign workers were employed in the emirate at the time of the invasion. Most of them fled the country, taking with them only what they could carry and losing their accumulated savings. In many cases the workers in Kuwait had been supporting large families at home, so many more in Bangladesh, Egypt, India, Korea, Morocco, Pakistan, the Palestine occupied territories, the Philippines, and Sri Lanka suffered a sudden deprivation of their main source of income. Since the Iraqi army sealed off the border with Saudi Arabia, most of the refugees traveled through Iraq to the border with Jordan; at the peak period, some 14,000 people were arriving in Jordan daily.[61]

WORLD REACTION

On 2 August, the day of the invasion of Kuwait, U.K. Prime Minister Margaret Thatcher was in Aspen, Colorado, where she and U.S. President Bush were scheduled to speak at the Aspen Institute of International Affairs. Thatcher immediately put herself on the front line of action, issuing a call for "concerted international action to force Iraq out of Kuwait." On the next day, on her way back to the U.K., she made an unscheduled stop in Washington to stand beside Bush and proclaim the U.K.'s resolve to work with the United States in liberating Kuwait. Some have speculated that Thatcher's determination, and the consequent reliability of the U.K. as an ally, might have influenced Bush's early reactions to the events.[62]

---

60. United Nations, *Iraq-Kuwait Conflict*, p. 217.

61. Ibid., pp. 18-19.

62. On this episode, see William H. Kincade, "On the Brink in the Gulf. Part 2: The Route to War," *Security Studies*, 2, no. 15 (1992): 319.

Arab leaders did not immediately abandon their efforts to seek a negotiated solution. Building on Iraq's 3 August declaration that its troops would withdraw from Kuwait, Egypt and Saudi Arabia attempted to organize an Arab summit in Jeddah during the first week in August. Scenarios for a peaceful solution covered a wide range of possibilities: from a change in the border in favor of Iraq, to extensive financial payments to Iraq, to significant changes in Kuwait's government. But the summit never took place: a public statement definitely announcing its cancellation was issued on 6 August. Why? It is doubtful that an Arab summit could have found a solution acceptable to all Arab parties; it is likely that it could not have found a solution acceptable to both Iraq and the West, which had clearly stated that the only acceptable solution was a complete and total Iraqi withdrawal and a return to the status quo ante. Western countries declared their intentions both individually and collectively, under the guise of resolutions by the U.N. Security Council (three of whose five permanent members are Western countries: France, the UK, the United States). Then, on 8 August, the United States announced its deployment of military forces to Saudi Arabia, thus signaling the West's determination to stem Iraqi aggression. Two days later, twelve members of the Arab League also voted to send troops.

The U.S. announcement, and the corresponding deployment of U.S. troops in Saudi Arabia, were in response to that country's official call for assistance in protecting against a possible Iraqi invasion. According to official U.S. reports, the Iraqi troop dispositions on 6 August were two divisions on the border with Saudi Arabia; one in Kuwait City; and eight in the northern half of Kuwait.[63] Although these forces were clearly more than what was needed to occupy Kuwait, their disposition on 6 August would not appear to indicate an immediate intent to invade Saudi Arabia.

Nevertheless the United States has publicly stated that it initially sent troops to Saudi Arabia only to prevent further advances by Iraqi troops. This mission fully coincided with Saudi views of the situation. In fact, Gen. Khaled bin Sultan, who commanded the Arab forces in the Coalition and who is a senior member of the Saudi royal family, candidly states in his autobiography that King Fahd believed that the invasion of Kuwait directly threatened Saudi Arabia's survival, and that the kingdom would have to ask for help to defend itself.[64] Indeed, King Fahd is quoted as stating: "After Kuwait, Saddam will attack the eastern side of Saudi Arabia, otherwise why all these big forces, and why this surprise?" and "The real reason Iraq attacked Kuwait was to own all the Arab Gulf countries, starting with Kuwait, continuing with Saudi Arabia, Bahrain, Qatar, UAE, Oman, and so on. That is why the Iraqi military attacked Kuwait with such large forces . . . the second round, after a few days,

---

63. U.S. Department of Defense, *Conduct of the Persian Gulf War*, chapter I.
64. bin Sultan, *Desert Warrior*, pp. 19-21.

would have been to take part of Saudi Arabia and then continue the whole plan."[65]

According to bin Sultan, the Saudis had considered the options well in advance, ruling out exclusive reliance on the military forces of Arab and Muslim allies because of their lack of mobility and long-range deterrent capabilities.[66] This is confirmed by the account that General Schwarzkopf gives of Saudi Arabian King Fahd's decision to invite U.S. troops. "I showed the king a series of photos of Iraqi tanks at the Saudi border," recounts Schwarzkopf. "Then I outlined our plan to defend the kingdom [with U.S. forces]. . . . The king and his advisors began debating among themselves the pros and cons of bringing us in. . . . The discussion among the members of the royal family present was very brief. . . . King Fahd . . . turned to Cheney and said in English simply: 'OK.'"[67] As bin Sultan puts it: "the Cheney mission to Riyadh of August 6 merely put an official, public seal on something which had already been decided. The King had already made up his mind."[68]

The Iraqi response to the U.S. troop deployment (code-named Operation Desert Shield) was to announce on 8 August the annexation of Kuwait, which was declared the nineteenth province of Iraq. This action was a clear provocation, meant to signal Iraq's defiance of the West, the U.N. Security Council, and the Arab countries that had called for an Iraqi withdrawal. Had Iraq always intended to annex all of Kuwait, or was the total annexation a response to Desert Shield? Perhaps future historians will be able to answer this question. Iraqi statements prior to 7 August do not indicate any intention to annex Kuwait. Rather, they advocate a scenario in which a newly installed puppet government would comply with Iraq's will. On 2 August, for example, Baghdad Radio had announced that "we will withdraw when the situation becomes stable and when Kuwait's provisional government asks us to do so. This may not exceed a few days or a few weeks."

Saddam Hussein may have been surprised by the harsh international reaction, particularly its rapidity and breadth. In an attempt to regain the initiative, on 12 August he announced the peace plan to which he would stick throughout the crisis: withdrawal from Kuwait in exchange for a total solution to all the region's problems—including the Palestinian question. This "linkage" between issues was categorically rejected by Israel and all the Coalition countries, but gave rise to a debate concerning the partial and selective enforcement of U.N. resolutions regarding the Middle East. We quote from Saddam Hussein's speech:

All the questions of occupation in the entire region, current or future, should be resolved on the same basis and according to the same principles, those of the Security

---

65. Saudi Press Agency, *Asdah al-Moukef al-Saudi*.
66. bin Sultan, *Desert Warrior*, pp. 22-24.
67. Schwarzkopf, *It Doesn't Take a Hero*, pp. 304-305.
68. bin Sultan, *Desert Warrior*, p. 26.

Council. . . . [We favor] an immediate and unconditional withdrawal of Israel from the occupied Arab territories in Palestine, Syria, and Lebanon; a withdrawal of Syria from Lebanon; and a mutual withdrawal between Iran and Iraq in addition to the steps to be taken in Kuwait. . . . [Regarding Kuwait it is necessary to] take into account Iraq's historical territorial claims and the will of the Kuwaiti people. . . . [Withdrawal] should start with the occupation that took place first. Then all the U.N. resolutions should be applied . . . The measures taken by the Security Council against Iraq should be also applied to whoever does not comply with these resolutions. . . . [We request] the immediate withdrawal from Saudi Arabia of American troops and of all other troops that have taken part in this conspiracy. They should be replaced by Arab troops whose composition, nationality, mission and positions should be defined by the Security Council. . . . [We demand] an immediate suspension of all resolutions regarding sanctions and the embargo against Iraq.

On 15 August, Iraq accepted Iran's conditions for a permanent end to the Iran-Iraq War, thus freeing up troops that would otherwise have had to defend that border. Iraq accepted that Iran would control one shore of the Shatt al-Arab, perhaps feeling that this was a minor concession now that it controlled the Kuwaiti coast and the islands of Bubiyan and Warba. In retrospect, the concessions to Iran may have made it more difficult for the Iraqi leadership to envisage a total pullout from Kuwait without retaining some control of the disputed islands. Thus, what appeared at the time to be a move to increase Iraq's flexibility may in fact have limited it.

By this time, U.S. military planners had begun to think that Iraqi troops in Kuwait were digging in and that offensive action might be required to remove them; an initial concept was developed during the second week of August and presented to U.S. President Bush on 16 August, but this initial plan was unsatisfactory because of the limited forces available.[69] Vigorous enforcement of a total economic embargo against Iraq started on 16 August. The next day, the Iraqi president "invited" all Westerners in Iraq to stay, in effect turning them into hostages. On 18 August, Iraq announced that Westerners would be used as "human shields" to protect key facilities against attack. On 19 August, Saddam Hussein explicitly linked release of the hostages to a U.S. force withdrawal and a pledge not to use force against Iraq. It appears that the Iraqi president counted on the use of hostages to delay any immediate military moves by United States and to gain time.

The taking of hostages was met with outrage in the West and likely contributed to a hardening of Western public opinion—as did the Iraqi television broadcast of Saddam Hussein patting the head of a young British boy whose family was among the hostages. Television footage showing the plight of tens of thousands of immigrant workers forced to leave Kuwait and travel through Iraq to Jordan, where they were kept in refugee camps, did nothing to improve Iraq's image. Nor did the measures taken against the embassies that

---

69. Schwarzkopf, *It Doesn't Take a Hero*, p. 315.

had chosen to remain in Kuwait after the 24 August deadline declared by Iraq for the closing of all foreign missions in the emirate.

In September, Saddam Hussein embarked on what appeared to be a campaign to create divisions within the nations arrayed against him by exploiting his hostages. A series of political figures traveled to Baghdad to discuss the fate of the Westerners, and Iraq announced some piecemeal releases.

But meanwhile political leaders in the United States, Europe, and the Middle East were at work forging the political consensus that would lead to the creation of the Coalition. USSR President Mikhail Gorbachev sent a personal envoy, Yevgeny Primakov, to Baghdad twice in early October, but was unable to obtain any softening of the Iraqi positions. U.S. Secretary of State James Baker visited the capitals of the major countries, including the USSR, and on 8 November the United States announced a major increase in its military forces deployed in the Gulf. On 18 November, Saddam Hussein announced that all Western hostages would be released before Christmas. Was this a signal that Iraq was seeking a negotiated solution? No concessions were forthcoming from the West, and a visit by Iraqi Foreign Minister Tarik Aziz to Moscow on 26 November also had no visible results. The plan for the military operation that would later become Desert Storm was presented to U.S. President Bush during his Thanksgiving visit to Saudi Arabia, and was approved by him. A week later, on 29 November, the U.N. Security Council authorized the use of force if Iraq did not withdraw by 15 January 1991. The next day Bush proposed a meeting between Baker and Aziz. Iraq's initial response was favorable, but it soon became apparent that its main interest was to postpone the meeting as long as possible, presumably in order to delay any Coalition military moves.[70]

On 3 December, the United States declared that it could not wait indefinitely for economic sanctions to compel an Iraqi withdrawal. On 6 December, Saddam Hussein announced that all Western hostages were free to leave because, in his view, they had fulfilled their role of delaying a Coalition offensive. Again, this move appears inexplicable. It may have been a peace feeler, but Iraq continued to insist that the visit of Baker to Baghdad could not take place until 12 January 1991, and on 18 December, Iraq proclaimed that it would not withdraw. The two sides finally managed to agree on a meeting between Baker and Aziz in Geneva on 9 January. The meeting was long but inconclusive, with both sides restating their well-known positions and Aziz refusing to accept a letter from Bush to Saddam Hussein.[71]

---

70. It has been argued that U.S. president Bush's offer of a meeting between Baker and Aziz was not serious and that it was merely a consequence of his concern that U.S. citizens and those of Coalition countries would see the White House as too bent on war. See Kincade, "On the Brink in the Gulf. Part 2: The Route to War," p. 301.

71. The text of the letter, a restatement of well-publicized U.S. demands for withdrawal, is reproduced in Sifry and Cerf, *The Gulf War Reader*, p. 178.

Apparently sure of the ability of his troops to fight well on the ground, or believing that the Coalition would not actually initiate military action, the Iraqi president rejected a last-minute peace initiative by U.N. General Secretary Perez de Cuellar, who travelled to Baghdad on 13 January.

The Role of the United Nations

The United Nations provided the umbrella under which the Coalition countries forged their policies. Ever since its creation after World War II, the United Nations has proved to be a paper tiger. Many of its resolutions have been openly flouted by powerful countries, including Israel and South Africa. However, it proved to be a useful forum for Coalition nations to build consensus both among themselves and with passive allies (such as the USSR) in the effort to liberate Kuwait. As U.S. President Bush stated subsequently:

The Coalition became essential from the very first days. Unilateral U.S. response to Saddam's invasion could well have gotten us crosswise with the Soviet Union, with other Arab countries, and even with Europe. It was essential that other countries join in, and that the United Nations be involved. . . . the aggression was so clear, and contravened so directly the U.N. purpose, the U.N.'s stated objective, that we all felt we could and must get the U.N. to pass a resolution. In so doing, not only could we bring together the Coalition that would commit forces, but major powers such as China would be committed.[72]

Had the mechanism of the U.N. Security Council proved ineffective in building the Coalition, we don't doubt that an alternative forum would have been found, for example an ad hoc alliance to liberate Kuwait. But such a step was not necessary, and the Coalition acted under the aegis of the United Nations, to enforce Security Council resolutions.

It is likely that Iraq dismissed the effectiveness of the United Nations, on the basis of its repeated failure to enforce resolutions calling for the withdrawal of Israel from the territories occupied in 1967. Even if Iraq did understand the importance of the United Nations as a forum for building the Coalition effort against it, there was little it could do to stymie that effort, since it lacked a reliable ally among the permanent members of the Security Council, who alone have veto power.

The Security Council acted quickly and decisively to condemn the Iraqi invasion of Kuwait, to call for Iraqi withdrawal, and to propose steps that would force a withdrawal.[73] Taken together, the resolutions show the determined will of the West and its Arab allies to obtain an unconditional withdrawal, and to foreshadow the harsh cease-fire conditions that would be imposed on Iraq after its military defeat.

---

72. Quoted in U.S. News & World Report, *Triumph Without Victory*, p. 82.

73. The U.N. resolutions have been widely reproduced, e.g., in U.S. Department of Defense, *Conduct of the Persian Gulf War*, Appendix B.

In retrospect, it is clear that Iraq should have interpreted these resolutions as handwriting on the wall, and sought a solution based on withdrawal. There was a hiatus between the trade embargo imposed on 6 August and the authorization to use force on 29 November. During this time there was considerable debate within Coalition countries regarding the effectiveness of economic sanctions and their ability to compel an Iraqi withdrawal from Kuwait.

U.S. Reactions

The Bush administration's reaction to the 2 August invasion of Kuwait was unequivocal: it refused to accept the aggression and demanded unconditional Iraqi withdrawal. On the morrow, after approving executive orders prohibiting transactions with Iraq and freezing of its U.S. assets, President Bush told his advisers that the invasion could not be allowed to stand.[74] Although it was not widely reported by the media at the time, President Bush declared a national emergency on 2 August: "I . . . find that the policies and actions of the Government of Iraq constitute an unusual and extraordinary threat to the national security and foreign policy of the United States and hereby declare a national emergency to deal with that threat." This measure gave Bush the authority to call up certain reserve military forces.

During the early days, there was considerable discussion and doubt about the measures that should be taken to compel Iraq to withdraw: proposals ranged from relying on economic sanctions that might take years to have effect to an immediate and massive military strike. However, the national consensus on undoing Iraqi aggression was extremely strong. While control of oil resources was a key factor shaping U.S. policies, the public debate tended to refer to moral arguments. Proposals to obtain a partial Iraqi withdrawal by ceding Kuwaiti territory to Iraq were too close in spirit to the politics of appeasement practiced by U.K. Prime Minister Neville Chamberlain prior to World War II (agreeing to accept German territorial demands in exchange for promises of peace). On 9 August 1990, Bush rallied public opinion by explicitly comparing Iraqi President Saddam Hussein to German dictator Adolf Hitler, pointing out that the politics of appeasement had not prevented World War II: "Appeasement does not work. As was the case in the 1930s, we see in Saddam Hussein an aggressive dictator threatening his neighbors."[75] And again on 23 October: "There's a parallel between what Hitler did to Poland and what Saddam Hussein has done to Kuwait." Hence the United States refused to participate in any negotiations based on the acceptance of Iraqi demands. Thus, in a matter of days U.S. and Western perceptions made a

---

74. Quoted in U.S. News & World Report, *Triumph Without Victory*, p. 48.
75. *Washington Post*, 9 August 1990.

dramatic about-face: the reformable dictator of the late 1980s became the demon aggressor of the early 1990s.[76]

The Iraqi leadership either did not understand enough about the United States to predict its reaction, or believed that the United States would not intervene militarily, preferring to rely on economic sanctions. Apparently, Saddam Hussein assumed that the United States would be deterred from military intervention by a continuing "Vietnam syndrome." In fact, the United States has a long history of armed intervention ranging from the bombardment of Tripoli in the early nineteenth century to the invasion of Panama in 1989.

It is true that the United States has not used military power to redress every situation of which it disapproves. For example, in recent times the United States has not used force to "stand up for what is right and to condemn what is wrong" (as President Bush expressed himself on 8 August 1990) in South Africa, Latin America, eastern Europe, or China; nor to enforce U.N. Security Council resolutions calling for Israeli withdrawal from the territories occupied during the Six-Day War (1967). However, it is clear that no vital U.S. interests were at stake in any of these situations. In fact, it can be argued that U.S. economic and geopolitical interests were favored by the existing conditions in certain countries, however much the status quo conflicted with the ideals of the U.S. Constitution.

Thus, its reluctance to use force to export its democratic ideals should not have been taken as a sign that the United States would fail to use force to protect its vital interests in an economically and geopolitically important region such as the Persian Gulf. In fact, it had spent over 10 years preparing the capability to wage war in the Gulf,[77] creating the Central Command headquarters structure specifically to deal with potential conflicts in the Middle East and potential threats from the USSR or, later, Khomeinist Iran. While Central Command had only limited naval forces directly assigned to it, it could quickly assume operational control over designated forces from other commands in case of a crisis.

In July 1978, a presidential directive identified a strike force of 100,000 troops, including 2 aircraft carriers and 200 Air Force planes, to respond to regional contingencies. On 1 October 1979, President Carter announced that rapid deployment forces would be used to meet contingencies anywhere in the world. On 5 December 1979, the U.S. Marines announced that 50,000 men would be organized to spearhead the rapid deployment forces. And eight days later, the U.S. secretary of defense announced that ships carrying heavy equipment and supplies in dehumidified storage for three Marine brigades would be stationed in remote areas around the world. Such ships were used to deliver equipment to Saudi Arabia from Diego Garcia (an island in the Indian

---

76. An assessment of appeasement policies in light of the Gulf crisis of 1990-1991 is in Kincade, "On the Brink in the Gulf. Part 2: The Route to War," pp. 295-329.

77. For a general discussion, see U.S. Department of Defense, *Conduct of the Persian Gulf War*, Appendix D, especially pp. 29-35.

Ocean) within 15 days of the invasion of Kuwait. On 23 January 1980, U.S. President Carter stated: "Any attempt by any outside force to gain control of the Persian Gulf region will be regarded as an assault on the vital interests of the United States and will be repelled by any means necessary, including military force." This became known as the Carter Doctrine. On 1 March, a joint services rapid deployment task force was established to protect U.S. national interests, including assured access to oil. This force later selected training centers in California to support realistic terrain and environmental training for desert conditions. In 1981, military construction and improvements were approved for existing facilities in Diego Garcia, Egypt, Kenya, Oman, and Somalia.

On 1 October 1981, U.S. President Reagan declared that "there's no way the United States could stand by and see that [Persian Gulf oil] taken over by anyone that would shut off that oil." On 1 January 1983, the rapid deployment task force became the U.S. Central Command, which would control U.S. forces in the Middle East. President Reagan stated on 6 April 1984: "Given the importance of the region [the Middle East], we must also be ready to act when the presence of American power and that of our friends can help stop the spread of violence." During 1988 and 1989, Central Command planners revised their plans for the Middle East specifically to address the U.S. capability to counter an Iraqi attack on Kuwait and Saudi Arabia. On 17 January 1989, the U.S. secretary of defense defined maintaining access to regional oil supplies and promoting the security and stability of friendly states to be U.S. regional goals in the Middle East. In the fall of 1989, the Defense Planning Guide, a primary tool for linking strategy and resource planning, called for additional attention to the defense of the Arabian Peninsula against strong regional threats and Central Command realigned its planning priorities.[78]

On 16 April 1990, U.S. Central Command published an outline plan dealing with an Iraqi invasion of Kuwait and Saudi Arabia.[79] In July, the U.S. Naval War College's annual games included as one scenario an Iraqi attack and occupation of Kuwait and Saudi Arabia.[80] Also in July, U.S. Central Command staff (including General Schwarzkopf) war-gamed the scenario of an invasion of the Arabian Peninsula. This exercise, code-named Internal Look, was in progress when the first intelligence reports of Iraqi troop movements arrived.[81] Also in July 1990, a plan containing the overall personnel and equipment requirements, as well as the strategy required for a successful defense of Kuwait, was being reviewed by military commanders, concurrently

---

78. Cohen et al., *GWAPS: Planning*, p. 20; and Col. Richard M. Swain, *"Lucky War": Third Army in Desert Storm* (U.S. Army Command and General Staff College Press, 1994), p. 4.

79. Cohen et al., *GWAPS: Logistics*, p. 58.

80. Cohen et al., *GWAPS: Chronology*, p. 2.

81. Ibid., p. 4.

with exercise Internal Look. This plan formed the basis for the initial U.S. deployment in Saudi Arabia.

U.S. policy was clearly articulated by Bush on 5 August: "What's emerging is nobody [the leaders of other countries] seems to be showing up as willing to accept anything less than total withdrawal from Kuwait of the Iraqi forces, and no puppet regime. . . . I view very seriously our determination to reverse this aggression. . . . This will not stand. This will not stand, this aggression against Kuwait." On 8 August, the United States announced the deployment of troops to defend Saudi Arabia against attack.[82] On 16 August, U.S. warships in the Persian Gulf and Red Sea were ordered to enforce U.N. economic sanctions against Iraq.[83]

Despite calls from some quarters[84] to give ample time for sanctions to have their effect, the administration's position hardened considerably as the months passed. While no peaceful solution was found, Coalition military forces grew in strength and Iraq deployed additional troops in Kuwait. As the autumn wore on and President Bush became more determined to force Saddam Hussein's withdrawal, the fear of a compromise settlement grew in Washington. On 23 October, Bush clearly stated his position on this matter: "There can never be compromise, any kind of compromise, with this kind of aggression. . . . These are crimes against humanity. . . . It isn't oil that we're concerned about, it is aggression, and this aggression is not going to stand."[85] In fact, it seems fair to say that "as for diplomacy, Washington never did see a role for it in settling the Gulf Crisis."[86]

After the congressional elections on 4 November, Bush clearly signaled his intention to use military force if necessary (according to the account given by General Schwarzkopf in his autobiography, Bush had apparently decided on 31 October that offensive operations would be needed[87]). Already on 6 October a U.S. Central Command assessment had stated that additional forces would be required to force Iraq out of Kuwait, and this had been presented to Bush on 11 October.[88] On 8 November Bush said: "I have today directed the Secretary of Defense to increase the size of the U.S. forces . . . to ensure that the

---

82. Ibid., p. 11.

83. Ibid., p. 24.

84. See, e.g., Admiral William J. Crow, Jr., "Give Sanctions a Chance," and Zbigniew Brzezinski, "The Drift to War," both in Sifry and Cerf, *The Gulf War Reader*, pp. 234 and 251 respectively. For a discussion of sanctions, see Chapter 3, section "Would Economic Sanctions Have Worked?"

85. On U.S. fear of a compromise settlement, see Elaine Sciolino, *The Outlaw State: Saddam Hussein's Quest for Power and the Gulf Crisis* (Wiley, 1991), pp. 232-234.

86. John Newhouse, "The Diplomatic Round: Misreadings," *The New Yorker* (18 February 1991). See also Kincade, "On the Brink in the Gulf. Part 2: The Route to War," pp. 300-301.

87. Schwarzkopf, *It Doesn't Take a Hero*, p. 370.

88. Ibid., pp. 359-361.

Coalition has an adequate offensive military option should that be necessary to achieve our common goals." On that day the United States announced that 100,000 more troops and 700 more top-line M1 tanks would be added to the forces in Saudi Arabia; some of these forces were NATO units stationed in Europe.

On the following day, the additional troop deployment was explained in detail and turned out to be more than twice the initial report. The United States sent to Saudi Arabia 110,000 men and 1,000 tanks from VII Corps (nearly half its forces in Europe); 17,000 men and 450 tanks from the First Infantry Division; 3 additional aircraft carriers and 1 additional battleship; 60,000 more Marines, bringing the Marine strength up to some 90,000 men, nearly half the total of this elite corps. In fact, the United States eventually committed nearly half of its active ground forces, combat aircraft, and carrier task forces to the Coalition.

Later in November, Bush signaled his resolve. Speaking to U.S. troops in Dhahran, Saudi Arabia, on 22 November: "We're not walking away until our mission is done, until the invader is out of Kuwait." On 30 November: "I am not suggesting discussions that will result in anything less than Iraq's complete withdrawal from Kuwait, restoration of Kuwait's legitimate government, and freedom for all hostages." Commenting on his decision to send Secretary of State Baker to Baghdad to meet with Iraqi President Saddam Hussein: "[The visit] is to be sure that he [Saddam Hussein] understands how strongly the President of the United States feels about implementing to a tee, without concessions, the U.N. position. . . . Never has there been a clearer demonstration of a world united against appeasement and aggression."

U.S. public opinion generally supported Bush's hard line. *New York Times*/CBS News Poll results in early August 1990 and early January 1991 reflect only a 5% drop in support for sending U.S. troops to the Gulf (66% to 61%). Yet a persistent and sizable number of those polled (41% in August, 43% in January) said that the government had not satisfactorily explained why the troops were sent.

Nevertheless, Bush pursued his inflexible policy, stating on 17 December: "no concession, no negotiation for one inch of territory. He [Saddam Hussein] has got to leave without conditions." On 3 January 1991: "No negotiation, no compromise, no attempts at face-saving and no rewards for aggression." The final confirmation of the United States' resolve came on 12 January, when Congress approved a resolution authorizing the use of U.S. military forces—a de facto declaration of war (the vote was 52 to 47 in the Senate, 250 to 183 in the House). Negative votes did not reflect a difference in principle but only one of timing; there was some sentiment in the Congress for giving economic sanctions more time before resorting to military action.

Soviet Reactions

As the only country possessing a military power even remotely comparable with that of the United States, the USSR was a key player in determining the progression of events. Iraq had perhaps counted on the goodwill of the USSR—an ally and its principal supplier of armored vehicles and missiles—to prevent a U.S. military attack. If it had, this was a miscalculation.

With the Soviet economy collapsing and attendant difficulties at home, the Kremlin had to keep a very low profile abroad. For the first time since the early 1950s, the United States found that it was the only superpower around, with responsibility for maintaining a certain degree of "world order"—and this in spite of its budget deficits and the effects of strong economic competition from Japan and Europe. As the U.S. Department of Defense put it: "the United States and many of its Coalition partners would not have been prepared to act so promptly and so decisively had the former Cold War circumstances still prevailed";[89] but perhaps they would not have needed to act, because in former times the USSR would have prevented Iraq from acting.

On 3 August 1990, U.S. Secretary of State James Baker and USSR Foreign Minister Eduard Shevardnadze issued a joint statement inviting all countries to take concrete measures to obtain the immediate and unconditional withdrawal of Iraqi troops from Kuwait. And on 9 September, U.S. President Bush and USSR President Gorbachev jointly stated: "Today we once again call upon the government of Iraq to withdraw unconditionally from Kuwait . . . Nothing short of the complete implementation of the United Nations Security Council resolutions is acceptable. . . . We are determined to see this aggression end."

The unusual nature of these joint declarations was indicative of the new nature of the relations between the two superpowers. Indeed, the Gulf crisis served as a litmus test of the "new thinking" in USSR foreign policy. Washington was able to confirm the definitive end of the practices that would have been typical during the Cold War, namely, the alignment of the USSR with Iraqi positions on the basis of bipolarity in world politics. Moscow made no attempt to protect its erstwhile client; in fact, Shevardnadze's speech to the United Nations in September was just as intransigent as Bush's.

Less visible but perhaps more important were U.S. attempts to test Gorbachev's willingness to abandon an international role and leave matters to Bush, de facto if not de jure. The USSR's position in this respect was less flexible: continued Soviet pressure to transfer responsibility for decisions regarding economic and military steps from the United States to the United Nations, and its repeated peace initiatives show that the leaders in Moscow intended to continue to play a role, behind the scenes if not publicly.[90] The United States thus faced an interesting challenge: how to operate in a world

---

89. U.S. Department of Defense, *Conduct of the Persian Gulf Conflict: An Interim Report to Congress* (July 1991), p. 21-1.

90. On this see Yevgeni Primakov, *Missione a Baghdad* (Ponte alle Grazie, 1991).

that was de facto unipolar while maintaining the de jure multilateral cover of the United Nations. And the real negotiations concerned the extent to which the United States would dominate world politics in the future.

By using the United Nations as a forum for consensus, the United States and its principal allies (France and the U.K.) were able to enlist the passive support of the USSR for their policies. The USSR approved all U.N. Security Council resolutions regarding the invasion of Kuwait and publicly stated that it would not oppose the Coalition's use of force to liberate Kuwait, although it regretted that such means appeared to be necessary. It also did not provide satellite-based reconnaissance data to Iraq; the availability of such data could have been helpful to Iraq in planning its resistance to the final Coalition ground assault.

However, the USSR did try to act as a mediator and may even have bluntly warned Iraq that it would face a massive military attack if it did not withdraw from Kuwait. USSR Special Envoy Primakov made several trips to Baghdad in October to meet with Iraqi President Saddam Hussein, but he was unable to obtain concessions that would meet U.S. demands. Unable to persuade Iraq to bend, the USSR finally gave its approval to the U.S. point of view. On 8 November, U.S. Secretary of State Baker and USSR Foreign Minister Shevardnadze issued a joint statement in Moscow which said that "[the use of force] could not be ruled out." The next day USSR President Gorbachev stated that "[all efforts to divide the Coalition] have failed and will continue to be doomed." On 26 November, he warned Iraq to withdraw or face "a tough U.N. resolution."

Reactions in the Arab World: Anti-Iraq Countries

The invasion of Kuwait was greeted with shocked surprise in Saudi Arabia, custodian of Islam's most important holy sites and of the world's largest oil reserves. The Saudis were suddenly confronted with the possibility that their rich, comfortable world could collapse under the treads of Iraqi tanks, as had the world of their neighbor. The stunned disbelief of the first hours was replaced by fear and consternation barely disguised by the media, which violently attacked the Baathist regime—after an initial silence meant to allow some time for the leaders in Riyadh to attempt a mediation. Saudi fears of an invasion were reinforced by U.S. forecasts of Iraq's intentions and capabilities.

Many Arab countries feared a rich, powerful, and dominant Iraq. It was this fear of Iraq's ambitions that motivated most Arab countries to tolerate, and some to invite, the West's intervention in the Gulf crisis. As General Khaled bin Sultan put the matter:

The Arab axis was formed because each of its three members saw Saddam's move as a deadly threat to its own vital interests. Saudi Arabia, Egypt, and Syria were united in a determination to defeat Iraq's bid for regional hegemony—a hegemony which would have undermined Saudi security and exposed it to extortion, marginalized Egypt in Arab affairs, and exposed the Syrian regime to extreme danger. Had Saddam not posed a deadly threat to the interests of these Arab states the Coalition would not have been formed and the war would not have been fought—or would have been fought very differently without Arab participation.[91]

The Bush administration moved quickly to gain Arab support against Iraq and adroitly exploited the long-standing enmity between Syria and Iraq. U.S. de facto recognition of Syria's de facto annexation of Lebanon was no doubt instrumental in obtaining Syrian support, just as the U.S. forgiveness of a $7 billion loan to Egypt certainly helped to secure Egyptian support; these countries quickly joined the Coalition, going so far as to contribute very significant military forces. In addition to armed forces, Egypt contributed by allowing Coalition ships and airplanes to cross its territory. Some 376 military supply ships passed through the Suez Canal during the course of the crisis and war, as did nearly 400 warships; over 30,000 planes flew through Egyptian airspace and nearly 4,500 landed and were serviced at Egyptian airports.

The centuries-old traditional rivalry for the leadership of the Arab world that involved Baghdad, Cairo, and Damascus also worked against Iraq.[92] Following the invasion of Kuwait, Egypt—concerned that it would lead to a complete change in the regional status quo, to its own disadvantage—led the way in forging the anti-Iraq coalition. Egyptian President Mubarak encouraged Saudi Arabia to take a strong stand, and used various mechanisms to mobilize Arab support against Iraq and to legitimize both the deployment of Arab forces in Saudi Arabia and the other Gulf countries as well as the recourse to American military intervention. Egypt's leadership in the Arab world had been badly damaged when President Anwar Sadat made peace with Israel; its attempts to reassert its position were stymied by the prestige of an Iraqi president capable of standing up to the mighty United States and of offering Arab countries without major natural resources (oil and gas) a social and political program tailored to their needs.

To justify its decision to join the anti-Iraqi coalition, Damascus accused Baghdad of distracting the Arab countries from their main goal (Arab victory in an Arab-Israeli conflict), noting that all Iraq had done was to weaken the Arab League and to provoke large-scale intervention by Western powers in an exclusively Arab conflict. This same argument had been used to justify Syria's aid to Iran during the Iran-Iraq War.

From a political point of view, neither Egypt nor Syria had any reason to support an Iraqi annexation of Kuwait, an event that could only result in the weakening of their own influence in the region. By annexing Kuwait, Iraq would have vastly increased its oil resources, and thus its capability to buy weapons and increase the firepower of its already formidable army. Egypt and Syria would naturally look askance at any settlement that legitimized Iraq's use of force to incorporate Kuwait and that gave Iraq the means to expand its

---

91. bin Sultan, *Desert Warrior*, p. 172.

92. For a cogent analysis of Middle Eastern interstate relations, see Evron, "Gulf Crisis and War," pp. 115-154.

military power. Thus Baghdad's calls for Arab unity were destined to fall on deaf ears in Cairo and Damascus.

Throughout the crisis, Egypt, Syria, and Saudi Arabia adopted a firm policy. Notwithstanding some disagreements among them, they clearly sought to accomplish two major objectives: to force Iraq out of Kuwait and to reduce Iraqi power.

Besides the necessity for the immediate withdrawal from Kuwait, Egyptian President Mubarak considered another point important: the necessity for Iraq to stop overthrowing other regimes by force. On 8 August he said: "I call on President Saddam and the Iraqi leadership to respond to an Arab umbrella and withdraw its forces from Kuwait and restore the legitimacy of Kuwait." Mubarak later stated: "The main point politically is not to interfere in the internal affairs of any country."[93]

In his 8 August speech Mubarak also claimed that Saddam Hussein had misled him by promising not to attack Kuwait: "I asked him [Saddam Hussein] outright if his troops were moving toward Kuwait, and he told me these were just routine movements and that the troops were 70 kilometers from the border. I asked him if he intended to attack, and he told me no." This irritated Mubarak: "You said you would not strike and you struck. And now you are turning to Saudi Arabia and saying 'I will not strike.' They will not believe you. . . . You are not accepting the Arab umbrella. Well, you are getting the foreign umbrella. American and French and British and other forces are being forced on you."

The conservative, in some cases religious, regimes that ruled Bahrain, Oman, Qatar, Saudi Arabia, and the United Arab Emirates had everything to fear from an expansion of Iraq. Thus, in addition to contributing armed forces, these countries helped defray the costs of the Coalition effort: Saudi Arabia pledged $17 billion (of which $3.5 billion took the form of in-kind assistance: food, fuel, housing, transportation, and so on), Kuwait $16 billion, and the UAE $4 billion. Saudi Arabia and the other Gulf states expected the United States and, more generally the Coalition, to preserve the political and territorial status quo in the Gulf, thereby legitimizing their existing social and economic systems.

While divisions appeared in the Arab Cooperation Council (Egypt, Jordan, and Yemen, in addition to Iraq) and the Arab Maghreb Union (Algeria, Libya, Mauritania, Morocco, and Tunisia), the Gulf Cooperation Council (Bahrain, Kuwait, Oman, Qatar, Saudi Arabia, and the United Arab Emirates: GCC) stood firm in preserving a high degree of cohesion in the face of Iraqi ambitions. This is not surprising, if one considers the high degree of dependence of the GCC on the status quo.

The stance of the Arab members of the Coalition hardened considerably in early November, when it became clear that the United States intended to use

---

93. Egyptian Ministry of Defense, *Al Kitab Harab Tahrir Kuwait* (Report on the War to Liberate Kuwait) (1992).

military force to liberate Kuwait. Saudi Arabian Foreign Minister Prince Saud al-Faisal on 14 November: "Any Arab meeting will yield no fruit, or result, unless Iraq agrees to abide by the decisions of the Cairo Arab summit and international resolutions that call for Iraqi withdrawal from Kuwait." A joint statement on 15 November by Egyptian President Mubarak and Syrian President Assad, in reply to Moroccan King Hussein's call for a "last chance" Arab summit: "Preconditions [not insisting on Iraq's withdrawal] made the convening of such a summit difficult, if not impossible."

Reactions in the Arab World: Pro-Iraq Countries

An important element in Saddam Hussein's strategy during the crisis was to try to mobilize the Arab masses' support, and to this end he raised several anti-American and anti-Israeli popular slogans. He was hoping that public support for him would force Arab regimes not to oppose his policy. In those countries where it mattered most, however—Egypt, Syria, and Saudi Arabia—this did not happen. Public backing for Saddam Hussein did manifest itself primarily in those countries whose governments lent their official support to Iraq—principally Jordan, Sudan, and Yemen, with the situation among the North African states varied.[94]

In fact, no Arab country actually supported Baghdad to the extent of sending its armed forces to help defend Iraq. Nor is there any sign that Arab terrorist organizations took significant actions against the interests of Coalition members. Some countries allowed volunteers to sign up and travel to Iraq; since these people were mostly untrained and unarmed, this action was just a token gesture.

Several Arab countries did express verbal support for Iraq, at least in the sense that they opposed the U.N. economic blockade and Coalition military action. Support for Iraq was strongest within the Palestine Liberation Organization (PLO), in Jordan (which depended on Iraq economically and emotionally), Yemen (a close political ally of Iraq whose interests were opposed to those of Saudi Arabia), Sudan, Libya, and Mauritania. In Tunisia, Algeria, and Morocco popular support for Iraq was also strong.[95]

Although the PLO was financed by Saudi Arabia (whereas Iraq had been unable to continue giving aid), its leader Yasser Arafat opted at once for the anti-Coalition and pro-Iraqi side. At the May 1990 Baghdad summit, Iraq and the PLO forged "an implacable front" against Saudi Arabia, Egypt, and the United Arab Emirates. Palestinians enthusiastically supported Iraq. It would be a mistake to think that the leadership of the PLO did not reflect the views and aspirations of the Palestinian people; it almost certainly did. One can wonder why the Palestinian people did not cast their lot with the Coalition by

---

94. Evron, "Gulf Crisis and War," p. 134.

95. Although King Hassan II of Morocco actually sent troops to Saudi Arabia on the Coalition side.

denouncing Iraq's invasion and contributing at least token military forces to the Coalition. The reasons could be disbelief, on the one hand, that—after years of neglecting their aspirations—Western countries would change their attitudes merely as a consequence of Palestinian support for the Coalition, or belief, on the other hand, that Iraq would win the confrontation and go on to liberate Palestine. Considering the military capabilities of Israel, the latter belief was never realistic, but one can understand how people who have been frustrated for decades may grasp at straws, no matter how frail the straws appear to be. Arafat stated on 7 January: "Welcome, welcome to war. Iraq and Palestine represent a common will. We will be together side by side and after the great battle, *inshallah*, we will pray together in Jerusalem."

After the PLO, Jordan offered the strongest moral support to Saddam Hussein before, during, and after the war. This support reflected the fact that the majority of its population was Palestinian and that it depended on Iraq economically. Thus the Jordanian leadership offered strong verbal support for Saddam Hussein's request that a global settlement of all Middle East problems be found, protested some aspects of the U.N. embargo on Iraq, and apparently looked the other way while small amounts of smuggled goods crossed the border.

While the governments of Yemen and Sudan officially supported the regime in Baghdad in some sense, they took no concrete steps to hinder the Coalition or to materially assist Iraq.

We cannot escape speculating that the reactions of Libyan leader Muhammar Gadhafi, traditionally a proponent of anti-Western activities, were subdued because of the U.S. bombing of Tripoli and Benghazi in 1986. In spite of his rhetoric, Gadhafi appeared to be a realist who understood the messages implied by U.S. actions: if the West is provoked to fight, it can deploy technically superior weapons.

In summary, in spite of Saddam Hussein's repeated calls for Arab unity, and much rhetorical support in some countries, Iraq received no active support from other Arab countries. Iraq's violation of the principles of the Arab League—which do not allow for the use of force to resolve conflicts—and the memory of U.S. reprisals against Libya in the past no doubt contributed to limiting Arab support for Iraq to words, words that proved powerless to prevent the hurricane of war from engulfing Iraq.

Europe's Reactions

The most striking feature of Europe's reaction to the invasion was its failure to act as a unified political body. Less than two years before the economic union envisaged for 1992, Europe once again proved its inability to speak with a single voice, even though all countries fully supported the central tenet of the U.S. position: Iraqi withdrawal from Kuwait. Differences among countries involved the appropriate means to bring about the withdrawal, and greater or lesser recognition of the legitimacy of some of Iraq's demands (for example, a resolution of the Palestinian problem).

United Kingdom

The United States and the U.K. have consistently been strong allies since World War II. In addition, the domestic situation at the time of the invasion of Kuwait favored U.K. intervention: Prime Minister Margaret Thatcher was under pressure because of unpopular tax policies and an unfavorable economic environment; she may have recalled that success in the Falklands War had bolstered her popularity at home and have hoped that success in the Gulf might have the same effect. But it was not to be: Thatcher was forced to resign before the start of hostilities.

However, even after her replacement by John Major, there could be no doubt that the U.K. would intervene militarily at the side of the United States.[96] On this issue even the Labour opposition supported the new prime minister before and during the war. The decision to send troops was approved on 15 September by an overwhelming majority in the House of Commons (534 against 55) and the U.K. contributed considerable military forces (air, land, and naval) to the Coalition. Public opinion polls in the U.K. consistently showed a majority, at times very substantial, in favor of the government's policies to deploy troops. The U.K. was also the only European ally of the United States prepared to withstand the Iraqi siege of Western embassies in Kuwait, keeping its ambassador in the U.K. compound long after all other diplomats, except for the Americans, had left.

France

France had strong social and economic ties to many Arab nations, in particular the North African nations, especially Algeria. Some 1.5 million Muslims lived in France in 1990.[97] In addition, France had consistently attempted to assert its independence of the United States during the Cold War (for example, by refusing to join NATO fully). Also, French public opinion was less favorable to a military intervention than U.S. or U.K. public opinion. In a poll taken by *Le Figaro* in November 1990, 36% were in favor of war and 57% against. One month before, only 45% had been against.

Thus the French positions were always less uncompromising than the U.S. positions, and French President François Mitterrand made several attempts to persuade Iraq to withdraw, going so far as to publicly state on 24 September at the United Nations: "Let Iraq declare its intention to withdraw its troops, let it free its hostages, and everything becomes possible." It is highly unlikely that

---

96. Jolyon Howorth, "United Kingdom Defence Policy and the Gulf War," in *The Gulf Crisis*, *Contemporary European Affairs*, 4, no. 1 (1991): 149-161.

97. International Labour Organization, *Migration* (1992), p. 5.

this statement was meant literally. Whenever specific actions were required, France consistently supported the U.S. position, for example, voting with the United States at the United Nations.[98]

On 14 January 1991, just days before the Coalition initiated military action, France proposed a last-minute peace plan in the U.N. Security Council. The plan envisaged an Iraqi withdrawal, followed by the deployment of an Arab peacekeeping force in Kuwait, followed by a U.N.-sponsored Middle East peace conference. It arguably offered Saddam Hussein an honorable way out of the crisis, although there is no reason to believe that he was prepared to accept it. This plan was immediately rejected by the United States and provoked the ire of some U.K. and U.S. commentators, who saw it as a sign that France was once again trying to follow its own path. But it is not clear whether the French proposal was a serious attempt to avoid imminent hostilities or a maneuver by Mitterand to rally domestic support; we can speculate that it is possible that the U.S. administration was not surprised by this proposal: Mitterand may have discussed it with Bush, explaining that a last public attempt to find a negotiated settlement was needed in order to unite French public opinion.

Less than 24 hours before the start of hostilities the National Assembly voted its overwhelming support in favor of French military intervention, and on 17 January Mitterand addressed the nation: "Unless there is an unexpected—and hence unlikely—event, arms will speak." But ambiguous statements by Defense Minister Jean-Pierre Chevenement raised doubts that French military intervention might be limited to Kuwaiti territory. These declarations gave rise to spirited debates in France and other Western countries, with the U.K. popular press violently lambasting the supposed French lack of resolve. On 20 January, Mitterand dissipated all possible doubts regarding French military and political objectives in the Gulf, stating that the liberation of Kuwait "presupposes, of course, military operations in Iraq itself. . . . It would be difficult to oblige Iraq to let go without attacking its military-industrial potential. Of course it must be destroyed." Chevenement later resigned and was replaced by Pierre Joxe: this change politically confirmed France's commitment to the Coalition, which was backed up militarily by the fact that it had sent essentially all of its elite volunteer armed forces to the Gulf, including air, land, and naval units.

Italy

Italian foreign policy since World War II had been broadly in tune with U.S. policy, though at times diverging on specific issues. During the Gulf crisis Italy generally supported Coalition policies and actions, but showed some reluctance to support military intervention. Italian authorities

98. Barbara S. Balaj, "France and The Gulf War," *Mediterranean Quarterly* (Summer, 1993): 96-116.

impounded 10 modern ships (including 4 frigates) that had been built by Italian shipyards for Iraq and which were still in Italian ports; these ships had been ordered during the years when Western support for Iraq was fashionable. Italy backed the various French and USSR peace plans, and its Parliament approved the use of Italian planes deployed in the Gulf area only 12 hours after the start of hostilities.[99] Italy possessed an excellent professional navy, and several ships were part of the Coalition force. The level of preparation of its planes turned out to be inadequate. No ground troops were sent because there were no volunteer units in the army.

Indeed, the Italian constitution includes language prohibiting the use of armed forces except in a defensive role, as do the constitutions of the other nations defeated in World War II. Article 11 of the Italian Constitution states: "Italy renounces war . . . as a means for resolving international controversies." It is thus perhaps not surprising that the Italian contribution was significantly less than that of France or the U.K.

Germany

After World War II the victorious Allies insisted that the German constitution include a clause prohibiting any future German aggression. Given the effort that Americans, Europeans, and Germans themselves have expended since 1945 in convincing Germany that it should never again attack another nation, it is not surprising that German public opinion strongly supported the German leadership's claim that its constitution prevented direct German participation in the military Coalition.

In addition to opposing direct German intervention, most Germans were broadly against the war. According to a poll taken as hostilities started, 79% of the population favored a negotiated solution to the crisis. Chancellor Helmut Kohl stated that he was "deeply distressed" by the news of the first Coalition air strikes against Baghdad.

However, leaders in Bonn did declare that Coalition countries "have a right to our solidarity, and we stand by them." Germany agreed to contribute to the war financially, pledging some $260 million initially and $6.5 billion later on. Also, Bonn sent air-defense forces to Turkey as part of its commitment to help defend NATO allies from potential attack. Furthermore, Germany provided in-kind assistance worth over $500 million, and U.S. troops and their families based in Germany reported receiving support from the local population.

Other European Countries

Belgium, Denmark, Greece, the Netherlands, Norway, Poland, Portugal, and Spain expressed their support for the U.S. position in varying degrees and

---

99. Laura Guazzone, "Italy and the Gulf Crisis: European and Domestic Dimensions," *The International Spectator*, 26, no. 4 (October-December 1991): 57-74.

contributed military forces, primarily naval units.   Czechoslovakia and
Hungary sent medical units.   Austria, Sweden, and Switzerland had a policy of
neutrality.   Sweden did join the Coalition by sending a medical unit to Saudi
Arabia.   In accordance with U.N. resolutions calling on all nations to help
enforce the resolution demanding the Iraqi withdrawal from Kuwait, Austria
and Switzerland permitted U.S. military transport aircraft to fly over their
territories, both before and after the conflict started.   No country expressed
any serious opposition to the U.S. position.

Other Countries' Reactions

Outside the Arab world and Europe, six countries (Argentina, Australia,
Bangladesh, Canada, New Zealand, and Pakistan) showed their support for the
Coalition by contributing air, land, or naval forces.   Honduras offered troops.
The African nations of Niger and Senegal sent troops, as did the Afghani
rebels.   Korea, Sierra Leone, and Singapore sent medical teams.

Turkey

As a secular, non-Arab state seeking to build closer ties with Europe,
Turkey could only support the Coalition.   Its support was encouraged by
economic assistance from the United States, which reimbursed Turkey for the
loss of revenue incurred when the flow of Iraqi oil to the Mediterranean
through Turkish pipelines was cut off on 7 August, in accordance with U.N.
economic sanctions.   Turkish support for the Coalition increased as events
moved toward war: large numbers of Turkish troops on the border of Iraq
constituted a threat that Baghdad could not ignore, and tied down potential
reinforcements far from the Kuwaiti front.   When hostilities commenced,
Turkey allowed NATO air bases to be used by planes that carried out attacks
deep within Iraqi territory.

Japan

After World War II the United States insisted that the Japanese constitution
include a clause prohibiting any future aggression.   Given the horrors of the
atomic bombing of Hiroshima and Nagasaki and the efforts that Americans and
Japanese have expended since 1945 in convincing Japan that it should never
again attack another nation, it is not surprising that Japanese public opinion
strongly supported the Japanese leadership's claim that its constitution
prevented direct Japanese participation in the military Coalition.   Japan did
agree to contribute to the war financially, pledging some $600 million
initially, and $10 billion later on.   Japan contributed about $500 million of in-
kind assistance.   As General Schwarzkopf put the matter: "Had it not been for
the Japanese, Desert Shield would have gone broke in August.   While Western

newspapers were complaining about Tokyo's reluctance to increase its pledge of $1 billion to safeguard Saudi Arabia, the Japanese embassy in Riyadh quietly transferred tens of millions of dollars into Central Command's accounts."[100]

Israel

Israel adopted a rather low profile during the entire crisis. Its interests were obviously best served by the destruction of the Iraqi military machine, parts of which (for example, the SCUD missiles) could threaten the Israeli population. Since the actions of all the other players in the crisis were inevitably leading toward war, Israel could afford to stand back and observe.[101]

Once war broke out, Israel was directly attacked by Iraq (via SCUD missiles). There was much speculation that Israel would retaliate and that such a retaliation might lead to the withdrawal from the Coalition of certain Arab nations, particularly Syria. However, we do not believe that retaliation would have been in Israel's interests. In spite of the myth of its invincibility, Israel could not have done anything more to prevent further SCUD attacks than the Coalition was already doing.[102] Nor would the addition of its air and missile forces to the Coalition have significantly increased the intensity of the bombing of Iraq. This is not to say that no one within Israel was in favor of retaliation; public statements by political and military leaders clearly show that at least some strongly favored retaliation. However, the vast majority favored a policy of no retaliation. In the end Israel did not retaliate, perhaps because its leaders saw the futility of any retaliation; perhaps because of U.S. political pressure; perhaps because the U.S. military denied IFF (Identification Friend or Foe) codes to Israeli warplanes, which thus risked being shot down by Coalition forces if they entered Iraqi airspace; or perhaps because Israel believed that its restraint would be rewarded by U.S. financial grants (after the war was over, the United States granted Israel $650 million to help defray its military expenses during the war).

We can only guess how Arab nations would have reacted if Israel had retaliated against Iraq. It is our hunch that, considering the fundamental political and economic reasons that led Arab nations to join the Coalition, it would have survived unscathed despite any Israeli retaliation. Indeed, General Schwarzkopf quotes Saudi Arabian King Fahd as stating privately in November 1990 that Saudi forces would remain in the Coalition if Israel were to defend itself against an Iraqi attack.[103]

---

100. Schwarzkopf, *It Doesn't Take a Hero*, p. 365.

101. Nurith Gertz, "Routine and Normality as Objects of Desire: Israel and the 1991 Gulf War," *Israeli Affairs*, 1 no. 4 (Summer, 1995): 128-149.

102. See Chapter 6, section "SCUD: Iraq's Most Publicized Weapon."

103. Schwarzkopf, *It Doesn't Take a Hero*, p. 373.

China

China is a permanent member of the U.N. Security Council. As such, it could have vetoed any of the resolutions that authorized Coalition actions against Iraq. However, China had no motivation for opposing Western policies, particularly in light of its attempts to rebuild the economic relations damaged by the internal repression that occurred in June 1989 (Tienanmen Square).

Iran

As a bitter enemy of the United States since the 1979 Khomeinist revolution, Iran could conceivably have opposed the U.S.-led Coalition effort to liberate Kuwait. However, several factors militated against this scenario. Iran lacked any military capability that could threaten the Coalition effort and, exhausted by the long war with Iraq, it had little will to enter a new conflict. As an Islamic religious state it had little in common with secular Iraq and, having painfully fought off Iraqi aggression for years, it had no interest in seeing Iraq's military power increased. Finally, as a non-Arab, Persian culture it had nothing to gain and much to lose from the realization of the Baathist dream of a pan-Arab nation.

On 15 August, Saddam Hussein—in a clear effort to curry Iran's favor—announced that he would release all prisoners of war, give up Iranian territory still occupied by Iraq, and accept Iran's conditions for a peace treaty ending the Iran-Iraq War. In essence, Iraq admitted its defeat by accepting the very borders for whose revision it had started the war in 1980.

This was the first of a string of diplomatic victories that throughout the Gulf crisis have permitted Iran to emerge from the international quarantine imposed on it in 1979 and to begin to resume the role of a regional power. Iran's decision to support the U.N. resolutions and to remain neutral during the war surprised some observers—despite the fact that Iran had much to gain from Iraq's defeat. But its persistent anti-Western (and particularly anti-American) rhetoric, its apparent violation of the trade embargo before the war, and its decision (officially announced in early February 1991) to send food and medicine to the Iraqi civilian population are indicative of the Iranian leadership's will to play each side against the other, to its own advantage.

While it had no motivation to support Iraq, Iran also had little reason to support the Coalition strongly. The clerics in Tehran must have been concerned that a dismemberment of Iraq would favor its two powerful neighbors, Syria and Turkey, and reduce the influence that Iran could exercise after the conflict. As President Rafsanjani put it on 20 January: "Those who wish that the Islamic Republic [Iran] support Iraq or enter the war on the Iraqi side would mean that they want Iraq to stay in Kuwait, and our borders with Iraq to extend to the strait of Hormuz. Is this not suicide?"

Thus Iran adopted a position of neutrality: it declared that both sides were wrong, viewed with suspicion a permanent U.S. military presence in the Middle East, and refused to aid Iraq in any significant way.

IRAQ'S REACTIONS

Iraq's rhetoric became increasingly harsh as the Coalition signaled its determination to liberate Kuwait through military means. On 30 September, Iraqi President Saddam Hussein declared: "The Iraqi armed forces are in all circumstances ready to defend the province of Kuwait as they are ready to defend all other provinces of the country." On 4 November, just before the U.S. elections, Information Minister Latif Nasim Jassim declared: "The world should know that Kuwait is the nineteenth province of Iraq and Iraq is not going to negotiate on Kuwait. . . . We are going to defend our nineteenth province on any condition, even if we have to fight a dangerous war. If the U.S. army enters Iraq it will never leave."

On 19 November, Iraq announced the deployment of 250,000 more men to Kuwait, and claimed that the United States would need 3 million men to defeat its 1 million. In fact, the announced deployment was largely a propaganda move, and these troops never really existed. As U.S. General Colin Powell put it on 20 November, this announcement was "part of Saddam Hussein's headline of the day program." However, part of the Western media did accept Iraq's announcement, leading to press reports that nearly 700,000 men were deployed in the Kuwaiti theater.

On 29 November, as the U.N. Security Council prepared to pass a resolution authorizing the use of force to liberate Kuwait, the newspaper *al-Thawra*, organ of the Baath Party, wrote that "the U.S. resolution prepared by the Security Council is not only a blatant violation of all standards of humanity, peace, and legality, but is a declaration of war on all the good and honorable forces in the world."

Meanwhile, demonization of the adversary became a permanent feature of Iraqi media (just as in U.S. and other Western media). On 7 January, for example, the *Baghdad Observer* referred to U.S. President Bush as "a narrow-minded and blinkered Dracula."

Saddam Hussein even attempted to escalate the conflict by calling for terrorist actions against Western interests on 7 January: "every struggler and fighter whose hand can reach out to harm the aggressor in the world . . . wherever the sons of the [Arab] nation exist. . . . The expectation is not a better life for the Iraqis, but for the whole Arab nation. . . . The battle turned today into an all-out battle. . . . where all people of goodwill have taken your [Iraq's] side and the evil ones the other side. . . . Victory is close."

The Iraqi president's rationale for resisting the Western military threat may have been that he felt he might withstand it.[104] Thus, on 9 January he

---

104. Kincade, "On the Brink in the Gulf. Part 2: The Route to War," p. 307.

declared: "If the Americans are involved in a Gulf conflict, you will see how we will make them swim in their own blood. . . . We are not of the type that bows to threats, and you will see the trap that America will fall into." As the U.N. deadline of 15 January 1991 approached, the scene was set for what Saddam Hussein called "the mother of all battles."

3

Was War Inevitable?

I fear we have only awakened a sleeping giant, and his reaction will be terrible.

—Japanese Admiral Yamamoto, 1941

Theoretically, the war was not inevitable, because a negotiated settlement was conceivable. In practice however, the historical backgrounds and emotional commitments of the involved nations and their leaders made negotiations fruitless. War became the only way to resolve the dispute.

As Clausewitz observed in 1832, war is a political act, a method for continuing political commerce after diplomacy fails: "the political view is the object; war is the means, and the means must always include the object in our conception."[105] It is normal and prudent to change objectives when one realizes that initially specified objectives cannot be attained. One is tempted to speculate that Iraq's objectives evolved through the crisis. The initial objective may have been nothing more than to replace the Kuwaiti government with one that would do Iraq's bidding, in order to get control of some territory (Bubiyan and Warba) and some disputed oil reserves, to ensure an increase in oil prices, and to emerge as the leading Arab country. These objectives were foiled by the strong U.S.-inspired world reaction, which imposed economic sanctions on Iraq and resulted in the deployment of Western military forces in Saudi Arabia. As a result, a second objective emerged: to link withdrawal from Kuwait to the other problems of the region, particularly the Palestinian issue, in order to obtain the support of the Arab masses, who perhaps could have forced their governments to support Iraq, which thus would come out of

---

105. Carl von Clausewitz, *On War* (Penguin, 1982), p. 119.

the crisis as the leader of the whole Arab nation. But emotional support in the Arab world was insufficient: Egypt, the Gulf states, and Syria failed to support Iraq.[106]

It is difficult to understand why Saddam Hussein did not pursue what some Western hawks called "the nightmare scenario": a slow withdrawal, perhaps only up to the disputed borders, accompanied by negotiations. It would have been politically awkward for Western leaders to start a war under those circumstances, and negotiations could have dragged on for years while the Iraqi army continued to be in a position to intimidate its neighbors. But this may not have been a viable option for Iraq. As Efraim Karsh and Inari Rautsi put it: "The invasion had been a desperate attempt to shore up the regime in the face of dire economic straits. Hence, an unconditional withdrawal, or even withdrawal with a cosmetic face-saving formula, were totally unacceptable from the outset, since they did not address the fundamental predicament underlying the invasion."[107]

In retrospect we can say that Iraq suffered a catastrophic defeat on all counts because its political objectives were out of proportion to its military power. In spite of its army being characterized as the fourth largest in the world, it bore no comparison to the fighting power of the largest. Iraq could have prevailed only if the West had been unwilling to use its military forces. But the Coalition set political objectives that were well within reach of its military power. Indeed, it appears that, as Gen. Colin Powell subsequently stated, at least in the United States, "there was, as close as possible, integration between political issues and political thinking and military issues and military decisions." And "[U.S.] political leaders . . . allowed the military to participate in the decision-making process from the very beginning."[108] The United States pursued, more or less openly, three goals that became those of the Coalition and, indeed, of the United Nations as a whole.[109]

First, to free Kuwait and restore the ruling family to power; in other words, to see that international law was respected and that aggression was not rewarded and was in some sense punished.

Second, to maintain the social, political, and, if possible, territorial status quo in the Gulf region. Now that the border between eastern and western Europe had ceased to be the world's most critical region, the U.S.

---

106. Lawrence Freedman and Efraim Karsh, "How Kuwait was Won: Strategy in the Gulf War," *International Security*, 16, no. 2 (Fall 1991): 5-41.

107. Karsh and Rautsi, *Saddam Hussein*, p. 239. But note that Saddam Hussein was able to survive an even worse economic situation for several years after the end of the war, which suggests that his fear of a revolt due to economic hardships may have been a miscalculation, if indeed he ever had such a fear.

108. Both statements are quoted in U.S. News & World Report, *Triumph Without Victory*, p. 95.

109. U.S. Department of Defense, *Conduct of the Persian Gulf War*, p. 38; Cohen et al., *GWAPS: Planning*, p. 2; Swain, *"Lucky War,"* p. 32; and Gallois, "Rivalry in the Gulf," pp. 60-61.

administration's vigilance was focused on the Middle East. The aim was to enable oil-producing countries to develop their main source of wealth in a stable manner and to profit from it without disrupting the purchasing countries' economies.

Third, to end Baghdad's nuclear and chemical ambitions and, if possible, destroy its weapons research and production facilities, so as to encourage other countries tempted to follow the same road to reflect on the risks involved. Militarily, Iraq had become a source of widespread concern, and not just to its neighbors. Until very recently, the Western powers, the USSR, and China shared a monopoly: the production and possession of the decisive weapon system composed of a combination of nuclear bombs and missile delivery vehicles. Fitted out with conventional high-explosive or with biological, chemical, or even nuclear warheads, today's missiles constitute a dangerous arsenal. Increasingly such weapons are in the possession of governments considered, rightly or wrongly, to be less responsible than the larger and industrially more advanced states. Of all these developing countries, Iraq was widely thought to be the most dangerous. The efforts it had made to acquire nuclear weapons capability and the work it had put into developing chemical and biological weapons had given rise to many concerns, especially in the West.

On 30 November 1990, U.S. President Bush summarized the Coalition's objectives as follows: "We seek Iraq's immediate and unconditional withdrawal from Kuwait. We seek the restoration of Kuwait's legitimate government. . . . And we seek the stability and security of this critical region of the world. . . . I'm deeply concerned about Saddam's efforts to acquire nuclear weapons."

We can speculate that there were some additional, not openly declared objectives: to bring about the downfall of the Baathist regime in Iraq; to establish a permanent U.S. military presence in the Gulf region; to prove the worth of NATO doctrines and weapon systems in actual combat conditions, and learn how to improve them for the future; even, perhaps on a subconscious level, to divert U.S. public opinion from domestic economic problems.

In spite of a statement contained in Bush's 9 January letter to Saddam Hussein, "the United States will not tolerate . . . the destruction of Kuwait's oil fields and installations,"[110] it appears that preventing this destruction was not one of the Coalition leaders' primary military objectives, perhaps because they feared that any attempt to liberate the oil fields before the destruction of Iraq's armed forces would result in high Coalition casualties, or perhaps because they (correctly) estimated that Iraqi engineers would be able to destroy the oil fields faster than any possible advance by ground troops. As General Schwarzkopf put the problem on 12 January: "If we really, truly get into a ground war, it is hard to envision that happening without damage to the Kuwaiti oil fields."

---

110. The letter is reproduced in Sifry and Cerf, *The Gulf War Reader*, p. 179.

There were, however, other factors, not directly connected with developments in the region, that made war in the Gulf likely to break out.[111]

THE END OF THE COLD WAR AND THE LEGACY OF VIETNAM

Among these factors, we single out the end of bipolarity and its impact on Middle Eastern politics. The Cold War (1945-1990) opposed the U.S.-led Western bloc to the Soviet-led Eastern bloc. The two main protagonists, that is the United States and the USSR, never engaged in direct hostilities. In our view, the conflict can be said to have been fought on economic grounds, with the sides attempting to attain either a qualitative or a quantitative military superiority that would allow them, at worst, to enjoy hegemony over their zones of influence and, at best, to extend their ideological, political, and economic power.

During the late 1980s, under the leadership of the new general secretary, Mikhail Gorbachev, the USSR entered a period of dramatic reform and change. This included détente with the West, welcomed by U.S. President Ronald Reagan in an almost complete volte-face. The two premier powers ceased to assume confrontational postures, as the United States sought to aid the USSR in its course toward democratic government and a market economy.

Absorbed with its domestic concerns and drastically reducing its sphere of influence, the USSR could no longer guarantee that vital U.S. interests in the Soviet zone of influence would be respected, as it had done in the past in order to ensure that the Cold War did not become World War III—an outcome that would have been catastrophic for both sides. The United States thus became responsible for ensuring that former Soviet allies and friends (such as Iraq) respected vital Western interests. In an earlier decade, Iraq might have had to fear Soviet reprisals for the invasion, but not American reprisals, since U.S. freedom to act would have been much more restricted.

The U.S. position in the Middle East was strengthened by the fact that the USSR counted on the United States and its European allies for economic assistance—both directly in terms of outright grants, and indirectly in terms of facilitations of trade and technical assistance in liberalizing and modernizing its economy. With the benefit of hindsight, we can see that while Saddam Hussein may have felt that the decline of the USSR gave him a free hand in the Middle East, correspondingly the administration in Washington no longer had to fear the possibility of Soviet opposition to its Middle East policy.

It has been argued, with regard to the effects on the region of changes in the international system following the collapse of the Berlin Wall, that Saddam Hussein had two conflicting perceptions about the newly emerging regional

---

111. For a comprehensive analysis of the origins and development of the Gulf crisis, see Roland Dannreuther, "The Gulf Conflict: A Political and Strategic Analysis," *Adelphi Papers*, no. 264 (Winter 1991-1992); and Freedman and Karsh, *The Gulf Conflict*.

role of the United States.[112] On the one hand, he assumed that the weakening of Soviet involvement would be followed by a symmetrically diminishing role for the United States, since the latter had been involved in the region only to counter Soviet influence. On the other hand, Saddam Hussein was concerned that American influence would in fact increase, and he inveighed against such a U.S. role.

In the event, massive U.S. military intervention against Iraq showed that concerns that the end of competitive bipolarity and the Soviet retreat from the Middle East would be followed by a symmetrical American retreat were unfounded. Similarly, the notion that the end of the Cold War would be followed by increased freedom of military behavior by the regional powers, unchecked by U.S. power, was not validated.[113]

Finally, the view that experience of the Vietnam War might make the United States reluctant to intervene, or that it might do so only ineffectually, overlooked the change in the U.S. Army made in response to its experience in Vietnam. This thorough reformation of what became a volunteer, long-service force stressed improvement in training, doctrine, and weapons, mostly directed at combat in Europe. Stress on this kind of war proved to be excellent preparation for fighting Iraq.

Furthermore, some in the United States felt that a clear victory in Kuwait would help to efface the memories of the defeat in Vietnam, while some in Iraq felt that resistance to the United States would bolster Iraq's standing as a leader of the Arab world.

PARALLELS BETWEEN THE UNITED STATES AND IRAQ

The country which most strongly opposed Iraq's invasion of Kuwait from all points of view, military as well as political, was the United States. It is axiomatic that wars cannot occur unless both sides are willing to fight, and have motives to do so. Some of the causal factors of the war applied to the United States as well as to Iraq: the desire to control oil resources and a belief in a just cause.

In politics, as opposed to morals and ethics, the concept of justice is somewhat relative, so when two nations are in conflict, each may believe that it is fighting for a just cause, no matter how diametrically opposed they are on principles. Although the idea may be difficult for Western readers to accept, many citizens of Iraq likely believed that the Iraqi cause was just, even as most citizens of the United States believed that the U.S. cause was just.

The Baathist regime in Iraq subscribed to a pan-Arab political vision, within which the wealth of the Kuwaitis was viewed as unjust, and its redistribution, even by force, as just. The 2 million residents of Kuwait enjoyed a per capita GNP of about $10,000 per year—three times that of the 18 million Iraqis.

---

112. Evron, "Gulf Crisis and War," pp. 128-130.
113. Ibid., p. 130.

Drawing attention to this disparity in resources, the Iraqi regime led a crusade on behalf of the poorer, relatively disadvantaged Arab countries against the wealthier and less densely populated Gulf states.

The United States, leader of the Coalition, of course had quite a different view of justice—but one as deeply held as the Baathist view. It is a common phenomenon for inheritors of ideologies based on revolutions to believe in their messianic mission to spread their enlightened thinking to less fortunate peoples—by force, if necessary; and it is often overlooked that the U.S. political system is the world's oldest surviving system born in a popular revolution (that of 1775-1783). The ideals of that revolution are still enshrined in the U.S. Constitution, and to a large extent affect national thinking. Thus it is not surprising that ever since the American Declaration of Independence, a large portion of the U.S. citizenry has felt it a duty to propagate around the world its fundamental belief that all men are endowed with the right to life, liberty, and the pursuit of happiness—at times resorting to military means to do so.

Those Iraqis who believed in the fundamental ideals of the Baath party must have felt that the invasion of Kuwait was justifiable, whereas many Americans surely felt that their intervention was justified by principles embodied in the U.S. Constitution. These contrasting views were expressed in statements by both sides. On 8 August 1990, for example, Iraq's Revolutionary Command Council declared that Iraq was ready to fight "in order . . . to rectify what time had wronged [the 1961 granting of independence to Kuwait] and to cancel the injustice and unfairness that had hit Iraq in the heart of its entity." In one occasion Saddam Hussein stated that his country had the honor of "bearing arms against injustice and the unjust and against atheism and atheists." A few days before the beginning of the air campaign against Iraq, he said the conflict would be "a showdown between the infidels and believers, between good and evil." The tone of U.S. statements was not much different. As President Bush put it on 28 January 1991: "It is a just war and it is a war in which good will prevail . . . The first principle of a just war is that it supports a just cause. Our cause could not be more noble. . . . We know this is a just war and a war we will win."

CLASH OF CIVILIZATIONS OR NORTH-SOUTH CONFLICT?

Less than a week after Saddam Hussein's invasion of Kuwait, large portions of the Arab populations in many countries proclaimed their support for his actions and protested against Western reactions. Although certain Arab countries joined the international effort to obtain Iraq's withdrawal from Kuwait, others—notably Algeria, Tunisia, Libya, Mauritania, Yemen, and Sudan—expressed opposition to the U.N. embargo of Iraq. Even ever-prudent King Hussein of Jordan went so far as to denounce the "foreign ambitions" of the anti-Iraq countries. According to the pro-Iraq view, the invasion and annexation of Kuwait was an Arab problem to be resolved by Arabs. Western intervention was seen as an attempt to smash Iraq's military power in order to protect Israel and to take control of the region's oil resources. On the Western side, the Iraqi aggression was considered a breach of the U.N. Charter and a gross violation of recognized international norms. The West considered the situation in the Persian Gulf to be an international problem, and influenced the United Nations to condemn Iraq and impose economic sanctions. Although some Arab countries accepted the West's position and joined the Coalition, even in those countries there is an Arab world-view that contrasts with the Western outlook.

These opposing views emphasize the fact that while Arabs and Westerners may look at the same world they do not always see the same things or draw the same conclusions from what they see. It is true that in addition to considerations of international law, powerful economic interests related to the control of oil were at stake in the confrontation between Iraq and Kuwait. Nevertheless, it cannot be denied that there is a dichotomy between Western and Arab perspectives, and that this dichotomy led to different interpretations of the same events.[114]

Some observers have characterized the Gulf War as a conflict between rich nations and poor nations, and considered it the first example of a North-South war.[115] But in fact conflicts between the "haves" and the "have-nots" form much of the fabric of history since ancient times. Although we recognize the recurrence of clashes between poor nations and rich nations throughout the course of history, it is our opinion that the clash of Arab and Western civilizations was a factor of at least equal importance in provoking the war. A major factor in this clash is the rivalry between the Judeo-Christian and Islamic traditions since Mohammed's thinking burst from the Arabian desert almost six centuries after the birth of Christ. Although not all Arabs are Muslim (some are Christian) and not all Muslims are Arabs (Indonesians, Iranians, and Pakistanis are far more numerous), the Arab world is dominated by Islam. The main factors of misunderstanding between Western and Islamic cultures can be traced back to the birth of Islam, and to a long history of military and cultural conflicts. Indeed, there can be no doubt that the attitude of Arabs and Westerners toward each other is influenced even today by events that took place in the distant past.

---

114. This section was originally written in 1991, well before Samuel Huntington's article on the same subject. See Samuel Huntington, "The Clash of Civilizations," *Foreign Affairs*, vol. 72, no. 3 (1993).

115. See, e.g., Vladimir Nosenko, "Iraq's Aggression against Kuwait in the Context of North-South Relations," *Mediterranean Quarterly*, 3, no. 2 (Spring 1992): 96-108; Edward J. Mortimer, "New Fault-lines: Is a North-South Confrontation Inevitable in Security Terms?," *Adelphi Papers,* no. 266 (Winter 1991-1992): 74-86. North and South mean, respectively, rich industrialized countries and poor underdeveloped countries.

Although some analysts are tempted to consider Islam as a destabilizing force in modern world politics, it is a fact that Islam is a religion practiced in large portions of Africa and Asia, and the future of North-South relations cannot be dissociated from the future of the relations between Islam and the West. These relations, in turn, cannot escape the historical constraints imposed by centuries of contact and conflict.

Yet this heritage of hostility did not make war inevitable. Neither old religious animosities nor the abandoned colonial empires dictated war. Rather, a major motive force in forming the Coalition was the recently taught lesson that the price and availability of oil depended on the Middle Eastern political situation. So whereas rich countries without oil wanted to make their supplies more secure, Iraq, rich only in oil, wanted to increase its income by eliminating a price-cutting competitor and by acquiring its output. If Iraq had not gambled on a fait accompli, it might have gained much of its objective by threat and negotiation.

LEADERS IN CONFLICT

For at least some Arabs, Saddam Hussein was a symbol of the Arab world's dignity, honor, and unity. He had crystallized and clearly expressed the emotions of hundreds of thousands of people regarding matters that to them were of enormous importance: opposition to foreign political and economic domination, a more equitable distribution of oil revenues, a solution to the Palestinian problem, and the strength and purity of Islam. Thus there were those who were willing to tolerate Saddam Hussein's acknowledged brutality and despotism, and to support his struggle against the Coalition.

From the beginning of the Gulf crisis the Iraqi president had counted on the support of the Arab masses. On 10 August 1990 he addressed all Arabs:

Iraq, oh Arabs, is your Iraq. . . . It is the flame of justice to dispel darkness. For these reasons, and under these circumstances, American forces arrived and Saudi doors opened in front of them, under the fallacious pretext that the Iraqi army would continue its holy advance. . . . Our denials and clarifications were in vain, which shows that there are deliberately aggressive intentions against Iraq. . . . Oh Arabs, oh Muslims and believers of the whole world, the day has come to rise and defend Mecca, which has been captured by the vanguard of American and Zionist forces. Rise against oppression, corruption, treachery, and attempts to stab us in the back. . . . Keep the foreigners away from our holy places, so that we may rise as one man to dispel darkness and unmask these leaders who have no sense of honor.

His 12 August speech offering a withdrawal from Kuwait in exchange for a total solution to all the region's problems—including the Palestinian question—was clearly meant to mobilize Arab public opinion in his favor. On 29 November he declared: "If war breaks out, we will fight in a way which will make all Arabs and Muslims proud. We are determined not to kneel down to injustice." When hostilities started, Saddam Hussein may have hoped to win in the streets of the Arab capitals a war that he could not win at the front.

On the Coalition side, U.S. President Bush appeared to view the conflict as one of good versus evil: "For me it boils down to a very moral case of good versus evil, black versus white. If I have to go [to war], it's not going to matter to me if there isn't one congressman who supports this, or what happens to public opinion. If it's right, it's gotta be done," he said on 2 January 1991. And he consistently maintained that Iraq must withdraw unconditionally: "The international community is united in its call for Iraq to leave all of Kuwait without condition and without further delay. . . . There can be no reward for aggression. Nor will there be any negotiation," he wrote to Saddam Hussein on 9 January.[116]

Undoubtedly, the personalities of the two leaders and their leadership styles figured prominently in the nature of their interaction and the crisis outcome. They shared certain qualities of personality and leadership style that tended to preclude learning and empathy while helping to sustain their angry face-off. President George Bush and President Saddam Hussein placed themselves on, and stayed on, a collision course.[117]

WOULD ECONOMIC SANCTIONS HAVE WORKED?

Imposed within days of the invasion of Kuwait, the U.N. economic embargo started to have an effect a few months later. On 13 November 1990, Iraq's minister of commerce announced a reduction in the rice ration from the 1.5 kilograms per person per month that had been declared at the beginning of the embargo to 1 kilo. While the minister claimed that stocks were adequate and that the rations had been reduced only in order to make supplies last longer, black market prices did not fail to rise. This market was supplied at least in part by government officials who bought in state stores and resold privately. Iraq had imported 60% of its rice and wheat before the crisis, and practically all its cooking oil, sugar, and tea. Thus all these items were subject to rationing.

Rationing was used by the regime as a propaganda weapon to denounce the "inhuman" aspects of the embargo. But the sanctions were primarily meant to put pressure on industry, in particular the oil industry, the government's main revenue source. By November 1990 some 40% of state enterprises had ceased operation as a consequence of the embargo. Oil production had been reduced by 75% and was barely sufficient to cover domestic needs and those of the army in Kuwait. Not a single barrel of oil was being exported from Kuwait or Iraq. Oil pipelines through Saudi Arabia and Turkey had been cut off, and the

---

116. Letter reproduced in Sifry and Cerf, *The Gulf War Reader*, p. 178.

117. Bush's and Hussein's personalities and leadership styles are analyzed and compared in Kincade, "On the Brink in the Gulf. Part 2: The Route to War," pp. 295-311.

Coalition naval blockade prevented industrial and consumer goods—not to mention arms—from reaching Iraq. The few leaks in the blockade were due to smuggling across the Iranian, Jordanian, and Turkish borders. Thus it appeared to some that economic sanctions might attain their goal, albeit slowly and at some peril for the Westerners being held hostage in Iraq.[118]

It is impossible to know whether sanctions would have worked or how much time might have been required for them to work. Three factors help to argue that they might have worked. First, Iraq was highly dependent on imports and needed oil revenues to pay for them. Second, apart from the arms market, Iraq was a small customer in global terms; therefore the embargo did not threaten to create economic problems for special interest groups in Western countries (unlike, for example, the situation with respect to U.S. farmers in 1980, who were unhappy with the wheat embargo imposed on the USSR after its invasion of Afghanistan). Third, Iraq was politically isolated, receiving support only from Jordan. The embargo thus had a good chance of being total, unlike those of Italy in 1935, Cuba in 1959, Rhodesia in 1965, and South Africa more recently, when allies of those countries openly violated the international sanctions.

On the other hand, the embargo had a serious weakness: it could not deprive Iraq of its oil supplies—an essential resource for an army. One can think of fighting, at least for a while, without clothes, spare parts, equipment, and even food; without oil and electricity, nothing can be done. The economic sanctions decreed against Mussolini's Italy and Castro's Cuba had very limited success largely because in those cases the international community could not reach the consensus required to cut off all sources of energy. Depriving Italian tanks and airplanes of fuel in Ethiopia in 1935, if the sanctions had been enforced, might have quickly ended Mussolini's imperial dreams. In the cases of Rhodesia and South Africa, lack of an international consensus delayed the effect of sanctions.

A review of the historical record[119] shows that sanctions have worked in 41 of 115 cases since 1914, including such partial successes as the measures imposed against Argentina after its invasion of the Falklands. In some situations sanctions required several years to achieve their purpose (14 years for Rhodesia and South Africa), and the average in the case of ambitious goals was nearly 2 years.

Although the embargo might have reduced Iraq's GNP by nearly 50%, it is not clear how long the regime could have survived this situation, if one

---

118. See for example Crow, "Give Sanctions a Chance," and Brzezinski, "The Drift to War," reproduced in Sifry and Cerf, *The Gulf War Reader*, pp. 234 and 251 respectively.

119. Kimberly Elliott, Gary Hufbauer, and Jeffrey Scott, *Economic Sanctions Reconsidered* (Institute for International Economics, 1990). A synopsis is published as "Sanctions Work: The Historical Record," in Sifry and Cerf, *The Gulf War Reader*, pp. 255-259.

considers that it has survived a worse situation for over five years after the end of the Gulf War.[120] In addition, even at the reduced level, Iraq's per capita GNP would have been much higher than that of most Arab countries. Therefore there can be no doubt that even in the best of scenarios it would have taken a long time for sanctions to work. Testifying before the U.S. House Armed Services Committee on 5 December 1990, CIA Director William Webster stated: "Industry appears to be the hardest hit sector so far. . . . Despite these shutdowns, the most vital resources—including electric power generation and refining—do not yet appear threatened. . . . Probably only energy-related and some military industries will still be fully functioning by next spring. . . . While we can look ahead several months and predict the gradual deterioration of the Iraqi economy, it is more difficult to assess how or when these conditions will cause Saddam to modify his behavior."

At the time several commentators pointed out that the real question was not "Will sanctions work?" but "Will the United States and the rest of the world have the patience to stick with them until they work?" Thus there was a lively debate in the West, with some arguing that more time should be given for sanctions to work, and others arguing that time was running out and that military steps should be taken. In the end most political leaders opted for war, judging, as Webster put it, that "[Saddam Hussein] appears confident in the ability of his security services to contain potential discontent, and we do not believe that he is troubled by the hardships Iraqis will be forced to endure."

As the U.N. deadline of 15 January 1991 approached, Iraq and the United States were on a collision course. Even though it was not obvious to all at the time, the presidents of the two countries had placed themselves in positions where no significant changes of direction were possible, given their respective temperaments and perceptions.[121] A number of U.S. "elder statesmen" had urged President Bush to give more time to sanctions; we do not know whether any of President Saddam Hussein's advisers had counseled some sort of conciliatory move, but many Western and Arab observers thought that some sort of partial Iraqi withdrawal might take place just before the deadline. Although there were minor antiwar protests in the United States, none compared with opposition to the Vietnam War, even in its early stages. There were no antigovernment uprisings in Iraq. Although the allies of the United States varied in the degree of their support for the Bush administration's position, none opposed it. Saddam Hussein had mustered little support in the Arab world or in the Third World, but he was prepared to go it alone. The collision, ultimately dubbed Desert Storm by military planners, became inescapable. Bush gave the tentative go-ahead for the attack on 11 January but reserved the final decision until the last minute.

---

120. See, e.g., Anne Reifenberg, "Bloody but Unbowed, Iraq Is Weathering U.N. Trade Sanctions," *Wall Street Journal Europe* (3 October 1996).

121. See Kincade, "On the Brink in the Gulf. Part 2: The Route to War," pp. 304-305.

4

The Balance of Forces

And so it is certain that a small country cannot contend with a great, that few cannot contend with many; that the weak cannot contend with the strong.

—Mencius, circa 300 B.C.

It has been argued that Iraq made a mistake when it stopped its advance at the border with Saudi Arabia, or when it did not attack U.S. troops during the early buildup of the Desert Shield force in the late summer and early fall of 1990. To have exploited its temporary military superiority by seizing Saudi Arabia's major oil fields and ports would have given Iraq a strong bargaining and military position. The argument is based on the observation that Coalition forces were weak and not well prepared for combat in the desert at that time. But on 6 August, only two Iraqi divisions were deployed near the border with Saudi Arabia. Nine other divisions were in Kuwait, but they were all about 100 kilometers away from the border.[122]

Not counting U.S. forces, Saudi Arabia and its close Arabian allies in the Gulf Cooperation Council could deploy a strong air force: 5 E-3 Sentry AWACS airborne radar surveillance and control aircraft and about 380 combat aircraft (including 72 Saudi F-15 air-superiority fighters), many equipped with advanced U.S. or French avionics and weapons; to this we can add the potential of 475 Egyptian combat aircraft.[123] Although the Iraqi combat air force of about 700 planes had a numerical superiority, its technical inferiority

---

122. U.S. Department of Defense, *Conduct of the Persian Gulf War*, Map I-2, p. 4.

123. Numbers from bin Sultan, *Desert Warrior*, p. 20.

was vast.[124]   An army in motion on highways is one of the most inviting
objectives a superior air force could have. The defending airplanes, flown by
well-trained pilots, could have wreaked havoc on exposed Iraqi columns
attempting to advance into Saudi Arabia—a huge country (with an area three
times that of Texas and five times that of Iraq) whose territory is open desert.
To reach the port of Dhahran and the principal oil fields would have had to
traverse 300 kilometers of desert under air attack.

Although U.S. and Saudi military planners[125] (who correctly plan for worst
cases[126] and had assumed that the Iraqis would advance with six heavy
divisions[127]) were concerned about this contingency, we believe that it is quite
doubtful that the Iraqis could have reached their objective with enough forces,
supplies, and morale to cope with the determined defense they would
inevitably have met. During the Iran-Iraq War, Iraq never demonstrated the
capability to conduct coordinated offensives more than 100 kilometers into
enemy territory. During the ground phase of the Gulf War, in the absence of
any threat from Iraqi air forces, the U.S. 24th Infantry Division (Mechanized)
advanced just over 350 kilometers in 100 hours, very fast movement by
historical standards.[128]   According to U.S. plans developed before the crisis,
"nine days . . . after hostilities began would be available before lead enemy
elements reached defensive positions near al-Jubayl [200 kilometers south of
the border]."[129]

With their usual penchant for colorful expressions, Western media referred
to the first U.S. forces deployed in Saudi Arabia as "speed bumps." Some of
the soldiers concerned feel otherwise. The first U.S. division to take up
defensive positions, along the road to Dhahran, was the 82nd Airborne. This
unit includes nine antitank companies, each equipped with 20 Humvees (4-
wheel-drive vehicles) armed with TOWs (optically guided antitank missiles); a
light armor battalion consisting of 56 Sheridan tanks armed with Shillelagh
heavy antitank missiles; and a helicopter gunship battalion with 21 Apaches.
The division planned to defend in depth by taking advantage of nontrafficable
and irregular terrain around some salt marshes, and by exploiting the 4,000-
meter range of the TOW, which far exceeded the 1,000 to 1,500-meter of both
the main guns and the machine guns of Iraqi tanks. The lack of armor on the

---

124. Cohen et al., *GWAPS: Weapons, Tactics, and Training*, pp. 19, 24-25; U.S.
Department of Defense, *Conduct of the Persian Gulf Conflict*, p. 13.

125. bin Sultan, *Desert Warrior*, p. 11.

126. Douglas W. Craft, *An Operational Analysis of the Persian Gulf War* (U.S.
Army War College, Carlisle Barracks, 1992), p. 1.

127. Brig. Gen. Robert H. Scales, Jr., *Certain Victory* (U.S. Army, 1993), pp. 44,
82; but early Central Command orders were based on a threat of only five divisions:
Swain, *"Lucky War,"* p.49.

128. Richard Hallion, *Storm over Iraq* (Smithsonian Institution Press, 1992), p.
135.

129. U.S. Department of Defense, *Conduct of the Persian Gulf War*, p. 43; and
Swain, *"Lucky War,"* p. 7.

Humvee is no disadvantage if it can shoot, hit, and move while remaining out of range of enemy fire (as Libyan forces in Chad learned to their dismay in 1987). In addition to the missiles mounted on vehicles, the division deployed infantry equipped with Dragon antitank missiles, dug into DIP (die-in-place) positions. Plans called for the helicopter gunships to be called in after initial engagements had shaped the battlefield.

Iraqi artillery could have seriously threatened the division's defensive positions, but Coalition air power, once deployed in strength, could have silenced the artillery rapidly. Indeed, close air support would have greatly multiplied the effectiveness of the 82nd Division's ground forces, both in a direct antiarmor role and by disrupting the Iraqis' extended logistic lines. Although the topic is controversial, some believe that each of the 82nd Division's nine battalions could probably have stopped one or two Iraqi armored battalions, thus holding up a one-to-two-division attack (the division was fully deployed by mid-September).[130]

In its invasion of Kuwait, Iraq gambled on winning without war, and lost. But at the time many observers thought that Iraq had some chance of winning its gamble. Attacking Saudi Arabian or U.S. forces would have immediately started a war, and denied the chance of winning the gamble that Western nations would lack the determination to fight to liberate Kuwait.

FORCE BUILDUP IN SAUDI ARABIA AND KUWAIT

On 6 August[131] the United States initiated its deployment to Saudi Arabia; 48 U.S. F-15C fighters from the 71st Tactical Fighter Squadron based at Langley Field, Virginia flew over 14 hours nonstop to Saudi Arabia, refueling in flight over the Atlantic Ocean. The U.S. aircraft carrier groups *Independence* and *Eisenhower* reached their stations in, respectively, the Gulf of Oman and the Red Sea on 8 August and were prepared for operations. Thus some 150 U.S. combat aircraft were quickly available for action; in fact, aircraft from the *Independence* could have conducted long-range strikes as early as 5 August.[132]

Iraqi forces increased steadily to about 420,000 at the end of September and then declined due to home leaves and desertions.[133] Figure 4.1 shows the buildup of U.S. forces.[134] It can be seen clearly that U.S. deployment took

130. This analysis is based on a personal interview with Lt. Col. John Blakeney, who was plans and operations officer for the division's tank battalion during the Gulf War.

131. Washington, D.C., time. The order was given at 0050, 7 August, GMT; Cohen et al., *GWAPS: Chronology*, p. 10.

132. U.S. Department of Defense, *Conduct of the Persian Gulf War*, p. 45; Cohen et al., *GWAPS: Chronology*, pp. 8-9.

133. See Chapter 8, section "The Opposing Forces."

134. Cohen et al., *GWAPS: Statistical Compendium*, Table 14, p. 51; Table 15, p. 53.

place in two phases, the first phase being complete for the air forces at the beginning of September, and for total forces at the end of October. At the beginning of November the Coalition announced a second phase of force deployment. The additional forces had been requested by U.S. Central Command on 9 October, and their deployment was approved on 7 November. Iraq attempted to match this deployment by increasing its forces in Kuwait, but was unable to do so significantly.

Figure 4.1
U.S. forces buildup

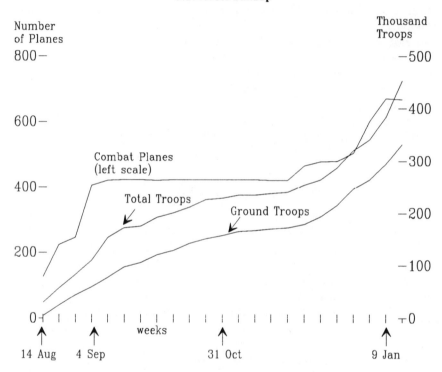

The first U.S. ground contingents arrived on 9 August: the Ready Brigade of the 82nd Airborne Division, whose weaponry included the lightly armored but big-gunned (152 mm) Sheridan M551 tanks;[135] the entire brigade was in position by 13 August, and a second brigade was in place eight days later.[136] U.S. Marines landed on 14 August and were ready for combat on 26 August: 17,000 men of the Seventh Marine Expeditionary Brigade, a mechanized air-

---

135. While very light for an armored vehicle, the Sheridan is considered a scout tank rather than an armored personnel carrier. Many improvements have been made to overcome problems noted during the Vietnam War.

136. U.S. Department of Defense, *Conduct of the Persian Gulf War*, p. 45.

ground task force.[137] On 21 August they were joined by 18 F-117 Nighthawk fighters.[138] On 7 September, the first U.S. Army heavy armored units were deployed;[139] specially designed U.S. ships unloaded their cargoes of M1 tanks and other vehicles within six hours. At that time, the equivalent of more than two divisions of ground forces had been deployed by the United States. By mid-September the Coalition had the capability to conduct offensive air operations against targets in Kuwait and Iraq; over 150,000 U.S. troops and their equipment had been deployed in Saudi Arabia, and Coalition commanders felt that there were enough ground forces to defend against any potential further Iraqi invasion.[140]

On 8 November, the United States, which then anticipated subsequent offensive actions, announced plans to draw on its NATO contingents to increase its total strength very significantly, deploying in Saudi Arabia a U.S.-based armored division, the Europe-based VII Corps (well over 100,000 troops), three additional aircraft carriers, one additional battleship, additional Marine forces, and more aircraft.[141] Another 18 F-117s were deployed in early December, and 6 more at the end of January.[142] Ground troops and their equipment continued to arrive throughout the conflict.

The first Egyptian troops arrived on 11 August; the Third Mechanized Division began deployment on 19 September and completed it on 6 October. A second Egyptian division, the Fourth Armored, was deployed from 19 December to 7 January 1991. Some 4,000 Syrian commandos started arriving in mid-August, and the Ninth Armored Division began its deployment on 1 November and completed it on 18 December.[143] According to U.S. air liaison officers attached to the Syrian forces, these troops were very well trained and professional. U.S. Air Force Sergeant Hans Erdmannn: "The Syrians didn't believe that Saddam would fight right up to the point when the war started. But when the war did start, they took it very seriously and trained accordingly and prepared themselves for it. It was not something they wanted to do, but it was something that was both politically and economically necessary."[144]

The first 12 U.K. Tornado fighters arrived in Dhahran on 10 August, as did a 70-man army communications post.[145] British warships were stationed in the southern Gulf by 13 August. Akrotiri airfield in Cyprus became an important staging base for U.K. logistics. Twelve more Tornados arrived

---

137. Cohen et al., *GWAPS: Chronology*, pp. 21, 26.

138. Ibid., p. 29.

139. Ibid., p. 51.

140. Cohen et al., *GWAPS: Statistical Compendium*, Table 14, p. 51; Schwarzkopf, *It Doesn't Take a Hero*, pp. 348-349.

141. Cohen et al., *GWAPS: Chronology*, p. 102.

142. Cohen et al., *GWAPS: Statistical Compendium*, Table 15, p. 53.

143. Cohen et al., *GWAPS: Chronology*; Egyptian Ministry of Defense, *Al Kitab Harab Tahrir Kuwait*; official reports; and personal interviews.

144. Personal interview.

145. Cohen et al., *GWAPS: Chronology*, p. 16.

toward the end of August, 18 more in mid-October; and the 10,000 men and 145 tanks of the U.K. Seventh Armored Brigade, the famous Desert Rats, were fully deployed on 3 November. Additional forces were added after 8 November, bringing U.K. strength on the ground up to 28,000 men and 221 tanks, comprising the U.K. First Armored Division; and, in the air, some 70 combat aircraft, including the ground-attack version of the Tornado. The First Division was completely deployed on 11 January and began to move toward its forward operating base on 14 January. It was declared ready for offensive operations two weeks later.[146]

The first contingent of 3,700 French ground troops and 12 planes started arriving on 6 September. These were later reinforced with another 5,100 men and 16 airplanes in mid-December. In addition some 6,800 French naval personnel were deployed.[147]

Contingents from smaller nations also arrived during late 1990 and early 1991.

RELATIVE RESOURCES: COALITION VERSUS IRAQ

The combined U.S., U.K., and French military expenditure during the ten years preceding the war was somewhere between 12 and 25 times Iraq's expenditure during the same period. Although Iraq spent an estimated 25% to 50% of its GNP on the armed forces in the decade before its invasion of Kuwait, while in 1990 the figure for the United States is 5.4%, for the UK 3.9%, and for France, 3.5%, the much larger GNPs of the Western countries meant that their military expenditures dwarfed those of Iraq.

Historically, attacks by what Toynbee[148] calls "external proletariats" on mature civilizations have been successful when the invaders were numerically superior. The numerical superiority of an external proletariat has been due essentially to the fact that in a society with a low level of development, many people can be enlisted as soldiers, whereas in a highly developed society, few people are willing to be soldiers. Indeed, the latter society cannot maintain its high level of development if too many people are engaged in military activities. The same factors applied to Iraq: in terms of numbers, Iraq's army was at least initially superior to the Coalition forces.

But one of the characteristics of an advanced civilization is the availability of capital and its use to ensure prosperity. The countries that comprise

---

146. Ibid.; Air Chief Marshal Sir Patrick Hine, "Despatch," *The London Gazette* (28 June 1991), second supplement; and U.K. Secretary of State for Defence, *Statement on the Defence Estimates* (July 1991).

147. Cohen et al., *GWAPS: Chronology*, p. 59; Service d'Information et de Relations Publiques des Armées, *Armées d'Aujourdhui*, no. 161 (June-July 1991), and *Terre Magazine*, no. 22-23 (March-April 1991).

148. Arnold Toynbee, *A Study of History* (abridged) (Weathervane, 1972), Part V, Chapter 29.

Western civilization (in particular the United States) have been investing very large amounts of money in their military establishments for many years. Thus, if threatened, Western civilization can draw on vast reserves of accumulated capital investments to defend itself. In physical terms, these investments are nothing more than stockpiles of high-technology weapon systems: planes, ships, tanks, missiles, smart bombs, and so on. A small number of highly trained Western warriors can use these vast capital investments to defeat a large external proletariat.

Thus industrial power and high technology provide the basis for a war such as that in the Gulf. In military operations on open terrain under comparatively clear skies, armored vehicles, airplanes, and high-technology weapons have a crucial role. Well adapted to the conditions prevailing in the Gulf region, Western armies depend more on machines than on manpower; that is, using the terminology of standard economic theory, they are capital-intensive institutions. By stating the total costs of weapon systems in terms of the manpower required to produce them, one can see that the human resources invested in the production of weapons for a high-technology, capital-intensive army far exceed those available to a low-technology, labor-intensive army. In the Gulf War, weapons that had taken many years of labor to build were used and consumed within seconds. The appropriate economic measure of manpower in this context is the fully loaded man-year, that is, the cost of one year of labor plus the cost of all the social benefits, working space, equipment depreciation, and so forth associated with the year of labor. In Operation Desert Storm, a single Tomahawk missile cost about $1 million (roughly the cost of 100 small automobiles), which represented something like 10 man-years of fully loaded labor. A Coalition pilot controlled a weapon system that required several hundred man-years of labor to produce (the F/A-18 Hornet cost over $40 million, and the next-generation U.S. Advanced Tactical Fighter will cost over $80 million).

Thus the efficacy of each Coalition soldier was magnified by the many man-years of labor that had gone into developing and building the weapon system he used. In contrast to the situation of past centuries, industrial states can today in effect accumulate vast reserves of offensive military manpower by stockpiling modern weapons, which represent long-term investments in military force. These stockpiles can be used rapidly, with devastating effects, as we have seen in the Gulf War.

Saddam Hussein may have been correct in believing that Western civilizations were unlikely to commit very large numbers of people to war. However, he did not understand that the technology of war has changed, so that extensive use of capital-intensive stockpiles of high-technology weapons allows small armies to defeat much larger ones.

To close this section we note that the total U.S. expenditure on the Gulf War has been estimated at $61 billion (these are costs incurred during Desert Shield and Desert Storm for personnel and equipment that would not have been incurred if the operations had not taken place).[149] This is a sum larger than the annual defense budget of any nation except the United States and USSR (other nations reimbursed the U.S. for $54 billion of the $61 billion total expenditure). The U.S. expenditure on the war exceeded Iraq's annual GNP. That is, the United States unleashed on Iraq military resources that would have required more than one year of work by the entire nation of Iraq to produce.

LOGISTICS

Within days of the Iraqi invasion of Kuwait, in response to an official Saudi Arabian request, the United States had concentrated sufficient air power in the Gulf area to have overwhelming air superiority. That this superiority existed in reality, and not just on paper, was conclusively proved during the war. Thus, from the beginning and throughout the campaign, the Coalition forces were immune to air attack. As a consequence, Coalition logistical forces were never threatened by air attacks and could carry out their mission with no disruption. In contrast, it has been estimated that 90% of the Iraqi capability to resupply frontline troops in Kuwait had been destroyed by Coalition air forces within two weeks of the start of the campaign (see Chapter 6, section "Air Strikes Against Logistic Support").

It is difficult to overestimate the advantage that Coalition forces enjoyed as a result of their massive superiority in logistics, which was due to the combination of Saudi Arabia's excellent port and road infrastructure and support (in the form of fuel, water, trucks, and so forth), and Coalition military transport ships, aircraft, and vehicles. Throughout history it has been a truism that "an army marches on its stomach." But food is only one of a modern army's needs. To it must be added clothing, shelter, medical supplies, recreational items, and—far exceeding human needs in weight and volume—fuel for myriad vehicles, ammunition for a multitude of weapons, and spare parts for high- and low-technology machines.

The ratio of support to frontline combat personnel was in the order of 6:1 for U.S. forces as a whole, with about 9% of U.S. enlisted personnel being supply and service handlers and 16% being administrators and clerks. There has been a steady downward trend in the proportion of frontline soldiers since the nineteenth century: in the Civil War, 93% of Union personnel were classified as holding "Military-type occupations"; this figure dropped to 34% for U.S. forces in World War I, and to 30% during the Korean War.[150]

A look at the effort involved in preparing the 48th Tactical Fighter Wing and its 66 F-111s for operations will help to understand the scale of the logistical effort. The first

---

149. U.S. Department of Defense, *Conduct of the Persian Gulf War*, Appendix P, p. 2.

150. *Historical Statistics of the United States* (U.S. Department of Commerce, 1975).

24 jets arrived in Saudi Arabia on 25 August, followed the next day by 300 support personnel—a small number considering that about 20 persons are normally required to support one aircraft.

Improvisation was the order of the day: people unrolled their sleeping bags and slept under aircraft wings and in shelters until an abandoned dining hall was cleaned up and converted to a mass dormitory. By the end of the first week four bombers were kept on ready alert 24 hours a day and 6 orientation sorties were being flown daily. Contracting personnel had to obtain supplies of water, food, transportation, equipment, and building materials. Over two million dollars were spent locally during the first month. Many cargo pallets were required for transport from the UK of spare parts and other essential equipment; a full complement wasn't available until two weeks after the first planes landed. Jet fuel was in critical shortage, and would have limited operations to 18 sorties per day.

It took a month to build up enough supplies for 7 days of sustained operations (with over 500 aircraft delivering 2500 tons of cargo), and 6 weeks for 30 days. Eventually 1400 people were deployed in Taif, over half of them maintenance personnel and over 8000 tons of munitions were moved.[151]

When making an attack, a U.S. mechanized division required some 2,700 tons of supplies per day, compared with 700 tons in 1953.[152] Forward logistic bases for the U.K. First Armored Division were prepared to provide daily supplies of 1,200 tons of ammunition, 450 tons of fuel, 350 tons of water, and 30,000 individual rations. The daily needs of this division were comparable with those of an entire army group during the 1944 landings in Normandy. By contrast, Iraqi logistical requirements were probably on the order of only 100 tons per division per day, given their static defensive posture.

As an example of the massive logistical efforts made by the Coalition countries, we describe the U.S. operation. Throughout the crisis a total of 406 airplanes delivered about 550,000 tons of cargo and over 500,000 people—the bulk of U.S. forces. The number of passengers and amount of cargo moved by air was equivalent to transporting all the residents of Oklahoma City and their belongings a distance of 12,000 kilometers. Airlift moved about 15% of the total U.S. dry cargo (that is, excluding petroleum products). Sealift delivered all the oil and the bulk of the dry cargo, accounting for 95% of the total cargo delivered. Thus, even in this modern war, sea power and cargo ships maintained their traditional supremacy in logistics. By the end of February 1991, an average of 1,000 large truckloads of cargo were arriving by sea every day. Over 220,000 tank rounds were supplied, of which only 3,600 were actually used during the war.[153]

---

151. 48 TFW, *Operation Desert Storm* (Taif, Saudi Arabia, undated), supplemented by personal interviews with officers and NCOs of this unit.

152. Trevor N. Dupuy et al., *How to Defeat Saddam Hussein* (Warner Books, 1991), p. 103.

153. U.S. Department of Defense, *Conduct of the Persian Gulf War*, Appendix F; and Cohen et al., *GWAPS: Logistics*.

Key components of the rapid U.S. deployment were the 24 prepositioned ships, mostly based at Diego Garcia Island in the Indian Ocean; these ships permanently carry ammunition, fuel, supplies, and equipment for the Army, Air Force, and Marines. With the exception of the Allied invasion of Normandy during World War II, which took two years to prepare, the logistical effort by sea for the Gulf War was the largest and fastest movement of material to a single operating area in the history of warfare.

Over 2 billion ton-kilometers of cargo were moved from ports to combat units: this is the equivalent of driving 10,000 40-ton trucks from one coast of the United States to the other. At the peak of operations, nearly 70 million liters of fuel per day were issued: enough to fill all the automobiles in a city the size of Pittsburgh or Manchester every day.

Telecommunications links proved inadequate to fully support the computerized logistics system; requests in some cases were consolidated daily and transmitted by courier to higher levels for processing. Processing delays, and the fact that units in the field had no way of knowing if a request had been correctly processed and shipped, undermined confidence in the system, resulting in multiple placements of many orders and an abuse of the priority system: 65% of all requisitions were submitted as high priority.[154] In addition, containers were often inadequately documented, and they had to be unpacked to determine their contents. Because logistics personnel were not deployed early, many containers sat in ports unprocessed, their contents unknown, thus adding to the confusion.[155] Finally, the United States had insufficient heavy equipment transporters (HETs) for its tanks (because it had primarily planned for a defensive war in Europe), and considerable ingenuity and effort were required to obtain enough of them.[156]

COALITION STRATEGY

General Colin Powell summarized the Coalition strategy very accurately at the beginning of the war: "First we're going to cut it [the Iraqi army] off, and then we're going to kill it."[157] The "cutting off" was an instance of a logistic strategy: this aimed to defeat Iraq's armed forces indirectly by depriving them of food, fuel, ammunition, and other supplies needed to defend themselves and their Kuwaiti conquest. The Coalition implemented this logistic strategy with a raiding, rather than a persisting, strategy based on air strikes. Instead of

154. U.S. Department of Defense, *Conduct of the Persian Gulf War*, Appendix F, pp. 48-49; Scott W. Conrad, *Moving the Force: Desert Storm and Beyond*, McNair Paper 32, Institute for National Strategic Studies, National Defense University, December 1994), p. 26.

155. Scales, *Certain Victory*, p. 75.

156. Swain, *"Lucky War,"* p. 157. Other logistical problems are mentioned in Lt. Col. Stephen J. Marshman, *Lessons from the Desert* (U.S. Army War College, Carlisle Barracks, 1993), pp. 217-220.

157. Cohen et al., *GWAPS: Effects and Effectiveness*, p. 159.

attempting to gain ground, a raiding strategy relies on hit-and-run attacks, which are well suited to air power.

The "kill it" was an instance of a combat strategy that aimed to defeat the Iraqi forces by direct attacks. This strategy was implemented initially with a raiding strategy and later, during the ground campaign, with a persisting strategy. During the air campaign Coalition air forces targeted and destroyed Iraqi airplanes, tanks, and artillery, using hit-and-run attacks. The subsequent ground campaign is a classic example of a combat persisting strategy based on an outflanking movement.

To summarize, the Coalition used all four types of strategy:[158]

1. Combat strategy, in which the enemy's armed forces are attacked directly.
2. Logistic strategy, in which they are attacked indirectly by striking their supplies, supply lines, and supply sources.
3. Persisting strategy, which aims at attacking to gain territory and defending to hold territory.
4. Raiding strategy, which strikes an enemy and then immediately withdraws, then strikes again.

Using this terminology, we can say that the Coalition strategy consisted of three phases, initially estimated to require about 32 days in total:[159]

1. An initial, primarily logistic, raiding phase to be executed by using air power (officially called Phase I—Strategic Air Campaign). This phase was initially expected to last about 6 days and it would be followed by:
2. A primarily combat raiding phase that would use a combination of standoff air power, close-in air power, ground artillery, and naval artillery (officially called Phases II and III—Air Superiority in the Kuwaiti Theater and Battlefield Preparation). These two phases were expected to require about 12 days and would be followed by:
3. A combat persisting phase to turn the Iraqi force, which would rely heavily on close-in air power and armored ground forces (officially called Phase IV—Ground Campaign), initially expected to last about 14 days[160] (but later revised to 6 days[161]).

Phases I to III combined both logistic and combat strategies, with the mix broadly shifting from targets far from the front to targets close to the front,

---

158. For an exposition of this approach to strategy, see Archer Jones, *The Art of War in the Western World* (Oxford University Press, 1989), pp. 54-65, 692-701, and *Elements of Military Strategy: An Historical Approach* (Praeger, 1996), pp. xiii-xv.

159. U.S. Department of Defense, *Conduct of the Persian Gulf War*, p. 134; and Cohen et al., *GWAPS: Planning*, Figure 1, p. 8.

160. U.S. Department of Defense, *Conduct of the Persian Gulf War*, p. 317; and Swain, *"Lucky War,"* p. 92. Slightly different numbers (total 14 days for the air campaign and 18 for the ground attack) were used by air planners: Cohen et al., *GWAPS: Planning*, p. 175.

161. Cohen et al., *GWAPS: Planning*, Figure 2, p. 8.

and from logistic targets to combat targets as the campaign progressed. Because of the large number of planes available, phases I, II, and III were executed simultaneously. The intensity of air operations was high, so the term *raiding* must be taken in a technical sense: Iraqi citizens and soldiers had the impression of living under a non-stop, continuous bombardment. Air superiority paralyzed Iraqi reconnaissance, logistics, and troop movements, while continual bombardment demoralized troops and destroyed equipment. Later, feints and distractions enabled an unchallenged concentration against weakness and the turning of Iraq's right flank.

During each phase, the Coalition systematically concentrated against Iraqi weaknesses. In the first phase, the Iraqi air-defense system, which was vulnerable to hi-tech weapons, and an overextended and cumbersome logistics system, which was susceptible to air attack. In the second phase, the immobility of the Iraqi forces exposed them to air attack. In the third phase, the open Iraqi flank invited a turning movement, favored by inferior Iraqi morale and, again, the lack of air defense and the vulnerability to air attack.

To these we can add what was perhaps Iraq's greatest weakness: its underestimation of the Coalition's capabilities. The Coalition had superior personnel and training; technological advantages in weaponry; better ability to acquire intelligence, in particular by using satellites; a sufficient level of political cohesion; and excellent political and military leadership.

The final Coalition ground attack was a classical example of a combined-arms land assault based on the time-honored strategies of distraction and outflanking (see 8, section "Coalition Strategy"). The Coalition had planned for the eventuality that Iraqi troops would defend Kuwait City. Many assaults against well-defended urban areas during the past 60 years have resulted in heavy casualties and widespread destruction. Modern firepower cannot be used selectively in built-up areas: if it is used, it tends to cause severe damage to civilian buildings, sometimes without significantly weakening the defenders. The Coalition's plans for liberating the city, if it had been defended, called for a siege of unspecified length, followed by an assault by Arab forces. The length of the siege would have depended on the situation of the civilian population and on the level of Iraqi resistance.

We can speculate that the perceived need to minimize Western casualties in order to maintain a high level of political support in Western countries may have been a factor in the plan's envisaged use of Arab forces for house-to-house fighting, as may have been the political value to have Arabs responsible for "collateral damage" and to give them the prestige of accomplishing the liberation. However, Kuwaiti military leaders felt (correctly, as it turned out) that the Iraqis would not stand and fight in populated areas, so a variation of the plan envisaged a swift liberation by Arab forces with little or no fighting.[162]

---

162. U.S. Department of Defense, *Conduct of the Persian Gulf War*, Appendix I, p. 42.

In accordance with the military principle of economy of force, the Coalition refrained from using its considerable strength in ground-based troops until the long air campaign had essentially ensured victory. Ground forces were not used so long as the air forces were achieving their objectives: destruction of Iraqi logistics, artillery, armor, and morale.

With respect to tactics, the Coalition relied heavily on concepts and methods developed by NATO and known as the AirLand Battle Doctrine: to defeat the enemy by conducting simultaneous offensive operations over the full breadth and depth of the battlefield.

IRAQI STRATEGY

Iraqi strategy was clearly based on lessons learned during the Iran-Iraq War, thus supporting the age-old adage that most armies are well prepared to fight the previous war: reliance on entrenched, static defenses and on Coalition unwillingness to absorb heavy casualties. A military obstacle system is intended to slow down an advancing enemy, so that it can be subject to artillery fire; to economize forces deployed forward; and to permit identification of enemy attacks in order to mount counterattacks, hopefully while the enemy is still negotiating the obstacle. The artillery would typically be placed out of sight of the obstacle system in order to conceal it from the advancing forces; thus the fire would typically be indirect. While armored vehicles can advance through massed artillery fire, logistical support vehicles cannot. Thus no serious advance can take place until enemy artillery has been silenced. An obstacle system not covered by massive artillery fire is of little use. It was the combination of obstacles and artillery that posed a threat to any potential Coalition advance—hence it became important to destroy Iraq's guns. According to Coalition combat engineers, the quality of Iraq's obstacle systems was not very high, either because the systems had been poorly built in the beginning (particularly in the west) or because they had been poorly maintained (wind erodes berms, fills in ditches, and exposes mines).

The typical fortification in Kuwait was composed of a trench, a berm, and some prepared positions for vehicles and artillery (usually a shallow hole surrounded by a berm for tanks and APCs, with ammunition kept nearby in a deeper hole covered by corrugated sheet metal and dirt). Map 4.1 was found in Kuwait by U.S. Lt. Curtis Palmer (Third Armored Divison); it was drawn by an Iraqi engineer and shows a battalion strong-point in the oil fields north of Kuwait City, about 20 kilometers from the Iraqi border and 3 kilometers from the coast.

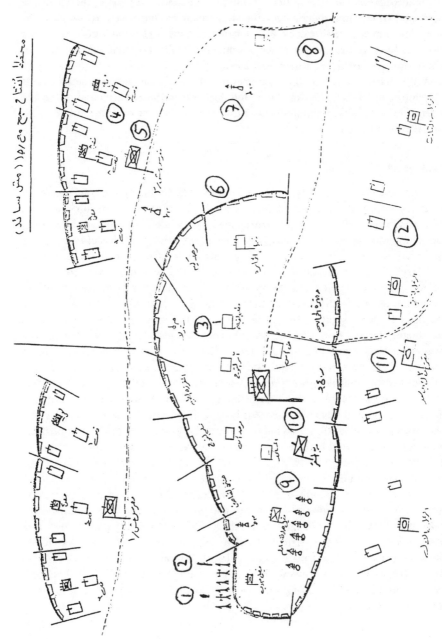

Map 4.1 An Iraqi map of a fortified position

Lieutenant Palmer states: "Note the conspicuous absence of mines, wire, booby traps, or other types of perimeter defense or early warning devices. I don't know why. Either they didn't have them or they didn't put them into place. If this was a properly prepared position, it would be nearly impregnable. If the combat vehicles had been properly camouflaged, the air threat would not have been so severe: pilots can't hit what they can't see."

Lieutenant Palmer provided the following legend for the map:

1. Medium antitank gun. Probably towed 152-mm used in direct-fire mode as per USSR doctrine.
2. Antitank rocket launcher (RPG-9).
3. Bunkers.
4. Mechanized platoon. Three platoons per company. Two vehicles forward, one back as reserve.
5. Mechanized infantry company.
6. Dark lines indicate trenches. Boxes were fighting positions for dismounted infantry.
7. Probably heavy anti-aircraft artillery, for example towed 57-mm. One section would contain 3 guns.
8. Roadway.
9. Heavy mortar platoon, part of the infantry company. No equipment was present when the position was overrun.
10. Infantry company.
11. Tank company.
12. Tank platoon.

Defending forces have an advantage over attacking forces, and force ratios of 3:1 in favor of the attacker are traditionally considered necessary for a successful attack. However, overall force ratios are meaningless. By concentrating its forces, a skillful attacker with numerical inferiority can gain a sufficient local superiority to defeat the defender in one point, and this local victory can lead to overall victory.

Iraq lacked the forces to establish a strong continuous front along its frontier with Saudi Arabia, so a proper defense would have required the ability to shift forces rapidly to the enemy's point of attack. Indeed, it is thought that the Republican Guard divisions north of the Kuwaiti border were intended to be used in this manner. But Iraq, because of its inferiority in the air, lacked intelligence on Coalition disposition and movements. Furthermore, Coalition air forces were able to disrupt troop movements and prevent Iraqi concentrations, even if Iraq had known where to concentrate a defensive counterattack. Thus Iraq was confronted with an insoluble strategic dilemma: not enough troops to defend everywhere and not enough intelligence or mobility to defend at points of attack.

The Iraqi army occupying Kuwait is estimated to have consisted of somewhat over 500,000 men, of which some 170,000 held the front lines on the border with Saudi Arabia and some 80,000 held front lines on the coast, while the rest constituted second-echelon and reserve forces. The front they were defending on the border was over 250 kilometers long, so the Iraqi troop concentration on the front was no more than 1,000 men per kilometer, a rather low concentration.[163]

Worse for the Iraqis, the Coalition had the undoubted advantage of initiative, defined as the ability to threaten or assail an opponent that cannot counterthreaten or counterattack.

Iraq did make some attempts to follow the fundamental principle of the art of war: concentration against weakness. Iraqi President Saddam Hussein appears to have understood that the only weaknesses of the Coalition were domestic peace movements; fear of heavy Western casualties; and, possibly, conflicting objectives among its members.

Unfortunately for Iraq, Saddam Hussein was unable to exploit these potential weaknesses. The reported brutality of Iraqi troops in Kuwait; inflammatory anti-Western and anti-Israeli speeches; threats to damage the environment and destroy Kuwaiti oil fields; calls for terrorist action against Western nations; the exhibition on television of maltreated Coalition prisoners of war; and repeated refusals to abide by the Geneva Conventions alienated Western peace movements and destroyed the credibility of their cause. Pro-Iraq movements in Muslim countries proved unable to do more than organize demonstrations.

Adroit exploitation of their own strengths allowed Coalition military forces to avoid heavy casualties. Clever maneuvering by Coalition political leaders, in particular U.S. President Bush and French President Mitterand, maintained the alignment of objectives of the Coalition nations. Good (in some cases excellent) leadership in the Coalition—combined with poor leadership in Iraq—defeated all Iraqi attempts to concentrate against weakness.

ORDER OF BATTLE

Both sides deployed large armies in the Gulf War. Table 4.1 summarizes the relative strengths of the two sides in the Kuwaiti theater of operations. Map 4.2 shows the deployment of the opposing forces when the Coalition launched its air attack against Iraq on 17 January 1991.

However, numerical comparisons alone mean little in modern warfare, since differences in firepower can be large and many other factors (such as mobility, adroit use of deception, morale, and so on) contribute to fighting power. While it is not easy to quantify these factors, it appears that Coalition ground forces had a very significant advantage in combat effectiveness. Although details of tank armor and armament are classified, a few estimates serve to give a feeling for the differences between the weapons employed by the two sides. Of the Iraqi tanks, somewhat over three-fourths were Soviet T-55 and T-62 models, with 200 mm armor and less than 1,200 meter range for accurate cannon fire; this tank is considered obsolete by Western standards and was no

---

163. Jones, *The Art of War*, p. 527.

match for any Coalition tank. The remaining Iraqi tanks were Soviet T-72 models, with armor ranging from 250 mm to 400 mm according to year of production and 1,500 meter ranges; the latest models of this tank were superior to the U.S. M60 tank but no match for the U.S. M1 or the U.K. Challenger.

Table 4.1
Order of battle

Country	Personnel[164] (thousands)	Tanks[165]
Iraq	336	3,500
United States[166]	454	1,900
Saudi Arabia	95	550
U.K.	45	221
Egypt	34	358
Syria	14	270
France	12	150
Kuwait	10	NA
Other	12	NA
Joint Arab total	158	1,178
Coalition total	676	3,449

Of the U.S. tanks, over 1,100 were late-model M1A1 or M1A1-HAs (these have built-in protection from chemical weapons and improved armor, compared with the older M1s). The Chobham[167] armor on the latest M1 models provided protection equivalent to 600 mm against sabot rounds and

164. Iraqi numbers from Cohen et al., *GWAPS: Planning,* Table 26, p. 203. U.S. numbers from Cohen et al., *GWAPS: Statistical Compendium*, Table 14, p. 51. Other numbers from official country reports and bin Sultan, *Desert Warrior*, p. 420. Our total is consistent with that given in Cohen et al., *GWAPS: Summary*, p. 7.

165. Numbers of tanks were not reported consistently. For example, the U.S. Department of Defense lists 20,000 personnel and 350 tanks for France, while official French Army documents list 8,800, 9,300, or 12,000 people and 150 tanks. According to the French Army, the discrepancies were caused by changes over time and reporting definitions (for example, certain partly armored vehicles were apparently counted as tanks by the U.S. but not by the French, and French naval personnel that were temporarily deployed were included in certain reports and excluded from others). Numbers in this table are derived from a combination of official sources.

166. U.S. strength ultimately increased to 541,736 people and 2,189 tanks. The number 1,900 is the authors' estimate for 17 January 1991.

167. This and other military terms are in the glossary at the back of the book.

1300 mm against HEAT rounds, and even the early models had armor equivalent to 350 mm against sabot and 750 mm against HEAT. The cannon on the M1 had a range of over 2000 meters, and its rounds could penetrate between 400 and 650 mm of armor, according to the model and choice of munitions; thus any M1 could destroy any T-72, while no T-72s could destroy late-model M1s.

Map 4.2
Initial deployment of forces

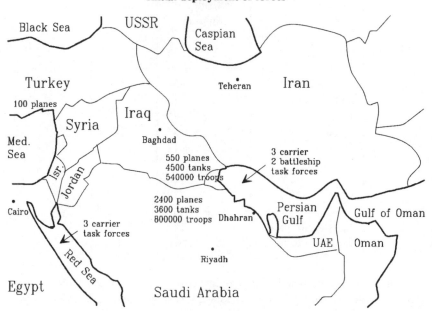

A considerable amount of artillery was present on both sides. Iraq deployed about 2,500 pieces, and the Coalition, over 1,500 pieces. Iraqi air forces, significant on paper with over 700 combat planes and 150 armed helicopters, played no role in the war.[168] By the beginning of February, the Coalition had deployed some 1,800 fixed-wing combat aircraft (a number far higher than indicated by contemporaneous press reports), of which approximately 1,300 were U.S. (about 350 carrier-based), and nearly 200 Saudi Arabian; there were over 1,600 helicopters (of which over 500 were ground-attack models, including 277 U.S. AH-64 Apaches, 145 U.S. AH-1S .Cobras, and 75 AH-1W Cobras).[169] An additional 600 planes were available in support roles, such as reconnaissance, airborne refueling, and so on. More aircraft were

---

168. Cohen et al., *GWAPS: Weapons, Tactics, and Training*, Table 3, p. 19.
169. Cohen et al., *GWAPS: Statistical Compendium*, Table 5, pp. 28-29 together with compilations from other official sources. AH-65 and AH-1S numbers are from Cohen et al., *GWAPS: Weapons, Tactics, and Training*, p. 233.

deployed during the war, with the U.S. contingent ultimately increasing to 1,600 combat aircraft. The United States sent to the Gulf area nearly half of its U.S.-based combat aircraft and most of its top-line planes.[170]

Iraq's navy consisted of some 13 fast attack boats armed with surface-to-surface missiles (including the French-made Exocet), plus a number of small motor boats. In contrast, the Coalition used over 230 ships from 20 nations in naval operations, including six U.S. carrier task forces (*America, J. F. Kennedy, Midway, Ranger, Saratoga,* and *T. Roosevelt*) and two U.S. battleship task forces (*Missouri* and *Wisconsin*).

Morale and training were critical factors in the war. The bulk of Coalition forces consisted of the best troops available: long-service professional soldiers, including numerous elite units with long traditions. In contrast, the bulk of Iraqi forces on the front lines was composed of young, relatively untrained conscripts, with a sprinkling of veterans from the Iran-Iraq War.[171] The veterans were mostly older men fed up with years of pointless fighting. Further in the rear stood the flower of Iraq's army: the Republican Guard.

As in all wars, leadership was a key factor. There was no overall commander of Coalition forces. U.S. Gen. Norman Schwarzkopf, a professional soldier with significant combat experience, particularly in Vietnam, commanded U.S. and non-Muslim forces. Saudi Lt. Gen. Khalid bin Sultan bin Abdul-Aziz commanded Muslim forces. Most of the other U.S. generals had seen combat in Vietnam, and all Coalition officers from NATO countries had undergone extensive combat simulation during training.

A Coalition Coordination Communications and Integration Center (C3IC, in military jargon) was used to ensure that the plans and efforts of all forces were coordinated. This center consisted of a group of Saudi and U.S. officers who provided briefings and daily updates on the Iraqi and Coalition situations to senior officers from all Coalition countries. Either General Schwarzkopf or Lieutenant General bin Sultan normally presided over these briefings. Briefing responsibilities alternated between Saudi and U.S. officers. Although the C3IC concept had never been tested, it worked well during the war. This center was augmented by seven liaison teams that were assigned to the several operating corps.[172]

Although future research may reveal otherwise, the evidence available to us indicates that what worked less well was General Schwarzkopf's decision to act himself as commander of the land forces (in addition to his role as overall commander), but to communicate with his two U.S. Army corps through General Yeosock, commander of the Third Army, a structure whose primary

---

170. Cohen et al., *GWAPS: Operations,* p. 49.

171. Craft, *An Operational Analysis,* p. 7 and personal interviews with U.S. soldiers who spoke with Iraqi prisoners of war.

172. Regarding the liaison teams, see Swain, *"Lucky War,"* p. 147.

mission was administrative. This arrangement went against the principle of simplicity and resulted in some communication problems.[173]

The supreme commander of the Iraqi forces, Saddam Hussein, had never received any formal military training, nor had he seen combat in the front ranks. During the Iran-Iraq War, experienced professional soldiers were thrust aside, and in some cases executed, in favor of politically reliable, but militarily inexperienced, members of the Baath party.

Formal training and simulated combat well prepared the general staff of the Coalition forces to confront a general staff whose doctrine was formed by combining the painful lessons of the Iran-Iraq War with misconstrued Soviet military principles.

---

173. Scales, *Certain Victory*, p. 141; and generally Swain, *"Lucky War,"* and specifically pp. 239, 274 note 75, 300.

5

Day 1 and the Battle for the Air

Find out where your enemy is. Get at him as soon as you can. Strike him as hard as you can, and keep moving on.

—Gen. Ulysses S. Grant

Coalition forces launched a massive aerial attack on Iraq at 0100 GMT on 17 January (4 A.M. local time); cruise missiles and Coalition aircraft using NATO ground-hugging flight tactics destroyed most of Iraq's air defense capabilities, preparing the way for an aerial bombardment that would last 38 days and render the Iraqi army incapable of seriously resisting Coalition ground forces. Thus, in retrospect, it seems fair to say that the first 24 hours were decisive. While air power has determined naval battles since World War II and it had been decisive in several previous ground battles, its contribution to the outcome of the Gulf War was greater than in any past conflict.

Supplementing the 1,300 combat sorties flown by Coalition fixed-wing aircraft, U.S. Air Force B-52s launched 35 Tomahawk cruise missiles, and U.S. Navy ships 106 during the first 24 hours. The B-52s that launched cruise missiles flew 35 hours round-trip from the United States, the longest air combat sorties in history.

Map 5.1 gives an indication of the number and nature of the Iraqi targets struck from the air on the first day. Some 400 combat sorties were flown during the first 4 hours. To put these numbers in perspective, note that the first day's sorties were about equal in number to those that had been flown against Hanoi in Vietnam during the intensive *two-week* bombing campaign around Christmas of 1972. If Washington, D.C., had been subjected to air strikes of the same intensity, the equivalent damage would have included

destruction of the White House, the Pentagon, the Capitol, all regional
telephone switching centers, all significant power plants, major military sites,
and numerous other targets.[174]

The beginning of the air campaign had been masked by deceptive measures.
Weekly sortie surges and periodic mass tanker launches created uncertainty
regarding Coalition plans. By 17 January the Iraqis had become used to
continuous Airborne Warning and Control System (AWACS) and fighter
patrols within their radar coverage. The actual strike forces on the first day
marshaled well out of radar range and entered Iraqi airspace with minimum
warning.

Map 5.1
Initial Coalition air attack

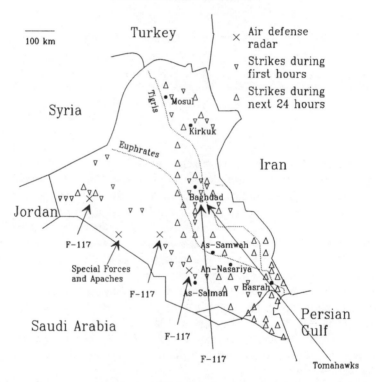

Iraq was known to possess first-rate antiaircraft systems, so there was
considerable anxiety on the first night concerning possible losses, with some
unit commanders predicting 10%—although high-level staff expected losses to
run around 0.5%. While surface-to-air missile (SAM) and antiaircraft artillery
(AAA) fire was heavy, countermeasures and training kept losses lower than

---

174. Hallion, *Storm over Iraq*, p. 267.

even the most optimistic estimates. Commanders were elated as the planes returned. Col. Tom Lennon of the U.S. 48th Tactical Fighter Wing (F-111 bombers): "I guess the greatest part of this whole thing was the first night, walking back into the command post and counting the airplanes as they recovered. . . . Going out and destroying one target is interesting, but recovering all the airplanes after the first night was great, it was a significant night for the air campaign. . . . It was the most exhilarating experience of the whole thing, I think."[175]

AIR AGAINST RADAR AND AIR DEFENSE

The first and most critical phase of the initial attack was directed against Iraq's air defense capabilities. The objective was to reduce as much as possible Iraq's ability to hinder subsequent Coalition bombing attacks. Iraq possessed a sophisticated air defense system comprising a French-built centrally controlled radar network; about 500 radars dispersed in 100 sites (which however did not cover the whole country); about 120 mostly Soviet-built SAM batteries; over 7600 pieces of mostly Soviet-built radar-guided and manual AAA; and about 300 air-superiority fighter aircraft, consisting of Soviet-made MiGs and French-made Mirages, and 2 Iraqi/Soviet-made AWACS.[176]

One of the main radar suppression weapons was the U.S. high-speed anti-radiation missile (HARM). This missile can home in on the radar emissions of a SAM battery. Most of the SAM systems deployed by Iraq relied on radar guidance. That is, a radar station on the ground is used to track the enemy aircraft and to guide the antiaircraft missile to it. As a countermeasure, when a SAM radar is detected, the aircraft launches a HARM; the HARM follows the radar signals emitted by the SAM battery and destroys the ground station (or at least the radar antenna). Some 2,000 HARMS were fired by Coalition forces during the war, of which 200 the first night and over half the first week.

However, the very first antiradar strikes were carried out by an entirely different weapon system: AH-64 Apache helicopters of the U.S. 101st Airborne Division attacked at 0238 local time, 22 minutes before the start of the main operation.

At 0220 hours two MH-53J Pave Low helicopters from the U.S. Air Force First Special Operations Wing crossed the Iraqi border acting as navigational pathfinders for two four-helicopter teams of AH-64 Apache gunships. The helicopters formed Task Force Normandy, and their mission was to destroy two Iraqi early warning radars that might detect low-flying F-15E strike aircraft heading for SCUD sites in Western Iraq. The choppers followed a circuitous route, using very-low-level flight techniques, descending into dry river beds and hugging the desert floor. The Pave Low crews had

---

175. 48 TFW, *Operation Desert Storm*, p. 25.

no difficulty locating the radar vans. Their job done, they veered off. At 0238, hovering some 5 kilometers away from their targets, the Apaches used missiles, rockets, and cannon fire to destroy the radars.[177]

The helicopter attacks opened up a 10-kilometer-wide radar-free corridor subsequently used by other Coalition aircraft. An F-117 Nighthawk (low-radar-cross-section or stealth aircraft) followed up the first attacks by destroying a hardened air defense control center in southern Iraq. At 0300 other Nighthawks struck communications buildings, command and control centers, and military headquarters in Baghdad. Large numbers of aircraft then attacked Iraq's air defense system, which, having been partially blinded by the initial attacks, was overwhelmed by the sheer number of Coalition planes and proved unable to mount a coordinated defense. Attacking aircraft carried radar jamming devices and antiradar HARM missiles. The most common antijamming measure is to increase radar power output, but this made the radar more vulnerable to the radar-homing HARM missiles. During the initial strikes, U.S. Navy planes released unpowered radar decoy drones, and the U.S. Air Force launched BQM-74 drones from two sites in Saudi Arabia.[178] The BQM drones were programmed to reach their targets in conjunction with F-117 and Tomahawk strikes, and to loiter over the target areas, simulating the radar signatures of bombers. In addition, U.S. Army long-range tactical missiles (ATACMS) were used to destroy air defense sites.

Strikes against Iraq's radar detection systems were so effective that no air raid sirens sounded in Baghdad, even as the roar of attacking planes and the explosions of bombs woke the city's population early in the morning.

Once the main radar system was rendered inoperative, low-flying Coalition planes concentrated their attacks on the main fixed SAM batteries, using either HARMs or precision laser-guided bombs delivered from planes protected by jammers and chaff. These tactics were extremely successful: during the first 6 days of the air campaign, radar-guided SAMs hit 8 planes; during the remaining 36 days, only 5 planes were hit.[179]

The final phase of the initial attack consisted of neutralizing the last component of Iraq's air defense system: its air force. In spite of the fact that the timing of the Coalition attack had been highly predictable (the first night after the expiration of the U.N. Security Council deadline), Iraq did not keep either its AWACS or a significant number of fighters on airborne patrol.

In accordance with NATO doctrine, Coalition plans called for extensive attacks on Iraqi airfields, cratering runways and destroying infrastructure

---

176. Cohen et al., *GWAPS: Operations*, pp. 79 and 81, and *GWAPS: Weapons, Tactics, and Training*, Table 1, p. 10; Table 2, p. 16; and p. 22.

177. U.S. Department of the Air Force, *Reaching Globally, Reaching Powerfully: The United States Air Force in the Gulf War* (September 1991), p. 18.

178. "BQM-74 Drones Operated by Former GLCM Unit Played Key Role in Deceiving Iraqi Military," *Aviation Week* (27 April 1992).

179. Cohen et al., *GWAPS: Summary*, p. 60.

needed to operate an airport: refueling facilities, radar, control towers, storage hangars. Some planes, notably the U.S. F-111s, used laser-guided conventional bombs, which can be directed at the middle of a runway and create large craters when they explode. Coalition forces had sophisticated special-purpose munitions specifically designed to make runways unusable (such as the British JP-233). Although such weapons are highly effective, some units preferred not to use them, because they require an attacking plane to fly a pattern more predictable than when laser-guided bombs are used.

On the first night, U.S. F-111 Aardvarks penetrated heavy defensive fire to deliver laser-guided bombs against a hardened aircraft shelter at Ali al-Salem airfield near Kuwait. Half the attack force was obliged to turn back by heavy enemy fire. Lt. Col. Dennis Erlter earned a Silver Star for continuing his flight. His account: "We were getting triple A, radar warnings, and SAM activity so I set the jet on automatic terrain-following radar when I saw the first launch of a SAM on the left side of the aircraft. The automatic system seemed to be flying us directly into the path of climbing AAA. I was forced to fly the jet manually at low-level because of that." During the weapons release, he received a second warning of a SAM approaching his plane. "I saw it coming at us at the same time we were trying to put our weapons through the door of another shelter, but that second SAM forced me to pull off at the last second. I released some chaff and the SAM blew up right behind us. Our bombs were still on target and they hit dead center."[180]

The same night another 6 U.S. F-111s and 4 Saudi Tornados attacked H3 airfield. U.S. Navy EA-6s and 4 F-14s provided air cover, while 10 Navy A-7Es carried HARMs. The F-111s used laser-guided bombs against chemical weapons storage bunkers, then the Tornados dropped JP-233 munitions on the runways. As the summary report of the U.S. 48th Tactical Fighter Wing (F-111Fs) put it: "Although air-to-air fighters get the glory for their engagements and tend to be credited with the victory against the Iraqi Air Force, devastating attacks against virtually every major airfield by Coalition air forces . . . left the Iraqis with no safe place to hide, and no alternative but to run to Iran. Saddam's hopes of having his air force ride out the war went up in those devastating strikes [which pierced hardened aircraft shelters]."

Thus the Coalition campaign against Iraqi airfields was very successful at achieving its objective: to remove the threat of Iraqi fighters attacking Coalition bombers. As U.S. pilots put it on 18 January: "We went in there and did exactly what we wanted" and "It's as if we had no adversary."[181] Within a few hours Iraq was left with no air defense capability except for isolated SAM batteries and uncoordinated AAA fire.

---

180. 48 TFW, *Operation Desert Storm*, p. 24.
181. Personal interviews.

DOGFIGHTING

On 17 January, U.S. fighter pilot Capt. Steve Tate was providing air cover for a squadron of bombers in Iraq—his first mission in the campaign:

A few minutes after the beginning of operations, around 3 AM, my radar showed a plane taking off and coming rapidly towards us. Soon he came up to the tail of one of my squadron's F-15s. I don't know if the bogey was chasing him, but I locked him up, confirmed he was hostile, and fired a Sparrow missile from 12 miles out. When the airplane blew up, the whole sky lit up. It continued to burn all the way to the ground and then just blew up into a thousand pieces.[182]

It was the first time Captain Tate had fired a missile at night. U.S. AWACS weapons controller Capt. Sheila Chewing describes one of her missions:

The mission I remember best was the first day's sortie on 17 January. The evening sortie had already been airborne and we were taking over from them. We were wondering what was going on and how the plan was really going. We came up, took station, things went as planned and everything was looking good. We were on station about an hour when we got contacts from some Iraqi fighters. We verified that they were hostiles. Then I called our fighters, giving them the range and bearing of the Iraqi planes. I fed them information until they told me they had them on their radars. So we vectored two F-15s onto the hostiles and they killed two MiG-29s.[183]

Very few Iraqi planes took to the sky to try to stop the Coalition attack. The few that did were rapidly shot down. Throughout the rest of the conflict there were practically no further attempts by Iraq's side to contest the Coalition's air supremacy: Iraqi sorties were down to 50 per day by the end of the first week, and soon became limited to attempts to shelter planes in Iran. Stringent measures were used to prevent friendly fire incidents in air-air combat: two independent forms of electronic identification had to be obtained before a Coalition fighter was authorized to fire its weapons. Only one Coalition aircraft was lost in air-air combat,[184] while 33 Iraqi fixed-wing planes and 5 Iraqi helicopters were shot down. Air supremacy was declared on the tenth day of the campaign.

That same day, 27 January, U.S. F-15 pilot Capt. Dane Powell was on a mission:

We were flying at about 20,000 to 25,000 feet [6,500 meters] in a defensive combat air patrol [CAP] for the AWACS and some tankers. My call sign was OPEC-2, since I was the second in a four-plane formation; call signs changed regularly and our squadron always had names of oil companies. We were about 40 to 60 miles [100

---

182. Quoted in Guy Gugiliotta and Molly Moore, "For Pilots, the Flush of Initial Combat," *International Herald Tribune* (18 January 1991).

183. Personal interview.

184. This emerged only from detailed postwar analysis. Cohen et al., *GWAPS: Effects and Effectiveness*, p. 111.

kilometers] north of the Kuwaiti border, due south of Baghdad. About halfway through our six-hour tour, AWACS asked us to move north, so we were just south of Baghdad, just outside the SAM ring there. Ten minutes later two of the four F-15s in our formation got low on gas and returned to the tanker [for aerial refueling].

It was now about 1200 noon local time. The AWACS notified us of possible hostiles that were about 100 miles east of our position; they were westbound. We immediately committed out on that heading, got our radars turned in the right direction, and we picked up the hostiles about 60 or 70 miles due east of us. At this time the other two F-15s considered coming back, but we had no indication that there were any more than two bandits, so the flight leader told them to continue toward the tanker, while our two planes continued with the intercept.

We confirmed that they were bandits and continued on a head-to-head intercept until they were about 35 to 40 miles away, at which point the Iraqi aircraft did a 180 degree turn and started running straight away from us—due east. I think our radars had locked onto their aircraft, probably triggering their radar warning receivers, and that's how they knew we were there. This was typical behavior for the Iraqis: they always turned and ran whenever we got to within 35 miles of them, so we usually couldn't catch them.

What we did different this time was to break our radar locks while leaving the radar in search mode, hoping that their radar warning indicator would turn itself off—and maybe they would turn back. In fact they did turn back to the northwest: they were close to the Iranian border by then, and probably had not been cleared to enter Iran. So they flew parallel to the border on the Iraqi side. We picked an intercept heading and went for them.

Until we got to within 20 miles of them, we thought the formation had one or two planes in it. But then the formation split apart and we could distinguish three individual aircraft on our radar scopes. We closed on a beam intercept, rolling out into a tail chase at about 15 miles behind the Iraqi aircraft. At that point we took our sort: prioritized the targets and assigned them to make sure we took separate guys. We took final locks and at this point the Iraqis descended from about 3,000 feet (which is where they'd been running) down to 50 feet, still heading northwest, toward Baghdad. One of the things that puzzled us about their actions is that they continued to fly at a medium airspeed: 350 knots—we should never have been able to run them down from the back if they had sped up. We had our throttles as far forward as they would go, afterburners on, so we were doing something like Mach 1.2, say 800 knots.

As we closed, my flight lead and I each took AIM-7 shots [fired AIM missiles] outside of visual range. Both of those missiles were misses. As we continued to close, I picked up a tally on the aircraft: by eye I visually identified them as three MiG-23 Floggers. The lead was about 5 miles ahead of the tail, with the third one off to the left between them. My radar was locked onto the Flogger to the left, my flight lead was locked on to the plane in the rear.

This whole time we'd been up at about 30,000 feet, simply because we knew we were in an area with heavy SAM and AAA defenses and we wanted to avoid ground fire. But at this point we both put the airplanes in steep dives, sinking down to around 6,000 feet. As I closed to within 2.5 miles of my contact I saw that the target was not in fact a single aircraft. He had a wingman: it was an F1 Mirage flying in close fingertip formation. I closed on their stern, and just as I was about to fire my second missile I saw the flight lead shoot an AIM-9 Sidewinder heat-seeking missile at his target. The missile made a straight beeline and blew up the Flogger: it just exploded in a fireball.

Two seconds after that I fired my own missiles: radar-guided AIM-7 Sparrows. Both the F1 Mirage and the MiG-23 were hit. The Flogger took a direct hit and just exploded in a fireball. The other missile detonated about 5 or 6 feet [2 meters] off the Mirage's wingtip, and that set off a secondary explosion. The plane just coasted into the ground and impacted 5 seconds later.

Then I looked back towards the right, at the flight leader and the remaining Flogger, and I saw that the flight lead had closed to within 9,000 feet of the MiG. He fired a second AIM-9, and that was also a direct hit. We saw this pilot eject and a parachute come out of the aircraft. There were no parachutes from the other aircraft.

By now we were at low altitude in an area with high concentration of enemy fire, so we egressed as quickly as possible—we ejected our fuel tanks to get rid of some drag on the aircraft, did essentially a vertical climb to get as high as possible, and then went back to our CAP.[185]

AIR STRIKES AGAINST SCUDS

Iraqi President Saddam Hussein's threat to use long-range missiles to attack Israel with chemical weapons had been taken very seriously by Coalition planners. As a result, SCUD launching sites were considered priority targets from the very first day. Coalition bombers were very successful in destroying fixed sites but not mobile launchers (see Chapter 6, section "Air Strikes and Ground Action Against SCUDs").

U.S. F-15E weapons-systems officer Capt. Jay Kreighbaum relates his mission on the first night of the war:

I went out the first night in a three-plane formation. Our entire squadron launched 18 jets in 6 3-plane formations to go against known SCUD sites. A typical fixed launching site consisted of up to six cement launch pads enclosed by a wire fence, with a single SCUD on each pad. There were three launchers at the site we went after, and each had a missile on it.

Our tactics the first night were low-altitude ingress all the way, and that's what we'd trained for. We launched at about midnight and our expected time at the target was 0305. In order to create an opening for us through the Iraqi radar coverage, an Apache gunship took out an early warning site right on our ingress route and we actually saw that blow up on the horizon in front of us, about 35 miles away from the ingress point.

Going in was uneventful. We didn't see a lot of air threats initially and didn't get a lot of radar warning receiver activity either. Of course we were pumped up—there were a lot of unknowns and we didn't know how good our training was or exactly what to expect. We were all expecting the worst. It was pretty black and there were very few lights; the ones we did see were isolated cars or buildings.

We updated our navigational radars off pre-planned offsets and went into the attack area. At a distance of 15 miles we lit the SCUD sights up [on the radar] and designated off that [set up the computer to release the bombs]. Everything was still quiet when the lead plane passed over the target and released his bombs. We were carrying Mark 20 Rockeyes—an unguided weapon, so we had no standoff capability: we just flew directly over the targets, level at 500 feet. The minute those first weapons

---

185. Personal interview.

went off, all hell broke loose: the bombs alerted them to our presence and they started shooting AAA.   The whole town of al-Queim, about a mile north of us, opened up—there must have been 70 to 100 AAA guns that started firing constantly toward our direction.   I don't think they were aware of our altitude and they were kind of firing in all directions.   Orange and red tracers were passing above and below the jet: it was pretty dramatic.

We pressed into the target, dropped our weapons on the SCUD, came off target. Number 3, the plane behind us, dove as he came off target and came within 90 feet [30 meters] of the ground, so we almost lost him.   But we all egressed the area—the AAA never ceased firing: they were firing as we passed over the horizon.   It was quite a show.

During the egress, two MiG-29s were launched out of Muddaissis.   I'm not sure if they were aware of us, but the leader was shot down by an F-15C and the other turned in to our stream.   So he came toward our flight and passed above us at an altitude of 4,500 feet while we were at about 300 feet.   He didn't try to shoot us—I think he was more scared than we were, having just seen his leader get blown up.   I don't think he was even aware of us.   He was doing about 600 knots, so we all locked our radars onto him.   One of our jets shot an AIM-9 at him, but it didn't guide.   We were in a defensive mind-set, so as long as he didn't threaten us, we didn't chase him.   As it turns out, shortly after he passed us, he ran into the ground: probably he was used to flying much higher, hadn't trained at night and lost control because of all the distractions he was experiencing—F-15s shooting at him and all kinds of radar threat indicators going off.[186]

AIR STRIKES AGAINST SUPPORT FACILITIES AND COMMAND AND CONTROL CENTERS

In addition to striking airfields, the initial Coalition attack targeted Iraqi command and control centers, communication systems, and logistic lines. Over 100 Tomahawk cruise missiles were launched to destroy military headquarters, communication links, and power distribution centers in Baghdad.   Several hundred bombing missions were directed against similar targets throughout Iraq.   The following accounts give the flavor of the pilots' experience and a sample of what they accomplished.

The first B-52 strike was flown from Diego Garcia Island.   It entered Iraqi airspace around 0200 local time on 17 January, one hour after the start of operations.   U.S. Capt. Carl Gramlick, plane commander and co-pilot:

We'd been waiting around for days, expecting to have a fair amount of preparation time.   It didn't work that way.   My commanding officer practically kicked the door in and told me we would be leaving in 20 minutes.   We were all scared to death.   It was a weird atmosphere.

Everything was routine except for things you can't simulate.   That night was the first time a B-52 had ever been in combat at low level.   You know you get all the briefings that Iraqi weapons are Soviet weapons and they paint them to be superhumans.   You always expect the worst.   And you've never really gone against

---

186. Personal interview.

them—just against simulators. But the fear of actually being shot at, actually dropping a full load of weapons at night, you're putting a lot of new factors in front of you.

We had the first estimated time of arrival over Iraq, 54 minutes after H hour. So it was getting pretty nerve-racking, especially after the second aerial refueling, when we started putting our personal weapons on, like a .38 pistol, and I remember putting on the survival vest, which mainly carries escape and evasion charts and extra water. When the navigator said "We are now in Iraq," that's when everyone really got scared. We were supposed to bomb a highway strip that could have been used as a forward airstrip for Iraqi fighters. In the premission briefing we were told that there was no AAA. It was supposed to be the proverbial milk run. We were at about 500 feet [150 meters] altitude when we entered Iraq. I put on night vision goggles and scanned the horizon—all I saw was detonations everywhere. We proceeded in; about half an hour later we were lined up on our target. We dropped cluster munitions from 1,000 feet [330 meters]. I'd never dropped a full load of weapons at night before. It was the most amazing thing I've ever seen: there were small white flashes under the nose—then all of a sudden the sky went poof, completely white. You didn't know if you were being shot at, it was so disorienting. The pilot was flying hard instruments, I was looking out as much as I could, backing him up. I saw AAA tracers, which I'd never seen before, and it looked real pretty, orange streaks going through the sky, and I thought they were flares, then I realized flares would be dropping, not shooting up.

"Oh my God, triple A at 11 o'clock, break right." So the pilot broke right; then the electronic warfare officer said, "Possible incoming missile at 4 o'clock." As I was turning to look for it, I felt a drop in the seat of my pants, as if the nose had fallen. It was the pilot pushing down to avoid the missile. It was an aggressive pushover, so I turned and looked at the instruments. The radio altimeter was shooting through 700 feet, and we were doing about 440 knots, heading down fast. This is where it kind of hit slow motion. I looked at the altimeter, saw it go through 600, spinning down, looked over at the pilot, and he was just fixated on flying the aircraft, avoiding the threat, and wasn't really sure how low he was going. I think he kind of lost contact with what was going on right then. At 500 feet I grabbed the yoke and started pulling; so did the pilot. I screamed, "Climb, climb, climb, climb," and so did the navigator and the radar navigator. The plane being as heavy with fuel as it was, it was just not responding and it kept sinking. I was sure we were going to hit. The plane eventually dished out at 60 feet above the ground [18 meters] and was wallowing, and I was just praying, "Don't have a wing drop." But it held, and all of a sudden all that thrust caught up with us and the speed of 440 just pushed this plane shooting up into the air. Now we all shouted "Pushover, pushover, pushover, we're heading back into the triple A." After that it was just get out while everyone was trying to regain their composure. The navigator had been getting ready to bail out, but then he looked at his instruments and realized he was below the ejection minimum, so he stayed with it.

U.S. Lt. Col. Miles Pound, pilot of an F-117 stealth bomber, whose modern airframe is at the opposite end of the technological spectrum from the B-52s:

The mission I remember best is the first one because it was the first time in combat and it was a brand-new weapon system. Of course a lot of testing has been done and a lot of money has been spent, and it's pretty conclusive that this new technology will work, but until you actually see it working for the first time in your favor, there is always that doubt. I was tense going up north to Baghdad, to say the least, and I think all of us were concerned.

Otherwise the first mission was very much like all of the missions that we flew. It involved departure from our base up to an air refueling point to meet a tanker. The tanker took me and my wingman all the way north to the border, then I was strictly on my own, flying up to Baghdad on a preplanned path that avoided known threats, finding the target, dropping the ordnance, refueling again, and flying home. It was about a six hour mission, which is like flying from Europe to the U.S., and all the time I was extremely busy. Being a stealth pilot is one of the most labor-intensive and time-constrained types of flying that I know. We have very strict timing constraints: to be where you are supposed to be all the time, exactly on time, and that has to be monitored by the pilot. For example, during a bomb competition in training in the U.S., the goal was to hit the target at an exact time; I dropped a weapon that landed .02 second from the desired time and finished third in the competition! That kind of precision lets us hit a target with multiple bombs at the same time without having any communication between separate airplanes.[187]

---

187. Operational details on F-117 missions—for example, altitudes and use of electronic countermeasures—are classified. However, the U.S. Department of Defense has revealed that F-117 missions against targets in Baghdad were flown at medium altitude (3,000 to 6,000 meters).

6

Military Operations: Day 2 to 38

Attack weakness. Hold them by the nose and kick them in the pants.

—Gen. George S. Patton

From to 18 January to 23 February 1991, Coalition air forces flew an average of about 2,800 missions per day (of which just over 1,000 were bombing sorties, and nearly 1,600 were combat sorties, the rest being combat support, such as providing refueling; see Chapter 9, section "The Air Campaign" for more details). In order to maximize the effectiveness of strike aircraft and to minimize their vulnerability to antiaircraft defenses, targets were attacked from several directions at once, and by airplanes taking off from different bases. Midair collisions and other undesirable conflicts (for example, overlaps in refueling schedules) could be avoided only by maintaining full detailed control in both space and time over virtually all Coalition airplanes.

Huge amounts of detailed data are required to coordinate military flights: refueling call signs, frequencies, times, locations, altitudes, targets, munitions, and more. These data must be disseminated among a number of users: electronic countermeasure support planes, escort or combat air patrol planes, AWACS or ground controllers, forward air controllers, and search and rescue teams. The assembled data, called an air tasking order (ATO), equaled the size of a phone book. The ATO is prepared by a computer system, and usually transmitted by a telecommunications network (with transmission time on the order of two hours). However, the two largest air forces in the theater had incompatible telecommunication systems, even though they belonged to the same nation, the United States. Various attempts to transmit the ATO via radio communications systems between the U.S. Air Force and the U.S. Navy failed to provide adequate performance, so the Navy received the ATO from the Air Force on floppy diskettes, via two nightly flights from Riyadh to the command aircraft carriers in the Persian Gulf and the Red Sea. The ATO was distributed to non-U.S. forces by a variety of means, including physical distribution, depending on where it was going and on available computer and networking resources.

The air campaign was planned by a relatively small staff reporting to U.S. Central Command Headquarters; the initial plan had been developed in late August 1990 by a team headed by Col. John Warden. Warden's intent was to win the war through unaided air power, but this unrealistic notion was quickly rejected by Lt. Gen. Charles A. Horner, Commander, Air Force Component, U.S. Central Command. Horner retained some members of Warden's staff and assigned them to a planning team led by Brig. Gen. Buster Glosson.[188] However, as late as mid-December, planners still had unrealistic expectations of what air power could accomplish: 50% attrition of Iraqi ground forces with four days of air operations, and 90% with nine days.[189]

The first two days of the campaign had been planned months in advance. After the first day, three teams, each consisting of six or seven multiservice, multinational specialists, had the task of planning strikes respectively three days, two days, and one day ahead. These teams received images collected by satellites and reconnaissance airplanes, and used them to select targets and types of planes to be utilized; they also suggested munitions to be used and approach patterns. Target lists were presented on a daily basis to the supreme Coalition command staff, reviewed, and approved.

Many bombing missions during the first few days relied on NATO low-flight tactics, specifically, flying through enemy airspace at altitudes around 60 meters by using a terrain-following radar-based automatic pilot up to about 6 kilometers from the target, then popping up to a couple of hundred meters to designate the target and release the weapon, then resuming low-level flight to exit. Low-level flight lessens the risk from radar-guided SAMs because a low-flying plane cannot be seen by radar until it is very close. On the other hand, low-flying planes are more vulnerable to AAA fire. Since SAM suppression was very effective, the AAA threat soon became the biggest one, and tactics were changed to medium-level flight, that is, around 3,000 to 6,000 meters, above most AAA fire. However, this reduced bombing accuracy made it more difficult to detect targets and unfavorably affected the operation of

---

188. Cohen et al., *GWAPS: Summary*, pp. 35-37, 47. A more detailed account is Cohen et al., *GWAPS: Planning*, pp. 126-127.

189. Cohen et al., *GWAPS: Planning*, p. 12, and *GWAPS: Effects and Effectiveness*, p. 202. Planners had assumed more sorties than actually could be flown, but even if the desired number had been flown, it would have taken two to three times longer than planned to achieve the desired attrition.

certain weapons (notably the Rockeye cluster bomb).[190]   Because of their inability to identify targets from higher altitudes, pilots of the A-10 close-ground-support planes moved down to 1,200 meters after the first two weeks; losses rose dramatically, from three damaged during the first two weeks, to six damaged and one shot down during the next two weeks, even though the number of sorties remained constant.   After that, A-10s flew only along the border.[191]

Many of the key strikes were made at night. As U.S. Col. Tom Lennon, commander of the 48th Tactical Fighter Wing, put it: "When you get down to it, I think the air war was won at night. During the day, operations were just to keep the Iraqis excited. . . . Up to the start of the ground war, almost all of the heavy stuff was done at night."

The intensive bombing rendered Iraq's air forces ineffective and destroyed its air defense system, military logistical system, electrical generating capacity, oil refining capacity, navy, many of its entrenched tanks and artillery, and its army's will to fight.   It did not destroy Iraq's unconventional weapons capabilities, its mobile SCUD launchers, or its communications and control systems.[192]

In addition to the strikes by Coalition air forces, 288 Tomahawk cruise missiles were launched by the U.S. Navy (106 the first day).   Weather was worse than expected and was a factor throughout the campaign, causing about a one-week slip in planned operations.   During the first 10 days, 40% of all scheduled attack sorties were canceled because of poor visibility or overcast sky conditions.   On the second and third days of the war, more than half of the planned F-117 flights could not bomb their targets because of low clouds over Baghdad, and all F-117 sorties were canceled on day 41.[193]

Support aircraft, such as airborne tankers used for in-flight refueling, were critical to the success of the air campaign, with some crews working 20-hour shifts.   Some 370 tankers (of which 336 were U.S.) flew over 12,000 sorties.[194]   Many missions would have been impossible without aerial refueling.   Enough fuel was delivered from airborne tankers to fill the gas tanks of every car in the states of Texas and Oklahoma.   Tanker operations were limited by airspace: at peak periods, no additional tankers could have

---

190. Cohen et al., *GWAPS: Summary*, p. 102; *GWAPS: Weapons, Tactics, and Training*, pp. 86, 89, 238; *GWAPS: Operations*, p. 260; *GWAPS: Effects and Effectiveness*, p. 161; and U.S. General Accounting Office, *Operation Desert Storm: Evaluation of the Air War* (2 July 1996), p. 3.

191. Cohen et al., *GWAPS: Operations*, p. 280, in conjunction with *GWAPS: Statistical Compendium*, Table 85, p. 323.

192. Cohen et al., *GWAPS: Effects and Effectiveness*, Table 25, p. 349.

193. Cohen et al., *GWAPS: Operations*, pp. 4, 193; *GWAPS: Summary*, p. 172; *GWAPS: Command and Control*, pp. 225-226.

194. Cohen et al., *GWAPS: Summary*, p. 190, and *GWAPS: Statistical Compendium*, Table 81, p. 316.

been used; airspace congestion around tankers limited the number of planes in a strike force and resulted in many near midair collisions.[195]

The 64 F-111Fs of the 48th Tactical Fighter Wing were among the key contributors to the air campaign. They flew over 2,400 combat sorties, dropping 3,300 tons of precision munitions and hitting 920 tanks or APCs, 245 hardened aircraft shelters, 160 bridges, 113 bunkers, and many other secondary targets.[196] The Pave Tack laser designation system was used to guide many bombs. This system is contained in an add-on pod carried in the plane's internal bomb bay, and its computer is interfaced with the aircraft's avionics. Images from the Pave Tack's infrared camera are recorded on video to permit subsequent battle damage assessment (BDA). The plane's Weapons System Officer (WSO, pronounced "wizzo") has a monitor that shows the image and range information, as well as crosshairs representing the laser designation—that is, the spot on which the pod's laser is shining. The laser beam is not visible to the human eye. After the WSO sets the crosshairs on the target, they stay there even if the plane maneuvers, because the Pave Tack computer receives data from the aircraft's inertial navigation system and uses this input to make corrections. Normally the WSO must make corrections only for drift or target motion. Once the bomb is released from the plane, a sensor in its nose picks up the laser light reflected off the target, and an onboard computer flies the weapon, which has fins at the nose and tail, to the target. The distance between the release point and the target depends on the type of weapon and the plane's speed, altitude, and attitude; but distances of well over 5 kilometers can be attained even with low-level flight patterns.[197]

While Iraqi fighters did not even attempt seriously to hinder the Coalition air campaign, there were some exciting moments for bomber pilots. F-111 Weapons System Operator Capt. Jerry Hanna recalls the mission of 20 January against an airfield:

We had attacked the taxiway intersection from about 18,000 feet [5,500 meters] and were egressing the target heading northeast. We were the last aircraft in a line of 20. Then on the radar warning receiver we heard a MiG-29 close in and lock on his radar. We immediately initiated a high-speed combat descent, the pilot folded the wings back and we went screaming downhill. Puking chaff, we went from 18,000 to 4,000 feet in a heartbeat! The adrenalin was really pumping. The pilot was busy trying to get the plane close to the ground, I was on the radio hollering at the AWACS that we had been jumped by a MiG and to get the fighters coming back in our direction. I got the terrain-following radar on so that it would take over when we got close to the ground. That guy had us locked up on his radar for 35 seconds; it felt like five years!" The F-111 evaded the MiG, then pulled back up to medium altitude to avoid AAA fire.[198]

---

195. Cohen et al., *GWAPS: Logistics*, pp. 179, 206, 207.

196. 48 TFW, *Operation Desert Storm*, supplemented by personal interviews.

197. Personal interviews.

198. Stan Morse, ed., *Gulf Air War Debrief* (Aerospace Publishing, 1991), p. 76.

SCUD: IRAQ'S MOST PUBLICIZED WEAPON

Iraq launched its first SCUD missiles 24 hours after the Coalition attack. On 18 January, at 0200 Riyadh time, Saddam Hussein kept his promise to attack Israel if Iraq was attacked. Six missiles were directed against cities in the Jewish state, but caused few casualties.

Official Israeli statements said that Israel reserved its rights, and would retaliate on its own terms. In fact it is not clear what form an Israeli retaliation could have taken. Israel surely had nothing to gain, and everything to lose, by attacking Iraqi civilian targets. Iraqi military targets were under intensive attack by Coalition air forces, and it seems unlikely that Israel's planes could have added much to this effort.[199]

It is reasonable to suppose that the first SCUD aimed at Israel was launched from a mobile launcher. We can imagine that a ball of fire scorched the desert floor, then turned into a graceful plume as the missile roared into the night sky. Sensors on a U.S. satellite orbiting high above the surface of the earth saw the moving speck of fire, as they saw everything, whereupon the satellite broadcast a burst of encrypted data. Dish antennas on the ground received the data; computers interpreted it and sent signals of their own. Alarm buzzers sounded, CRT screens flashed, printers clattered.[200]

Within a minute of the SCUD's launch, air raid sirens sounded in Tel Aviv. Its citizens had been briefed days before, and the city was prepared for the worst: a chemical warhead. One room in every house and apartment had been made airtight; each person carried a gas mask at all times; special antigas cribs would protect babies. Gases used against people must be heavier than air, because otherwise they would disperse quickly. Hence dangerous gases would tend to accumulate in underground bombproof shelters; therefore the population of Tel Aviv stayed above ground, preferring the risk of injury from explosion to the risk of gas. Most Israelis put on their masks.

The missile struck five minutes after the warning sounded. Its warhead was not chemical, and it was not sophisticated: 250 kilograms of explosive triggered on impact. It demolished a building on the outskirts of the city. Flying glass and debris injured several people. No one was killed, but everyone was frightened: Who knew where the next missile would fall, and what type of warhead it would carry?

Iraq's long-distance version of the SCUD was very inaccurate (on the order of kilometers) and carried a small warhead, so it was a weapon of no use

---

199. The fact that the Coalition used high-altitude tactics, and that the Israelis might have flown lower, is not necessarily determinant, given that Iraqi deception and camouflage for mobile SCUDs were excellent (see Chapter 6, section "Air Strikes and Ground Actions against SCUDs"). An Israeli ground invasion of the SCUD launching area would have been effective only if it had been massive, risking counterattack from significant uncommitted Iraqi forces in the north and likely provoking the entry of Jordan into the war.

200. Personal interviews.

against military targets, unless equipped with a nuclear warhead, as the original SCUD was designed to be in the 1950s by the USSR. However, it poses a significant terrorist threat to cities, ports, and other extensive areas of personnel or material concentration, as did the German V1 and V2 missiles in World War II. Since contemporary civilian populations are very sensitive to threats of this nature, the United States quickly introduced a new defense against the SCUD: the antimissile missile.

PATRIOT AGAINST SCUD

A blinding flash accompanied an explosion at the Dhahran air base in Saudi Arabia around 0448 local time on 18 January. Uninformed observers might have thought that an Iraqi missile had found its target. But it wasn't the case; the explosion came from the launch of a Patriot missile, whose initial acceleration comes from an explosive charge built into the launch container.

U.S. Army Lt. Charles McMurtrey:

They had just launched missiles at Israel and we were in our van in the highest alert state, looking for inbounds. [But nothing happened for a while.]

Everything was calming down, we were looking to come down off the alert and soldiers were starting to come down out of that high state of readiness. The adrenalin kind of started to slow down. Then we picked up the inbound, tracked it, identified as a SCUD, engaged, and shot it down. It was a thrilling experience.

For about half a second or one and a half seconds it was just dumb disbelief and a sense of wonder. Everything happened so fast that we were not consciously thinking about it. Then it sunk in. We looked at each other and shouted "Yeah," hooked into the battalion net, and gave an excited report that we had engaged and destroyed one inbound track. The battalion confirmed that they had seen the whole thing. Then we were whooping and hollering and making a bunch of noise in the van. It was wide open and real good. Then the realization hit us that more might be coming in, so we went right back to the scopes.

As soon as we got the all-clear stand-down, no more missiles in flight, the battery commander came over to the van and we had a little powwow, a lot of high fives and hand slapping. There was a lot of high-stepping, chest-stuck-out walking when we were relieved by the next shift.[201]

The Patriot appeared to have worked as planned the first time it had been fired in earnest.

A total of 32 Patriot batteries were deployed: 21 in Saudi Arabia, 7 in Israel (of which 4 were manned by U.S. forces), and 4 in Turkey. The Patriot was initially developed as an antiaircraft missile (SAM) and was later modified (primarily via computer hardware and software upgrades) to have a limited antimissile capability. The actual performance of the Patriot in its antimissile role is controversial. MIT Prof. Theodore Postol: "The Gulf War experience with Patriot has left us with a piece of military history that, not surprisingly, is

---

201. Personal interviews.

not as simple as early reports. In retrospect, it is clear that Patriot was misperceived as an 'unqualified success.'"[202]

During the war Iraq launched 88 SCUD missiles (46 against Saudi Arabia, 40 against Israel, 1 against Bahrain, and 1 against Qatar).[203] It appears that 47 entered Patriot interception zones and that 158 Patriot missiles were fired against them (it is normal procedure to fire two missiles against each incoming target, and some SCUDs broke up in flight, presenting multiple targets). Initial reports of kill ratios were very favorable, claiming that 45 of the 47 engaged SCUDs had been successfully intercepted. Apparently the software available to missile operators reported a successful interception whenever the Patriot detonated near the SCUD—although actually the SCUD might not have been destroyed. These initial reports were later revised: the kill rate was estimated to be about 70% for the Patriots based in Saudi Arabia, and about 40% for those based in Israel.[204]

But in fact there was a fundamental problem with the criteria used to define success. Proponents of the Patriot (including its manufacturer) counted a "kill" whenever the missile intercepted a SCUD and "either exploded the SCUD warhead in the air or destroyed its ability to make a damaging explosion when it hit the ground."[205] Denigrators of the Patriot's role as an antimissile missile (including some Israelis working on a competing missile) counted a "miss" whenever significant damage was observed on the ground after a SCUD attack. This damage could be due to debris from an intercepted SCUD, or from debris generated by the Patriot itself when it detonated. Even a successful interception did not necessarily render the SCUD harmless: debris from the SCUD and the Patriot had to fall to earth somewhere, and the impact from large pieces weighing hundreds of kilograms, falling at speeds on the order of several thousand kilometers per hour, caused considerable damage. For example, depending on its density, a chunk of missile the size of a Coca-Cola can could hit the ground at about the speed it would have if dropped from an altitude of one kilometer. It could have sufficient energy to penetrate 10 centimeters of concrete. The damage done by a falling fuel tank would be about that done by a very small car dropped from 500 meters.

Of the 40 missiles directed against Israel, 13 were fired before Patriot batteries had been installed. It appears that of the remaining 27, some 10 to 13 fell in unpopulated areas, and some 14 to 17 were engaged (with about half being intercepted). Total damage was 2 people killed directly, 248 wounded,

---

202. Theodore Postol, "Lessons of the Gulf War Experience with Patriot," *International Security*, 16, no. 3 (Winter 1991-1992): 119-171.

203. The number 40 for Israel comes from official Israeli reports; the U.S. Department of Defense reports 42 for Israel. Cohen et al., *GWAPS: Effects and Effectiveness*, Table 39, p. 337.

204. Ibid., p. 118.

205. Robert A. Skelly, vice president, public and financial relations, Raytheon Company, letter in *Science* (24 January 1992): 382, as corrected by Mr. Skelly in a private communication.

and nearly 10,000 apartments damaged.[206] Most of the SCUDs fired against
Saudi Arabia were intercepted or landed in unpopulated areas. Saudi Arabia
reported 1 person killed and 23 wounded from falling debris.

One non intercepted SCUD that landed on the mess hall of U.S. troops in
Dhahran caused many more casualties: 28 killed and 98 wounded. The SCUD
was not engaged because of a software problem (the computer lost the target as
a result of the cumulation of a series of small timing errors caused by the
mathematical expressions used to track the incoming missile).[207]

There have been several efforts to analyze Israeli damage data, in order to
evaluate the Patriot's effectiveness at reducing the SCUD's threat to civilian
areas. However, the data are of dubious reliability and the number of events
observed is too small to allow statistically valid conclusions to be drawn.
Thus there are no publicly available data that prove or disprove the proposition
that the Patriot was effective in reducing ground damage in civilian areas.
Nevertheless, it is likely that, at least for military sites in Saudi Arabia, the
Patriot did save lives and reduce damage.[208]

Regardless of its true effectiveness (whether measured in interceptions or in
reduced ground damage), the Patriot was widely perceived to be highly
successful during much of the war, and this perception boosted civilian and
military morale in the Coalition nations and Israel.

AIR STRIKES AND GROUND ACTION AGAINST SCUDS

The Coalition had not developed any specific scheme for finding and
destroying mobile SCUD launchers, having planned to deal with the SCUD
threat by destroying fixed launchers, support bases, and production and
support facilities.[209] After the war started, much attention was given to the
destruction of the mobile launchers, which were viewed as a political weapon,
in spite of the missile's insignificance as a military threat. Although all fixed
launching sites were destroyed in the first week, mobile launchers remained
active throughout the war. Map 6.1 shows the main areas from which mobile
SCUD launchers operated: these areas were called "SCUD boxes" in the
jargon of the U.S. Air Force. The circles indicate the areas that could be
targeted by the Iraqi missiles.

---

206. There have been several conflicting reports of Israeli casualties and damage.
The data presented here are taken from an official report provided by the Israeli
embassy in Bern, Switzerland.

207. Eliot Marshall, "Fatal Error: How Patriot Overlooked a SCUD," *Science* (13
March 1992): 1347.

208. This is the official U.S. view: see, e.g., U.S. Department of Defense,
Conduct of the Persian Gulf War, p. T-153. While it is disputed by some experts, we
subscribe to it on the basis of probabilistic arguments that are beyond the scope of this
book.

209. Cohen et al., *GWAPS: Summary*, p. 43.

U.S. satellites and JSTARS reconnaissance planes detected SCUD launches, and sometimes orbiting aircraft could actually see a missile as it rose in the sky. In addition, U.K. and later (from 7 February) U.S. special forces were inserted in SCUD launch areas, with the mission of locating the missiles and destroying them or calling in air strikes, sometimes designating the targets with lasers.[210] One U.K. group of eight men flew in on the night of 22 January, was discovered by the Iraqis two days later, but was able to flee. During their march toward the border, three men died, four were captured, and one escaped by walking 300 kilometers in seven days, without food and with little water.[211]

Map 6.1
SCUD launching areas

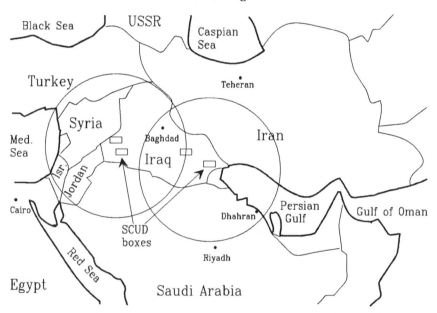

But all launches took place at night, and a mobile SCUD team could fire, drive away, and hide within 5 minutes; in addition, knowing that a SCUD launcher was located within an area as small as 2.5 square kilometers was not sufficient to allow it to be located at night even by a sophisticated plane such as the F-15E.[212] Furthermore, many of the sorties proved unable to locate

---

210. The extent to which these missions were successful is controversial.

211. A telling account is given in Gen. Sir Peter De La Billière, *Storm Command* (HarperCollins, 1993), Chapter 10.

212. For a controversial but in-depth analysis of the difficulty of locating mobile SCUD launchers, see Mark D. Mandeles, Thomas C. Hone, and Sanford S. Terry,

SCUDs and the planes dropped their bombs on other targets. Postwar analysis shows that only 3.5% of the bombing strikes[213] were devoted to the suppression of SCUDs, and only 15% of these (215 strikes) were specifically targeted at mobile launchers (as opposed to suspected hiding places, support facilities, and so forth).[214]   Although decoy SCUD launchers, some incorporating heat generators to simulate activity, further complicated the effort, the Coalition's ground and air anti-SCUD campaign, which included dropping mines by air to hamper the mobile launchers' movements, was quite effective, as shown by Table 6.1.

Table 6.1
SCUD attacks

Week	Number launched	Against Saudi Arabia[215]	Against Israel
1	33	18	15
2	18	6	12
3	4	0	4
4	5	2	3
5	11	8	3
6	17	14	3
TOTAL	88	48	40

During the war, the Coalition was confident that it was finding and destroying mobile SCUD launchers, with aircrews reporting 80 destroyed and Special Forces about 10. The continuing SCUD attacks were attributed to the fact that Iraq possessed many more mobile launchers than the originally estimated 36. However, postwar analysis showed that most of the items that were reported destroyed were in fact trucks or decoys (U.N. observers who oversaw the postwar destruction of Iraqi material reported that the best decoys were indistinguishable from real mobile launchers from 25 meters away). In fact, there is no proof that any mobile SCUD launchers were destroyed by fixed-wing aircraft operating independently, although some were destroyed by

---

Managing "Command and Control" in the Persian Gulf War (Praeger, 1996), pp. 79-80.

213. A strike is the delivery of a weapon against a specific target. There can be more than one strike in a sortie.

214. Cohen et al., *GWAPS: Statistical Compendium*, p. 418, Table 177.

215. The column for Saudi Arabia includes the two SCUDs launched against Bahrain and Qatar; as noted in the section "Patriot Against SCUDs," different official reports provide slightly different numbers.

or with the assistance of Special Forces.[216] The maximum number of missiles launched within one day never exceeded 14, which was less than the 19 mobile launchers known to have survived the war, so the available data are consistent with the hypothesis that Iraq started the war with no more than 25 to 35 mobile SCUD launchers.[217]

The unexpected persistence of the SCUD threat required the Coalition to devote a higher than planned number of sorties to searching for and destroying the launchers. At the time, U.S. Central Command planners worried that the diversion of sorties to SCUD suppression would affect the air campaign.[218] However, this turned out not to be the case.

A-10 pilot Capt. Tom Sheehy's account of his missions on 15 February:

During the first mission of the day we found no SCUDs—and that was kind of typical; you didn't expect to find SCUDs every day. They hid them pretty well, camouflaged, under overpasses, culverts along the roads, and that sort of thing. It was almost kind of a rare occurrence to really find one. They didn't do a lot of shooting of the SCUDs during the daytime.

Sometimes you would see some kind of SCUD associated equipment, like a fuel truck. They did some transporting during the day, and that's what we were looking for. . . . So those were our primary targets. Secondary targets were artillery sites, ground control, and early warning radar sites. Those were the sites that had been hit during the early days of the war, but sometimes they tried to repair them at night. So if we came along and saw a new radar antenna, we'd attempt to destroy that.

So here we are on the second mission of the day, talking to AWACS, heading up north. The weather was clear, it was 1130. High sun, clear weather, a beautiful day for flying. We crossed the border, didn't really encounter any threats and didn't really find anything in SCUD alley. Came southeast to look at Muddaissis airfield—it had been pounded real heavily early on in the war (as had H2 and H3 airfields). There was starting to be more activity south, so we checked that area out carefully and didn't see any SCUDs.

But about 2 miles north there was a SU-7 Fitter aircraft off the road, and they'd piled some sand up around it to make sort of a revetment. We destroyed that with 30mm cannon fire after we'd dropped cluster bombs on it that didn't do much. I took pass and started firing the cannon at about 10,000 feet [3,300 meters] and put a couple of hundred bullets into it—it exploded and burned in a big cloud of black smoke. We got some 23 and 37mm AAA in return, so we figured out we'd worn out our welcome and we kind of egressed to the southeast, to work the tanks and mechanized regiment.

As we were flying over at 20,000 feet, we heard AWACS directing other A-10s. He had a low and slow contact on his radar (we don't have a radar on the A-10, so we rely on AWACS for those airborne threats). Sometimes AWACS can even pick up large ground targets, including SCUD transporters. But typically we just searched with our eyeballs—we carried binoculars, just normal field glasses, to help spot targets

---

216. De La Billière, *Storm Command*, pp. 224, 226, reports the Special Forces missions.

217. Cohen et al., *GWAPS: Effects and Effectiveness*, pp. 330-340, and *GWAPS: Command and Control*, pp. 251, 253.

218. Personal interview.

without having to get down into the AAA threat, which was pretty dense mostly all over Iraq and Kuwait.

So the AWACS tells me to look basically below me, two miles ahead. I figured it was a helicopter, so I armed my air-air missiles (two AIM-9M). My wingman is about 1.5 miles [2 kilometers] behind in a wedge formation. We start descending to look for the contact visually. As I passed 15,000 feet, I saw some movement off my left wing. So I rolled into a little steeper dive and took a look. By then I was in about a 45 degree dive, and 2 miles ahead of me I visually identified an MI-8 HIP, a Soviet transport helicopter. I started firing 30mm cannon at it from about 10,000 feet altitude. It was low, about 50 feet off the ground, doing about 120 knots. I fired 200 rounds, recovered from the dive at 7,000 feet, and started climbing. My wingman reported that it was hit in the tail, but appeared to be still intact. I was maneuvering rapidly, avoiding some 23mm AAA around there. Then I told AWACS what was going on, and came around for another pass; this time I rolled in from 8,000 feet, and shot a couple hundred more rounds. This time it exploded and burned.

U.S. F-15E Weapons Systems Officer Capt. Jay Kreighbaum relates night SCUD patrols:

We never knew the source of the targeting data, but we knew we should search intensively along certain roads. We'd form two-plane formations where one jet had a laser designation pod and the other carried conventional munitions. The laser pod has an infrared imaging system with very good resolution, so that plane would search up and down the suspected area especially looking at culverts and other hiding places. At one time we even had directives to just drop weapons on one road every 20 minutes.[219]

AIR STRIKES AGAINST LOGISTIC SUPPORT

The destruction of Iraq's logistic support system was a primary Coalition objective; Map 6.2 shows air strikes against railroads and bridges.

The U.K. Buccaneer aircraft circled high in the sky above an Iraqi bridge. As it circled, the bombardier kept the crosshairs of his television display firmly fixed on the end of the bridge, close to land. Meanwhile a U.K. Tornado approached, released its bomb, and proceeded toward the next target. The laser beam in the Buccaneer struck the bridge exactly where the television crosshairs were centered. A sensor in the nose of the bomb saw the reflected light of the laser, and it too struck the bridge precisely where the cross-hairs pointed. A puff of smoke came up as the entire first span of the bridge collapsed.[220]

---

219. Both accounts are based on personal interviews.
220. This account is based on contemporaneous media pool reports.

Map 6.2
Air strikes against logistic lines

U.S. Navy A-6 pilot Lt. Col. Leif Larsen recounts his part in a 48-plane strike against a railroad yard near Basra on the first day of the war.

Crossing the coast inbound, we had F/A-18s shooting HARMs over our heads, missiles coming up from the ground and a lot of AAA. There isn't much time to worry. You're concentrating on getting to the point where you start your bomb run. The bombardier-navigator is concentrating on trying to pick up the target on radar and then getting a clear infrared picture of the target area.

We pushed into a 30-degree dive about 8 or 9 miles from the target that night. Coming down from 24,000 feet [7,000 meters] meant that we were going to release our weapons with a lot of kinetic energy. The bombardier-navigator had a good infrared picture by this time and could break out the target. The computer takes the target data from the systems, calculates the weapons release point. It doesn't matter if we're in a 20-degree dive or 40 degrees, or if we're doing 400 knots or 500: the computer solves the problem. All we have to do is center steering on the screen, step the system into attack and commit, so that the computer can let the bombs fly when we reach the correct point. I have readouts that tell me how far I am from the target, and from preflight briefing I know that the bombs should be dropping off about 2.5 miles from the target for this type of attack profile.

Our goal was for the bombs to drop at 15,000 feet. You can feel the bombs come off, but you also back the computer by pickling manually [pulling the bomb release trigger] just to be sure they're all off. You know it takes about 1.5 seconds to release all of them, so when the first one drops you say "One potato, two potato," and then you're ready to pull off. The aim was to have pulled out of the dive by 12,000 feet. At that altitude you're in the envelope of some of the lighter AAA, but it's only for 20 or 30 seconds, and then you're passing through 15,000 feet again in the climb.

We could see the bombs going off, but there was a light cloud layer so from certain angles you couldn't see the ground well enough to see where they were hitting. Bomb damage assessment we got later showed that 5 out of the 6 airplanes in my division were in the general target area, successfully cutting most of the tracks in that rail yard.[221]

Three or four highways and a single rail line ran from central Iraq to Basra. A highway ran from Basra to the Kuwaiti border, then split into two roads, one of which ran along the coast while the other went inland. Thus supplies could reach Iraqi troops in Kuwait only over a limited number of routes, and the key roads and railroads in Iraq crossed large rivers over bridges.

By the end of the campaign, 46 of the approximately 67 bridges eventually targeted had been destroyed, as had 32 pontoon bridges built to offset the Coalition raids. By the end of January the Coalition's campaign was successful in reducing Iraq's logistical capacity by about 90%. The resulting disruption of the distribution system resulted in shortages of food and even water, and contributed to the low morale that the Iraqis exhibited during the final phases of the war.[222]

AIR STRIKES AGAINST INDUSTRIAL INSTALLATIONS AND COMMAND AND CONTROL CENTERS

The bombing in the morning of 13 February of a Baghdad air-raid shelter housing (unbeknownst to the Coaltion) civilians created a sensation. Although several U.S. opinion polls taken before and after the bombing indicate no effect on public support for the war,[223] concern for the effects of such incidents on Western public opinion led Coalition leaders to sharply reduce the bombing of targets in central Baghdad; in the two weeks after the incident, only 5 were struck, compared with 25 in the preceding two weeks.[224]

However, this event demonstrated the Coalition's capability to destroy some of Iraq's most protected resources, if their location could be determined accurately enough, and this fact may have been noted by the Iraqis. Was it a coincidence that Iraq made its first partial peace proposal on 15 February, two days after the shelter was bombed?

---

221. This account is from Morse, *Gulf Air War Debrief*, p. 82.

222. Cohen et al., *GWAPS: Summary*, pp. 92-98, and *GWAPS: Effects and Effectiveness*, pp. 181-202.

223. Cohen et al., *GWAPS: Support*, pp. 149-151; and Philip M. Taylor, *War and the Media* (Manchester University Press, 1992), p. 212.

224. Cohen et al., *GWAPS: Summary*, pp. 22, 69, 219.

The bombing of the shelter in Baghdad was part of the Coalition's overall effort to destroy Iraq's command, control, and communication systems. A modern army of over 500,000 men, such as Iraq's, is a complex organization, larger than almost all private companies. Just as no private company can function without managers, telephones, facsimile machines, and electronic mail, so no army can function without command centers and communication systems. Radio communications are subject to jamming, so ground-based systems using copper or fiber cables are preferred. The Coalition targeted both the command centers and the cables.

Although the Coalition attacks disrupted the Iraqi communication system, it proved resilient and impossible to destroy in its entirety. Central Iraqi leadership retained the capability to receive information and issue orders to troops in the field.[225]

A notable strike against a highly hardened command center near Baghdad was carried out by F-111 Aardvarks of the 48th Tactical Fighter Wing on the night of 27 February, just a few hours before the end of hostilities. The destruction of this facility was achieved by using newly-developed GBU-28/B 2100-kilogram hardened penetrating laser-guided bombs; four were actually delivered to the theater and two used before the end of hostilities; others were in production. The bombs were flown to Saudi Arabia as they were produced: they were still warm to the touch from the heat of the melted explosives which had been poured into the casing. Previous attempts to destroy this bunker with 1,000-kilo bombs had failed, since it was built deep under the ground and protected by thick cement walls. But the 5.5-meter-long GBU-28, which was developed in a crash 17-day effort and built from surplus 203mm cannon barrels, penetrated 30 meters of earth in one test in the United States and 6 meters of concrete in another. Penetration is achieved thanks to the high mass and impact velocity of the weapon, which is fused to detonate several seconds after it hits the target. While most technical parameters of this bomb are classified, its speed at impact is certainly greater than 500 kilometers per hour, so when it hits it releases over six times more kinetic energy than that of two cars colliding head on at 100 kilometers per hour. Video tapes of the 27 February strike showed a garage door flying off seven seconds after the bomb struck, indicating it had exploded inside the bunker. "Sure would like to see that bunker now," said Master Sgt. Jerry Grace, who helped assemble the bomb in Saudi Arabia.[226]

Coalition forces struck indirectly at communication systems by destroying electrical power supply systems thought to power military facilities and weapons factories. Some 175 strikes were flown against power plants, and generation capacity was reduced to 12% of its pre-war level.[227]

---

225. Ibid., pp. 70-71.

226. Personal interviews with the aircrew who conducted the strike and with Sgt. Grace; and Sgt. Troy Prine, "The 'Big One'," press release by 48th Tactical Fighter Wing.

227. Cohen et al., *GWAPS: Summary*, p. 73; United Nations, *Iraq-Kuwait Conflict*, p. 276.

In addition, about 431 strikes reduced by 90% Iraq's oil refining and fuel production capability (as opposed to crude oil production facilities, which intentionally were not targeted). However, this had no effect on the war, because of the rapid collapse of the Iraqi forces during the ground war.[228]

About 970 strikes were directed against nuclear sites and chemical and biological weapons production and storage facilities. However, these sites were highly dispersed, camouflaged, and hardened, so the air campaign was not effective in significantly reducing Iraq's unconventional weapons capabilities.[229]

Finally, Coalition aircraft destroyed or severely damaged over 375 hardened aircraft shelters, damaging many Iraqi aircraft in the process; postwar analysis shows that 141 planes had been destroyed inside shelters, in addition to the 113 destroyed in the open, the 33 shot down in the air, and the 120 or so that fled to Iran.[230]

EFFECT ON CIVILIANS

Article 23(g) of the Annex to the 1907 Hague Convention Respecting the Laws and Customs of War on Land (the international law invoked during war crime trials after World War II) prohibits belligerents to "destroy . . . the enemy's property, unless . . . imperatively demanded by the necessities of war." Article 27 further prohibits attacks on "buildings dedicated to art, science, or charitable purposes, historic monuments, hospitals, and places where the sick and wounded are collected, provided they are not being used at the time for military purposes." Article 147 of the 1949 Geneva Convention on protection of civilians forbids "extensive destruction . . . of property, not justified by military necessity and carried out unlawfully and wantonly."

Bureaucracies around the world are known for their ability to invent arcane jargon, acronyms, and euphemisms. The U.S. military does not lack this skill. Thus unintended bombing of civilians was referred to as "collateral damage" by Coalition briefers, and they assured the world that all steps were being taken to "minimize collateral damage," that is, to keep to a minimum the number of civilians killed either because they were near military sites, or because bombs malfunctioned, or because pilots made errors, or because targeting personnel made mistakes.

There can be no doubt that Coalition forces did not deliberately target civilian areas. Nevertheless, errors were made and civilians were killed. For example, the UK acknowledged that a steering-vane malfunction caused a laser-guided bomb directed at a bridge on 16 February to strike a nearby civilian area; Iraq claimed that 130 civilians were killed. According to official

---

228. Cohen et al., *GWAPS: Summary*, pp. 76-77.

229. Ibid., pp. 80-82.

230. Cohen et al., *GWAPS: Effects and Effectiveness*, p. 154 footnote 98, and Table 10, p. 156.

U.S. reports, 20% of the precision bombs released by F-117 Nighthawks did not hit their target. That is, about 400 tons of bombs from the F-117s alone may have caused collateral damage; the total explosive tonnage contained in all the SCUDs fired by Iraq was around 20 tons—20 times less than the stray bombs from the Nighthawks. Official Iraqi sources claimed a total of around 2,300 civilian deaths.[231]

The day-to-day life of civilians was perhaps more affected by the Coalition's destruction of much of Iraq's industrial infrastructure than it was by the few stray bombings of civilian areas. Within days of the start of the war, large portions of Iraq, including Baghdad, had no electricity; as a consequence, there was no running water, so some residents of Baghdad had to seek water directly from the river running through the city. Furthermore, sewage disposal systems were not functioning correctly and basic foodstuffs were rationed, as was gasoline.[232] Some quotes from Iraqis:

People have started hating these air raids. They live in constant horror, fearing death in their shelters. Their faces are pale, their bodies tremble from the unknown. This is the reality.

People are trying to preserve themselves. Only a few gasoline stations are open and people are living on hoarded food, no electricity or water.

We were at home in Doura [in Baghdad]. There was an air raid every two hours. The planes came three times. There were no casualties in our quarter, but people are terrified. No one was expecting this to happen. We have never seen anything like it. My children screamed all night. They all piled up on top of me.

Food and water are no longer available. . . . There is no diesel for pumps or generators. . . . Everybody is afraid.

Even shaving in the morning is impossible. Where do you get the water?

Old habits die hard. I still automatically switch on the light when I get home. Nothing happens of course. I still turn on the tap and expect water. Nothing.[233]

Although there was no material discomfort in Riyadh and Tel Aviv, residents of both cities suffered from stress and psychological discomfort due to the threat of SCUD missile attacks, as did the residents of certain other Saudi and Israeli cities. Since the use of chemical warheads could not be ruled out, residents were advised to keep a gas mask readily available at all times. Schools were closed and the Israeli economy was disrupted for a few days; in

---

231. The U.S. Census Bureau assumed 5,000 civilian deaths: Frank Hobbs, *Population Estimates for Iraq* (Center for International Research, U.S. Bureau of the Census, January 1991). A New York-based human rights group estimated 3,000 civilian deaths, on the basis of extensive interviews: Middle East Watch, *Needless Deaths in the Gulf War: Civilian Casualties During the Air Campaign and Violations of the Laws of War* (Human Rights Watch, 1991), p.19. Similar figures are confirmed by John Mueller, "The Perfect Enemy: Assessing the Gulf War," *Security Studies*, 5, no.1 (Autumn 1995): 103.

232. United Nations, *Iraq-Kuwait Conflict*, pp. 188, 275-276.

233. *International Herald Tribune* (22 January 1991).

addition, a 24-hour curfew was imposed on Palestinians living in the territories occupied by Israel during the 1967 war, in effect subjecting to house arrest people who had committed no crimes. The curfew started on 17 January and lasted until 5 February.

AIR STRIKES AGAINST DUG-IN TROOPS

Iraq started the war with some 3,500 tanks, 3,100 APCs, and 2,500 artillery pieces in the theater, approximately 20% less than estimated by Central Command at the time.[234] Over half of all air strikes were devoted to reducing the strength of Iraqi troops on the ground (see Table 9.1). More emphasis was given to Republican Guard units in the rear than to frontline troops, which caused some concerns among ground troop commanders.[235]

However, it proved remarkably difficult to estimate the effectiveness of air strikes against tanks and other equipment, with theater and Central Intelligence Agency (CIA) sources differing by a factor of 3, because theater estimates were based on pilot reports and analysis of gun-camera videos, while CIA reports were based on analysis of satellite photographs that could not necessarily detect partial destruction of equipment.[236] In-depth postwar analysis indicates that Central Command estimates were about 20% high, offsetting the too-high estimate of Iraqi strength, so that theater *relative* (percent) estimates of equipment attrition were approximately correct.[237] Table 6.2 shows these estimates.

Coalition forces used F-111, F-15, A-10, and A-6 aircraft against tanks—with the F-111s and F-15s flying only at night. B-52 bombers were used against logistic sites and other targets. The use of the F-111s against tanks was not planned at the beginning of the war; a first test mission was carried out in the early morning of 6 February, with 2 F-111s dropping 8 220-kilo laser-guided bombs, hitting 7 tanks or APCs. From then on, strikes were flown almost every night; the largest single night total was scored on 14 February, when 46 F-111s hit 132 tanks and APCs (at the time, it was thought that most hits resulted in kills; postwar analysis shows that the success rate was only 35%-40%[238]).

A U.S. F-111 pilot explains night antitank missions: "Looking at videos from aircraft that had overflown the dug-in vehicles at night, we noticed that the bulldozer scrapes left a distinctive infrared signature. The subsurface soil was a different makeup of dirt: it absorbed heat and cooled off at a different

---

234. Cohen et al., *GWAPS: Effects and Effectiveness*, Table 11, p. 170.

235. Cohen et al., *GWAPS: Operations*, pp. 287-290, p. 200 footnote 129. A detailed account is given in Swain, *"Lucky War,"* pp. 185-189.

236. Cohen et al., *GWAPS: Effects and Effectiveness*, p. 34, and Table 13, p. 211.

237. Ibid., pp. 218-219.

238. Cohen et al., *GWAPS: Effects and Effectiveness*, p. 36.

rate than the surrounding sand. At night you could see it clearly on the Pave Tack [the laser guidance unit on the F-111]."

Table 6.2
Percent cumulative Iraqi equipment losses in the KTO

Day	Tanks[239]	APCs	Artillery
5	0	0	3
10	2	3	11
15	14	8	14
20	21	18	21
25	25	22	31
30	41	28	51
35	45	29	57
37	48	30	58
38	51	31	59

From briefings of the U.S. 48th Tactical Fighter Wing (F-111s):

The different areas of Iraq and Kuwait were divided into tank kill boxes, about 100 kilometers by 35. Each unit designated to kill tanks would have its own box. We put two or four planes in a box for a twenty-minute period. Within the box were groups of targets. Our Army Ground Liaison Officer provided us with precise coordinates and briefed us on preferred targets, for example three armor units and one artillery unit. This type of information was critical to the success of the mission.

From an air crew perspective it was a fairly simple mission. We'd take off, refuel in the air, and leave the tankers to enter the box at a designated time. We'd update our inertial navigation system prior to entering the box, so when we turned on the laser guidance system it would cue into the target area. Generally, there would be many targets displayed on the system's view screen and the hard part was figuring out which one to hit. Prior to weapons release, the targets were just hot spots in the scope, little white dots. You wouldn't know what it was, but it was obviously a target due to the formation: line, V, circle. So I'd pick one and fire the laser, which gives the pilot steering and release information. The pilot would pickle off [release] the bomb and it would follow the laser into the target. After release, we'd continue towards the target, and as we got closer I could see that it was indeed some sort of vehicle, armor or maybe artillery. We'd blow up one, sequence to the next target, blow it up, and so on until we were out of bombs. Then we'd return to base. Mission time was about four hours.

We had the ideal conditions for these tactics to work. By this point in the war the threat was low, mostly unguided 23 and 37mm AAA; SAMs were ineffective due to

---

239. These are the U.S. Central Command estimates, based largely on analysis of gun-camera videos, as presented in U.S. Department of Defense, *Conduct of the Persian Gulf War*, Table VI-4, p. 188. They differ slightly from the numbers given in contemporaneous Central Command briefings.

our countermeasures.   The armor was revetted and concentrated which made
formation identification much easier.[240]

Day after day Coalition bombers flew unhindered over the Iraqi trenches,
dropping tons of bombs. Even when no one was killed, the nearly continuous
bombing made it difficult for Iraqi troops to sleep and sapped their morale.
EC-130 planes loaded with radio transmission gear were used to broadcast
messages designed to weaken Iraqi morale on a wide range of frequencies.
Starting in January, Coalition aircraft used loudspeakers to broadcast calls for
surrender, and dropped leaflets guaranteeing the safety of any surrendering
soldiers. Over 1 million leaflets were dropped in Kuwait on 12 January, and
over 250,000 on Baghdad on 20 January. Later, leaflets announcing a
bombing were dropped on specific units, which were then bombed, and then
showered with more leaflets reminding them that they would be bombed again.
In one case, an entire battalion surrendered to a helicopter patrol when the
attached loudspeaker aircraft announced that "death from above" was
imminent.

There can be no doubt that the continuous, heavy Coalition bombing
reduced the fighting capability of the Iraqi army and made possible the rapid
success of the Coalition ground assault. Prisoner-of-war debriefing suggested
that morale was already poor after one week of bombing, and that B-52 strikes
were particularly demoralizing.[241] Even if only some of the tanks in a unit are
destroyed, reconstituting an effective fighting force is not easy: there is a great
deal of teamwork involved in modern mechanized fighting, and rebuilding an
effective team requires practice—something that was impossible under the
threat of Coalition air raids.

The diary of an Iraqi lieutenant in an air-defense battery close to the Iraq-
Kuwait border reveals the difficult conditions of those subjected to the
bombardment. On 17 January one of the unit's bunkers suffered a direct hit
and burned, the next day a supply bunker was destroyed. Troops relied on
heavy rain to collect enough water to drink, cook, and wash. By 20 January
food was running short, but superior officers could offer no solutions. Day
after day Coalition planes flew overhead, out of range of the anti-aircraft guns,
dropping bombs and photographing the site to plan the next day's bombing.[242]

Another diary opens every day with words like: "The intensive enemy
bombardment continues. O Lord, protect us." On 2 February:

Two enemy airplanes came towards us and started firing at us one after the other, with
bombs, automatic cannon, and rockets. Death passed close to me. It wasn't further
than a meter from me. The bombs, cannon fire, and rockets never stopped. One of
the rockets even hit our bunker and went through it. Shrapnel flew inside and we

240. 48 TFW, tank killing briefing (undated) and personal interview.
241. Cohen et al., *GWAPS: Operations*, p. 250.
242. Adapted from Douglas Jehl, "Life in Wartime: An Iraqi Soldier's Diary,"
International Herald Tribune (6 March 1991).

shouted Allah, Allah, Allah. One tank was burning and three others were destroyed. These moments were very difficult. Time passed and we waited for death. The ammunition dump of a nearby battalion exploded. One of the shells fell into a trench, but fortunately no one was in it. The attack lasted 15 minutes, but it felt like an hour.[243]

U.S. AIR RESCUE

Extensive resources were dedicated to air search and rescue: the capability to find and recover pilots behind enemy lines. MH-53J Pave Low helicopters and A-10 planes were devoted to these tasks. Since many pilots were captured immediately after parachuting to the ground, only seven search and rescue missions were flown, resulting in three saves. The first save, on 21 January, is described in detail below. On 23 January, a Navy helicopter rescued a pilot who had ejected over the Persian Gulf. During the night of 17 February, two Army Blackhawk helicopters, whose crew used night-vision goggles, picked up an F-16 pilot 100 kilometers behind enemy lines, evading a SAM as they returned to their base.

On 27 February, during the ground attack, helicopters from the U.S. 101st Airborne Division attempted to rescue a downed U.S. pilot, and lost one of the helicopters to Iraqi ground fire in the attempt. Of the crew, five were killed, and three were injured and captured as POWs, including Maj. Rhonda Cornum, a female medical officer.

U.S. F-14 pilot Lt. Devon Jones recounts his mission in the early morning of 21 January:

We were escorting an EA-6 Prowler that was on a HARM mission. We were working between 26,000 and 30,000 feet [8500 meters] when I saw a SAM coming up through the clouds. I added power and rolled into the SAM, as briefed, to give it tracking problems. As we rolled down, almost inverted, the SAM tracked us, came up toward our tail and detonated with a bright, white flash. The F-14 shuddered and kept rolling right.

The plane started to go into a flat spin and I was getting thrown around, helpless. Lots of eyeball-out negative g. I couldn't see my instruments; the only thing I could sense was light or dark. It was light in the clouds, dark when we were outside. It was obvious that I was not going to recover the aircraft, so I pulled the handle.

I wasn't in a very good seat position, but the seat worked like a charm. As I came down, I passed in and out of clouds. The ceiling was only 150 feet. It was just too dark to see the ground—it came up and hit me very hard.

Now reality finally hit me, in a big way. I was down on the ground, inside Iraq. I could see my plane's crash site and the ball of flames. There's an initial shock that goes through you that has nothing to do with survival training. I thought, "Geez, I'm going to be a POW. My family's going to go nuts. They'll probably rip my fingernails out and shoot me!" After that, though, some survival training started seeping through. I started looking for a bush or tree to hide the seat and parachute,

243. Adapted from Service d'Information et de Relations Publiques des Armées, *Terre Magazine*, pp. 55-57.

but there was nothing. Just a big dirt—hard dirt, not sand—parking lot. So I wadded up my parachute into a small ball and put it under the seat pan.

Then I made a radio transmission and started walking away from the crash site. I kept looking for places to stop, but there was nothing—no mounds, no hills. I walked for 2.5 hours. Finally I came to a little vegetation, small bushes really, and a few small mounds. I thought the only chance I had was to try to dig into one of those mounds and hide. There was a blue cylindrical tank about 3 kilometers away on a dirt road.

By 1000 hours I'd finished digging a hole with my knife. I got into it, took off as much gear as I could, and scrunched down. I laid my radio on the edge of the hole and tried to get comfortable. About 1100 I heard a truck. It was a farmer's truck and it pulled up to the tank. Two guys got out, but they drove away three minutes later.

At 1205 I turned my radio on, as I had done every hour. Suddenly, I heard American voices: "Slate-46, how do you read?" It was my call sign! I answered, and they were able to locate my position approximately. The rescue plane made a couple of passes, setting off flares, and I saw the last one. He came down and I saw it was an A-10. I brought him in with standard aviator talk. He didn't see me, but flew right over me at 100 feet and noted the position in his inertial guidance system.

"I've got to get some gas," he called. "Minimize your transmissions and come back on in 30 minutes." He headed south toward the border. Meanwhile, he had given my position to the rescue helicopters and they began heading toward me. As the planes came back, everything seemed to be heading to a big crescendo. I think the Iraqis may have monitored our transmissions, and I had mentioned that I was close to the blue tank. About 800 meters to the south I spotted a truck, an army truck, with the canvas covers. I think we all saw it at the same time because the A-10 called, "We've got a fast mover on the dirt road." This truck was coming right at me, down in my hole.

I had a moment of panic there. But hey, the A-10s have those huge cannons and the helicopters have .50 caliber machine guns. Within three or four seconds, the A-10s rolled in on the truck, maybe 30 meters above the ground. They opened up with their 30mm cannon. By the time they each finished there was nothing out there, just flames and dust, about 100 meters from me.

For the first time, I looked to the east and saw the Pave Low helicopter, about 2 meters off the ground, watching the A-10s. I started talking to him. I had never seen such a beautiful sight as that big, brown American MH-53. He got about 50 meters away from me, and I popped out of my hole for the first time. I grabbed my gear as he landed about 20 meters away. One of the Special Forces guys jumped out and waved me on. I jumped in and off we went, 250 kilometers to go at 140 knots at 6 meters altitude!

Pretty impressive machines. Just what you'd expect from these Special Forces people with lots of guns hanging off them. There was a second helicopter 30 kilometers south, flying cover. Big spines on these guys, I'll tell you, being 250 kilometers into enemy territory during the day, in a helicopter. I had been on the ground exactly 8 hours. The A-10s had been airborne 8 hours for the rescue mission, and the helicopters had been up 3 hours.[244]

---

244. Adapted from Morse, *Gulf Air War Debrief*, p. 96.

IRAQI TREATMENT OF PRISONERS

Coalition pilots captured by Iraqi forces were mistreated, in violation of the Geneva Conventions. For reasons which are difficult to understand, Iraq actually broadcast television images of the captured POWs in which it was clear that they had been beaten. The following reminiscences by a captured U.S. pilots are just one example of Iraqi treatment of POWs. U.S. Marine Harrier pilot Capt. Russell Sanborn, shot down on 9 February:

I suddenly felt this loud thump on the left side of the plane. It immediately started spinning and inverting out of control. However, I still struggled with the aircraft for a few seconds in hopes of saving her. But the fire light was on and I knew she was a goner. So, I got myself into a good body position and pulled the handle to eject—and out I went.

I was on the ground no more than 10 minutes before the Iraqi welcoming committee reached me. I was blindfolded, had my hands tied behind my back, and was thrown in the back of a truck. They drove for a while, then took me off and made me run a gauntlet of soldiers. They lined up and hit me with their fists, with sticks, and with their rifle butts. For the last 18 or 19 days we had been bombing them. The guys I saw looked pretty tired and ragged. They needed somebody to vent their frustration against. And I happened to be the unlucky one. They screamed insults at me in Arabic and broken English. I fell down a couple of times. They would quickly pick me up and push me forward. But I never lost consciousness. Then they placed me back on the truck, stopped, and repeated the procedure again. Then they did it a third time. By then, I was hurting.

Later, I was interrogated by professionals. Again, I was tied up and blindfolded. Whenever they picked my chin up, I knew they were going to hit me. So I would tuck my chin in and roll my shoulders forward to protect my face as much as possible. I would also feel what thumb they had pressed on me and brace myself. If it was the left thumb, then I knew it was the right hand coming around to strike me.[245]

THE CAMPAIGN ON THE SEA

Carrier-based airplanes contributed significantly to the Coalition effort, flying some 15% of total sorties including 20-35 maritime attack sorties every day.[246]

In addition to contributing to the air war, naval forces maintained a tight blockade that prevented Iraq from receiving any supplies by sea; destroyed most of Iraq's small navy; and directed fire against land installations (using missiles and guns). The overall plan of operations called for the Coalition naval forces gradually to move north as they cleared mines.

---

245. Adapted from Military History Magazine, *Desert Storm* (Empire Press, 1991), p. 130.

246. This section is based on U.S. Department of Defense, *Conduct of the Persian Gulf War*, Chapters IV and VII; U.S. Department of the Navy, *The U.S. Navy in "Desert Shield"/"Desert Storm"* (15 May 1991); and Hine, "Despatch," pp. G43-G44.

In order to enforce the U.N. embargo, Coalition vessels intercepted over 10,000 ships, boarded over 1,600, and diverted nearly 100. Modern radar systems and their associated computers aboard ships were used to track thousands of merchant vessels. Each was challenged, identified, and if necessary warned, boarded, and in some cases diverted. The United States deployed 10 Coast Guard boarding teams who had considerable experience with drug interdiction boardings. Coalition units attempting to board a ship confronted it with overwhelming force: three or four warships surrounded the challenged vessel while a helicopter gunship hovered nearby. In some cases a Special Forces team rappelled down ropes from helicopters onto the challenged ship.

On 28 October 1990, the USS *Reasoner* intercepted the Iraqi merchant *Amuriyah*, which had refused to answer radio calls. HMAS Darwin forced the Iraqi vessel to turn but it resumed its original course. F-14s and F/A-18s from the USS *Independence* made low passes but the master remained uncooperative and refused to accept a boarding party. *Darwin* and *Reasoner* fired warning shots, which only caused the Iraqi crew to don life-jackets. A 21-man U.S. Marine team rappelled onto the Iraqi ship and encountered no resistance. When Navy SEALs [Special Forces] arrived in boats, the Iraqi crew attempted to use water cannon to prevent them from boarding. The crew then resisted passively as the vessel was searched. One crew member who attacked a Marine with an axe was disarmed and restrained. Inspection revealed no prohibited cargo, so the vessel was allowed to continue on its course.[247]

Once hostilities started, airplanes and helicopters based on U.K. and U.S. ships attacked the Iraqi navy; by 28 January nearly 20 ships had been sunk or severely damaged. A week later the number was 35, with an additional 30 damaged, and the Iraqi navy was considered ineffective because all ships capable of firing surface-surface missiles had been destroyed or disabled. Eventually over 140 Iraqi vessels were destroyed. In keeping with the proud traditions of Britain's Royal Navy, at the time hostilities ceased, the nine Coalition ships in the most forward positions were all British.

On the night of 29 January, with poor visibility because of the weather and oil fires, a U.S. Navy A-6 located four suspicious vessels south of the Faw peninsula. With their lights out, the ships were heading towards Iran. An orbiting E-2 surveillance plane assumed control of the A-6, determined that the ships were hostile, and authorized an attack.

The A-6 dropped a 228-kilo laser-guided bomb on the lead vessel, scoring a direct hit. The other Iraqi ships scattered, but the A-6 dropped another bomb on a second boat, destroying its superstructure and stopping it dead in the water. An F/A-18 joined the attack, scoring a direct hit on the third boat. The U.S. planes had no more ammunition, so the E-2 called for additional planes. Two Canadian CF-18s were released from Combat Air Patrol and strafed the fourth boat with their 20-mm guns as it fled towards Iran.

---

247. U.S. Department of Defense, *Conduct of the Persian Gulf War*, p. 75.

Three boats were destroyed, while the fourth was later located in an Iranian port with substantial damage to its superstructure.[248]

Some 276 cruise missiles were launched from U.S. surface ships cruising in the Persian Gulf and the Red Sea. An additional 12 were launched from U.S. submarines. The 18 406mm guns of the battleships USS *Missouri* and USS *Wisconsin* were used to shell fortified Iraqi positions and tank formations close to shore. These guns, originally built in the 1920s, and now aimed by modern fire-control computers, fire a 1-ton shell at some 40 kilometers, achieving very high accuracy thanks to the use of remote-controlled drone aircraft as spotters and ship-based radar to track the outgoing round and to correct subsequent fire. The *Missouri* had not fired a shot in combat since 1953 when it opened fire on 4 February. The two battleships eventually fired some 1,000 tons of 406mm ammunition, the equivalent of more than 500 A-6 bombing missions (in total weight, albeit not in explosive content, since bomb casings are typically lighter than artillery shell casings).

A considerable portion of the navies' efforts was devoted to countering the threat of mines. Modern sea mines can take very different forms: they can be moored on lines (like the classic World War I or II mines), floating on or below the surface; they can be free-floating, drifting with the current; they can sit on the bottom in shallow waters. They can be triggered by contact, by detecting the propeller noise of an approaching ship, or by detecting the disturbance in the earth's magnetic field caused by the passage of a ship. Sophisticated models can be programmed to explode only after a certain number of ships have passed. Thus a minesweeping vessel might pass over a mine without causing an explosion, whereas the following ship would trigger the mine. Modern warships rely on forward-looking sonar (side-scan sonar) to detect mines and on divers to defuse or detonate them. Some ships (in particular Italian ones) deploy wire-guided unmanned submarines to detect and neutralize mines. These devices have sonars, television cameras, explosives for neutralizing mines, and cable cutters for cutting mooring lines so that mines float to the surface for destruction. Mines that sit on the bottom are particularly hard to detect. Eventually about half of the estimated 1,000 mines laid by Iraq were detected and neutralized. However, mines continued to threaten naval operations throughout the war.[249] Map 6.3 ilustrates the minefields.

Even though several U.K. and U.S. mine clearing vessels had been at work clearing a channel for the battleships USS *Missouri* and *Wisconsin* and other ships since 15 February 1991, two ships were damaged by mines on 18 February: the USS *Tripoli*, a Marine troop and helicopter carrier, and the USS *Princeton*, an Aegis class missile cruiser. No one was killed, and neither ship sank thanks to good damage control efforts by the crews, who had to work in a

---

248. Ibid., p. 266.
249. Ibid., p. 309.

mixture of water, paint, and paint thinner in the flooded compartments on the
Tripoli and in a mixture of fuel and water on the *Princeton*. Both ships were
able to proceed under their own power, although the *Princeton* was sufficiently
damaged that it was ordered into port.

Map 6.3
Iraqi minefields in the Persian Gulf

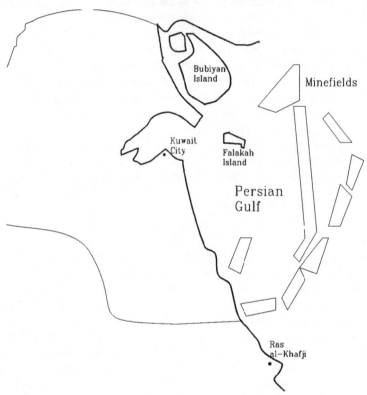

Continued mine-clearing efforts allowed the *Missouri* to reach its designated
position on 23 February, from which it shelled Falakah Island. The next day
the battleship fired some 130 tons of ammunition in one hour. On 25
February, it shelled and did very significant damage to an Iraqi tank brigade
near Kuwait International Airport. In general, fire from the big guns of the
Missouri and the *Wisconsin*, directed by remotely piloted vehicles (RPVs), was
very effective against Iraqi positions.[250]

Apart from one apparent attempt to send Mirage jets, possibly carrying
Exocet missiles, to attack the Coalition fleet (both planes were shot down by a
Saudi fighter pilot while they were still over land), Iraqi forces made only one

---

250. Personal interviews with U.S. Marine officers who saw the targeted sites.

attempt to attack Coalition ships. On 25 February a Chinese-made Silkworm missile was launched, perhaps against the USS *Missouri*. The U.K. frigate HMS *Gloucester*, performing its functions as a picket ship, fired Sea Dart missiles that intercepted and destroyed the Silkworm at a distance of a few kilometers (about 30 seconds before it would have flown by the *Gloucester*). The Sea Dart system thus had one chance to exhibit its antimissile capability.

IRAQI REACTIONS TO THE COALITION OFFENSIVE

Iraq's reactions to the massive Coalition air attack were, as Coalition military briefers put it, "limited." Because of to the effectiveness of the Coalition's actions, no air response was possible. Artillery strikes against Coalition forces were severely hindered by Iraq's lack of aerial reconnaissance capabilities and were quickly silenced by Coalition counterfire. A massive ground attack could have been envisaged, but would have been subject to aerial attack by the Coalition.

Thus there was little that Iraq could do. We review here in more detail what Iraq could not do, and what it did do, which can be summarized as: send its air force out of the country, fire artillery sporadically , mount a probing attack, but mostly just hunker down.

Anti-air Defense

Iraq was unable to use its air forces to threaten Coalition aircraft. Since Coalition attacks had destroyed Iraq's central radar and control facilities on the first day of the war, its only remaining air defense capabilities were uncoordinated SAM and AAA fire.

Coalition radar jamming and HARMs proved successful in severely reducing the effectiveness of Iraq's SAMs, which were all radar-guided. A SAM battery operator can detect the launching of a HARM, and has the choice to wait for it to strike his radar or to turn off the radar, thus rendering his battery ineffective. Coalition forces typically flew about 100 missions per day dedicated to suppressing Iraqi air defenses. At one point over 200 HARM missiles were in the air simultaneously, all homing in on Iraqi radars. Only 10 Coalition aircraft were downed by SAMs, even though thousands of SAMs were fired.

Similar measures were used against radar-aimed AAA. These measures were so effective that on 1 February, 80% of the F-4 Wild Weasel missions (which carried most of the HARM missiles) reported that they had detected no radar emissions. Thus optically aimed AAA constituted the main Iraqi threat to Coalition aircraft. The main countermeasure to this threat was simply to fly at higher altitudes. While many Coalition bombers had carried out their initial attacks using low-level flights, after the first few days of the campaign all switched to medium altitudes (3,000 to 6,000 meters), flying above small-arms fire and much of the AAA. Figure 6.1 shows how the Coalition relentlessly improved its aerial supremacy, driving the combat loss rate down by tactical measures and by progressively destroying Iraq's air defenses.

Figure 6.1
Coalition combat air loss rate

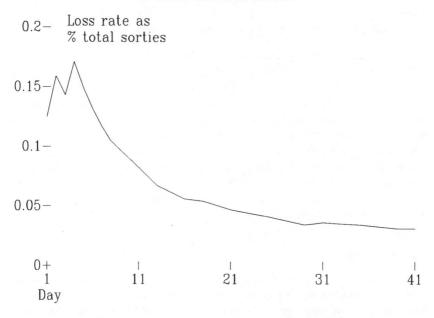

Overall, Iraqi air-defense proved incapable of inflicting serious losses on Coalition aircraft. A rather high U.K. loss rate during the first week of the campaign (4 combat losses out of 250 combat sorties—1.6% versus 0.21% for the Coalition as a whole or 0.15% for the non-U.K. planes) cannot reasonably be attributed to bad luck: a straightforward computation shows that the probability of 2 or fewer losses in 250 sorties is about 99% if the average loss rate is 0.2%. The U.K.'s lack of a laser-designation system for its Tornados, in conjunction with reliance on low-level flight patterns during the first week, may account for some of the losses. Without this system, planes have less freedom to maneuver as they approach the target and can be more easily brought down by AAA. But it is quite likely that there is no single explanation for the Tornado losses.[251] Indeed this is the UK's official view.[252]

The overall U.K. loss rate was 0.4%, about the same as Italy's and about 5 times greater than the loss rate for U.S. bombers. However, this rate was still

---

251. Cohen et al., *GWAPS: Summary*, p.63.

252. U.K. Secretary of State for Defence, *Statement on the Defence Estimates* (July 1991).

lower than what had been expected before the campaign started.[253] Hence the official U.K. view that "fewer aircraft were lost than might have been expected from the number of sorties flown."[254]

Air-surface Attack

On 24 January a Saudi fighter pilot destroyed two Iraqi Mirage jets that apparently were equipped with Exocet missiles and might have been attempting an attack against Coalition ships. This was the only known attempt by Iraq to use its air forces to attack Coalition forces on the ground or the sea.

Fleeing Airplanes

From 22 January to 9 February a considerable number of Iraqi air force planes flew into Iran, a neutral country, evading Coalition fighters. Because of the short flight time and the low Coalition priority assigned to attacking planes flying away from the combat zone, most planes that attempted to flee into Iran succeeded. The Coalition estimated that over 120 Iraqi planes, mostly late-model, high-performance MiGs and Mirages, had reached Iran, leaving the Iraqi air force with essentially no modern air superiority fighters. Iran admitted that some Iraqi planes had reached its territory, but gave much lower numbers than the Coalition. In the absence of any official information from Iraq, we can only speculate on the reasons for these flights into Iran.

The fact that by the end of the campaign, Coalition aircraft had destroyed or severely damaged over 300 hardened aircraft shelters lends credence to the theory that Iraq may have been motivated to take desperate measures to protect its remaining airplanes.

Figure 6.2 illustrates the plight of the Iraqi air force: when it took to the air, it experienced very high loss rates (a total of 5%, some 150 times greater than the Coalition loss rate). Coalition planes started attacking and destroying hardened bunkers on Day 7, an action that may have motivated Iraqi leaders to order pilots to fly their planes to Iran. By Day 9 the Iraqi air force had conceded defeat in the air and flew very few sorties, except attempts to fly planes to Iran.[255]

Iran did not return the planes after the conflict, preferring to keep them for its own use.[256] Considering the bitter enmity between the Iraqi and Iranian

---

253. Some estimates of losses were as high as 5%: Cohen et al., *GWAPS: Summary*, p. 53.

254. U.K. Secretary of State for Defence, *Statement on the Defence Estimates*, p. 19.

255. Data concerning the number of Iraqi planes flying to Iran are subject to considerable uncertainty.

256. Daniel Pearl, "Hiding and Seeking: Iraq's Best Planes Are Mainly in Iran," *Wall Street Journal Europe* (30 April 1998).

regimes, it seems unlikely that Iraq's leaders would have sent the planes to Iran for safe-keeping. However, a miscalculation on their part cannot be excluded.

Figure 6.2
Iraqi air sorties and loss rate

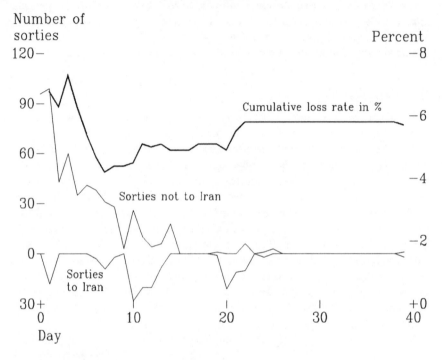

Terrorist Attacks

At the beginning of the conflict there was serious concern in Western countries that Iraq, as well as Arab political movements allied with Iraq, could launch a serious terrorist campaign against Western interests. Thus Western countries took steps meant to disrupt the organized sabotage and terrorist capabilities of Iraq, for example, expelling many Iraqi diplomats during the Gulf crisis.

In fact there was no significant terrorist activity during the Gulf War, perhaps because Western counter-measures were effective, or perhaps because the individuals who perform terrorist actions were not inspired to come to Iraq's aid. The only visible terrorist actions were those of a well-known Greek left-wing organization, which damaged several U.S.-owned properties in Athens (no one was injured or killed).

This lack of effective pro-Iraqi terrorism should be contrasted to the tremendous effectiveness of the actions that the Irish Republican Army (IRA) took on 20 February: a series of well-placed bombs and threats succeeded in forcing the closure of most of London's subway system, virtually paralyzing the city.

Nonetheless, the mere threat of terrorist activities did discourage many people in the West from traveling. U.S. companies in particular severely reduced business travel. As a consequence, the world air transport industry registered a loss in business between 15% and 20% while the war lasted. Other sectors of the Western travel industry (hotels, restaurants, and so forth) suffered comparably. This industry appears to be the only industry outside of Kuwait or Iraq that was damaged by the war.

ARTILLERY ACTION

A considerable amount of artillery was present on both sides. Iraq deployed over 3,000 pieces and the Coalition over 1,500 pieces. It thus appeared that Iraq had a numerical advantage in artillery. However, Coalition forces also deployed some 200 multiple launch rocket systems (MLRS), thus narrowing the gap. Both sides possessed artillery tracking systems, each consisting of a radar system coupled to a computer. In addition to their ability to monitor outgoing fire and its impact points, these systems can observe incoming shells and compute the points from which they have been fired; these coordinates can be used to call in air strikes or to direct artillery counterfire against enemy batteries. However, some Iraqi troops appeared incapable of using counterbattery radar, or perhaps did not believe in it. Furthermore, the combination of counterbattery radar with the mobile MLRS system acting as a team gave the Coalition superior counterfire capability.

U.S. Marine artillery officer Lt. Col. Rob Rivers:

They had some good radars, and they had acquired us [that is, our location]. At one time during the ground campaign we captured one of their radars and went inside. We checked the azimuth [direction of fire] it had computed, and it corresponded exactly to the position one of our artillery battalions had shot from. So they had us [located], but didn't believe it. They probably wanted two radars to give the same coordinates in order to double-check. But they had spaced them so far apart that the two radars couldn't be used together. So there was no way to check the one radar's reading. They had the gear, but didn't know how to use it.

The range out there made the difference. We were able to outrange everything they had, except for some Austrian artillery they had, and of course their multiple rocket launcher systems. But everything else we could outrange and cover with fire. Their problem was that they didn't have adequate training for the gun crews. They really had no precision. They were very lax. When you shoot a round and you're one mil [a unit of measurement for angles] off, your round will fall 2,000 meters away from a target at 20 kilometers. So we saw rounds impact a couple of kilometers away, and said, "Oh well, a round's impacted." They really had no precision in their artillery.[257]

---

257. Personal interview.

In addition, Coalition artillery benefited from the support of aerial reconnaissance, which both significantly increased the precision of its fire and helped determine targets to fire at. Iraq, lacking any aerial reconnaissance capability whatsoever, could only fire its artillery blindly, and wait for the inevitable counterstrike. Every time the Iraqis fired their artillery, they revealed its position and opened themselves to attack from Coalition artillery or air forces. By 19 February, Coalition briefers reported that in some cases the Iraqis no longer responded to Coalition artillery fire, in order to avoid revealing their own positions.

U.S. Marines had started conducting artillery raids at the outbreak of hostilities. These were always directed at specific targets, such as command and control centers or radar sites. A typical raid was carried out by two groups of artillery, one of which would fire at the target and withdraw, while the other group stood by to counterfire on any Iraqi artillery that responded to the first group's shelling. Additional coverage and counterstrike capability was provided by airplanes.

Lt. Col. Cliff Myers describes one set of raids:

We had been deployed near the Kuwaiti border on 15 January and had started conducting a series of artillery raids as soon as the hostilities commenced. In these raids light armored vehicles (LAVs) would escort maybe two batteries of artillery up to the vicinity of Observation Post 6 [see Map 6.4]. One battery would fire on a couple of high-priority targets, in the hopes that it would evoke a response from the enemy—so that our air that was on station could attack and destroy that enemy artillery. Destroying their artillery was a very major concern of ours, because of the numbers of artillery pieces that they had. We also wanted to destroy some of their counterbattery radars, so as to have greater security for our own artillery once the ground war started.

When we conducted an artillery raid on the night of 25 January, we had a response that we had never anticipated. We sent one battery of artillery up to within a couple of kilometers of the berm [the first line of fortifications], and it fired up into the vicinity of al-Jaber airfield in Kuwait. We fired about 20 artillery rounds just after midnight that night, and suddenly the air that came in to help us was taking SAM shots and AAA fire up to 19,000 feet [6,000 meters], which is very, very high for AAA. This indicated that there was really a high-value target around there that we didn't know about—the strong Iraqi reaction surprised us a little. In retrospect, it looks like we hit the lead elements of a division that was coming down to attack south along the border. By the luck of the draw we may have forced them to do something prematurely.[258]

RAS AL-KHAFJI AND OTHER MAJOR GROUND ACTIONS

During the night of 29 January, Iraqi armored forces launched five or six probing attacks along three axes, as shown in Map 6.4; the forces deployed along each axis were about brigade size (roughly 3,000 men). The Iraqis

---

258. Personal interview.

achieved tactical surprise thanks to a number of factors, including the short distance of the advance, quick movement, and cloud cover.[259]

Map 6.4
Iraqi attacks on 29 January

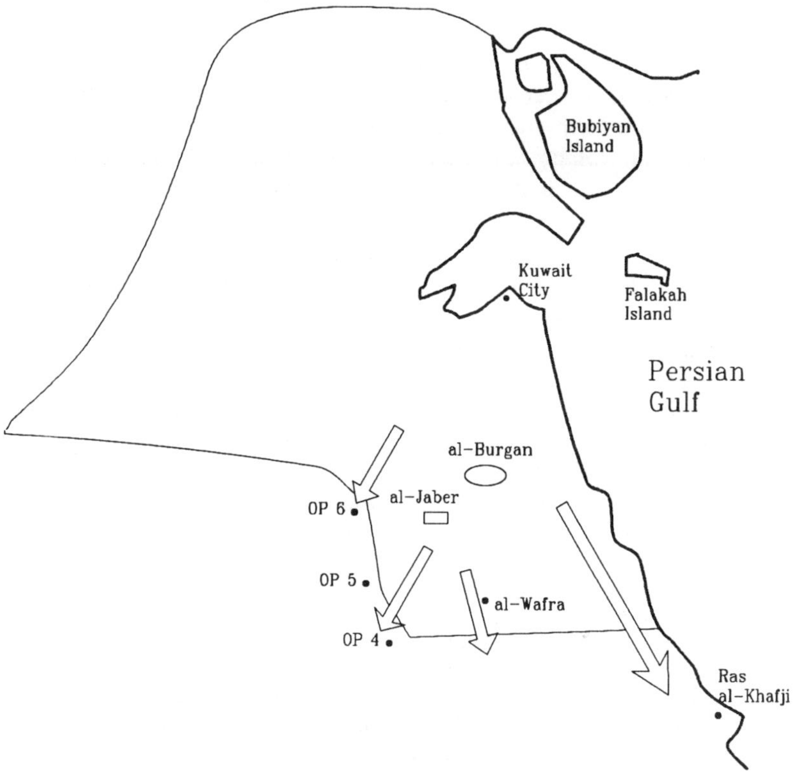

The first attack occurred in the west; units of the U.S. Marine First Light Armored Infantry Battalion (LAI) engaged the Iraqi forces, calling in artillery and close air support from AH-1 Cobra helicopters, AV-8 Harriers, and A-10 Warthogs in addition to using their own TOWs mounted on LAVs. At about

259. This section is based on personal interviews with the cited U.S. Marines who participated in the battle; on U.S. Marine First Air Naval Gunfire Liaison Company, *After Action Report for the Battle of Khafji 29 January-1 February 1991* (which includes detailed maps of troop movements), *After Action Report, Liberation of Kuwait*, report of Capt. J. R. Braden and report of Capt. D. R. Kleinsmith, and *Command Chronology for the Period 1 January Through 31 January 1991*; and on U.S. Department of Defense, *Conduct of the Persian Gulf War*, pp. 174-176. Our description differs from previous ones with respect to certain details. For example, see Michael Gordon and Bernard Trainor, *The Generals' War* (Little, Brown, 1995), Chapter 13.

the same time, another LAI battalion repulsed the probe coming from al-Wafra. The LAI was meant to be a reconnaissance and screening force, and was not designed to stop attacks by heavy armor; thus it had no armor, although it had antitank weapons. Nevertheless the LAI succeeded in stopping the Iraqi attacks, and the LAV performed very well its first time in combat. By the time the fighting ended, some 33 Iraqi tanks and 29 APCs had been destroyed. Eleven U.S. soldiers were killed in two friendly fire incidents. One involved a Maverick missile launched from an A-10 Warthog: the missile lost its intended target and instead destroyed an LAV, killing seven soldiers; four others were killed by friendly ground fire.

The third Iraqi column advanced farther east, around 0200 hours on 30 January, toward the town of Ras al-Khafji, which had been abandoned by its residents. U.S. SEALs (Navy Special Forces) and Marines called in close air support until they were engaged by direct fire as the Iraqis advanced. They then retreated. Two six-man U.S. Marine reconnaissance teams remained in the town while an Iraqi battalion occupied it in the early morning of 30 January—these Marines were not captured and were able to provide valuable intelligence to Coalition forces planning their counter-attack.

U.S. Marine Captain Fleming of the First Naval Air and Gunfire Liaison Company reports on the events at 2100 on 29 January:

The forward observer ran back to report "TRACKS!!" We got all our equipment on top of the bunker for easy use and access. Almost at the same time a round (tank, mortar, or artillery) landed to our immediate west. At the same time the upper silhouette of a machine gunner with a large caliber weapon on top of an APC loomed at the edge of the berm 200 meters to our northwest. He turned and began firing on us. Several dismounted infantry engaged us from the opposite coastal side as they topped the berm. We were being invaded. We headed to our Humvee, started loading it, returned fire, and took off as soon as everyone was in. As we drove over a little ridge we came under small arms, machine gun, and tank fire. We sped on, hit the coastal highway south, joined another reconnaissance team, and stopped to regroup and redeploy in Khafji to direct air strikes. This position also came under fire, so we sped out of the city and spent the remainder of the night outside Mishab [about 25 kilometers south of Khafji]."[260]

Just after midnight, another Iraqi probe 30 kilometers northwest of Khafji was repulsed by a Marine LAI battalion, again supported by air power. Around sunrise, yet another column attacked in the west, once again without success. In the early afternoon of 30 January, an Iraqi mechanized battalion concentrating at the Saudi border north of Khafji was attacked by air and ground forces, and withdrew to the north.

---

260. U.S. Marine First Air Naval Gunfire Liaison Company, *Command Chronology for the Period 1 January Through 31 January 1991*, report of Capt. Fleming.

The Coalition counterattack to recapture Khafji was conducted by Joint Arab Forces supported by U.S. Marines. Several plans were discussed during the day on 30 January, and Saudi commanders decided to launch an attack into the city from the south during the night. The main attacking units were elements of the Saudi Arabian National Guard with attached Qatari tanks: one battalion would attack from the northwest to cut off the city and prevent escape as well as reinforcement; another battalion would attack from the south; one battalion stood by to clear the city; and another was kept in reserve. The first step consisted of launching a four-to-six-hour probing attack from the south at 2100 on 30 January; its purpose was to elicit an Iraqi response, which would be observed by the two reconnaissance teams in Khafji, providing information for planning the full-scale action to recapture the town. While these probes were taking place, an advanced electronic reconnaissance aircraft, the U.S. JSTARS, was used to observe the advance of two or three Iraqi divisions sent to exploit the partial breakthrough at Khafji. Ground attack aircraft were called in, and the Iraqi reinforcing columns were bombed for 10 hours during the night. Badly weakened by this attack, they withdrew the following morning, leaving the forces in Khafji on their own.

Joint Arab Forces launched their main counterattack at dawn on 31 January, supported by U.S. Marine artillery fire, Coalition air force strikes, and information provided by the two reconnaissance teams still in the town. U.S. Marines provided antitank weapons to cover the flanks, went in as point (vanguard) in some cases, provided artillery and close air support, and recovered the reconnaissance teams. The Marines used laser designators on Iraqi positions and vehicles, guiding Hellfire missiles from Cobra helicopters and bombs from AV-8 Harriers.

Saudi and Qatari forces advanced into the city from the south, firing all available weapons furiously. As the Saudi forces advanced, U.S. Marine artillery fire and aircraft were called in to destroy many Iraqi vehicles. Cobra helicopters flew right down the streets to provide additional firepower. Saudi casualties during this attack, which lasted until 1300 hours and cleared the southern third of the town, were 10 dead and 45 wounded. Later in the afternoon, the Saudis swept the main coastal road. Map 6.5 illustrates these events.

While the attack from the south was going on, other Saudi forces attacked Iraqi formations north of Khafji. The better part of an Iraqi brigade was attempting to enter the city. Saudi tanks, APCs armed with TOW missiles, and U.S. Marine AV-8 Harrier jets inflicted heavy losses on the Iraqi forces, which were forced to withdraw.

No significant ground action took place during the night of 31 January while Coalition forces conducted heavy bombing raids north of the border in order to block any movement of Iraqi forces to reinforce the units in Khafji. On the morning of 1 February, Saudi forces swept the city from north to south, clearing it completely.

Some of the house-to-house fighting had been intense; about 10 Saudi and Qatari vehicles were destroyed. Coalition casualties were 18 dead and 32 wounded. Iraqi casualties were 32 dead, 35 wounded, 435 prisoners; some 90 Iraqi tanks and armored personnel vehicles were destroyed.[261]

Map 6.5
Coalition counterattack on Ras al-Khafji

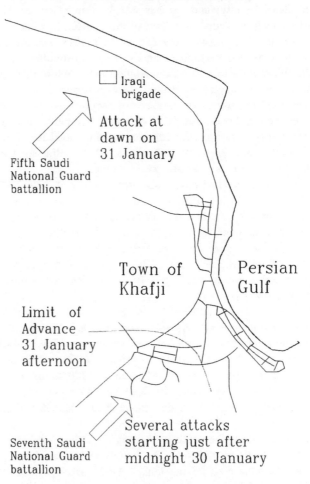

An Iraqi company-sized attack in the vicinity of Khafji was repulsed on 2 February. On 9 February, 300 Afghani resistance fighters, mujahidin, were assigned to Khafji as a defensive force.

---

261. Casualty numbers from bin Sultan, *Desert Warrior*, p. 387.

Several U.S. Marine enlisted men, NCOs, and officers were decorated for their actions in support of the Joint Arab Forces during the battle of Khafji. We give only one example: "Upon arrival west of Khafji, Capt. Aaron Horney immediately moved his team forward to support the assigned Saudi tank company. Within three minutes of arrival, Captain Horney had destroyed 5 Iraqi tanks and APCs by controlling a section of Marine AV-8s onto the enemy forces. Dismounted [enemy] infantry was forced to break and run several minutes later after Captain Horney directed numerous A-10 strafing runs, thus crumbling the Iraqi enthusiasm."[262]

Lt. Col. Cliff Myers, commanding officer of Task Force Shepherd, a reinforced U.S. Marine Light Armored Infantry Battalion, describes the fighting in the west:

I had three companies deployed: one in the vicinity of each of Observation Posts 4, 5, and 6; each company had about 30 light armored vehicles (LAVs), a kind of APC.

When the Iraqis attacked on 29 January, we saw them coming on the north-south road to Ras al-Khafji. We really didn't pick up the movement further west though, and it turns out they attacked through the border at Observation Post 4 (OP-4). Around 1800 local time, all of a sudden we detected some radio jamming—which had not happened before. At the same time, my people reported tank movements: 4 or 5, then 10, then about 50 tanks in the vicinity of OP-4. We counted those tanks with the thermal sights that were on the antitank variant of the LAV: it had a periscope that stuck up over the berm.

About three hours later they started making movements around OP-4 and were trying to break out. There was a reconnaissance team in OP-4 and they were in contact with the company that was opposite the post: Delta Company. The recon team had asked for assistance to get out of there. They had a couple of jeeps and a truck; they fired a couple of rockets at the tanks, maybe hitting one tank, and pulled back as Delta Company moved up.

By the time the company reached OP-4, the tanks were starting to come through the border, so they got into a fight that lasted several hours. They sort of repositioned a little bit to the southeast so that they could confront the enemy head on and started maneuvering as a company. I had antitank LAVs with me, and that was the only kind of weapon system in our task force that could kill tanks. The enemy tanks were T-62s and T-55s, not T-72s, so we could stand off and kill them with TOWs without coming within range of their cannon. The LAVs maneuvered dynamically, looking for the right place to take a shot, then immediately moving on to another position. We shot at the tanks and had a couple of hits with the TOW missile system, but air was the thing that really helped us that night.

We got the word back to the First Marine Division that we were under attack by tanks and called for all the air support that we could get. What happened was the airborne command post that was flying at that time was talking to us and they diverted the aircraft that were going further up north into Kuwait City and possibly to Iraq to our assistance. The initial aircraft were A-10s. Our forward air controller, Corporal Zowalick, a young man whose call sign was "Cowboy," was given all those aircraft to use. He controlled all that air that night and did a phenomenal job at the risk of his own life—he received a Bronze Star for his actions.

---

262. Citation presenting the Bronze Star Medal to Capt. Horney.

There were several tanks killed by Maverick missiles immediately. It soon looked like the Iraqis were not as aggressive as they had been when they first came through the border. Then we had the first friendly fire incident, with an A-10 dropping a Maverick on an LAV. But we continued to use the air, and by about midnight we had pretty much established a secure area and I decided to pull Delta Company back and insert another company there, so they'd have a chance to get some more ammunition and rest—they'd been fighting for nearly fours hours by then.

I moved Alpha Company up to the vicinity of OP-4. They continued to fight the enemy with the use of both Marine Corps Harrier aircraft and Air Force aircraft. There was one time about 0200 hours when Headquarters asked me what I needed. I said more air, and within a minute we had planes stacked up that we used throughout the night. At this point in time the tanks were no longer on the Saudi side of the border; those tanks that had made it through the hole had been destroyed, and we were really working on the tanks that were on the Kuwaiti side of the berm.

When daylight came (around 0500) we started using Marine Cobra helicopters, which also carry TOW missiles. That way we could relieve the other aircraft and let them continue their missions further up north. By about 1100 on 30 January it was all over: we'd destroyed about 22 tanks that night around OP-4.

The same time this was taking place at OP-4, similar things were occurring around OP-6. Charlie Company was up there and they were being attacked by tanks and vehicles. They were using air to stop that attack also. In both cases the combat multiplier for us was air.

One of the significant things that came out of that is that we learned a great deal about the Iraqis' training, morale, and state of mind. We got a lot of key indicators of what we could expect in the future. That night, for example, we captured an Iraqi lieutenant from the tanks that were attacking us. He said that as soon as we started engaging him he had sent a runner to order some BTRs and BMPs (APCs) that were about 2 kilometers back to come forward and assist them. But the people got in their BTRs and BMPs, started them up, turned them to the north, and wouldn't come and fight. This was truly a great indicator of their will and desire to fight. Little did they know that it was just LAVs that they were fighting—most any machine gun can penetrate an LAV and stop it, let alone some of the weapons that BMPs and BTRs have. They missed an opportunity, and we never gave them another one.

The LAVs are not really designed to fight tanks. We were put into a position where there was no one really right behind us except for our logistics effort, so we really had to stand and fight. It was good for our morale. It showed us a lot of deficiencies in the Iraqis, which turned into positive things for us. From some tanks that we captured, we had a good idea of the state of maintenance of the Iraqis. It was not good at that time.[263]

In the absence of official Iraqi information, we can only speculate on Iraq's motivation for launching these attacks. Possible reasons include (1) a probing attack to search for Coalition weaknesses; (2) an attempt to inflict heavy casualties on Coalition forces; (3) an attempt to seize the initiative and occupy Saudi territory; (4) an attempt to provoke the Coalition into a ground attack.[264]

---

263. Personal interview.
264. Cohen et al., *GWAPS: Summary*, p. 19.

Considering the overall numbers of men available to the two sides, the action at Ras al-Khafji can only be characterized as a minor skirmish. Nevertheless, it was a significant event. As Marine Lt. Col. William Grubb, commander of the U.S. air and artillery support liaison officers put it:

The battle of Khafji was, in my opinion, the most significant battle of the war. It proved that Coalition Arab forces could stand up to and defeat the Iraqis. After the first three hours, U.S. forces provided only air and artillery support. The counterattack was all an Arab show. It was a tremendously significant battle because that's the point where the Iraqis threw what they could at us, and they didn't even wind up fighting Americans. They wound up fighting other Arabs, and the morale of our Arab forces was really improved. Any chance the Iraqis had to win ended at Khafji. It was their best shot, and not only did it not work, it didn't even require us to commit our top of the line forces; it didn't even get us out of rhythm—we continued to shift our forces west as if nothing had happened. After this battle, it was only a matter of finding the opening and knocking them out. It was a good rehearsal for us.[265]

The outcome of a military action can be judged only in terms of the objectives it is supposed to achieve. If the objectives are achieved with reasonable losses, it is a victory. If the objectives are not achieved, or losses are excessive, it is a defeat.

The Coalition's objectives were clear: to repulse the Iraqi probes with a minimum of Coalition casualties while destroying a significant amount of Iraqi equipment. These objectives were achieved, so the Coalition's action can be characterized as a victory.

Iraq's objectives are unknown. Testing the outcome of the action against the possible Iraqi objectives listed above, we conclude that the attack might be considered a partial victory for the first objective (no Coalition weakness was found), and a defeat for all other objectives. It can only be characterized as a major defeat in terms of the third objective.[266]

On the basis of typical Iraqi tactics during the Iran-Iraq War, we are tempted to conjecture that the three probes were meant to discover weak spots in the front that could be exploited by follow-on forces. Coalition superiority was such that U.S. Marine light infantry forces, aided by air power, were able to repulse two of the probes; air power successfully prevented exploitation of the penetration to Khafji, and the entire exercise ended in a debacle for one or two Iraqi divisions. Coalition morale was boosted by these events, and no doubt Iraqi morale was further eroded.

The Marines' success at repulsing the western Iraqi probes was a tremendous achievement and one of the many untold stories of this war.

Ground action after Ras al-Khafji was limited to border skirmishes. For example, on 6 February, Coalition troops saw Iraqi trucks or troops on three

---

265. Personal interview.
266. Gordon and Trainor, *The Generals' War*, p. 287, also conclude that this event was a major defeat for Iraq.

separate occasions and shelled them.   On 10 February, an Apache helicopter destroyed a command bunker.   Skirmishes increased in frequency and intensity as the campaign continued.   Starting in mid-February, as part of the overall deception plan, the U.S. First Cavalry Division began a series of cross-border raids in the area where the Iraqi, Kuwaiti, and Saudi Arabian borders meet, in order to give the impression that the main attack would be in that area. Massive artillery raids, feints, demonstrations, and reconnaissance-in-force missions were conducted.

CONCLUSION

Iraqi troops were devastated after 38 days of bombing; the official U.S. Department of Defense report on the war says it well: "At the end of over a month of bombardment Iraqi forces remained in Kuwait; however, most were in poor condition with heavy desertions, low morale and a severely degraded capability to coordinate an effective defense." In some cases, corps, division and brigade commanders lost touch with their commands.   Stockpiles of supplies were depleted or destroyed, and the road nets over which replenishment had to pass were degraded.   Desertion rates were substantial.[267]

The actual bomb tonnage dropped on Iraqi troops in Kuwait was not extraordinarily great compared with other conflicts, but use of precision-guided munitions greatly increased the effectiveness of bombing in comparison with earlier wars.   In World War II, during the German drive on the Meuse, a 5-kilometer front was bombed for one day, with a total of 54 tons of bombs (10 tons per kilometer per day).   During the Normandy breakout by U.S. troops, an 8-kilometer front was bombed for one day with a total of 4,200 tons of bombs (525 tons/km/day).   During the Gulf War, a 250-kilometer front was bombed for 38 days, with about 1,000 tons of bombs per day (150 tons/km/day).

Lt. Curtis Palmer, an engineer with the U.S. First Infantry Division:

Most of the equipment on the ground that we encountered had already been destroyed by aircraft.   There were troops there, but they hid in their bunkers until we got there. Bunkers were not touched much by the air campaign.   But anything that was above the ground and an airplane could see, like a truck or jeep, was gone, destroyed.   The planes were thorough.   Everything had been hit, including motorcycles.   I can understand why they wouldn't go outside with A-10s swooping around.

U.S. Marine Lt. Col. Frank Kabelman, also an engineer:

The minefields that we encountered had been fairly well prepared, but unfortunately for them, that was six months before our attack.   The problem for the Iraqis was that the defenses had not been maintained well: I could see some of the mines and I could tell that engineers had not been in the minefields making sure that they were relatively

---

267. U.S. Department of Defense, *Conduct of the Persian Gulf War*, p. 190.

invisible. There wasn't a lot of maintenance done, and that's possibly because of the air campaign. You don't want to be out there working in the minefields with A-10s hovering over your head. Fortifications in that kind of soil are very difficult to maintain. With the wind blowing, ditches get filled in pretty quick, berms get cut down. The air played a big part in keeping them from being able to maintain those barriers.

Sgt. Ricky Wheeling of the U.S. First Armored Division, referring to prisoners taken on the front lines:

We had a 30 minute artillery barrage, and the next thing we knew you could see what looked like little ants coming out of the sand. Some 200 POWs came walking up to us. Their weapons were broken: the stocks were taped together; they had socks wrapped around their feet because their boots were worn out. Those that spoke English told us that they had had nothing to eat for the past three weeks except for a loaf of bread and three onions. If they had been fed and well supplied, we might still be there fighting, because there was no way we could see their positions in the sand. We ran over places with our tracks and didn't even know it was a foxhole until we were on top of it. Guys in there with RPGs [rocket-propelled grenades] and the will to fight could have caused a lot of casualties.

An Iraqi general taken prisoner:

During the Iran war, my tank was my friend because I could sleep in it and know that I was safe. During this war my tank became my enemy: none of my troops would get near a tank at night because they just kept blowing up.

Another captured officer: "I surrendered because of the B-52 strikes." "But your position was never attacked by B-52s," exclaimed the interrogator. "That is true," replied the prisoner, "but I saw one that had been attacked." A division commander: "You know why our men gave up. It was the airplanes."[268]

The Coalition's air supremacy denied Iraq any reconnaissance capability. Thus the ground forces assembled behind the front lines were able to perform a massive undetected redeployment, moving far left in order to prepare an outflanking maneuver that apparently was not expected by the Iraqis.

In addition Coalition ground attack aircraft and counterbattery fire had wreaked havoc on Iraqi artillery, leaving it powerless to deliver mass fire against advancing troops.

---

268. Personal interviews with the cited U.S. soldiers; and U.S. Department of the Air Force, *Reaching Globally, Reaching Powerfully*, pp. 38 and 43 for the Iraqi quotes.

7

Political Reactions: Day 2 to 38

He whose generals are able and not interfered with by the sovereign will be victorious.

—Sun Tzu

POLITICAL REACTIONS IN WESTERN COUNTRIES

Popular support for the Coalition's military offensive ran high in Western countries, as measured by public opinion polls.[269] It appears that the U.S. president and other Coalition leaders had convinced a substantial majority of their citizenry that Operation Desert Storm was indeed, to use another phrase of the Bush Administration, a "Just Cause" (the name assigned to the invasion of Panama).

However, public opinion ran across a broad spectrum: in the U.K., support for the war was even stronger than in the United States; in Germany, opposition to the war was quite strong; most other nations were somewhere in between these two extremes. The pacifist movement never had any effect on the policies of Western governments, most of whose leaders continued to make uncompromising statements. Nor did the Gulf War cause any economic hardships in the West.

In conjunction with the beginning of military operations, Western governments conducted an intense campaign on the political front, in order to ensure the continued support of a large portion of the public. President Bush appeared on television just after the beginning of the Coalition air strikes,

---

269. Taylor, *War and the Media*, pp. 48, 75, 129, 135.

explaining to the American people his decision to initiate hostilities because economic and diplomatic means had not succeeded in modifying Iraq's intransigent position in spite of five and a half months of intense international efforts. In Europe, the foreign ministers of the European Economic Community met in an emergency session on 17 January. In addition to repeating a call for Iraq to withdraw immediately from Kuwait, in order to avoid further suffering for the Iraqi people, the ministers expressed support for the French proposals for an international Middle East peace conference.

The Iraqi SCUD missile attack against Israel on 18 January provoked a series of lively pro-Coalition reactions and contributed to a significant improvement of the Jewish state's image in many Western capitals, an improvement reinforced by the Israeli government's decision to forgo immediate retaliation.

But the outbreak of war did highlight differences that had been present for some time within several governments, European ones in particular, regarding the objectives and final goals of the military intervention against Iraq. French Minister of Defense Chevenement, who had consistently taken a position different from that of French President Mitterand regarding the crisis and the role that should be played by French military forces during the conflict, resigned on 29 January, declaring that "the logic of war is driving us ever further from the objectives established by the United Nations." In Italy, apart from the clear antiwar position taken by the pope, Minister of Foreign Affairs De Michelis took pains to distance himself from the Anglo-American call for the destruction of Iraq's military potential, thus exposing a certain ambiguity in the foreign policy of a country that, while it participated in military operations, later did not hesitate to support various Soviet peace initiatives.

Indeed, concern that the U.S.-led military operations might go far beyond the U.N. mandate was clearly present also in the minds of the Soviet leaders. On 26 January, just before leaving Moscow for Washington in order to meet Bush and Baker, Alexander Bessmertnykh, the newly appointed foreign minister, after reaffirming the USSR's commitment to support the U.N. resolutions against Iraq, stated: "I am concerned there may be a danger of the conflict going more in the direction of the destruction of Iraq, which was not in the spirit of the U.N. resolutions." Three days later, Vitali Ignatenko, Gorbachev's spokesman, restated the Soviet concern that the conflict might go well beyond the original objective of liberating Kuwait and announced a peace initiative similar to the one that several Coalition countries had proposed, without success, at the United Nations.

On 4 February, during a plenary session of the Communist Party's Central Committee, General Secretary Gorbachev was asked to take "the necessary additional steps before the international community and the U.N. to end the bloodshed." This was the prelude to a series of Soviet initiatives that resulted in the arrival on 11 February in Baghdad of Yevgeni Primakov, Gorbachev's special envoy. Primakov was well versed in Middle Eastern issues and knew

Saddam Hussein well; he had traveled to Baghdad in October of 1990 as part of a series of USSR attempts to find a negotiated solution to the crisis.[270]

However, public opinion in most Western countries was substantially in favor of a continuation of the war, particularly after the third week of hostilities. In Germany, France, Italy, the U.K., and above all the United States, polls showed a strong alignment of public opinion and government policy.

POLITICAL REACTIONS IN ARAB COUNTRIES AND IRAN

Some 24 hours after the beginning of hostilities, the first Iraqi SCUD missiles landed in Israel. After months of more or less veiled threats, the Iraqi leaders kept their promise to attack the Jewish state as a reprisal against a Coalition attack on their territory. Saddam Hussein clearly hoped that an Israeli retaliation would lead to divisions within the Coalition, the withdrawal of Arab forces from the Coalition, and, perhaps, Iranian intervention.

The damage caused by the first Iraqi SCUDs was limited: a few people were wounded and some buildings destroyed, but the news that an Arab state had finally managed to strike at the very heart of Israel was greeted with joy by the populations of many Arab states. Official reactions of Arab governments varied, with the Coalition members taking a low or even anti-Iraq profile, thus providing one more example of the split that has often existed between the sentiments of Arab populations and the actions of their governments. The Saudi Arabian media ignored or minimized the Iraqi attack against Israel. Egypt and Syria stressed that the attack on Israel did not affect their positions, thus signaling the failure of the Iraqi attempt to divide the Coalition by creating an Arab-Israeli conflict, even before Israel's policy of restraint rendered the question moot.

In Algeria, where support for Saddam Hussein was strongest, large anti-Western demonstrations were organized right after the start of war. In Jordan, at one or two critical moments there was some concern that King Hussein might lose control of the country. The heavy Coalition bombing of targets deep within Iraq surprised and outraged the Jordanian population, who had perhaps expected a straightforward Coalition advance into Kuwait. But the moral support for Iraq expressed in North Africa, Jordan, and the Occupied Territories remained at the verbal level and had no effect on either the military or the political fronts.

In contrast, Iran emerged as a political force of considerable importance. While primarily protecting Iran's economic and political interests, and always taking an anti-American attitude, the Iranian leaders maintained a position delicately balanced between the two contending sides. Iran prevented Iraqi planes that landed on its territory from flying again, and encouraged the provision of medical aid and food supplies meant to alleviate the hardships

---

270. Primakov, *Missione a Baghdad*.

suffered by Iraqi civilians. In addition, Iran favored a negotiated solution to the conflict, making concrete proposals for a cease-fire at the beginning of February.

Thus Iran and the USSR were, albeit for different reasons, the most active nations in the diplomatic arena.

POLITICAL REACTIONS IN IRAQ

Reliable information on public opinion in Iraq is extremely hard to obtain. Apparently a majority of the population was pleased when Kuwait was annexed, since they viewed its sheiks as corrupt, decadent spendthrifts and since they expected to benefit from Kuwait's riches. Popular support may have wavered once bombs started falling on Baghdad: Saddam Hussein's late-February announcements of withdrawal were greeted with spontaneous outbursts of joy, such as firing guns in the air (a traditional Iraqi expression of happiness). Reports given by Iraqi prisoners of war have to be taken with a grain of salt, since they may have said what they thought their captors wanted to hear. For what their testimony is worth, many POWs who were conscripts said that they thought the invasion of Kuwait was wrong, and that they had no idea why they were occupying it.[271] On the whole, it is clear that the Iraqi population did not have a determined will to hang on to Kuwait. Coalition military leaders noted repeatedly that the Iraqi soldiers had poor morale and showed little will to fight.

Once hostilities started, Iraq's political objective was undoubtedly to split the Coalition by exploiting dissensions within Western nations and the long-standing hostility of Arabs toward Israel. But attempts to exploit Western peace movements failed miserably for at least three reasons: Iraq's bellicose rhetoric, SCUD attacks on Israel, and public display of brutalized POWs. Attempts to bring Israel into the war in the hope that this would drive out the Coalition's Arab members also failed.

On 15 February Iraq made a proposal that was a restatement of its prewar position—with new demands added. It announced its willingness to withdraw from Kuwait in compliance with Resolution 660, but under the following conditions: that all remaining U.N. Security Council resolutions be abrogated; that Coalition troops simultaneously withdraw from Saudi Arabia; that Israel withdraw from the Occupied Territories; that Iraq's historical territorial claims be guaranteed; that a new form of government be considered for Kuwait; that Coalition nations pay war reparations to Iraq; and that all Iraq's foreign debts to Western and Gulf countries be forgiven.[272] These were conditions that could have been dictated by a winner, not proposed by a loser.

Western political leaders quickly rejected Iraq's conditions, with U.S. President Bush characterizing the Iraqi proposal as "a cruel hoax" and going so

---

271. Personal interviews with U.S. troops who captured Iraqi POWs.
272. United Nations, *Iraq-Kuwait Conflict*, p. 27.

far as to call for the overthrow of Saddam Hussein. A few days after this proposal, Foreign Minister Tarik Aziz began a series of trips to Moscow. The main purpose of this shuttle diplomacy appears to have been to attempt to obtain a negotiated settlement whose conditions were less harsh than unconditional withdrawal. In addition, this effort may have been intended to delay what appeared to be an imminent ground attack.

SOVIET PEACE PROPOSALS

On the other hand, efforts to mediate the conflict and bring it to an end appeared to become necessary also for Gorbachev, who was coming under increasing pressure from Communist Party hard-liners and Red Army officers for having essentially abandoned a key Soviet ally in the Middle East (as Saddam Hussein's Iraq had been since the 1970s) and for having permitted large U.S. military forces to deploy within a few hundred kilometers of the USSR's borders. Thus, when Aziz reached Moscow, he found the Soviet president ready to act as a mediator.

On 18 February, Aziz flew back to Baghdad, carrying a peace proposal from Gorbachev. The contents of this proposal were not made public. It seems safe to assume that the Soviet peace proposal irritated U.S. leaders because, if it had been accepted, it could have supplied Saddam Hussein with a face-saving diplomatic way out of the conflict before the Coalition ground forces could administer the coup de grace to the badly weakened Iraqi army. Indeed, General Schwarzkopf recounts in his autobiography that he came under some pressure not to delay the ground attack past the initially planned date of 21 February, in order to avoid giving the Soviets and the Iraqis more time to work out a deal.[273] On 19 February, Bush rejected the proposal, on the ground that it was inconsistent with the Coalition's objectives.

Nonetheless Italian and German political figures made statements supporting the Soviet proposal, actions indicating that it had the potential to undermine the Coalition's cohesion. But Saddam Hussein rejected the first Soviet proposal in an aggressive speech on 21 February, thus ensuring that the Coalition would remain solid.

But just a few hours later, Gorbachev's spokesman Ignatenko confidently announced Iraq's acceptance of a new Soviet peace plan. It seemed that the USSR was determined to play a key role in resolving the crisis. Indeed, Aziz had returned to Moscow, where on 21 February he accepted a plan whose main points were: unconditional Iraqi withdrawal from Kuwait; no linkage between withdrawal and other issues; Coalition POWs to be released immediately; U.N. economic sanctions to be lifted after the Iraqi withdrawal was two-thirds completed; no explicit Iraqi recognition of Kuwaiti independence; no acceptance by Iraq of its obligation to pay war reparations; no explicit timetable for withdrawal.

---

273. Schwarzkopf, *It Doesn't Take a Hero*, p. 443.

Aziz's acceptance of this proposal is a convincing argument that the air campaign had been effective—up until then Iraq had steadfastly refused to withdraw unless its move were linked to other issues. We can speculate that the Soviet proposal might have been accepted by Western leaders before the 15 January deadline, but, given the reality of the military situation, it was too little, too late after more than a month of war. The hawks in the Coalition were undoubtedly relieved that Saddam Hussein did not himself announce acceptance of the plan, thus missing a chance to introduce some political divisions within the Coalition. Aziz and the leaders in Moscow continued negotiations and, during a press conference on 22 February, a new plan was announced: unconditional withdrawal to start on an unspecified date and to be completed within 21 days; the evacuation of Kuwait City within 4 days; immediate release of Coalition POWs; abrogation of the U.N. resolutions upon completion of the withdrawal; and creation of a neutral interposition force to supervise the withdrawal. The Soviet spokesman noted that the plan had not yet been approved by the leadership in Baghdad and that its terms were subject to negotiation with the Coalition; he also made the point that his country was part of the international community dedicated to upholding U.N. resolutions.

It is difficult to avoid expressing admiration for the extraordinary political moves that Gorbachev made when he presented his peace plans. These moves, albeit unsuccessful, were arguably the most ingenious and brilliant diplomatic initiatives of the Gulf crisis. With these well-crafted proposals, Gorbachev attempted to counter the patient diplomatic efforts of Bush—efforts that had resulted in the creation of the Coalition and its decision to wage war to liberate Kuwait—and to reassert the USSR's role as a superpower, entitled to influence the course of events, even if it had not participated militarily. But in reality the proposals were the swan song of Soviet foreign policy—both in the Middle East and as a superpower. It would have required far more moral and military resources than those then available to the USSR—already in the terminal stages of the economic, political, and strategic decline that resulted in its demise—in order to deny the United States the advantages that its leaders foresaw in a decisive victory that was by then within reach.

Bush's reply to the Soviet proposal was another political masterpiece. On 22 February, he thanked the Soviets for their efforts, accused Saddam Hussein of having started a scorched-earth policy, and stated the Coalition ultimatum for a cease-fire: immediate and unconditional withdrawal from Kuwait, beginning no later than 1200 EST on 23 February and completed within 7 days; a public statement by Saddam Hussein accepting these terms; the evacuation of Kuwait City and the liberation of all Coalition POWs within 48 hours; and Iraqi assistance in clearing minefields. Bush thus regained the initiative on the political front and imposed conditions that, if accepted, would have meant a clear political and propaganda defeat for Iraq. Objectively, the Soviet proposals differed little from Bush's demands, but by this time Coalition military forces were ready to start their ground attack; furthermore, the Coalition's political leaders insisted that all U.N. resolutions had to be accepted by Iraq, thus refusing any compromise that called for abrogation of the resolutions.

But Iraq did not make any attempts to start a withdrawal and signalled its defiance by launching SCUD missiles on Tel Aviv just as the ultimatum expired. Last-minute attempts by Gorbachev to postpone a ground attack were of no avail; the USSR announced that, while it regretted such an attack, it did not condemn it. Iran also declared that Iraq should have given a practical sign of acceptance of the terms by initiating a withdrawal, and indicated that it would continue to remain neutral. The Coalition thus had a green light to start the last phase of its campaign: the land battle.

8

The Land Battle: 100 Hours

Everything is very simple in war, but the simplest thing is difficult.

—Carl von Clausewitz

Coalition forces launched a massive ground assault on Iraqi positions at 0100 GMT on 24 February. The offensive was completely successful and Coalition forces ceased hostilities at 0500 GMT on 28 February, by which time all of Kuwait had been liberated, the southern third of Iraq had been occupied, and the capability of the Iraqis to threaten other countries had been eliminated.

A battle involving hundreds of thousands of people is an extremely complex event; it can be viewed and described from many vantage points. There is a great deal of motion and confusion in any battle: plans change and people are under stress, get temporarily lost, and encounter unexpected enemies. Division commanders, battalion commanders, company commanders, and private soldiers receive different information, see different things, and live different battles. Some units see strenuous action, others don't. A huge amount of information can be collected from official accounts and personal interviews: to describe a battle it is necessary to winnow the information, summarize it, and simplify it—processes that can lead to distortions. The available facts are filtered through the writer's mind; hence no description can claim to be infallibly objective and impartial. Thus it is unlikely that there will ever be a definitive account of this battle, any more than there has ever been a definitive account of such classic battles as Waterloo.[274]

---

274. For an in-depth discussion of the difficulty of reporting a battle, see John Keegan, *The Face of Battle* (Penguin, 1978).

In fact there were really two rather distinct components to the 100-hour land battle. U.S. Marines and Joint Arab Forces-East advancing into Kuwait faced fairly well prepared field fortifications manned by Iraqi troops who made some initial attempts to resist the Coalition advance. Joint Arab Forces-North advancing into Kuwait encountered very light resistance. French, U.K., and U.S. Army forces advancing along the left flank into Iraq faced very poorly prepared field fortifications and troops offering practically no resistance to the initial advance. While the U.S. Marines and Joint Arab Forces-East faced Iraqi troops who quickly dispersed, so that resistance lessened as the Coalition advanced into Kuwait, the opposite was true of the U.S. Army units advancing on the left: they encountered stiff resistance from Republican Guard units during the last two days of the ground battle. Thus radically different pictures of events can be given, depending on which geographical area and which day are emphasized.

It is our intent to describe the battle from two points of view: that of the detached observer who sees events in their entirety and in hindsight, and that of the individual soldier who participated in specific actions. We do not claim to have identified all the units that participated in hard fighting. Our set of descriptions can be considered a somewhat random sample of individual experiences, one that attempts to provide a cross section of what real soldiers saw and lived through.

We start our description of the Gulf War's 100 hours of ground combat with the living conditions and events just prior to the assault.[275]

LIVING CONDITIONS

Ever since World War II, the U.S. armed forces have had the reputation of providing more equipment and logistical support to its troops than other armies. In line with this reputation, U.S. troops in the Gulf were well provided for: in addition to essentials like food and water (eight liters or more per day per person), soldiers received sunglasses, sun cream, lip salve, and even antiperspirant lotion for feet. U.S. Chief Warrant Officer (CWO) Wes Wolfe worked with the principal Saudi food contractor, Zahir Masri, to set up mobile mess halls serving pizzas, hot dogs, hamburgers, and french fries. The burgers were dubbed "wolfburgers" and the mess halls "wolfmobiles." Considerable attention was paid to preventive medicine, such as food and water sanitation, insect control, and avoidance of heat stress. Two sets of desert uniforms were available for every combatant by the end of February; for the entire force, there were 390,000 pairs of desert boots—with 1.4 million on order by 20 February, just in case. Contracts for the extra boots were worth $63 million, and the United States spent nearly $1 billion on clothing alone. Hundreds of thousands of photo image maps and 116 million map copies were

275. The following account is based on personal interviews with Coalition soldiers cited elsewhere in this book.

produced. The cruise ship *Cunard Princess* was used to provide rest-and-recuperation tours, and commercial vendors of telecommunications services offered a variety of popular services (such as phone calls to the United States).

Living conditions on the front lines, however, were not luxurious, since the forces slept in bunkers dug out of the sand and ate MRE rations (officially called "meals ready to eat," a name that some soldiers characterize as three separate lies). In the words of one Egyptian soldier: "We tried them the first night. I don't know how the American soldiers eat them."

In contrast, the French Foreign Legion made it a point to live up to its country's reputation for fine food and wine. Officers ate freshly cooked food served on porcelain dishes and drank wine out of crystal glasses. The lunch menu on 18 February: boiled potatoes, pheasant paté, duck liver, Emmenthal cheese, and goat's cheese; dinner: tuna, hare paté, duck paté with green peppercorns. Moreover, the harsh desert of the Gulf region was considered almost a playground by the Legionnaires, many of whom had been on campaign in tropical regions, where for many days troops slog through jungles on foot, carrying all their supplies.

But the most luxurious living conditions were probably those of the 8,000-strong Kuwaiti contingent: spacious tents, uniforms washed daily, sheep and rice and fresh fruit prepared by Egyptian cooks—all forming an interesting contrast to the U.S. living conditions.

U.S. troops, however, were unique in one respect: about 7 percent of them were women (30,000 Army, 4,700 Navy, 4,000 Air Force, and 1,200 Marine).[276] Women held such assignments as administrators, air traffic controllers, logisticians, mechanics, technicians, security guards, truck drivers, and pilots. A number of women commanded brigade, battalion, company, and platoon-sized units.

Living conditions in the frontline Iraqi trenches were quite different. Continual bombing rendered sleep difficult, if not impossible, and disrupted supply lines to the point that some soldiers received less than one liter of water per day and were not fed every day. It would appear reasonable to assume that many Iraqi soldiers were affected by illness and disease.

THE OPPOSING FORCES

Coalition ground strength was around 575,000 soldiers organized primarily in 14 divisions and 10 brigades (counting U.S. armored cavalry regiments as brigades), with about 3,700 tanks and 1,500 artillery pieces.[277] At the time, Iraqi strength was estimated at 43 divisions and 6 brigades, comprising

---

276. Cohen et al., *GWAPS: Support*, p. 126.

277. Cohen et al., *GWAPS: Statistical Compendium*, Table 14, p. 51, shows U.S. Army and Marines at 390,691. Adding other ground forces (from Table 4.2) and subtracting for Marine aviators and Marines positioned on ships gives a total ground force of about 575,000.

540,000 men, 4,200 tanks, 2,800 APCs, and 3,100 artillery pieces.[278] Map
8.1 shows the disposition of forces in mid-January.[279]

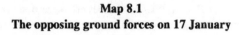

Map 8.1
The opposing ground forces on 17 January

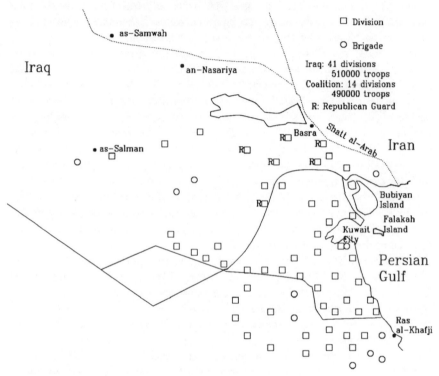

However, many Iraqi divisions were below nominal strength when they first
deployed, and were further weakened by desertions before the war started. It
is likely that only about 336,000 Iraqis were present in the theater on 15
January, with some 3,500 tanks and 2,500 artillery pieces.[280]

---

278. Cohen et al., *GWAPS: Summary Report*, p. 8. Subsequent estimates are 41
divisions and 4 brigades: Scales, *Certain Victory*, p. 161.

279. Different sources show different dispositions. This map and the subsequent
ones are based on Scales, *Certain Victory*, p. 161; and Cohen et al., *GWAPS: Effects
and Effectiveness*, p. 164.

280. Cohen et al., *GWAPS: Summary*, p. 10, and *GWAPS: Effects and
Effectiveness*, pp. 166-170.

Desertions after the air campaign started are estimated at about 25-30%;[281] deaths from air attacks were between 1% and 6%;[282] total casualties during the air campaign are estimated at 10% (about 11,000 dead and 23,000 wounded).[283]

Map 8.2
Relative ground-unit strength on 23 February

Thus by 23 February Iraqi forces had been reduced to approximately 220,000 men and the Coalition had about a 2.5 to 1 numerical advantage on

---

281. Cohen et al., *GWAPS: Summary*, p. 107.

282. Reports by captured Iraqi senior officers; see Les Aspin and William Dickinson, *Defense for a New Era: Lessons of the Persian Gulf War* (U.S. House of Representatives, Committee on Armed Services, 1992), p. 32. Losses reported by captured officers for four divisions and two brigades are about 5 percent killed and 5 percent wounded; see Gordon and Trainor, *The General's War*, p. 352.

283. Cohen et al., *GWAPS: Summary,* p. 107 and 249 footnote 19; and *GWAPS: Effects and Effectiveness,* p. 220. But a lower rate is proposed by John Heidenreich, "The Gulf War: How Many Iraqis Died," *Foreign Policy,* no. 90 (Spring 1993), p. 117, who gives ranges of 700 to 3,000 dead and 2,000 to 7,000 wounded.

the ground. Iraq had perhaps 60,000 men along the front lines, 60,000 defending the coast, 25,000 around Kuwait City, 15,000 along the east-west part of the Iraq-Kuwait border, and 60,000 Republican Guards in the north.[284]

The air campaign had reduced Iraqi equipment to some 1,700 tanks and 1,000 artillery pieces, respectively half and two-thirds of the Coalition levels. Considering the technological superiority of Coalition tanks and artillery, the Coalition possessed a very significant superiority in force when the ground attack was launched. At that time, the strength of Iraq's frontline troops had been reduced by approximately 50 percent, that of the second echelon by about 25 percent, while the Republican Guards in the rear remained relatively intact. U.S. plans assumed that VII Corps would have an advantage of 11 to 1 at the breach site and 2 to 1 when it encountered the Republican Guard.[285] Map 8.2 illustrates this situation.

Coalition ground forces were organized into five major groups. From left to right, the principal units were:

1. XVIII Airborne Corps: French Sixth Armored Division, U.S. 82nd and 101st Airborne Divisions, 24th Mechanized Division, U.S. Third Armored Cavalry Regiment, 12th and 18th Aviation Brigades (armored cavalry regiments are nearly brigade-strength; aviation brigades are ground-attack helicopter units).
2. VII Corps: U.S. First Armored Division, Second Armored Cavalry Regiment, 11th Aviation Brigade, Third Armored, First Infantry, and U.K. First Armored Divisions, U.S. First Cavalry Division. This corps had over 1,400 tanks and 1,200 Bradley APCs.[286]
3. Joint Arab Forces-North: Egyptian Third Mechanized and Fourth Armored Divisions, Syrian Ninth Armored Division, Egyptian Ranger Regiment, Syrian 45th Commando Regiment, Saudi 20th Mechanized Brigade, Kuwaiti Shaheed and al-Tahrir Brigades, Saudi Fourth Armored Brigade.
4. I Marine Expeditionary Force: U.S. First and Second Marine Divisions, plus the U.S. Army's First (Tiger) Brigade of Second Armored Division.
5. Joint Arab Forces-East: Saudi Tenth Infantry Brigade, UAE Motorized Infantry Battalion, Omani Motorized Infantry Battalion, Saudi Eighth Mechanized Infantry Brigade, Bahrain Infantry Company, Kuwaiti al-Fatah Brigade, Saudi Second National Guard Motorized Infantry Brigade, Qatar Mechanized Battalion.

The composition of individual units varied a great deal. In general, a U.S. armored division had about 350 tanks, a comparable number of APCs, 72 guns, 8 MLRS launchers, and 42 helicopter gunships (AH-64 Apache). An armored cavalry regiment had about 125 tanks, a comparable number of APCs, 24 guns, and over 20 helicopters. A mechanized infantry division had about 230 tanks, about 360 APCs, 72 guns, 8 MLRS, and 21 helicopter gunships. Each corps had additional artillery and MLRS. Some units were heavily reinforced. For example, the U.S. 24th Infantry Division (Mechanized) had

---

284. Authors' estimates.
285. Swain, *"Lucky War,"* p. 106.
286. The Bradley is more properly called an IFV. (See the Glossary).

26,000 soldiers, 249 M1A1 tanks, 218 Bradley APCs, 843 M113 APCs, 90 helicopters (including 18 Apaches), 114 guns, and 36 MLRS launchers.

A full-strength Iraqi armored division had about 300 tanks (400 for Republican Guards), 250 APCs, and 84 artillery pieces. Mechanized divisions had about 220 tanks, 250 APCs, and 84 guns. Infantry divisions had about 44 tanks, 50 APCs, and 54 guns. Of the 43 Iraqi divisions deployed in the theater of operations, 31 were infantry, 8 were armored, and 4 were mechanized infantry. An additional 2 armored brigades were also present. Of the divisions, 8 were Republican Guards, of which 2 were armored and 1 was mechanized.

COALITION STRATEGY

The strategy used by the Coalition for the ground attack can be summarized in two words: "distraction" and "outflanking." Distraction consists in acting in such a way that the enemy cannot concentrate his forces against the planned attack by drawing his attention to the wrong place. It is often the key to concentrating against weakness on the offensive. Distraction was provided by U.S. Navy and Marine maneuvers threatening an amphibious landing on the coast of Kuwait, by Joint Arab Forces and U.S. Marines actually making ground attacks not far from the coast, and by the First Cavalry Division conducting a feint attack in the area where the borders of Kuwait, Iraq, and Saudi Arabia meet. These ground attacks were meant to fix Iraqi forces in position, preventing them from detecting the outflanking maneuver of the Coalition left wing and from redeploying to meet it. They were also intended to create surprise by focusing Iraqi attention on a frontal assault in Kuwait while other Coalition forces prepared for a flanking attack in Iraq. In summary, we can say that the intent of Coalition planners was for the U.S. Marines and Joint Arab Forces to gain the attention of the Iraqi commanders in Kuwait, convince them that the main attack was coming north along the Kuwait border, and therefore gain an element of strategic surprise in the west, where VII Corps would attack.

Iraqi defenses against an amphibious assault were extensive, with some reports suggesting that they were more formidable than those encountered by U.S. Marines during World War II. In the end, U.S. commanders felt that an amphibious assault ran the risk of incurring high casualties, so although plans were ready, it was decided not to launch an amphibious attack in the early stages of the ground war.

Napoleon once said: "The nature of strategy consists of always having, even with a weaker army, more forces at the point of attack or the point where one is attacked than the enemy has."[287] This principle provided guidance for the

---

287. Quoted in Hans Delbruck, trans. Walter J. Renfroe, Jr., *History of the Art of War Within the Framework of Political History*, vol. 4, *The Modern Era* (Greenwood Press, 1985), p. 428.

Iraqi defense as well as for the Coalition attack: the Iraqis fortified their front line and the Kuwaiti coast.

For assailing weakness, the Coalition followed the traditional rule: if the defenders are well concentrated (the Iraqi situation), the flank is the weak point. In this case, the western flank, because the coast was fortified. Ideally, the force going around the western flank would have aimed at reaching the rear of the whole Iraqi force, cutting it off from its base, thus compelling it to capitulate when it found it impossible to fight its way through the Coalition forces in its rear. This would have been a classical turning movement and envelopment.

Although the Coalition's plan has sometimes been described as a turning movement[288] and primary sources describe the Coalition plan as an envelopment,[289] we have seen no indication that a true envelopment of all Iraqi forces was ever planned, or perhaps even considered.

Indeed, several factors prevented such a decisive move. A true envelopment of all Iraqi forces would have required Coalition troops to cross the Euphrates River north of an-Nasariya, then turn east, advancing to within 30 kilometers of the Iranian border before moving south to Basra. Such a movement, if considered, was no doubt ruled out on both political and military grounds. On the political side, deployment of Coalition troops so near Iran might have provoked its entry into the war. On the military side, the marshy nature of the terrain south of the Euphrates effectively protected the Iraqi rear from ground attack, and the deep penetration into Iraq would have required additional forces in order to prevent the Republican Guard in the north from moving west and cutting the enveloping forces' supply lines.

What was planned, and in fact executed, was to send a powerful Anglo-American armored force (VII Corps) through the weak western part of the Iraqi line. This had the objective of reaching the rear of the forward Iraqi forces in Kuwait and of assailing them on their flank (carried out by the U.K. First Armored Division), and of attacking the deep reserve provided by the Republican Guard (carried out by the U.S. First and Third Armored Divisions, and Second Armored Cavalry Regiment).[290]

As Richard Swain convincingly argues,[291] the Coalition plan was a compromise—as was the AirLand doctrine on which it was based—between two concepts of military operations: the indirect approach, which sought to win with a minimum of firepower by maneuvering to surround the enemy; and

---

288. For example Swain, *"Lucky War,"* p. 88.

289. U.S. Department of Defense, *Conduct of the Persian Gulf War*, p. 315; Schwarzkopf, *It Doesn't Take a Hero*, pp. 362, 366, 382; Scales, *Certain Victory*, pp. 129-130, 138-140.

290. U.S. Department of Defense, *Conduct of the Persian Gulf War*, p. 315; Schwarzkopf, *It Doesn't Take a Hero*, p. 383; Scales, *Certain Victory*, pp. 148-149; Swain, *"Lucky War,"* pp. 73, 77, 83, 88, 92.

291. Swain, *"Lucky War,"* pp. 72-73.

the direct approach which sought to overcome the enemy with superior firepower, to be achieved through maneuver and concentration against weakness.

Map 8.3 shows the outline of the Coalition's planned ground attack, together with the sectors assigned to each of the Coalition's main ground units.

Map 8.3
The Coalition ground attack

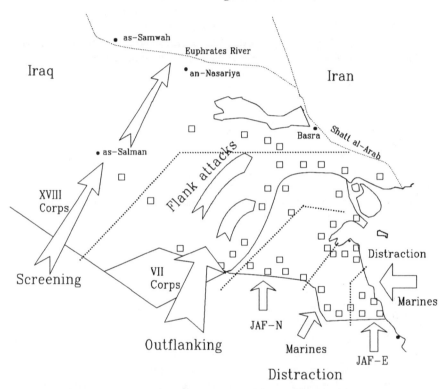

Prior to the VII Corps attack, further west of the opposing armies, Franco-American airborne and armored forces (XVIII Corps) would pass completely around the Iraqi flank, go north towards the Euphrates, and screen all the other forces advancing around the flank from any interference from Iraqi troops coming from the west or northwest. Some elements of XVIII Corps (French forces and U.S. airborne forces) had primarily a screening role: to prevent Iraqi forces in the north from moving south to reinforce the troops deployed in the theater of operations. Other elements (the U.S. 24th Infantry Division (Mechanized)) had the role of penetrating far into Iraq to attack the rearmost Iraqi divisions. The remaining elements (U.S. Third Armored Cavalry

Regiment) had the mission of protecting the left flank of the main maneuver carried out by VII Corps.

As the attack developed, it became evident that the Iraqi forces were actually everywhere weak, except in the rear, just south of the Euphrates, where the Republican Guard had some success in fulfilling an often ridiculed mission for a reserve: to cover a retreat in case of defeat.

The initial distraction provided by Joint Arab, U.K., and U.S. Army and Marine armored forces turned into breakthroughs when they pierced the front in several places. The Coalition plan called for the main breakthrough to be performed by VII Corps on the right flank of the Iraqi lines, while the direct attack at the center and left by Joint Arab Forces and the U.S. Marines was primarily meant to fix Iraqi forces in place, to prevent them from redeploying to stymie VII Corps' turning movement. The mission statement for Joint Arab Forces and the U.S. Marines was:

To hold the enemy's tactical and operational forces in place by breaching the Iraqi defenses in Kuwait and encircling Iraqi forces in the southern part of Kuwait and in Kuwait City. U.S. Marine forces would destroy enemy forces and seize key objectives southeast of al-Jahra, while protecting the right flank of Joint Arab Forces-North. Meanwhile, U.S. Navy and Marine forces in the Gulf would create a deception through amphibious exercises and feints before and during the ground offensive. The specific mission of I Marine Expeditionary Force was to attack into Kuwait west of al-Wafra to hold and destroy Iraqi forces to their front, hold Iraqi tactical and operational reserves to prevent reinforcement of Iraqi forces in the west, block the retreat of Iraqi forces from southeast Kuwait and Kuwait City, and help Arab forces enter Kuwait City.[292]

As events unfolded, the Iraqi resistance in Kuwait crumbled rapidly, and the U.S. Marines and Joint Arab Forces quickly advanced right up to Kuwait City, thus providing an additional breakthrough.

In order to maintain momentum and exploit Iraqi weakness, the Coalition command allowed generals in the field considerable latitude in modifying plans. However, even though Coalition tactical plans were modified quickly during the course of the fighting (by some accounts at least five times), the actual ground attack differed little from the planned attack: the main difference resulted from the overwhelming initial success, which allowed the plan to be accelerated. The plan anticipated that U.S. Marines would reach Kuwait City three days after the start of the ground attack (which they did), but that Arab forces would require a few more days to liberate the city. In fact no additional fighting took place.[293]

Central Command planners had initially considered a plan for a frontal night attack directly north, toward Mutla Pass northwest of Kuwait City, but had not

---

292. This detailed statement was provided at our request by the Office of the Commandant, U.S. Marine Corps.

293. Cohen et al., *GWAPS: Planning*, Figure 2, p. 8.

recommended it. In early September, Central Command had developed a plan calling for an outflanking maneuver through the western desert, and on 6 October, General Schwarzkopf requested additional armored forces to carry it out. The one-corps frontal attack plan was presented to U.S. President Bush, Secretary of Defense Cheney, and General Powell on 11 October. It was pointed out that this plan entailed a risk of high casualties. Cheney then directed efforts to focus on preparing an attack through the western desert.

On 15 October, General Schwarzkopf ordered his planners to start refining this concept, which would require an additional army corps to conduct the flank attack. On 22 October, in Riyadh, the new two-corps plan was presented to General Powell who approved it. On December 19 and 20, the plans were reviewed by Cheney and Powell in Riyadh, approved by Cheney, and later approved by Bush once again. However, the actual start of the ground attack required Bush's specific approval, which was given in February.[294]

The general idea of the Coalition's ground attack plan was not particularly original. What is admirable about it is not its general outline, but the meticulous attention to detail with which it was put together and executed, and its painstaking adherence to the tactical realities: the strengths and weaknesses of both sides. One example of attention to detail and good knowledge of the military realities is provided by the Coalition's building, well before hostilities started, enough facilities to house 100,000 prisoners of war. These facilities were later used; had they not been planned and built, it would have been difficult to deal with the large number of surrendering Iraqi soldiers. More broadly, it is one thing to conceive of a a flank attack and quite another to pick out the exact terrain favorable to the movement, to marshal the right units in the right places at the right time, and to adapt the plan to unforeseen events.

Successful execution of the Coalition's plan, which called for low Coalition casualties, had two prerequisites. First, Iraqi strength had to be significantly reduced, particularly in the front lines. This reduction was accomplished by the aerial campaign against dug-in troops. Second, significant Coalition forces had to be concentrated on the northwestern (left) flank of the Coalition front, without Iraq's detecting the movements and reinforcing its own right flank. This concentration was made possible without detection by the fact that Coalition air supremacy denied all reconnaissance capability to Iraq, which thus could have no knowledge of Coalition troop deployments. Extensive and successful Coalition deception efforts were instrumental in ensuring the plan's success. The movement of Coalition troops was massive: over 100,000 men and some 2,000 tanks moved some 250 kilometers, together with logistical supplies for 60 days of fighting—more than a million tons.

---

294. The summary account presented here is based on information provided at our request by the public affairs staff of U.S. Central Command; on U.S. Department of Defense, *Conduct of the Persian Gulf War*, p. 90; and on Schwarzkopf, *It Doesn't Take a Hero*, pp. 356-362, 395. A more detailed account is given in Gordon and Trainor, *The Generals' War*, Chapters 6 and 7.

Coalition political and military leaders had to weigh conflicting risks when taking the decision to move from a purely aerial campaign to one involving ground forces. The main risk in postponing an attack was that a partial Iraqi withdrawal from Kuwait might have created strong political pressure for a cease-fire, and that Iraq might have taken advantage of a cease-fire to reinforce its remaining defensive positions. Another motivation to start a ground attack was given by reports that Iraqi troops were arbitrarily arresting, torturing, and killing Kuwaiti civilians. The main risks in launching the ground attack were the casualties that might be suffered by Coalition forces when penetrating Iraqi lines or liberating Kuwait City, and the possibility of a setback (or even a defeat) for the Coalition if its troops became bogged down in front of Iraqi defensive lines.   Thus the focus on VII Corps's outflanking manuever: a classical example of bypassing and avoiding enemy strength.   VII Corps concentrated on attacking rear echelon troops in less fortified positions from an unexpected direction, thus exploiting a relative weakeness in the Iraqi dispositions.

Already in October 1990, the month of February had been selected as a possible date for a ground attack, and an analysis conducted in early November indicated that mid-February would be the most advantageous time.   On 8 February, General Schwarzkopf picked 21 February as the optimal date, with three or four days of latitude.   On 14 February, the ground attack was rescheduled to 24 February.

Many factors contributed to determining the timing of the ground attack. From an overall military point of view, a key factor was General Schwarzkopf's judgment that about half of the Iraqi tanks and artillery in the theater of operations had been destroyed: Coalition plans called for attaining this objective before starting the ground assault. Additional factors were the commander's judgment that Iraqi will and capability to fight were eroded, and that Coalition forces were adequately prepared. The calendar was a factor: specifically, the approach of seasons with usually less favorable weather, and of an important Muslim religious period (the Ramadan fast, which was to start on 17 March).   More specific military factors were the short-term weather forecast: four to five days of clear weather was considered desirable in order to ensure that the effectiveness of close air support would be maximized; and the arrival at their assembly point of the last combat units on 21 February.

A political factor was introduced by the last-minute Soviet peace proposals and the possibility that Iraq might announce a withdrawal.

The actual decision to launch a massive ground attack was made less than 24 hours in advance—and was communicated to unit commanders around midnight local time on 23 February.   The formal "execute order" went out at 0100 hours Riyadh time on 24 February.

From a tactical point of view, the main Coalition concern was how to advance rapidly past the Iraqi field fortifications, in order to avoid being subjected to artillery fire.   Land mines posed a very significant threat to

Coalition forces. It is estimated that Iraq laid around half a million mines, covering most of the front and extensive areas in Kuwait. There were two major Iraqi defensive belts: the first paralleled the border with Saudi Arabia roughly 10 to 15 kilometers inside Kuwait, and was composed of continuous minefields varying in width from 100 to 200 meters, with barbed wire, antitank ditches, berms, and oil-filled trenches. The second obstacle belt was similarly constructed and formed the main defensive line. It was about 20 kilometers behind the first line in some areas and merged with it in others.

Extensive breaching exercises had been performed by Coalition troops against mock-ups of the most formidable obstacles, reconstructed from satellite and aerial reconnaissance photographs. Minefields would be cleared by a combination of MICLICs (a rocket that deploys some 800 kilograms of explosive in a chain some 100 meters long; when the explosive is detonated, it destroys obstacles and conventional pressure-activated mines in its path) and tanks pushing rakes and rollers. Dirt walls and ditches would be breached by armored bulldozers.

THE FIRST MOVES: DISTRACTION AND OUTFLANKING

Deception has been part of war for millennia, so it is not surprising that both sides used decoys and other means of deception. Iraq painted fake bomb craters on runways, and ground units constructed fake positions, including dummy missile sites, boats, artillery, and tanks. When the Iraqis learned that these ruses were ineffective against night raids that used infrared targeting systems, they began burning tires near the decoys to simulate heat signatures. Although the decoy positions did draw Coalition fire that could have been directed against operational units, it does not appear, in retrospect, that the overall effectiveness of the air campaign was significantly reduced. The Coalition also built mock artillery pieces and tank turrets, but these were never attacked by Iraq.

On the other hand, Coalition deceptive maneuvers appear to have been successful in reducing Iraqi resistance to the ground assault. Among the deceptive measures was the creation of distracting "ghost divisions" by U.S. Marines and U.K. forces; these "divisions" consisted of a limited number of troops equipped with some artillery and an extensive network of radios and loudspeakers simulating full-strength divisions. Needless to say, these ghost divisions maneuvered far away from the actual planned point of attack, creating fictitious threats against the enemy lines. Surpassing every other ruse, the main Coalition distraction was to create the impression that a U.S. Marine amphibious landing was planned. This impression was created by well-publicized training maneuvers, ship and aircraft movements, and naval gunfire. As a result, at least six or seven Iraqi divisions were tied down defending the coastline.

The net effect of all the Coalition deceptive measures, was that when the Coalition forces swept in from the west, they found Iraqi defenders oriented to the east and south, open to attacks from the flank and rear. U.S. Lt. Curtis Palmer, relating a conversation with an Iraqi brigade commander: "The first indication he got that something was there was the noise of our tanks. I don't think he even got word of our artillery fire. It was dark when we came through, so they heard us far before they saw us. When you're in the ground, in a trench or bunker, you can hear noises far away."[295]

Due to Iraq's sabotage of Kuwaiti oil wells, a great deal of smoke was present on the battlefield when the ground assault was launched. But the winds, which had initially been blowing the smoke toward the advancing Coalition forces, shifted during the ground assault, blowing back toward the Iraqi positions and thus hiding the rapid maneuvers of the Coalition forces. Furthermore, the superior low-visibility and infrared target-acquisition and vision systems available to the Coalition allowed its forces to see through the smoke better than the Iraqis could.

In addition to not obtaining any significant advantage from the smoke that they had created, the Iraqis suffered from the lack of any capabilities to reconnoiter the battlefield; to hamper Coalition logistics; and to fire artillery at specific targets (rather than general areas—without reconnaissance capability, specific targets could not be identified).

Several preparatory steps had been taken by the Coalition well before the actual beginning of the ground attack. For example, U.S. Navy SEALs had conducted reconnaissance missions on Kuwaiti beaches since 16 January. U.S. Army Special Forces had conducted long-range helicopter infiltration into Iraq in order to determine whether the ground would permit heavy tanks to pass, and to collect other information not available by air reconnaissance. About one week before the actual assault, a team of Marines had infiltrated Kuwait on foot in order to gather information on the types of mines that would be found during the initial attack. They had crawled into the minefields at night in order to determine the density of the mines, whether they had antihandling devices, whether they were chemical or antipersonnel, and so forth. There was no other source for this kind of detailed information—satellites and aerial reconnaissance cannot provide it. Certain types of modern mines have detonators that are not sensitive to the overpressure from blasts of explosive clearing devices such as the MICLIC. If such sophisticated devices had been found, the point of attack would have been moved to avoid them. Similar actions had been conducted by Saudi Forces a few days before the ground attack.[296]

Lt. Col. Frank Kabelman, commander of the First Combat Engineer Battalion, attached to the U.S. First Marine Division describes his troops' activities:

295. Personal interview.
296. bin Sultan, *Desert Warrior*, p. 402.

Five of my best NCOs, accompanied by a reconnaissance team, infiltrated in by hiding during the day and moving at night and early morning. It took several days to get into position. Then, with the infantrymen providing cover, the combat engineers crawled into the minefield, basically probing by hand from side to side and back and forth, at several points. Most of the people got Bronze Stars for valor, and they were well earned.

Thanks to the efforts of those young Marines, we had a real feeling of confidence when we went up against those minefields. We knew that we were facing simple pressure mines and that our equipment could deal with them. We knew that the fields had not been maintained, and we knew that they had not been prepared with a high level of competence. So we knew we could get through them fairly quickly. Even though we didn't know how well they would be covered by artillery fire, we knew we wouldn't be exposed for long.

Sgt. Luis Adrianzen, one of the people on that mission:

I was attached to an experienced reconnaissance team. It took us about 6 hours to move 19 kilometers into enemy territory. Our mission was to stay there 3 days, getting as close as possible to the obstacles and, if possible, going right into the minefields. We took a pretty light load, considering the amount of time we were going to stay, but it still weighed over 20 kilos what with extra water, batteries, communication gear, and so on.

We were in position about 0300 and we could hear the enemy talking right in front of us. We thought we had come right up on top of them, but at night sounds travel far in the desert—we were actually about 150 meters away from the fence that delimited the minefield. They had dogs, and that scared us, but they didn't detect us. We dug in to holes and camouflaged ourselves during the day. The way we had set up our holes, we could see the Iraqis walking up and down, and anytime a jet came overhead, they would sneak down into their holes.

About 2000 that night we came out of our holes and did some reconnaissance, looking for what we could find. We noticed that the wire barriers were thicker toward the north. There were a lot of Iraqis patrolling, so we couldn't actually go into the minefield, but I know one of the other engineers with another team was actually able to get into the minefields and see what the mines looked like; mostly they were surface laid so you could walk right up to them. We moved further east, then dug in to holes again and hid the following day.

By the second day I felt pretty comfortable out there. At first I had been scared, not knowing what was going on. But by the second day I was comfortable. That evening we did a little more reconnaissance, then packed up our gear and pulled right back to the rear, which we reached at 0300. Then we were debriefed by our officers.[297]

Following up on their previous activities, U.S. Navy SEALs swam ashore on Kuwaiti beaches just before the start of the main attack, detonating explosives and calling in air strikes against bunkers. This was a diversionary maneuver designed to make the Iraqis believe that an amphibious landing was imminent. In addition, U.S. Army Special Forces sent teams deep into Iraqi to observe possible troop movements. Some teams were discovered and

---

297. Personal interviews.

recovered; others remained in place hundreds of kilometers behind the lines until Coalition ground forces arrived.[298]

U.S. Army Capt. Edward McHale recounts a mission for which team members received Bronze Stars:

We were a long-stay-behind-the-lines team, a special reconnaissance team. We were placed near the western flank of the Tawalkana Republican Guard division to watch them, see what they would do, and report to VII Corps, who would eventually come up to our positions. My team consisted of six men; we had specialized light weapons and some antitank capability.

We were surreptitiously flown nearly 150 kilometers behind the Iraqi lines in MH-53 Pave Low helicopters a day before the ground war started. We flew low, fast, and at night. The ride was interesting because the rear door was always open and as we flew along we passed over columns and revetments of Iraqi vehicles; they didn't know we were there until we flew right over them—it was kind of interesting to see them waking up and looking at us.

It was kind of like rolling dice: either we got there and everything was good, or we might have got dropped into a not-so-good situation. We were quite fortunate that nobody was there where we landed, so we were able to get on the ground, hide ourselves, and set up our satellite communications so that we could report directly to VII Corps.

From our hides we observed minimal traffic; some Iraqi scouts were in the area but they didn't find us. If the Iraqis had started to move to meet VII Corps, we would have detected it, but they were being bombed substantially and were never able to make any kind of movement. It would have been inherently dangerous if they had moved right up to our positions. But our technique for hiding was good, and it should be possible for someone to walk right over us without finding us—we practice that in training. Unless they are very observant they wouldn't see us within a meter of our location. But that's if everything goes right for us and there's no bad twist of fate or anything.

We stayed in hiding for four days, then helicopters came to extract us. The biggest danger was when we were flying back and some air-defense radars from Iraqi troops retreating toward the Euphrates locked on to us. We took evasive maneuvers and no shots were fired.

This was our first mission in an out-and-out conflict. Everybody thought that they would be more fearful, but we train so realistically that the fear level was quite low and it was almost business as usual. What we'd done didn't really hit us until after we were back.

U.S. Army Chief Warrant Officer-3 Richard Balwanz:

My team was an eight-man reconnaissance group. Our mission was to conduct a special reconnaissance along Highway 7, a major road which runs from Baghdad down to an-Nasariya and then to Basra. We were supposed to gather information on movements along the highway and transmit them in real time [immediately] to XVIII Corps command. They wanted to know what was coming down that road and what was retreating. On the evening of 23 February our team was inserted into this area by a Blackhawk helicopter. We were on the ground at about 2230 hours, but we had to

---

298. Both of the following accounts are from personal interviews.

walk about 5 kilometers to reach the place we wanted to be. We were carrying extremely heavy packs: about 70 kilograms each—it was quite a burden on us. We finally reached the area near Highway 7 and dug hide sites. Each hide was about 3 meters by 3 wide and 1 meter deep, covered with a camouflaged cap that blended into the terrain. Digging the holes and filling sandbags was quite an arduous task, but it was all uneventful. It was a clear night, there was no sight of anyone, and we were pretty confident that we were in an isolated area and would be able to carry out our mission. We finished digging the holes about 0600 hours, just as it was beginning to get light. We moved into our hide sites and began our observation of the highway. There was a small village nearby, just off the road. We were very close to the highway, so we could identify the equipment moving along it at night through our night-vision goggles.

The hide sites were set up along the sides of a canal or drainage ditch. This canal was anywhere from ankle- to chest-deep. The dirt excavated from the canal had been piled up along the sides, creating two walls, and we had dug into those walls because the soil was softer there. We had one hide site on the north side of the canal, the other on the south side. There were four-man teams on each side of the canal.

About 0900 we heard some voices. They belonged to children who were playing out in front of our hide site. One of my men could see them by looking out through our observation porthole. There were two six- or seven-year-old girls and a three-year-old boy. I felt pretty confident that we were well camouflaged, but I was somewhat concerned. The voices got closer and after about 30 minutes the children recognized some disturbance in the earth. They came up and looked directly into the hide site, screamed, and took off. Two of my guys jumped out of the hide site and trained silenced weapons on the fleeing children. They asked me what they should do and I immediately told them that shooting civilians was not our job. What had happened had happened, and we weren't going to take the lives of unarmed civilians, especially not children.

So the children ran off and I called my men out of their hides. We gathered up our equipment and I called XVIII Corps on the radio requesting emergency evacuation. I told them we'd been compromised and they told me they'd see how they could get us out of there. Then I moved my team up the canal, 200 or 300 meters farther away from the road, into a place where the canal was shoulder-deep. We set up there and continued to watch the highway. At that point we realized that we were in an area with a lot of agriculture: wherever we looked, we could see people out in the fields. After about 45 minutes I realized that the people in the area gave no indication of our presence: they just went about their business. I thought that if the girls had told somebody, then somebody would have come to investigate. But nobody did, so I called headquarters again and canceled our emergency evacuation. I explained that I planned to stay in the canal until nightfall, then move to a different area. Our hides had been compromised, but our mission had not necessarily been compromised.

So we continued to watch the highway and I sent an activity report in at 1200 noon. At that time most of the guys were resting, because we had been up all night digging the hide sites. I was watching the highway and the surrounding areas when we got walked upon again. This time there were some boys with an adult. The children saw us first: they just walked into that area by chance. They ran off and got the adult. He walked up the wall of the canal and was so close I could have touched his pant legs. I said "hello" to him in Arabic. He answered something that I wasn't able to understand. If I had tried to shoot him or to drag him down into the canal, the people in the fields around us probably would have seen him disappear. So I let him walk off, hoping that he would keep quiet. He walked into the town.

A little while later, he came back with about 30 of the local people. They were all armed with some sort of long hunting rifle. They began to walk toward us along the canal. A couple of minutes after that, a convoy of vehicles came up the highway. There were three 2.5 ton trucks and a Land Rover-type command vehicle. They stopped on the road directly in front of us, some 500 meters away, and about 150 Iraqi soldiers started to get out: a company. This time I knew that things didn't look very good. I called XVIII Corps on our tactical satellite radio, told them that contact was imminent, and requested close air support and emergency evacuation. They replied that air support would arrive in about 20 minutes. We gathered up all the equipment we were carrying: there was a lot of classified material, radios and so on. It was heavy and would have hampered us if we tried to escape. I decided to destroy all the equipment apart from water, personal supplies, ammunition, and one radio: the one we needed to communicate with XVIII Corps. So we piled the equipment up and set an explosive charge with a one-minute fuse.

We moved back up the canal, away from the road. At one point the canal made a 90-degree turn, like an elbow, and that's where we stopped, about 1 kilometer from the highway. As we began moving, the Iraqis tried to outflank us on the right and left. Some of them were even with us, although they were out quite a ways—maybe 500 meters. Then there were approximately two platoons moving up the canal itself. As soon as we moved, we came under a heavy volume of small-arms fire. It pinned us down for a few moments. It kind of set us back—it was a large amount of fire. But then our explosive charge blew up. The Iraqi soldiers who had been moving up the ditch were right next to it: they were less than one minute behind us.

We were being outflanked, so it looked pretty bad for us. I directed the men who had grenade launchers to open fire on the outflanking elements. One reason I hadn't fired up to this time is that there were still a lot of civilians in the area: women and children who had come out to gawk and sit around. I really didn't want to get involved in shooting at civilians. But once we came under fire, I had to return the fire. So we lobbed two or three rounds into the flanking elements. It was done very effectively: we stopped the flanking movement almost immediately. But we were now tied down in a firefight. Air support was still some 20 minutes out, so it was a very bad situation. Everybody's morale was kind of low. The situation was so grave at one time that I recall seeing a couple of men who were very good friends waving good-bye to each other. We knew we couldn't get out until we had close air support. There were 150 Iraqi soldiers plus some 30 armed locals maneuvering against us. We were under attack and we were fighting back.

The thing that helped us was that we were in a very good position to defend ourselves. The terrain outside the canal was flat and open and the only way they could get to us was to come across it. These Iraqi soldiers were not Republican Guard or frontline troops. It was more like a militia or reserve unit for that local area. As a result, they were poorly trained. To our benefit, when they maneuvered against us, they stood upright and never tried to get down or fire and maneuver. They just stood up and walked openly in the desert. If people of our own caliber of training had come against us, things would have gone differently. Also, if they'd had any sort of heavy machine guns, mortars, or indirect fire weapons, it would have been very very difficult for us to hold out against them. They may have had that type of weaponry, but if they did, they left it behind in their vehicles on the road. At first they probably figured that we were such a small force, they could just walk up and take us.

So the battle went on. Of the eight people I had, five were trained as snipers. We didn't have sniper weapons with us, but snipers are superior marksmen. I told them to take their time, aim well, pick out their targets, and that's what they did. Within the first few minutes they probably shot 40 Iraqis at distances of 500 meters or so—very good shooting with open-sight rifles. This kind of set the Iraqis back and made them realize it wasn't going to be easy. So they regrouped, gave out a loud sort of Arab battle cry and tried to charge us. We peppered them with two or three rounds of M-16s and drove them back. Then we continued with the fire from my snipers: we could engage them at a range where they couldn't fire at us effectively.

So it was sort of a stalemate for a while, until the first sortie of F-16s arrived. This was close to an hour after we had called for it. I could hear the pilots on our radio, but I couldn't talk to them. During the move away from our hide sites we had lost a very critical piece of equipment: a whip antenna for the tactical satellite radio. Without that antenna, we could hear the planes but we couldn't talk to them. My communications specialists tried to jury-rig a system by pointing our dish antenna directly at the planes as they flew by. This was partially successful: the pilot could hear us, but the signal was all broken up. So those first aircraft really didn't do anything to eliminate the threat. They flew south of us toward the camp from which the Iraqi soldiers had come, and bombed it. When those bombs started falling, the civilians departed the area pretty rapidly, even though the bombs weren't very close. That air strike also made the Iraqis keep their heads down, because they became kind of leery: they knew then that we had some help in the area.

Then one of my sergeants turned on the survival radio he happened to be carrying. This is the type of radio carried by Air Force crews. He turned it on to voice mode and began calling for help just out of desperation, because the other radio was broken. None of us really thought it would work, because it was just a small radio. But an AWACS plane picked up our signal. They contacted the F-16 pilots and told them to switch frequencies. So then we could talk to the pilots with that small hand-held radio, and we used it to control the close air support for the rest of the day. By that time, the first planes were out of fuel, but another sortie was on the way in.

At this time, the Iraqi soldiers near the road were flagging down vehicles in order to get reinforcements. There were anywhere from 30 to 50 soldiers and half a dozen vehicles down on the road. So the first air strike that we called in was against these vehicles on the road. The planes dropped cluster bombs and did a very effective job. The vehicles and people on the highway were totally destroyed. As soon as that happened, our morale was bolstered quite a bit. This strike might have destroyed any heavy weapons they had left in the vehicles: I saw a lot of secondary explosions that could have been from ammunition left in the vehicles.

At that point we began calling close air support; against the flanking units and also against the units maneuvering up and down the canal. We brought in what we call "danger close" strikes, with some bombs falling within 100 meters of our location in the canal. But these Iraqis, unlike some of the ones that were involved in the main fighting, didn't give up. They were pretty mad that we were in their backyard, and they were real game. When the aircraft would leave, they would regroup and attack. As the day progressed, we had several sorties come in to help us out.

The canal itself was not straight: it wove around like a snake. From where I stood, I could only see maybe 5 or 10 meters before it bent out of sight. I was very concerned that a unit could work its way up that canal and be on top of us before we could react to them. So I called an air strike along the canal. As soon as the strike was over, I and one of my sergeants walked shoulder to shoulder down the canal, basically running a counterattack on the elements moving up the canal against us. My hope was that after the air strike they would be in disarray and that we could catch the point element by surprise, fire on them, and drive them back down the canal. And that's exactly what happened. We went about 100 meters down the canal, around a bend, and there was the point element: three soldiers hunkered down. They actually had their weapons lying beside them. As we stepped around the bend, they reached for their weapons. Of course we were ready, so we got the drop on them and shot the three of them. When the remainder of the force behind them heard the gunfire so close, they withdrew.

Air strikes continued to give effective support for the remainder of the day. The Iraqi troops made no night attacks; the detachment was able to call in and board a helicopter in the dark, and was evacuated with no casualties. Chief Warrant Officer Balwanz received the Silver Star for this action and was called to brief the U.S. Congress; his men received Bronze Stars for valor.

Map 8.4
First Coalition moves on the ground

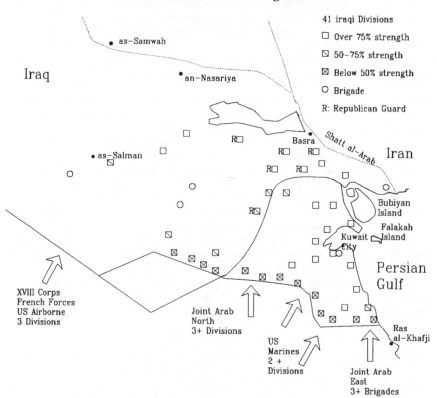

The Coalition ground assault began on 24 February, before dawn. U.S. Marines made the first moves, against the Iraqi divisions deployed along the border with Saudi Arabia. Soon afterward, Joint Arab Forces-East attacked the Iraqi left. Later in the day, Joint Arab Forces-North struck the center of the Iraqi lines. These moves constituted pinning attacks, designed to distract attention from the Coalition's planned outflanking maneuver. Just after dawn, units of XVIII Corps (French and U.S. Army forces) hit the Iraqi right, initiating the outflanking maneuver. Map 8.4 illustrates the situation.

The first moves of the ground assault consisted of attacks meant to fix Iraqi forces in place. Task Force Ripper of the U.S. First Marine Division, consisting of two infantry, one combat engineer, one tank, and one artillery battalion began the main assault at 0400 local time on 24 February by breaching the obstacle belts and advancing toward Kuwait City. The Marines used bulldozers and M60 tanks equipped with plows to demolish dirt obstacles, and their improved triple-shot version of the MICLIC together with M60 tanks equipped with rollers to clear minefields—which were extensive in this area. A few tanks were disabled by mines, but the task force penetrated the first line of defenses without encountering serious opposition; artillery was used sparingly in order to conserve ammunition for future fighting. The Second Marine Division started its breaching operations at 0530, preparing the way with a 15-minute artillery barrage. They received counterbattery fire; used radar to determine its source; and returned fire, silencing the Iraqi artillery. Joint Arab Forces-East started advancing at 0800. Farther west, the U.S. First Cavalry Division, the theater reserve, conducted a feint attack.

U.S. Marines, acting as an infiltration force, advanced 12 to 14 kilometers into Kuwait during the night of 22 February. Brig. Gen. John Admire (who was a colonel during the war):

During the next day we just simply harbored in, we dug our defensive positions and camouflaged ourselves as best we could in the desert. We were somewhat surprised, to be honest, that the Iraqis never did discover us—or at least if they did know that we were there, they never made any attacks on us, never acknowledged our presence in any way.

The night of the 23rd, at about 2100 hours, we penetrated the first barrier. Our estimate was that the Iraqis would probably defend very lightly at the first defensive barrier. We felt that their major effort would be at the second one, because we knew that probably in between the two barriers would be our most vulnerable time—we would be subject to their counterattacks plus their supporting arms fire. In fact the resistance was very light. We went across the old-fashioned way, literally on our hands and knees, probing for mines with bayonets; we finished crossing by 0400 on the 24th. For four or five months one of our major concerns had been those formidable Iraqi defenses, and we had practiced and trained at penetrating these with tanks, APCs, tanks with plows, explosive devices, with supporting arms fire, but all of a sudden our mission was to do this with no armor, no mechanized assets, no explosive devices, total secrecy, no supporting fire—so we literally walked across on foot, or in some cases crawled across. Then we opened up lanes for the follow-on forces; we surprised the Iraqis and confused them: for a time we were operating behind their lines.

While most of the Coalition attack was conducted by armored forces, there were some infantry actions. Col. James Fulk, commanding officer of Task Force Grizzly of the U.S. First Marine Division:

We were an infantry infiltration force; our mission was to screen the left flank of Task Force Ripper. Everybody was on foot; we had two tracked vehicles with line charges and tanks with mine plows that we would use only if we got into trouble crossing the first minefield. Our mission was to cross clandestinely, so we didn't want to use the line charges or tanks. As an infantry unit, we were concerned about the timing and the distance we had to go from the Kuwaiti border to the first minefield: about 18 to 20 kilometers. So I had authority to go in two days prior to the ground war starting. At midnight on 22 February I had two infantry battalions 20 kilometers into Kuwait, right up against that first mine belt.

We went to ground, dug in so nobody could spot us. We kept still during the day and probed into the minefields during the nights of 22 and 23 February. Our job was to get through the first minefield and all the way up between the two mine belts to clear that area for Task Force Ripper, so that they would not run into any dismounted infantry or direct-fire antitank weapons at the first mine belt.

A stripped-down Iraqi battalion was defending the first minefield. They had been subjected to three days of air attacks, artillery raids, and broadcasts from loudspeakers urging them to surrender. Every time a vehicle moved on their side of the barrier, we called in an air or artillery strike. They didn't know where these were coming from, because we were well hidden. Nobody actually surrendered until we came up to the minefield and started firing machine guns on the other side as we were attempting our breach. At that point they gave up: we captured about 300 prisoners on the night of 23 February. We gave the Iraqi prisoners chemical lights, and they showed us the way through the antitank minefield, but we discovered that there was an antipersonnel minefield behind their defensive positions. We hadn't expected that, and it was probably put there to keep the frontline Iraqi troops from retreating. We didn't want to clear the field with line charges or tanks because we didn't want to be detected, so we ended up having to get on our hands and knees and probe our way through that anti-personnel minefield—that took us most of the night.

Staff Sergeants Reseifo and Mitchell led the way through the minefield. What you do is to get down on your hands and knees and probe gently forward with your bayonet until you hear a clunk when you hit a mine. This is a very dangerous operation, since the mine can explode and injure you, so you probe very delicately and slowly: it took almost eight hours to work through the 60-meter-wide minefield. Once they found a mine, they just marked it and moved around it, leaving it in place. So they created a meandering path through the field. Our heavy weapons, machine guns and mortars, were mounted on little carts that were pulled through by hand.

By 0400 on 24 February we had some 2,700 Marines on the other side of the minefield, ready to head north up toward al-Jaber airfield. The Iraqis thought that the ground war was just starting, but we were already some 35 kilometers into Kuwait, in their rear. The second barrier system was 16 to 18 kilometers further up, and our mission was not to create a breach in it but to move north just to the edge of the second set of minefields so we could bring direct fire to bear and call artillery fire into the al-Jaber airfield if it turned out to be heavily defended.

The Iraqis started to fire artillery at us, but whenever they fired, we called in air strikes, so they could never adjust their fire. As soon as they fired a ranging shot, it was observed by an airborne forward air controller, he marked the battery, and called in AV-8s or F/A-18s to take it out. We were so far forward that we had no artillery support, and being on foot, we had no counterbattery radar, so we relied on air to locate and suppress their artillery positions. It was very effective: the Iraqis were never able to mass their fire against our positions. We had conditioned them so that whenever they fired on us, we would fly not two or three airplanes against them but an overwhelming number of airplanes against them, so they would abandon their artillery.

Task Force Ripper came up on our right flank to breach the second barrier system. They could move very fast through the first barrier because they knew we had cleared the way and were protecting their flank. The Iraqis didn't want to commit their armor against my infantry and kept it in reserve, but Ripper went through the second minefield so quickly that they were shocked and overrun.

Colonel Fulk's unit later moved up to secure al-Jaber airfield on 25 February and suffered 1 killed and 12 wounded from Iraqi 122mm rocket fire. Lt. Col. John Garrison of the U.S. First Marine Division:

The mission of my infantry battalion was to advance through the minefields and berms ahead of the armored attack and screen the right flank of the armored task forces Ripper and Papa Bear. We had been told on 14 February that the attack would start in 10 days, but we didn't know exactly what we would be asked to do or if we would be transported behind the lines by helicopters. We only got our final orders a few days before the attack: we would do everything on foot, wearing NBC suits [protection against chemical weapons] and carrying 35-kilogram loads—mostly extra ammunition.

We cut the first berms and crossed into Kuwait on 22 February. We really didn't know what enemy forces we would find, but we didn't run into any in Kuwait. We stopped when we reached the obstacle belt: the minefields and barbed wire. We didn't know at that point where we would go through. We had had photographs and so forth, but it wasn't clear enough. Partly because of the smoke from burning oil fires, we really had no idea of the size of the enemy or their location.

On the night of 23 February, my reconnaissance came back and reported that there was a place that appeared to be a weak spot in the minefields and obstacle belt. This report came in just an hour before we were supposed to step off into our final march to attack. The trick was to try to get everybody through the barriers without getting hung up and being exposed to fire from machine guns and artillery. The bad news about having found a weak spot was that the enemy probably knew about it also and might have had a lot of artillery targeted there.

So we got up to the spot; it appeared to be a good place to cross, but nobody had actually been through yet or knew what the enemy strength or disposition was on the other side. Two company commanders and some men got up and actually stepped through the minefield, cut through a piece of barbed wire that constituted the last of the obstacles, and made it to the other side without being detected. Engineers dug out by hand whatever a man couldn't step over, so that we had a clear track. What that meant was that we had a way to get through for everybody that was on foot. By now it was nearly daylight, and we began to move through. The men just sort of stepped in each other's footsteps and did a very good job. They were quiet, cautious, and nobody triggered a mine or got hung up on an obstacle. We got 600 Marines across in less than an hour.

One company went pretty much undetected. By the time the second company came up, they started taking some enemy fire. The Iraqis had now realized we were coming, vacated their positions, pulled back, and started firing at us from 1,000 meters or less. We called in artillery and air strikes. But at this point my dilemma was that I had wanted to get all the troops through that were on foot, because they take longer. The problem was that by doing that, I couldn't get any of my vehicles across, and they had the .50-caliber machine guns, 40mm grenade launchers, and TOW missiles.

Those were the only heavy defensive weapons we had—no tanks, no armored vehicles. So when we started taking fire, I thought to myself "Well I've made a mistake: I should have gotten the vehicles through first so that they could hold off a counterattack." For a few moments there I was really concerned about getting my TOWs, machine guns, and grenade launchers across.

I had a tank with me that had a plow to clear a lane through a minefield. The problem was that that particular tank had thrown a track and was not available. So it was a real dilemma: how to get the vehicles across. There wasn't really time to probe along with a mine detector and clear a lane by hand. Fortunately the reconnaissance team leader told me he thought he knew a place where we could get the vehicles across. I asked, "Why do you think that," and he said "Well, I just do." We took my Humvee, and he got on the hood and I got in the side, and we just drove through the place where he thought it would work. And it did. So all my vehicles could follow.

Now I had all my equipment across and we could take up defensive positions. By this time the Iraqis that were there were pretty much in retreat, and we dug in. This was a big shot in the arm: Task Force Ripper was waiting to go, and when they heard the news that we were able to get through, it was comforting to them to know that their flank was secure. At the same time it was a big psychological thing, because they knew that somebody could get through and not everybody was going to get cut to pieces. If we could do it, they could do it.

U.S. Marine Brig. Gen. Carlton Fulford (who was a Colonel during the Gulf War), commander of Task Force Ripper:

The concept of our second breaching operation was identical to the first: the Third Tank Battalion was in the lead in order to gain fire superiority, First Battalion Fifth Marines was on the left, and First Battalion Seventh Marines on the right, both tasked with making two breaches each and passing their forces through quickly, in order to be in a position to stave off a counterattack. The difference between the first and second breach was that the first one had been relatively unopposed. As we reached the second line of defenses we began to receive a significant amount of artillery fire, both on our lead and flank elements. The artillery fire was inaccurate, and it seemed that the Iraqi forces were unable to adjust their artillery in order to really do any damage—the incoming rounds fundamentally fell harmlessly.

They did have a couple of observers in towers, but we destroyed those with Hellfire missiles from our Cobra helicopters, so they had no eyes to adjust the artillery. But their ineffective use of artillery was a surprise, because that had been their most lethal weapon against the Iranians and we feared their artillery capability considerably.

With the exception of the artillery fire, the only other thing that caused us some difficulty at the second breach was the influx of prisoners. After we fired the MICLICs and began to cross the breach, we got a trickle of Iraqis surrendering, about 60—and these 60 were actually fired on by their own forces with mortars and artillery. But as the mortar and artillery fire decreased, the number of POWs increased, to the point where we called up a battalion to take control of them and move them quickly out of the field so we could continue our attack toward Kuwait City. We took about 8,000 POWs in three or four hours.

U.S. Marine Col. Richard Hodory, commander of Task Force Papa Bear:

We did our breach about three or four hours after Ripper had gone through on our left. I had assumed that Ripper going through would have unnerved the rest of the Iraqi forces and that they would be waiting for us with white flags in the air as we closed on the obstacle belt. That was not the case. They did put up resistance and fire on us as we tried to do the breach. There were no berms in our area, only minefields; we used tanks equipped with plows—they dig down and throw dirt out of the way as they move forward. We only had enough assets [equipment] to create two lanes, and one of them soured when the tank that was doing the proofing hit a mine and closed that lane down. We think the mine didn't go far enough [away from the path] when it hit the plow, so it fell back down in front of a track. It was a field with sophisticated Italian mines—the plastic kind that are hard to detect and harder to deal with than normal mines because the MICLIC line charges won't set them off unless they are very close to the center of the charge.

Since I wasn't going to wait, we put the entire task force through on one lane. We were able to do that because the Iraqis were unable to mass artillery fire against us: our helicopters had destroyed their observation towers and our air campaign had had quite an effect on their artillery. The Iraqis shot mortars at us, but they were close and my Marines could see them and just shoot them. Some of the Iraqis were brave in the beginning. But once we got behind them, once we were through the minefields and started to open up the beachhead, their resolve quickly collapsed and the white flags came up. The fact they had the white flags indicated to me that they were probably going to put up token resistance until they saw that the situation was lost.

Brigadier General Fulford:

We were able to move right on schedule because of the lack of resistance at the first breach and the ineffectiveness of their artillery fire at the second breach. Our initial objective was al-Jaber airfield. It had been put out of commission during the air campaign and there were no known Iraqi planes operating out of it. But we wanted to gain it so we could restore it to operational conditions and use it. We moved north and then did a 90-degree turn left to attack the airfield.

We began the attack on the airfield around 1530—at that point we were still the only force that had passed through the minefield and was north of the breach. As we were making the attack we continued to get increasing resistance in terms of direct tank and antitank missile fire from the right flank of our formation, north of al-Jaber. We killed somewhere around 10 or 11 tanks, including T-72s, on our flank as we were maneuvering to seize the airfield. As we got to its outskirts, intelligence indicated that we were about to be counter-attacked from the north.

At that time the remainder of First Division forces were just coming through the breach and there was a pretty good gap on our right flank between us and the forces coming through the breach. So rather than going into al-Jaber airfield, we formed a perimeter defense outside it in order to be prepared to defend ourselves against an enemy counterattack and be ready to link up with First Division forces and close the gap. The flank was actually a burning oil field, with about 150 burning wells, so you couldn't see into it from the smoke and haze. We weren't real sure what was in there on the Iraqi side.

During the night we did get additional intelligence indicating that there would be a counter-attack coming through the smoke of the oil field. The rest of the division had come up during the evening, but there was still an 8 to 10 kilometer gap between my right flank and the rest of the division.[299]

Why did the Coalition attack against supposedly well-fortified positions succeed so spectacularly well? The following quotes provide the key reasons.[300] U.S. Marine Lt. Col. John Garrison:

Probably we came up on the Iraqis so fast that their artillery couldn't react. They were good at targeting and putting the artillery down, but they needed time to do it because of their very centralized control. The guy at the top has to make the decision and of course he's talking to lots of people, so you have to wait your turn to talk to him. I think that by the time they realized what they could have done, we had moved out of the target area. It seems strange to think it would take them an hour to get artillery down, but time goes really fast in those circumstances. I think they were surprised by where we came through, when we came through, and the fact that we kept moving. Also, maybe there wasn't an inclination there, for whatever reason, for that particular unit to want to lay down artillery fire.

The air was certainly a factor—the reason that we had an easier time of it than we could have had was because of the air campaign. The whole thing was really a combined arms campaign. Before we crossed the border on 22 February, I had called in B-52 strikes on the area we would assault. The bombs were falling 25 kilometers away, and the ground was shaking so badly where we were that I was rising off the ground.

U.S. Marine Lt. Col. Frank Kabelman:

The Iraqis were unable to bring mass artillery fire on a certain point. Artillery was one of Iraq's great strengths in the Iran-Iraq War. But in Kuwait there was no coordinating authority to turn the guns to a given point, so they could not fire a massive barrage on the right point at the right time—for example, between the first and second obstacle systems when our troops were exposed.

Although it is nearly impossible to quantify precisely the amount of artillery destroyed before the ground campaign, most experienced officers agree that the air campaign contributed to eliminating the threat from the Iraqi artillery and that, overall, aircraft had destroyed much of the Iraqi artillery before the ground war. U.S. Marine artillery officer Lt. Col. Rob Rivers:

The Iraqis were unable to use their artillery effectively to slow down our advance. Number one, when they saw air coming, they ran. They didn't hang around when they saw planes: they got away from the equipment because they knew the aircraft would go after it. Second, we moved so fast, they didn't expect us. We went into one brigade command bunker just south of the al-Wafra oil field, and there was still hot coffee sitting on the tables: they had no idea that we were going to push north so quickly. The speed of our advance even surprised us!

---

299. All personal interviews.
300. All personal interviews.

Brigadier General Fulford:

I think they were prepared to fight until we made the second breach. In fact, they did fight until we made the second breach. In retrospect their tactics, as they had been with the Iranians, were to use minefields to slow our advance and then mass artillery on top of us and attrit us. We knew that, we were concerned about it, I thought they would be much better at it than they were. That was their tactic and as soon as they saw that those minefields were not going to hold us up (it took us just over an hour to breach each minefield), then they began to give up by the thousands.[301]

While the first breaching operations were taking place, the French forces and U.S. airborne troops of XVIII Corps advanced deep into Iraq on the left flank, with the U.S. 101st Airborne Division penetrating half-way to the Euphrates river.[302] The French deployed 130 helicopters and 150 tanks, quickly advancing 20 kilometers past the Iraqi border. The first line of fortifications had already been breached on 23 February with no fighting. At 0530 on 24 February, General Janvier ordered: "Everyone, forward and good luck." "It was like the start of a Grand Prix," said one trooper. "A real old-fashioned cavalry charge," said another.

The first substantial Iraqi position was reached by the French at 1200. Two battalions took up positions on either side of the enemy triangular fortifications, then unleashed a torrent of rocket and cannon fire on them. "Gentlemen, adjust your hats and ribbons. We have the honor of charging. Good luck," ordered one unit commander. Forty-four AMX 30 tanks moved forward, accompanied by other troops. But there was no serious Iraqi resistance: some automatic rifle fire, a few rocket-propelled grenades (RPGs), and then the few defenders left in the fortifications came out with their arms in the air. Nearly 100 prisoners were taken in minutes. Some revealed that an entire brigade on the front lines had deserted en masse when the first intensive artillery barrage hit their positions.

Yasser, a 19-year-old deserter from the front lines who had walked two days through the desert said: "We haven't had food in days. Our officers just left us there." Youssef, an Iraqi POW from Mosul, drafted 10 years before stated:

No one wants to fight anymore. The division was ordered to retreat at 2 A.M. last night. But they told us to stay here to hold this position. We fell asleep in the bunkers and were woken up by your planes. When we saw your helicopters, we ran out with our hands in the air. But nothing happened, so we went back inside. Are you going on to Baghdad? No? Too bad, that's where you should go.

Kharez, a recently drafted 55-year-old:

---

301. All personal interviews.

302. The description of French operations is based on Service d'Information et de Relations Publiques des Armées; *Terre Magazine*, pp. 26-35 and I-VII, and *Armées d'Aujourdhui*, no. 161 (June-July 1991): 27-29.

They didn't even give me military pants. I've been here 10 days, I haven't slept for a week because of the bombs, and now I have no food or water. We came out of one war with Iran to get into another one. We can't continue like this.

In the words of a French colonel:

They surrender with their hands in the air, shocked to see Frenchmen in front of them. They thought they would be fighting Arabs. Saudis or Kuwaitis that they could eat alive. When they saw us, they fell off their horses. They said: "This isn't our war. It's Saddam's."[303]

French and U.S. helicopters ranged far forward, suppressing artillery fire. By nightfall the French forces had advanced 50 kilometers, as planned, suffering only one man wounded and taking nearly 1,000 prisoners.

In conjunction with the French attack, the U.S. 101st Airborne Division began its advance, creating a forward operating base 150 kilometers into Iraq; over 300 helicopter sorties ferried men and material into this base (called Cobra), the largest helicopter operation in military history. This base was later used to support and resupply U.S. forces who penetrated deep into Iraq as part of the outflanking movement. Also at this time, the U.S. 24th Infantry Division and Third Armored Cavalry Regiment started their advance on the Iraqi right flank. Later in the day, at 1600 hours, the Egyptian Third Mechanized Division and Saudi forces of the Joint Arab Forces-North corps also breached the lines, striking the Iraqi center. In total over six divisions launched attacks to the north along the Kuwaiti-Saudi front, which was held by only nine Iraqi divisions, all reduced to below 50 percent strength by the aerial campaign. In addition to their numerical advantage, Coalition troops enjoyed considerable superiority in weapon systems and in morale.

Iraq's reaction to the attack was to proclaim defiance, with Radio Baghdad reporting heavy Coalition casualties. These reports appeared to be yet another attempt to create a propaganda victory by denying the reality of the Coalition's successes. But the initial attacks were so successful that Coalition leaders launched VII Corps forward nearly 15 hours ahead of schedule.

BREAKTHROUGH

Starting at 1430 local time on 24 February, 10.5 hours after the U.S. Marines' first moves and well ahead of schedule, Coalition forces went through and around prepared Iraqi defensive positions and onward to attack the enemy's unprepared flanks. The movements are shown in Map 8.5.

A total of five divisions (four from VII Corps and the U.S. 24th Mechanized from XVIII Corps, with the First Cavalry Division of VII Corps being held as theater reserve) overran the four Iraqi divisions holding the

---

303. Service d'Information et de Relations Publiques des Armées, *Terre Magazine*, pp. V and VI.

Saudi-Iraqi border; all four Iraqi divisions had been reduced to below 50 percent strength by the aerial campaign.

Map 8.5
Breakthrough, 24 February

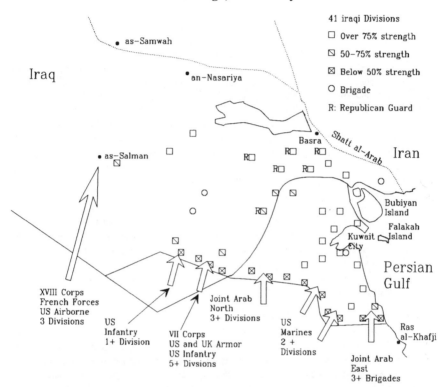

"This is the job I came to do. I just hope I don't die of fright," said a young U.S. soldier as he closed the hatch of his tank and prepared to advance into Kuwait. Elsewhere, at the same time, an experienced U.K. veteran of the Falklands war advised a young recruit: "If you can still spit, you're not too nervous to fight."[304] And so the tanks rolled forward, supported by AH-1 Cobra and AH-64 Apache helicopters, and A-10 Warthog ground-attack aircraft. U.S. A-10 pilot Capt. Todd Sheehy, describing his missions on 24 February:

The ground forces had such overwhelming power that they didn't really need a lot of air support. So for us it was kind of characterized by a lot of holding, a lot of waiting. But we were there in case they needed us: A-10s flew 24 hours a day, and could be anywhere on the battlefield within 10-20 minutes.

304. Personal interviews.

The first day I went out west, where the XVIII airborne was making its big sweep to as-Salman. I flew three missions that day, from King Khalid Military Complex. The first mission was early in the morning. I landed and got rearmed and refueled in 30 minutes. It was an amazing operation: you never shut down your engines or got out of your airplane. First they pumped you full of gas: 11,000 pounds [5,500 liters] in 10 minutes, then you got a full load of weapons in about 15 minutes. Meanwhile, you were sucking down some water and having a snack.

We took off for the second mission. We were only about 15 minutes from the target area. This was kind of the classic mission where A-10s were doing what they were meant to do. Kind of close to the battle line, where good guys were meeting bad guys. We were talking to people on the ground, since we had been handed off to an air liaison officer: an Air Force officer attached to a ground unit. He calls in the air support. Sometimes, not this time, we also had forward air controllers in OA-10 aircraft, and they had phosphorus marking rockets to indicate targets.

Our ground liaison was with an armored cavalry regiment, and the really amazing thing was the speed that they were moving across the desert, and the length of their formation. It was just a huge column sweeping across the desert. They were encountering pockets of resistance here and there, bypassing the smaller ones, which sometimes fired artillery. They called us in primarily to suppress those. We came in at 45-degree dive angles, releasing cluster bombs at 10,000 feet [3,000 meters] or 500-pound [230 kilo] Mark 82 bombs. We had various kinds of fuses: contact or 20-foot [6 meter] radar fuses. The radar ones worked best against artillery sites.

The air liaison officer was directing us: the artillery sites were in close contact with the army, and they were shooting back at the Iraqis. So that was our target mark: where our shots were impacting. We could actually see the muzzle flashes of the enemy artillery. We attacked three separate artillery sites, and they stopped firing.

Also there were some revetted tanks; our people had lots of direct-fire weapons, like TOWs, and also lots of Apaches and Cobras, but sometimes they called us in for second echelon armor. The tanks were in deep revetments, and there were many decoys. You really had to be sure it was not a wooden model, and we used our eyeballs to identify targets: I would typically fly directly over at 10,000 feet and look straight down with binoculars. We usually used Maverick missiles, which are really designed as standoff weapons, but we didn't use them that way. We used them because of their high accuracy and 95% kill rate. We destroyed three or four tanks and strafed some APCs.

Threats were primarily 23mm AAA, which we mostly could stay above; small arms, which we were well above; and hand-held heat-seeking missiles. But the altitude we were at, our use of the sun to mask our position, and our countermeasures—the flares [which attracted the heat-seeking missiles away from us]—allowed us to work around the threat.

Also, we didn't stay over any target area too long. Generally I would roll in first, with my wingman staying higher up, to provide support and warn me if he saw a missile coming up. Then we would reverse and he would go in. Typically we would approach from different directions, to keep them guessing. The key is not to become predictable.

One of the Republican Guard commanders in an armored division said: "The A-10 was a deadly accurate, ubiquitous threat. The black jet rarely missed with its weapons. The most fearful thing was that it loitered around the target. We never knew where it was going to strike or when. We knew they were there—sometimes you could see them or hear them, but they kept us guessing."

U.S. Apache pilot Lt. Col. William Bryan:

Our greatest concerns were the Iraqi shoulder-fired air-defense weapons. We could get around the sophisticated long-range systems by flying at low altitudes and letting the ground clutter mask our signature. But with the man-pack SAMs one person in a hole in the ground can take you out. We also knew that the enemy had over 5,000 armored vehicles, each of which mounted a heavy antiaircraft machine gun, and he had large numbers of 23mm and 57mm cannon. But as long as we stayed 3 kilometers away we were generally out of range, and in any case we were flying below 8 meters.[305]

A U.K. soldier provided an infantryman's view of ground-attack aircraft: "At one point . . . we had two American Apache helicopters come over us. They had no lights on or anything, and they were about 6 meters off the floor. It scared the shit out of us. We were in the trenches sleeping and these two black things just appeared overhead. We didn't hear them until they were right on top of us; we shit ourselves."[306]

As usual in modern warfare, the actual advance on the ground was preceded by violent artillery fire, delivered by cannons and MLRS systems. Five artillery battalions (120 guns) and an MLRS battalion fired for two hours on the 1-kilometer fortified front breached by the U.S. First Infantry Division, saturating it with some 11,000 artillery rounds during the afternoon of 24 February. Engineers used tanks equipped with rakes and rollers to prepare a path guaranteed free of mines.

Lt. Curtis Palmer, an engineer with the U.S. First Infantry Division:

There were no serious fortifications or visible minefields where we went through—just a big berm. We were kind of disappointed: no ditches filled with oil or anything. We'd been out there since late December doing every possible type of breaching exercise, talking about how to burn the oil. They'd constructed a huge obstacle out there for training—a copy of a section of the Iraqi fortifications. It had a wire obstacle, a simulated minefield, a berm, and a ditch.

But the actual berm we hit didn't even slow us down: we just knocked it down and went. If we'd encountered heavy artillery fire, we would have called in our own artillery and aircraft to suppress it, but luckily we didn't—if the enemy has effective artillery, the breach is not going to be successful. Aircraft had already destroyed most of their artillery. There was one unit still functioning when we came to the breach, delivering sporadic fire. They got swamped by our counterfire. They had prepared defensive positions, but had no will to fight. I don't know if they were all dead or had withdrawn because of our massive artillery barrage. They probably ran away.[307]

Less than 12 hours later, at 0200 on 25 February, the first elements of the U.K. First Armored Division exploited this breach to enter Iraq (see Map 8.6).

305. Captain Sheehy's account is based on a personal interview. Colonel Bryan's account is from Morse, *Gulf Air War Debrief*, p. 160.

306. From Nicholas Benson, *Rat's Tales* (Brassey's, 1993), p. 84.

307. Personal interview.

They were followed at 1145 by the U.K. Seventh Armored Brigade. The first contact with the Iraqis occurred at 1630 when a major communication site was destroyed: enemy trenches and bunkers were cleared. A counterattack by a company-sized tank unit was defeated and all the Iraqi tanks were destroyed. By 2000 the Seventh Brigade had reached its initial objective. The other major component of the First Division, the Fourth Brigade, then advanced, destroying 12 tanks and 11 guns and occupying its objective at 0200 on 26 February. Fighting continued during the night, with the Seventh Brigade destroying 18 tanks and advancing as planned, and the Fourth Brigade capturing 2 divisional commanders as it advanced.

Map 8.6
U.K. forces' ground advance

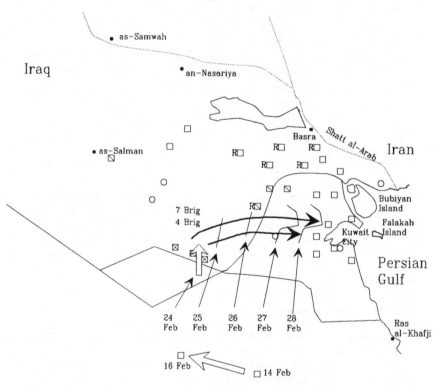

Major Simon Knapper of the Staffordshire Regiment described the first major action by U.K. forces:

There was a main command site, and then off to the right-hand side an area of bunkers and trenches. Thirty seconds before H Hour the tanks [Royal Scots Dragoon Guards] opened fire, destroying the vehicles and generator. . . . The tanks led us to exactly the right places and in the last 300 meters, the Warriors [APCs] broke forward of the protective screen of tanks and opened fire with their chain guns. We debussed [got out of the APC] the men on site. I followed the troop commander's tank in, in the middle of the two forward platoons.

One Platoon had nothing on the first position but there was stuff they could see in depth, so we then moved Two Platoon in to take on the depth position. We had this constant debussing and re-embussing [getting back into the APC]. I re-embussed One Platoon and then put them in to the right, where they took on the command bunker and cleared that. Then we re-embussed Three Platoon from their first position and put them down in the center. All the time there was this incredible noise of firing; cannon fire and small arms and tracer bouncing everywhere.

As somebody identified another enemy position, what we would do then was say: "Right, put fire down on it now, put tracer on it now." Then you'd see tracer go off in the dark, and you'd see where it was striking and roughly where they were firing from. Then you'd confirm that it was them who had just fired and say: "Right, was anyone taking rounds? Did anyone take that tracer?" Once we'd confirmed that we were not doing a blue-on-blue [friendly fire incident] we went in.

Sergeant Dixie Oliver gives a different view of another assault later in the campaign:

The trenches were very well concealed: they were flush with the ground, and where we had stopped, we were right amongst them. So I told the platoon commander quickly about them, and then I immediately debussed [got the men out of the APC]. I went straight out of the back, had a quick look round, and there was a trench just to the right of the wagon [the Warrior APC]. I cleared it with fire; I couldn't get in it because the entrance was too small, but I checked inside and there was nobody there.

We got a section [group of men] on the ground to sweep through. The Warriors were to move behind us, covering us with chain gun and 30mm cannon. We shook out and moved forward in extended line. There were loads of fighting holes in the ground which we systematically cleared with fire, although we didn't find anyone in them. Then, on our right, we spotted the enemy in some bunkers. As we swept round to take them on, they surrendered, so I ordered the guys to cease firing.

But there was still an Iraqi APC with a machine gun mounted that no one had cleared, off to our right. We crawled to the lip of the scrape that the vehicle was in. Then they covered me as I moved forward, lifted the commander's lid, and dropped a white phosphorus grenade in. When it had gone off, we ran round the back and opened the doors and sprayed automatic fire in.[308]

Meanwhile, the U.S. Third Armored Division, Second Armored Cavalry Regiment, and 24th Infantry Division (Mechanized) turned the Iraqi right flank and penetrated deep behind the front (see Map 8.7). The mission of the 24th Infantry Division was to advance all the way to the Euphrates river and to block any possible retreat by Iraqi forces. In order to ensure adequate logistic support for their rapid advance, the division's engineers marked combat trails with blinking yellow construction lights mounted on tripods bounded by fluorescent material. Each tripod was labeled with an eight-digit location coordinate obtained from the Global Positioning System (GPS) satellites.

---

308. Both accounts adapted from Benson, *Rat's Tales*, pp. 1, 110.

Initial resistance to VII Corps's advance was light: the obstacles were easily breached and Iraqi artillery fire was very light. The First Cavalry Division, still the theater reserve, conducted feints in the triborder area, and U.S. Marine amphibious forces also staged demonstrations, tying down up to 10 Iraqi divisions deployed along the coast.

Map 8.7
VII Corps initial advance

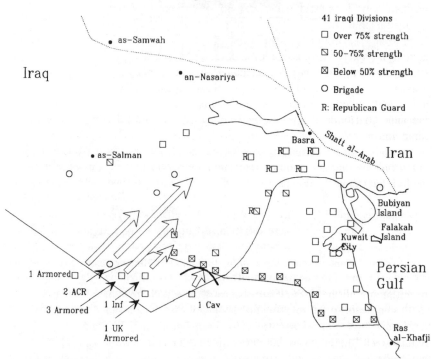

Lt. Col. Terry Tucker, commander of the Fourth Squadron of the Seventh Cavalry Regiment: "I personally spent something like 30 days driving up and down the frontline area to make sure I knew the place we would penetrate and that it was well scouted. We were the easternmost unit of the Third Armored Division. Navigating in the desert is just like on the ocean: there are no visual clues, so the satellite-based Global Positioning System was very important." Indeed, commanding hundreds of vehicles moving at high speed across the desert from inside a cramped Bradley APC must be a difficult task. The map representing troop positions is large, and must be updated continually. The space available to Lieutenant Colonel Tucker inside his vehicle is so small that we can think of no civilian example that would give an equivalent feeling—even the smallest passenger car is less cramped.

A U.K. soldier provided a good description of conditions in the Warrior, the British equivalent of the Bradley APC:

It is a bit hot in the driver's compartment because you're sitting right next to the engine. You're wearing a lot of clothes as well, because you've got your normal desert suit on, then you've got your NBC suit [protection against chemical agents], plus an anti-flash mask and gloves. On top of that you're wearing a helmet. It's like walking from the cold into a nice centrally heated room where the heat suddenly hits you. You're drinking water virtually all the time. With the hatch down it's nearly unbearable. You're just cracking up because of the heat.[309]

The Third Armored Division was moving on the right flank of the First Armored Division. Colonel Tucker's cavalry squadron was on the right flank of the Third Armored Division, which was moving in divisional wedge: Second Brigade out front, Third on the left, First on the right. The squadron's lead elements were in the middle of the Second Brigade wedge. The helicopters were way out in front. The squadron's mission was flank screen: preventing attacks on the flank. Alpha Troop (a company-sized unit) was in the lead, Bravo Troop was second. Alpha was in a flying L formation. Sergeant Denninger's and Sergeant Jones's sections were in the lead. Denninger was at the corner of the L, leading the division forward. Jones' mission was to maintain contact with the division. Lieutenant Vassalotti was behind Denninger, and Captain Davie (Alpha Troop commander) was between Jones and Denninger. Lt. Michael Vassalotti speaks of the first day of their advance:

Sergeant Denninger and Sergeant Jones stumbled on a trench. We wound up that night stopping about 1700 hours and we set the first screen line facing a high mountain. So there were guys running around the hilltop all night. And Sergeant Myers and Sergeant Hunt saw most of that: these guys wanted to surrender and started coming down. As I recall, they were up on a clothesline changing clothes. I could see them going in and out of bunkers, exchanging clothes. Then they started coming towards us slowly. We saw that through our night vision devices. [The unit moved the prisoners to the rear and continued its advance the following day and night.]

We stopped at 0545 the following night. No one got any sleep. The next day we were supposed to hit checkpoint 101, where we would come together with the First Infantry Division. Things were moving so fast the checkpoint had been moved, so we had some trouble finding it. We initially mistook the Second Armored Cavalry Regiment (ACR) for the First Infantry Division. Finally we followed the aerial scouts. There was a lot of confusion and a lot of motion. Some people gave directions in mils, others in degrees, which occasionally caused problems. We didn't always know where other people were, or relative positions. We were afraid of friendly fire, especially from other corps.[310]

---

309. Ibid., p. 94.
310. Personal interviews.

At one point a Scout helicopter pilot landed to talk to Second ACR tanks that appeared ready to fire at his squadron. The rendezvous was finally successful and the entire corps turned east. Lieutenant Colonel Tucker's squadron continued its rapid advance toward the Republican Guard divisions, whose destruction was one of the main missions of VII Corps. He related: "We were rolling as fast as Bradleys would run for hours at a time. It was a race. We even had to slow down for the logistics train. After a while we stopped taking prisoners of war. When we passed Iraqis who wanted to surrender, we just pointed toward the rear, telling them to walk that way."

Map 8.8
Marines repulse counterattack

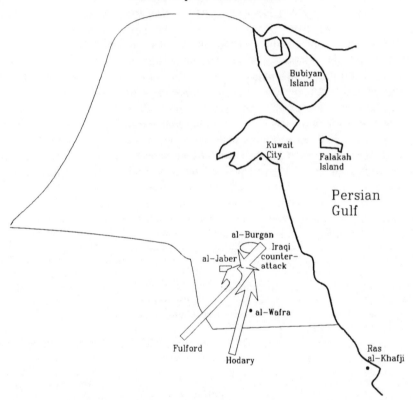

At this point a total of 14 Coalition divisions were committed, leaving one division in reserve on the ground. The reserves were reinforced on 25 February, when the U.S. Fifth Marine Expeditionary Brigade (which is nearly divisional strength) disembarked from amphibious ships and deployed on land. Of the 14 divisions, 3 (French and U.S. airborne) were devoted to the extreme left flank, 5 (U.S. and U.K. armored) were devoted to the breakthrough just left of the Kuwaiti border, and 6 (Joint Arab and U.S. Marine) were devoted to a northerly attack on the Saudi-Kuwaiti border. Both U.S. Marine divisions repulsed repeated counterattacks, destroying or capturing nearly 200 tanks (see Map 8.8).

U.S. Marine Brig. Gen. Carlton Fulford: "We were in defensive positions around al-Jaber airfield in the early morning of 25 February when the Iraqis launched a counterattack through the burning al-Burghan oil field on our right flank. Light armored infantry which had been streaming forward fell back to address the counterattack and I called in TOWs to assist. After a tense hour, hour-and-a-half fight that counterattack was brought under control and was no longer a threat."

U.S. Marine Col. Richard Hodory, commander of Task Force Papa Bear, a mechanized force with about 45 tanks, described his experience of this counterattack:

We were positioned on the right flank of the First Marine Division and our task was to guard the flank, because there was a gap between us and the Joint Arab Forces-East advancing along the coast. We would advance north toward Kuwait City airport while screening the flank. At 0630 I called my battalion commanders in for a meeting—it was extremely foggy—real fog, not smoke. Visibility was probably 50 meters. The tank battalion was oriented almost due east on the right, I had one mechanized infantry battalion in the middle, and the other mechanized infantry battalion on the left was prepared to link up with Task Force Ripper. Two of the battalion commanders arrived, and we gave them their orders. At about 0800 the third battalion commander was able to find me: he had had trouble in the fog with all the bunkers in that area.

As I was giving him his mission and describing what we expected to be doing, out of the fog rolled in this T-55 tank along with two APCs. Our thermal sights didn't pick up the Iraqi vehicles because of the fog, so they came right up to us before we saw them. The first tank was the lead of an Iraqi mechanized regiment, and the commander was in it. He said their orders were to attack the forces near al-Jaber airfield, that he wanted to surrender, but that the rest of the force he was leading in the counter-attack did not want to surrender. We quickly grabbed him and those of his staff who were willing to defect. The commander spoke very good English, so we attempted to get him to tell us what the codes were for his radios, but he wouldn't. We got our Kuwaiti interpreter on the radio anyway to ask the rest of the force to surrender as well, but as soon as he was on the radio, it seemed like they shut them off or stopped using them. So they really had no command and control and got confused.

Meanwhile, another tank was coming around behind us. We were somewhat fearful because we had heard of fake surrenders around Ras al-Khafji, so we weren't sure what this guy was doing. One of my Marines grabbed a light antitank weapon, jumped in a vehicle, drove out to intercept it, and shot it.

That kind of started the battle, because the rest of the force that was behind those first vehicles opened up on us as they closed in through the fog. They started shooting at our command post (which of course is not supposed to be engaged in combat) with tank guns and heavy machine gun fire. At the same time they were hitting the southernmost portion of First Tank Battalion. We had rounds coming through, it was very chaotic, we weren't sure what was going on there—but obviously a counterattack of some measure was occurring. We took immediate action, ordering tank and infantry forces to wheel to the southeast to catch the force that was coming at us from the flank. At the same time the air officer was able to get a section of attack AH-1 Cobra helicopters that were armed with both TOW and Hellfire missiles—they came in from the south. Between the ground forces and the Cobras we managed to destroy some of the vehicles.

By this time the fog started to lift at a tremendous rate. So we caught this Iraqi formation out in front of us all strung out, not in any tactical formation, but moving forward as if uncertain of what was in front of them. The combined action of my tank companies, antitank weapons, and the helicopters caught them in a V where there was no escape. The Cobras were hovering to the south without advancing; each acquired a target, shot, and dropped down to leave a clear field of fire for another helicopter. They went back three times for ammunition reloads.

Because of the lack of command, the Iraqi vehicles were just milling around getting shot up, and didn't seem to have any idea of what to do. It was not a coordinated attack; some continued to advance, some stopped, and a few tried to turn around but were engaged and shot. Since the fog had lifted completely, we were able to get Marine fixed-wing airplanes in with Rockeye cluster bombs. They went deep to catch formations coming in from the northeast and destroyed numerous tanks. The battle lasted until about 1300; we destroyed over 100 tanks and APCs.

U.S. Marine Capt. Mark Schulte, pilot on an OV-10 Bronco observation plane described how he saw this battle:

The second day of the ground war, we found an Iraqi tank brigade. The fog had moved in real good that morning, and we had clouds everywhere. The guys on the ground, part of the First Marine Division, thought that they had enemy movement to the northeast.

We arrived on station at about 0900 and started looking. We could see our troops, but just to the north of them the clouds were still there, the fog was still there. We'd head out for a mile, make a lazy turn back to our troops. We finally found the Iraqi tank brigade, maybe 40 tanks. The first thing we did was to ensure our friendly forces knew from where the enemy was coming so that they could set up defenses. We immediately started calling for bombers. Being Marines, the AV-8 was the aircraft of choice for us. The clouds were clearing up nicely, so anyone we called in would see these guys coming.

Initially, the Iraqis were coming in a column, which is tactically pretty stupid. I guess they were trying to pass themselves off as surrendering. We circled over them, realizing that might not have been too smart either, but we just had to know. Eventually, we determined in our minds that they were not surrendering. We advised the First Marine Division that these people were probably going to attack.

At about that time, the tanks started spreading out into an attack formation. Finally, they sent a round downrange, which pretty much started the engagement. Since I was in contact with the ground at the time, I asked the ground-based forward air controller whether he knew of any air on station. He replied that there was a division of Cobras at a checkpoint, and could I get them? So we flew over to the Cobras and escorted them back to attack the southern flank of the Iraqi brigade.

The four Cobras used TOW missiles. They took out at least eight tanks. After they'd expended their TOWs, they went back behind friendly troops. We'd fly high over our own line and started calling up air support. As soon as we got the jets in we'd fly back out there and take out the rear elements. We got a pair of Harriers each time, and each Harrier would make two runs. As they finished, we'd fly back and try to call up some more. We did that about three times.

After about 2.5 hours, the engagement was just about over. The guys on the ground took out a lot of tanks themselves, and they also designated targets for Hellfire-armed Cobras. The Iraqis were very brave. They didn't all just up and surrender. These guys mounting the counterattack just kept coming, even when our tanks and air just overpowered them.

Brigadier General Fulford:

We spent the remainder of the day on the outskirts of al-Jaber airfield fighting randomly with tank units from a brigade that was dug in on a little rise just to our north. We were waiting for another Marine task force to come on line and attack the airfield, while we continued to move north toward Kuwait City. They arrived about 1500 hours and we started to move again. At that time the smoke and haze was so thick that you couldn't see more than a couple of feet [60 centimeters] in front of you. We moved about 2000 meters, which got us up onto the ridge line and in the midst of the dug-in tanks. We felt it wasn't prudent to keep moving through that without any visibility at all, so we held up for the night.[311]

The Joint Arab Forces[312] advancing up the coast encountered very light resistance during 24 February as they advanced through areas that had been shelled by the U.S. battleships: on 23 February the USS *Wisconsin* had fired some 700 tons of ammunition in preparation for the attack (see Map 8.9). Large gaps had been opened in the frontline defenses during the morning of 23 February, so the second line of fortifications was quickly reached and the breaching effort started in the afternoon. U.S. Navy ships and Marine aircraft provided support during this advance; two Saudis were killed and four were wounded in an air-ground friendly fire incident.

The breaching operation was continued on 25 February, but heavy and accurate Iraqi artillery fire forced a pullback, with 6 soldiers killed and 21 wounded. Airpower was called in to silence the artillery (with U.S. Marines on the ground using laser designators to guide bombs), and the USS *Missouri*'s remotely piloted vehicle (RPV) was used to detect Iraqi columns and call in air strikes.

Iraqi counterattacks were repulsed throughout the day, and the second line was overrun around 1630 local time on 25 February. Iraqi resistance collapsed

---

311. Captain Schulte's account is adapted from Morse, *Gulf Air War Debrief*, p. 172. The remaining accounts are based on personal interviews.

312. Since we have not been able to obtain information from Arab sources, this account is based on U.S. Marine First Air Naval Gunfire Liaison Company, *First Anglico After Action Report* (which includes detailed maps of troop movements). First ANGLICO was part of First Surveillance, Reconnaissance, and Intelligence Group, I Marine Expeditionary Force; this unit was attached to the Joint Arab Forces-East and its soldiers called in supporting fire.

at that point, and the Joint Arab troops were able to move rapidly to Kuwait
City, which they reached in the evening of 26 February.

Map 8.9
Advance by Joint Arab Forces-East

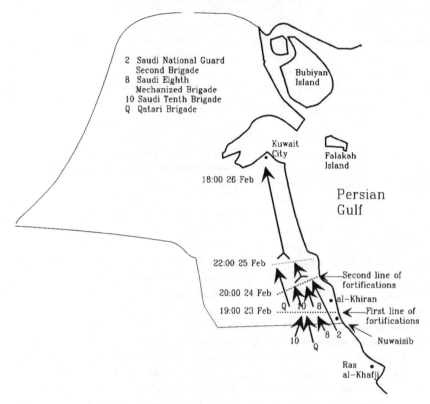

U.S. Marine Lt. Col. William Grubb noted:

When you hit the Iraqi main defensive positions, it seemed that as long as they had
good artillery support, they would fight. But as soon as you killed their indirect fire
assets, then their frontline guys didn't have any more heart for it. Concerning the
Arab units in the Coalition, I can say that some of them were superb; there were others
that were not as good, either because of lack of training or poor leadership, but
General bin Sultan ran as good a battle as anyone in the war. They usually knew how
to use the equipment they had, and were smart enough to shape the battlefield to
conform to their training and doctrine.[313]

On 25 February, French forces continued their advance on the Coalition's
extreme left flank, reaching their ultimate objective: as-Salman airfield, which

---

313. Personal interview.

they secured that evening. The entire town was under French control by the following morning. Heavy direct fire was used to reduce enemy positions during the advance, and A-10s were called in to destroy entrenched enemy armor. These movements are illustrated in Map 8.10.

While intact Iraqi forces in the rear may have been well prepared to fight off a frontal assault advancing from the south, they proved incapable of maneuvering and redeploying to meet the Coalition flank attack; the front-line divisions, severely weakened by the aerial campaign, proved incapable of effectively resisting the Coalition's frontal attacks.

Map 8.10
French forces' ground advance

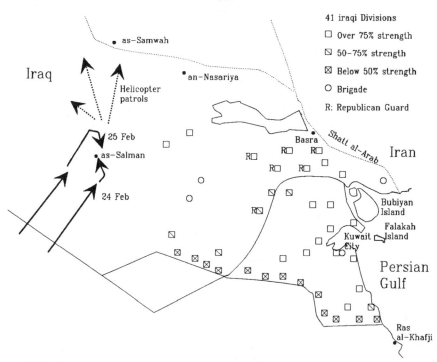

Iraqi forces retreated to Kuwait City, intermingling with occupation troops based there. The combined forces became disordered, and attempted to escape in the early morning of 26 February. But Coalition aircraft dropped mines in front of and behind the columns, blocking their advance or retreat, then pounded them repeatedly, causing heavy casualties.

U.S. Marine Brig. Gen. Carlton Fulford:

We resumed our advance at 0600 on 26 February, again with tanks in the middle, and that day we moved from our starting point about 2 kilometers north of al-Jaber airfield to the outskirts of Kuwait City. Through the entire time we were fighting tank units along the way. I wouldn't classify it as heavy: there were no heavy concentrations, but there were tank battles somewhere along my front almost always. We accounted for a little over 100 tanks during that movement from al-Jaber to the outskirts of Kuwait City.

These tank battles were primarily one-on-one, and we engaged them both with TOW missiles from Cobra helicopters and direct fire from our own tanks. The helicopters accounted for about 40 tanks—they were a tremendously brave, courageous group of aviators: the smoke and the haze was such that we couldn't see on the ground, yet because of their concern for our safety, the pilots were up there continuously and provided a significant number of kills. In retrospect the lack of visibility helped out our tanks because we were able to engage at a range that negated any advantage that the T-72s might have had over the M60s. Our crews were better trained: in general it would be one round, one hit for us—and the hits were almost always catastrophic: as soon as our round hit, the enemy turret would go flipping up in the air and the tank would be a ball of fire.

The Iraqi tank rounds or Sagger missiles mostly skipped off the dirt or harmlessly exploded somewhere without hitting anything at all. We owe some of that to the Good Lord, some of that to the Iraqis' lack of training, and certainly a great deal to the courage of our young Marines who fired coolly and with determination. It was very difficult for the young people up front to determine what was a threat and what was not: there were empty vehicles, people trying to give up, people fighting. If we'd shot at all the empty vehicles we saw during our advance, we'd probably still be there today. The thermal night sights helped a lot, because we could tell whether a vehicle was hot or not, and hot meant it was a threat. But those young Marines up front were able to identify what was a threat and what was not, and to address the threats very effectively. And I'm still amazed at their ability to do that.

Early in the afternoon we used the remotely piloted vehicle [RPV, an unmanned drone reconnaissance aircraft] to identify an Iraqi tank brigade and called in fire from the battleship USS *Wisconsin*. I saw about 60 tanks on the monitor: they were located on the northwest corner of Kuwait International Airport, in a formation obviously poised for a counterattack. We called in the naval gunfire, and they started putting shells right in the middle of that formation, and you could see the Iraqi tankers just crawling out of their tanks and running as fast as they could to get away from that target area. Those one-ton shells did a considerable amount of damage to that Iraqi tank brigade.

We attacked due north and arrived right outside Kuwait City during the evening, setting up a night defensive position and blocking any movement of Iraqi tanks that might have occurred during the night. As we made that move north, my right-flank battalion began to have considerable contact with the Iraqi tanks that were in and around the international airport itself. Our zone of action took us to within about 1,500 meters of the airport gates so my right flank was exposed to fire from the airport and we asked that Task Force Papa Bear on our right speed up its attack and close the gap on our flank.

The battalion on their left flank moved up and had a pretty substantial tank battle with the remnants of the Iraqi brigade located in the airport.[314]

---

314. Personal interview.

Starting at 1200 on 26 February, the Second Marine Division initiated its final attack. The U.S. Army's Tiger Brigade, attached to this division, reached the Mutla Ridge, high ground northwest of Kuwait City, and added its firepower to the air strikes that were continuing to pound the blocked Iraqi columns attempting to retreat from southern Kuwait and Kuwait City. By the evening of 26 February, the Iraqi right flank, in the west, had been turned by French and U.S. Army forces; the French covered the left flank of the Coalition forces that broke through the Iraqi right. A good portion of the Iraqi left flank, in the east, had been overrun by Joint Arab Forces, assisted by the U.S. Navy and Marines, and the first Coalition forces had entered the outskirts of Kuwait city (see Map 8.11).

Map 8.11
Breakthrough

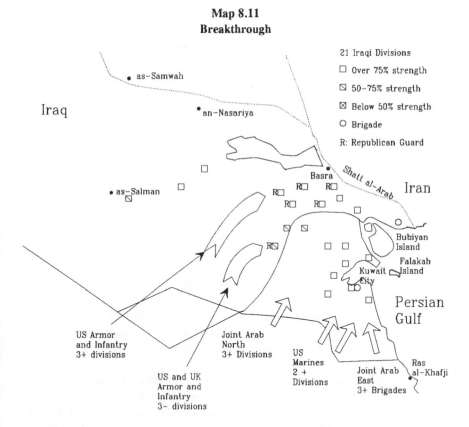

The Joint Arab Forces forces advancing at the western end of the Kuwaiti border encountered very light resistance.[315] Iraqi soldiers in this sector

---

315. This account is based on Egyptian Ministry of Defense, *Al Kitab Harab Tahrir Kuwait,* and on interviews with U.S. Air Force air liaison officers attached to Joint Arab Forces-North.

surrendered in large numbers, probably because they had been severely demoralized by intensive bombing.

Starting at 1100 local time on 24 February, Egyptian commandos penetrated the barriers formed by trenches filled with burning oil and initiated obstacle clearing operations. Egyptian, Kuwaiti, and Saudi forces moved up to the obstacle belt in force during the afternoon of 24 February, breached it at dawn on the next day, and advanced some 20 kilometers. The Egyptians prepared to repulse any Iraqi counterattacks by digging in; later in the day, they launched a feint attack on their left flank and moved additional forces forward. By the end of the day, 600 square kilometers of Kuwait had been liberated in the sector assigned to Joint Arab Forces-North (see Map 8.12). Egyptian forces took some incoming artillery and called air support to suppress it.

Map 8.12
Advance by Joint Arab Forces-North

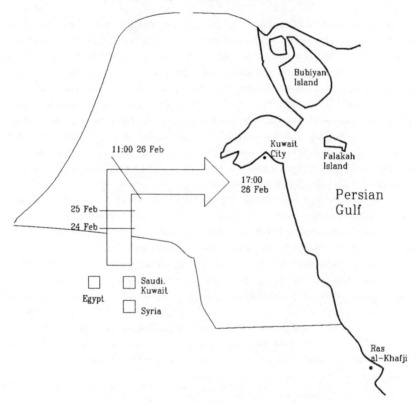

Syrian forces, acting as a reserve, followed the Egyptians on 25 February. The Syrians were equipped with Soviet tanks, as were the Iraqis, so in order to avoid friendly fire incidents, Coalition commanders maintained a good separation between the Syrians and the other Coalition forces.

On 26 February, the Egyptians, Kuwaitis, and Saudis advanced north into Kuwait about 40 kilometers by 1100 hours, then turned right and reached the outskirts of Kuwait City by 1700. The Syrians advanced about 40 kilometers into Kuwait but did not encounter any opposition.

Map 8.13
The final phases

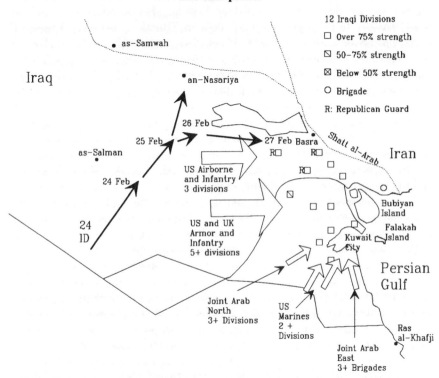

When night fell on the third day of the Coalition's ground offensive, its grand strategy based on outflanking had been realized. The 6 Coalition divisions advancing in the south faced only 5 Iraqi divisions. The 5 divisions of VII Corps that had broken through west of the Kuwaiti border were reinforced by 2 U.S. airborne divisions from the extreme left flank, and this massive force turned right to attack the 15 Iraqi divisions remaining operational in the northern part of the theater of operations. Meanwhile, Iraqi forces further south had collapsed more rapidly than expected, and so the U.S. Marines and the Joint Arab Forces were able to advance quickly towards Kuwait City, as shown in Map 8.13.

General Schwarzkopf provides an example of the varying views of a battle. In his autobiography, he stresses his initial disappointment at what appeared to him at the time to be an excessively slow and deliberate advance by VII Corps. But later, when the war was over, he concluded: "I'd been too harsh in my criticism of VII Corps's slow progress during the ground battle. It is easy to second-guess in the isolation of a war room deep underground where you are not faced with the enormous task of moving huge forces over strange terrain in foul weather against an unknown enemy. I knew that there wasn't only one right way to fight a battle." In fact, it appears that headquarters staff and VII Corps staff had different views of the situation. Headquarters believed that VII Corps should be in pursuit mode, exploiting the Iraqi defeat by bypassing pockets of resistance. VII Corps staff believed that they should be conducting a deliberate and concentrated attack against largely intact and very capable forces: the Republican Guard, some 200 kilometers behind the start line. The right flank of VII Corps's extended logistic line could have been attacked by the Iraqi divisions positioned on the border with Kuwait.[316]

In addition, although VII Corps's attack had started 15 hours ahead of schedule, it proved impossible to maintain that advance. The initial attack had been planned for 0600, when there would have been 12 hours of daylight left: night breaching operations had not been practiced. Instead, the attack started at 1500 the previous day, and some operations were slowed down during the night (for example, passage of logistic vehicles through cleared lanes in minefields). Considering the risks of advancing in darkness (including friendly fire) and of the corps's formation becoming strung out, corps commanders decided to halt for the night (with the approval of Central Command staff).[317] Thus, during the second day, much of VII Corps's attack was only a few hours ahead of schedule. In the early morning of the third day, General Schwarzkopf ordered VII Corps to accelerate its movements, and its lead elements attacked the Republican Guard in the late afternoon of that day (26 February), more than 12 hours ahead of initial plans, which had called for

---

316. Schwarzkopf, *It Doesn't Take a Hero*, pp. 456, 461, quote p. 482; the VII Corps account is from Swain, *"Lucky War,"* pp. 236-239, 247-250, 254-255; Lt. Col. Peter Kindsvatter, "VII Corps in the Gulf War," *Military Review* (January, February, June 1992); and interviews with Maj. Gen. John Landry (who was a brigadier general and VII Corps chief of staff during the war) and Brig. Gen. Stanley Cherrie (who was a colonel and VII Corps operations and plans officer during the war). General Schwarzkopf's account must be read with the understanding that he had a tendency to explode in towering rages (as reflected in his nickname "Storming Norman"); see Scales, *Certain Victory*, pp. 43, 404. An excellent account of the entire situation is given generally by Swain, *"Lucky War,"* specifically pp. 112-114, 232, 239, 274, 300, 340.

317. Swain, *"Lucky War,"* p. 236.

it to begin its attack on the morning of 27 February and to "destroy the Republican Guards" on the following day.[318]

Farther west, at the same time, elements of XVIII Corps controlled Highway 8 from as-Samwah to an-Nasariya. By nightfall, 26 Iraqi divisions had been destroyed, and the U.S. 24th Infantry Division (Mechanized) had reached the Euphrates valley, cutting off the retreat of Iraqi forces. Over 30,000 POWs had been taken at this point.

Starting at 1400 hours on 26 February the 24th Infantry Division (Mechanized) began its final 80-kilometer attack toward the Euphrates river. The division had previously advanced about 170 kilometers against light resistance. During the attack, stiff resistance was encountered. Hundreds of Iraqi vehicles were destroyed in night fighting. One U.S. M1 tank survived multiple hits by antitank rockets as it advanced to the Euphrates; its commander, Lt. Col. John Craddock, received a Silver Star for this action. Heavy Iraqi artillery fire was inaccurate and was suppressed by counterbattery fire. The division advanced so fast that fuel tankers could not keep up; it was forced to halt during the night, refueled by midnight, and resumed its advance the next day. At 0600 on 27 February, the division's Second Brigade attacked Jalibah Air Base (70 km southeast of an-Nasariya) and secured it four hours later. A tank battalion, 80 antiaircraft guns, and 20 aircraft were destroyed, as were large ammunition and fuel stocks. U.S. Capt. Steven Sicinski related:

We were on the far left flank of the 24th Infantry Division. In the afternoon on 27 February we moved toward Tallil airfield, near an-Nasariya on the Euphrates River. This was a key area. Now every other armored unit was beginning to line up, although we were still the lead element.

We conducted a raid into the airfield. It was pounded heavily with wave after wave of sorties. This was a combination of A-10 Warthogs, F-15s, and F-16s. Two company teams went in and destroyed lots of personnel and equipment. We caught half a dozen planes on the ground, helicopters, air defense weapon systems, and APCs. It was real quick. The entire attack at Tallil lasted only 15-20 minutes. It was very violent and quick.

Sgt. Daniel Stice:

The airfield was a threat to us because of its communication equipment and radar equipment for the Republican Guard. I had nine tanks from Alpha Company, and Delta Company sent nine plus another platoon. We lined up and moved out very fast: 60 kilometers per hour. The air and artillery had prepared the area. When we got in there, we had to maneuver to avoid these massive berms. They had bunkers filled with RPGs and other supplies.

I fired the first main-gun round at a truck blocking the front gate and went right through with my tank. To our right, and to our front, there were probably 20 to 25

---

318. Ibid., p. 120 gives the time for attack as H+74, which would have been 0700 local time on 27 February. Cohen et al., *GWAPS: Planning,* Figure 2, p. 8, gives the date of "destruction" as G+4, which would have been 28 February.

Iraqi helicopters. We had rounds going off everywhere. They hit everything we aimed at, helicopters, planes, radar disks. Plus we took out a lot of enemy soldiers there with our machine guns. We just leveled the place.

Captain Sicinski:

After the attack on the airstrip, that raiding force joined the remainder of the brigade and we started moving east along Highway 8. We were taking lots of prisoners by this time. They put up very little resistance.

We later learned that the raid into Tallil had more significance than we first realized. What it did was to unhinge the entire Iraqi defenses. They thought we were going to attack north along the Euphrates Valley to Baghdad. This triggered a lot of movement by the Republican Guards and their heavy armored units. It enabled VII Corps and the air forces to close in and hammer them.[319]

Map 8.14

VII Corps attacks Republican Guard

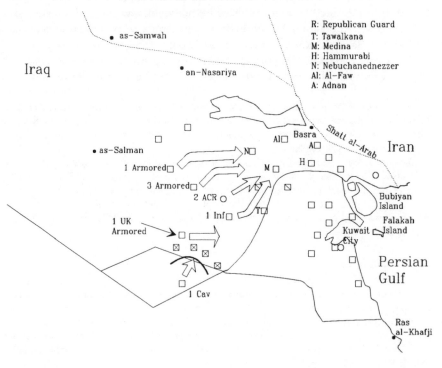

319. Adapted from Military History Magazine, *Desert Storm*, p. 154; and Maj. Jason K. Kamiya, *A History of the 24th Mechanized Infantry Division Combat Team During Operation Desert Storm* (24th Infantry Division (Mechanized) Public Affairs Office, 1992).

Meanwhile, Coalition forces had continued to advance during the night of 25 February, and attacked the flower of Iraq's troops: the Tawalkana, Medina, and Hammurabi mechanized Republican Guard divisions. The Eagle Troop (a company-sized unit) of the U.S. Second Armored Cavalry Regiment (a brigade-sized force) encountered elements of the Tawalkana Division on the afternoon of 26 February. The troop's 9 M1 tanks led the attack, followed by 14 Bradleys. They engaged at nearly 1,500 meters and advanced for 23 minutes, destroying 28 Iraqi T-72 tanks and 16 APCs without suffering any losses. This was the battle of 73 Easting (so called from the map coordinates where it took place). There were pockets of stiff resistance through 27 February. At 1130 on that day the Second Brigade of the U.S. First Armored Division engaged a brigade of the Iraqi Medina division. The 166 M1s of the U.S. brigade started shooting at over 3000 meters, advancing as they fired. In about half an hour some 40 Iraqi armored vehicles had been destroyed, and within an hour some 61 tanks and 34 APCs. Apache helicopters and A-10 and F-16 airplanes contributed to the battle, which lasted about 2 hours and resulted in the destruction of 300 Iraqi tanks and APCs, with only 2 U.S. Bradleys being hit by Iraqi RPGs, resulting in one dead and serveral wounded. This was the battle of Medina Ridge.

Armored vehicle combat doctrine calls for the vehicles to position themselves so that they can mutually support each other. Usually vehicles will fight in pairs—the wingman concept. The lead APC or tank takes up a position, gets set for a shot, and shoots. If it misses, the supporting vehicle will try to shoot; then both move to a new position. In the Gulf War, Coalition vehicles tended to form lines, sitting still and firing for a while before moving on. They adopted this tactic because of the poor visibility and their ability to engage beyond the range of Iraqi fire. The terrain was very flat and provided few places for concealment.[320]

Map 8.14 shows the general movements of VII Corps. In order to give the flavor of the actual combat experiences, we will focus on one hard-fought encounter, in which the Fourth Squadron of the Seventh Cavalry Regiment (the regiment that suffered the death of 225 men, including its commander, Gen. George Armstrong Custer, at the hands of the Sioux Indians) took on the advanced positions of the Tawalkana Division. The squadron, which has the strength of a reinforced battalion, is known as the 4-7 in military jargon. The 4-7 was the division cavalry unit for the U.S. Third Armored Division. The squadron's mission was to find and fix the enemy while protecting the division's flanks. Lt. Col. Terry Tucker: "Our mission was reconnaissance and screening. We operate over the distance of an entire division. We're twice the size of a tank battalion. We have about 1,100 people and 400 vehicles: 27 tanks, 80 Bradleys, 100 other armored vehicles, and 8 Cobras. A battalion operated over a distance of 3-5 km in width and about 4-5 km in depth. When we crossed into Iraq, the squadron covered the width of the

---

320. Personal interviews with U.S. VII Corps soldiers.

entire division, about 19 km, and we also covered the flank, at one point along 42 km."[321]

It was late in the afternoon on 26 February when the Seventh Cavalry's Fourth Squadron encountered the Tawalkana Division (see Map 8.15). A severe sandstorm reduced visibility to nearly zero without thermal sights. Helicopters could not fly. The squadron had been in a flying L formation, and came into a 5-km gap between the Third Armored Division and the Second Armored Cavalry Regiment. The lead elements of the squadron were Bradley APCs from Alpha Troop, commanded by Capt. Gerald Davie; Third Platoon, commanded by Lt. Michael Vassalotti was on the right, and Second Platoon, commanded by Lt. Daniel King on the left. The squadron scrunched down to a 1-km front, so Second Platoon shifted behind Third, with First Platoon and the rest of Bravo Troop still in a long line. They ran into mostly linear formations of BMPs (a Soviet-made APC) with tanks here and there. The BMPs were separated by about 75-100 meters. Positions were well prepared and the vehicles were well dug in. It was later learned that helicopters could have flown right between two entrenched BMPs without seeing them until abreast of them.

Map 8.15
U.S. Third Armored Division attacks Tawalkana Division

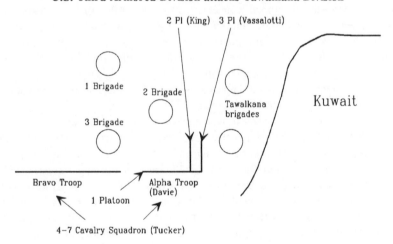

Lieutenant Vassalotti gives an account of the action:

The Cavalry squadron was like the outstretched fingers of a hand, while the division behind us was like a fist. [We were supposed to find the enemy, leading the division to him. But] when you stick your finger out to find a fire, you might get burned. We

---

321. Personal interview.

thought we would make contact that morning. I'd shaved, to make sure my gas mask would fit tightly, so I didn't suck up gas and die.

As we advanced, we started to see tank tracks, which was kind of spooky [because we were in APCs, not tanks]. We stopped to refuel at about 1500 hours, and made contact right afterward. Sergeant Jones called the first one in, then Sergeant Denninger, then my platoon sergeant (Baker). We were in field recon formation.

Sgt. Roland Jones:

We'd come over this little ridge and started going down it when my gunner, Corporal McLane, spotted dismounted infantry out front. I told him to engage and reported on the radio. He fired two bursts, then said he saw a vehicle out there, but he wasn't sure what kind. I told him to engage it, and we did. By then we knew it was a BMP. I reported it up, and it blew up after about 20 rounds. From then on, all we did was just traverse a little bit more to the right and we'd shoot at another vehicle. We'd destroyed two BMPs and one tank when Lieutenant Vassalotti came over the radio and said that we needed to move south because we were intermingled with Second Platoon. They'd come up to reinforce us after we made contact.

Lieutenant King:

My platoon was ordered to take up position roughly 200 meters behind the lead platoon for the division. We began getting contact, and everyone's adrenalin started to rise. We started to hear reports and the platoon sergeant from the Third Platoon screaming "BMPs," identifying vehicles, and calling in scout reports. Immediately we started moving forward to try to assist that platoon. As soon as we got up on line, parallel to the enemy, my gunner started tapping me on the back, saying, "I got something, will you come and take a look at it." So my platoon became engaged, began to shoot. Really the realization of what was going on hadn't happened yet. It was still very cold and very much like training. My gunner had acquired a very large object on the thermal imager. We discussed what it was. It seemed bigger than a BMP. We raised our TOW missile, fired, and it exploded almost right away—which meant that the large target we were looking at was much closer than we thought. I put my head up out of the turret and saw a T-72 tank in a fireball about 300-400 meters away. My gunner and I started to give each other high fives and jumping up and down the turret, saying, "This is outstanding." "Wow, did you see that," and then we started getting back to business. The first impression was sort of a lot of adrenalin, a lot of excitement.

Sergeant Jones:

So we moved south about 500 meters and took up positions again. We shot another BMP and another tank. I had my head out of the hatch, looking out to my front, trying to see what was out there. The weather was bad, and I really couldn't see anything without the thermal sights. Just as I started to drop back into the hatch, I saw some sparks and dirt fly off the front of my vehicle—I knew we were being shot at. I told the driver to back up. He put it in gear, but all the transmission did was to whine. It was like it was in neutral. I told him to put it in forward and try to move that way, but it wouldn't move forward either.

I called Sergeant Denninger and told him we were sitting ducks and that we needed some help to get out. So he started moving toward us, as did Lieutenant Vassalotti.

Sergeant Denninger pulled up right in front of my vehicle, shielding it. We abandoned the Bradley, jumping out. I ran around the back to make sure my driver, my gunner, and my observer were getting out. I got up to my driver, and he was trying to pull out his protective mask, which was hooked up to a filter system in the vehicle. I told him: "Forget it. We ain't got time." I grabbed him and threw him off the track [vehicle].[322] No sooner had I thrown him off than the turret was struck by a Sagger missile.

Cpl. Darrin McLane:

Sergeant Jones shouted at me to get out. I had still been trying to load, but as soon as I heard that, I jumped out of the hatch. When I was about half-way down, in the air, there was a huge explosion behind me. My whole right side felt it, and I caught some shrapnel in the arm. I hit the ground and staggered a couple of steps, then started running. I don't know if it was a Sagger or an RPG that hit my track [vehicle], but a couple more seconds, and I'd be toast.

Sergeant Jones:

I was thrown about 20 feet by the shock, landing on top of my observer. As I was getting up, I heard my driver screaming for a medic. We grabbed him and ended up getting in Lieutenant Vassalotti's Bradley. Then we started heading back to the troop baggage trains, towards the medics.

And that's when we were shot twice by a T-72. The first round hit just behind the driver, below the turret. It was like, "What was that?" It was smoky inside. First I thought that the fire extinguishers had gone off. I started checking everyone else to make sure they were OK. My driver had caught some more shrapnel. Everyone had been injured in some sort of way. I had flash burns to the side of my head and the back of my neck. Lieutenant Vassalotti also caught flash burns on the face and shrapnel in his eyes.

Everyone was hurt, but we were still going. Then the second one happened. I'm thinking, "Oh God, let's hope there's not a third one." And luckily there wasn't. One of our Bradleys had taken out the tank that was shooting at us.

Corporal McLane:

We caught a lot of flash burn. It was real loud. The explosive in the 25mm casings started blowing up. I inhaled smoke and I couldn't breathe. A sergeant grabbed my flak vest and pulled on me saying, "Breathe, breathe, you'll be OK." I caught my breath. Sergeant Jones and I were burned in the face. My driver caught a piece of casing across his eye. It was pretty hairy.

Lieutenant Vassalotti:

We went to our troop trains, and I remember seeing Sergeant Jones carrying his driver over his shoulder. Medics took our guys and started taking care of them and me.

---

322. In military jargon, a tracked vehicle like an APC is often called "a track."

Sergeant Hunt:

My platoon leader, Lieutenant King, and I started engaging infantry. His gunner noticed that some of the infantry was carrying little suitcases—Saggers. Our machine gun wasn't working, so we were using the chain gun with high explosive rounds. Then we heard that Sergeant Jones had been hit, and also our platoon sergeant's track [vehicle]. I was popping in and out of the hatch, trying to lay my gunner on targets and trying to pay attention to all the vehicles around me. I was watching Sergeant Jones get evacuated, and saw the two rounds go through Lieutenant Vassalotti's Bradley.

Something exploded right off my rear deck. As I scanned around, I saw a tank round just going through Sergeant Myers' track [vehicle]. I saw it exit the Bradley, and I saw him come rolling out onto the ground. I pulled around to try to get him and his people into ours and evacuate them. My loader was in such a hurry to go help them that he tried to run out with his headset still on—he nearly broke his neck. There was one guy stuck in the turret of Sergeant Myers' Bradley, we couldn't get him out.

Sergeant Myers:

I'd opened the hatch to look for an incoming A-10. When I saw it, I dropped down and closed the hatch. Something hit us, and all I saw was a big flash and a big wind, and the next thing I knew I was burning. I jumped out the hatch, and the next thing I knew Sergeant. Hunt and another guy were pulling me back to a track [vehicle]. My flak jacket absorbed a lot of shrapnel and flames.

Sergeant Hunt:

I pulled back over the ridge line into an armor unit and we got the wounded evacuated.

Sergeant Rousey:

I was with the platoon sergeant in Bravo Troop. We went to the north of Third Platoon to support them. We took up the flanks. Hunt and Myers were to the south. The first engagement I had, I was up with binoculars trying to see what I could see, and I couldn't see a damn thing. Then my gunner finally said he had a hot spot. I asked him what it was, but he couldn't tell. So I jumped down and looked in the sight, looked up to make sure my gun was pointed in the right direction. It was, so I told him, "OK, kill it." We had two engagements like that, then got the word to shift south. We did, then sat and waited for the platoon sergeant to make his move. I looked over at him, and saw what looked to me like just a mist shoot out the back of their turret.

At first I was wondering what the hell happened, and then I saw their loader just literally come flying out of the back of the track [vehicle] and land on the ground. I saw the sergeant fall off the top of the Bradley and then it registered: "Shit, they've been hit." I told my driver: "Get me up there now." We got there, parked the vehicle in front to try to protect them. I called on the radio, then jumped down and we started evacuating them. Our wingman was providing protection. We got hung up when we went to get the gunner out of the Bradley. He was unable to move on his own, because his leg was basically gone. It took three of us to pull him up out of the turret and lay him on the ground. We placed a tourniquet on him. He died, but we gave him mouth to mouth and he started breathing again. That's when we took his vest off, and that's when I found that he had two holes going through his chest. Every time the guy who was giving him mouth to mouth would blow air into him we would see the blood and bubbles coming out of his chest.

Then the medics came forward and started taking care of Sergeant Egan, transferring him to their vehicle. There was nothing to be done for Sergeant Gentry. We covered him up with a poncho. They evacuated back to the aid station.

I can't really describe how I was feeling then, because it doesn't register. Afterwards, when you started thinking that you had to go do it again, that's when all the fear registers, and the reality of what you've already done, what you've seen, and what's happened to the people that you're used to standing next to. It's like a different part of life that you never hope to experience.

I was now the platoon sergeant. It's something you don't expect to happen—to lose your leaders and take their place. Suddenly I was the platoon sergeant and had to figure out what to say to these guys because they've had people die that they're used to listening to. Our instructions were to get consolidated and move out again, so the only thing I could say to them was, "It's hell and we got to go do it again."

Sp. Bryan Moore was one of the medics who went up to the front in an M113 vehicle to evacuate the wounded. Moore's vehicle pulled right up to one of the stricken Bradleys. Specialist Moore:

I heard these shouts over the radio: "I'm hit, I'm hit," so we knew we had casualties, but we didn't know where they were. We got our orders to move forward to pick them up. Usually we're accompanied by an armed vehicle as an escort, but there wasn't one around, so we just went forward to find the casualties, into the battle. Visibility was awful, we couldn't see anything. The terrain was bumpy. After about 1.5 kilometers we could really hear that war was getting close. All of a sudden, out of nowhere, I saw some 30 M1 tanks coming like a wave. A tank fired, it was loud. We stopped and let them come forward, then followed them. A Bradley had fallen back, and it guided us to where the casualties were.

We got out of our M113 and saw the wounded. Sergeant Gentry had a poncho on him—his leg was twisted grotesquely. Our people started working on him, then I got out too, without my mask or my weapon. I went over to Sergeant Egan. He was in real pain, and told me something was wrong with his leg. I tried to give him some morphine, but in all the madness took the wrong kind, and it wouldn't come out of the tube. Then I called for one of the other guys to give him a shot with a syringe. I'd seen a wound below his kneecap, so I started cutting his gas suit off. Then I saw a pool of blood around his boots, so I took them off too. When I took his sock off, I saw that every bone from around the ankle area was sticking out of the skin. He was bleeding real bad, so I splinted and bandaged his leg. His pulse was very faint in the foot.

There was a lot of noise of guns and missiles and I was getting really scared. I thought I might not get out of there alive. We loaded Sergeant Egan into our track [vehicle], and were getting ready to leave when the sergeant major screamed at us that we had to pick up Sergeant Gentry's body. He was dead. Two guys jumped out and tossed him on another vehicle, and we got out of there fast.

By now it was pitch dark. Sergeant Houston, the track commander, passed out from heat exhaustion, so I was in charge. We looked at a compass and drove south. Finally we got to some artillery and asked him where 4-7 Cav was. He pointed back behind, and as I was about to drive off, he said, "But there's an aid station right over there." So I drove over there, and it was our aid station. We dropped the ramp and got the casualties inside.

Now we felt like we were back home. Then the sergeant told us we had to go back out there again. So we went back up to the assembly point, but we didn't have to go into battle again. It was a pretty hair-raising situation for me, and I hope I never have to go through it again.

Corporal Garcia, a medic at the aid station:

I had re-enlisted in Germany just so I could go to Saudi Arabia, because I'd always worked in a hospital, and wanted to go do John Wayne-type stuff. We were driving along when we heard over the radio that our troops were engaging. So we stopped, and started setting up the aid station. It was chaos for the first 15 minutes. We heard, "We've got wounded," so we got the tent set up, then the medics started pulling out the chests and setting up. We had the aid station set up within 15 minutes, just as the first casualty came in.

We heard an M113 pull up outside and the medics shouting: "Check it out. Start an IV. Is he breathing?" The first couple of wounded were not real urgent; they were treated outside. Then the first serious case came in, and it took us 45 minutes to treat him: start IVs, give medication, stop bleeding, dress wounds, bandage, report, pack his stuff onto a litter, and call a helicopter for evacuation to the rear. We figured that we were in real trouble if it was going to take us 45 minutes for each patient, so we had to start moving faster.

We split into two teams, one working from the waist up, the other from the waist down. We did the second patient in 15 minutes. It was chaos in there. It was hot, so I took off my protective gear, figuring we were safe. We treated eight patients inside, and there were more outside that were less serious. I wasn't afraid until after we were done and I realized it could have been a lot worse. The worst thing I was scared about was not being able to do my job.[323]

Unbeknownst to Garcia, the MLRS battery near his aid station took some Iraqi counterbattery fire.

The Bradleys completed their withdrawal, and the Iraqi positions were overrun later in the day. During the 45-minute action, the 14 Bradleys of Alpha Troop got credit for destroying 18 APCs and 6 T-72 tanks; 5 Bradleys were hit and 2 men killed: Sgt. Kenneth Gentry and Sgt. Edwin Kutz.[324] The men of Alpha Troop received numerous decorations, making the unit the most heavily decorated company-sized unit in the theater. Sgt. Raymond Egan recovered from his wound but needed grafts from his stomach to his leg, bone grafts from his hip, and skin grafts from his thighs. If he had not got back to a field hospital within four hours, his foot would have had to be amputated.

---

323. All personal interviews.

324. Subsequent investigation determined that three of the five Bradleys had been hit by rounds fired from U.S. M1 tanks and that both deaths were due to friendly fire. The two sabot rounds that pierced Lieutenant Vassalotti's retreating vehicle and the one described by Sergeant Rousey were attributed to U.S. M1 tanks.

Sergeant Hunt:

We started the battle in daylight. By the time we got everybody evacuated it was pitch black. All you could see was tracer rounds flying all over the place. Our lieutenant told us to go west. We started heading that way, then saw some MLRS go off 900 meters in front of us, so we didn't want to go that way. We tried to get our bearings straight, and regrouped.

Sergeant Denninger:

When you heard that your buddies were getting hit, it didn't really register until that night, when we reconsolidated, till after it was all over.

The 4-7 Squadron was the only unit to fight every day of the ground war. On 27 February, the day after Alpha Troop was hit, it sent up two teams of helicopters. Each team consisted of two AH-1 Cobras and three unarmed Scout observation helicopters. Chief Warrant Officer-2 Jackely piloted one of the Scouts and directed the other helicopters in his team. The Cobras typically flew at 3 to 10 meters altitude and up to 90 knots velocity. Each shift lasted 2 to 2.5 hours, with 1 to 1.5 hours spent on station and the rest of the time spent flying to and from the forward air refuelling point (FARP) and reloading. There was no antiaircraft fire, although many AAA weapons that had been destroyed by the air force were visible. But Iraqi tanks did attempt to shoot at the helicopters, which were greatly feared by the Iraqi troops.

The battlefield was extremely mobile, with FARPs moving around all the time. Chief Warrant Officer Jackely:

One time we landed to get rearmed. An ammunition truck drove by and the guys asked us what we needed. We told them, and they just pushed it off the truck and drove away.

We started off in the morning. It was totally confusing. We weren't sure where the enemy was or who we were after. For three days we had just been collecting prisoners, and then somebody decided to shoot. So we took off, and got assigned to the battalion that was furthest forward. There had been a lot of fighting, so the brigade would stop about every 30 minutes and unload a bunch of artillery, and that would cause heavy smoke to our front. They were worried about security, so they started putting us off on their flanks.

We worked around one flank, and found that the brigade had walked around a brigade-level command post: a bunch of bunkers and BMPs. I guess our helicopters made more noise than the ground guys, because suddenly T-55s started coming out of defensive positions and running. Because of smoke and rain, visibility was about 500 meters, which made it difficult to use the Cobra's weapons. So I'm jumping up and down on the radio telling the brigade commander that he's got T-55s moving across his flank. The Cobras fired their rockets at them, which only made them stop. By that time one of our Bradleys had come up literally under a Cobra—I don't think he saw the helicopter or viceversa. The APC fired two TOWs into a tank, and it was just a burning, smoking wreck. About that time another truck came up from behind—it was an ammunition truck. The second Cobra put an antitank round into it. It exploded, overturned, and burned for about an hour. Then we put some TOWs into bunkers.

We were stumbling across things because visibility was so bad. Every time we'd say, "There's something out in front of you," the ground forces would stop and expect us to go out there.

Later in the day, right after they finished an artillery barrage, they ordered us forward. We moved up on a ridge line and started identifying targets. First of all we came across some bunkers and people came out waving white flags. But there was some small arms fire further ahead, so we moved up and found a tank company in defensive positions. That's when we started getting engaged with small arms fire, and one of the Cobra guys said that through his sight system he could see some of the T-55s swinging their turrets toward us. We heard a loud noise, and one of the Cobra pilots thought it was a problem with his turbine, but actually it was a sabot round that had passed just next to us. So we engaged and killed two or three tanks and a BMP with TOW rounds.

Lieutenant Sperling, a Cobra pilot in the other team:

The squadron had been in contact with the enemy all night, on and off. We went up in the morning and flew forward, reaching a whole line of M1s just behind a ridge line. Artillery was firing over our heads. When it stopped we moved over the ridge to see what was there. Our OH-58 Scout helicopter was about 500 meters in front and to our right when we crossed the ridge line. He started screaming on the radio that he saw a T-72 traversing his turret toward him. So he started flying to the left, away from it. Then we came up and we could barely see the turret—the tank was well dug in. I fired a TOW into the berm; it penetrated the dirt and blew the turret about 25 feet [7 meters] into the air. It was a hell of a shot.

Then there was a truck coming straight for the M1s. I don't know whether it was some psycho who thought he could blow up the M1s with some ammunition in the back of the truck or what. But I fired on that, and that seemed to have burned for about six hours that day, because they were using it as a navigation marker for the rest of the day.

It was only after we went to the forward aerial refueling point (FARP) to rearm and everyone was asking what happened that my pilot and I realized that we hadn't just destroyed a vehicle, we'd killed some people too. That was the first time it really hit me hard. I think about it every once in a while.

After that, we fired on a couple of bunkers. I remember looking down and the guys on the M1s were loving it. It was like they were watching a show. They were on top of their tanks cheering and stuff.

Chief Warrant Officer Jackely:

We hit one tank from about 3,000 meters: all the ammunition inside it exploded, and the hatches all popped open and flames shot out of the top of the turret about 10 feet [3 meters]. We stayed until sunset, firing rockets to keep them buttoned up. Then an entire battalion of M1s came over the hill, and that was the last I saw of those guys.

Lt. Horst Herting, of the Alpha Company (M1 tanks), Fourth Battalion, 23rd Armor Regiment, attached to the First Brigade, Third Armored Division:

The night of 26 February is when all hell broke loose. We'd heard on the radio about 4-7 coming in contact, and we were getting close to the logistics assembly area to refuel. As we were refueling, our scouts came in contact with the Iraqis. We pretty much came in line and supported them as best we could. We got aviation assistance then our left flank came to assist their scouts.

The next day we started receiving intelligence reports that the enemy was going to come over to the battalion's left flank, which was where we were at. So I referred that to the company commander, and I moved over into a saddle between two mounds, popped up, and started engaging them as we came up over the ridge, holding them off. I requested assistance, and Third Platoon came over, and we held that flank and just continued to fire. From that point on, we just started slowly moving forward.

At midday we came into contact again. This time the Third Battalion of the Fifth Cavalry Regiment was engaging. Their scouts were just having a field day out there. We started to get frustrated, because we'd been out there in a line for 45 minutes, just sitting and waiting for something to happen. I remember we were thinking to ourselves, "Why don't you just let the tanks go in there?" because we have much more firepower, and those guys were diddling around, dancing all over the place. Finally they prevailed and we continued on. From that point on, anything we came in contact with, we engaged. Infantry followed, collecting all the prisoners.

They fired at us, but we were out of their range of accurate fire. My first kill was 2,800 meters, and the second 2,300. In the Second Platoon I think they engaged something at just over 3,000 meters, which was way beyond our expectations.

Other acts of valor were performed far from the front. Sgt. Shane Jensen of an air defense unit received a Bronze Star for valor:

We were in a convoy when someone came on the radio and said they needed help. At first it was hard to understand them, because they were talking all confused and everything. I guess they were in another convoy that was up in front of ours. Anyway, I guess they had stopped for fuel or something and two guys got out of their vehicle and stepped right on a land mine. They were hurt pretty bad and they were afraid the one guy might even be dead.

They needed to get a MEDEVAC in, but the helicopter couldn't land because both of the guys were in an area that had mines all around and they didn't know where they were. So they called and asked if someone would volunteer to lead a mine rake. So me and this lieutenant said yes, we'd to it. So I stole my first sergeant's Humvee and we went out to get them.

When we got there, they were messed up pretty bad. The one guy died like just two minutes after we got there. We saw the helicopters flying over us, so we popped some smoke and about four of them flew over and then finally one came in. They put the one guy in a body-bag. They told me the other guy made it through.[325]

By 27 February, XVIII Corps and VII Corps formed a solid northwest line of 8 divisions attacking 11 Iraqi divisions to the east, while Joint Arab Forces and U.S. Marines advanced from the south with 6 divisions, liberating Kuwait City. At this time over 29 Iraqi divisions had been destroyed. The U.K. First

---

325. This account is based on personal interviews, except for Sergeant Jensen's, which is from *Pathfinder* (July/August 1991): 30.

Division had advanced 290 kilometers, destroying or capturing 200 tanks, 100 APCs, and 100 artillery pieces, and taking 7,000 POWs. By comparison this division had committed to combat 180 tanks, 260 APCs, 90 artillery pieces, and 18 antitank helicopters. The Coalition had still not committed all its reserves: U.S. Marines from the amphibious landing force were not involved in the fighting.

However, no ground forces stood between the Iraqi army and its lines of retreat into Iraq; this was due on the one hand to the fact that no Coalition forces had driven to the north of the Republican Guard, and on the other hand to the fact that the Republican Guard had not advanced south to confront the advancing U.S. Marines and Joint Arab Forces. Furthermore, envelopment from the air did not take place either: air forces were not allowed complete freedom to assail the retreating Iraqi forces because ground forces wanted freedom to use their helicopters and moved the boundary within which air strikes were controlled by ground forces (the fire support coordination line) past Iraqi forces. However, few air strikes were called in by ground forces and few helicopter strikes took place.[326] Thus the Iraqi forces were able to retreat largely unhampered.

U.S. Marine Brig. Gen. Carlton Fulford:

By dawn on 27 February we were right on the outskirts of Kuwait City itself and the light armored infantry battalion went in and cleared the international airport. There was no substantial resistance at that point. Later that day we learned that the cease-fire order had been given and were told to hold our positions and evaluate the equipment and weapons in our area, and that's the way we spent the remainder of our time in Kuwait.

At the beginning of the ground war, intelligence showed that there were something like 17 Iraqi divisions in our path. If we'd had to fight just half of those, it would have taken a considerable amount of time. I think that the fact that we were delayed about half a day at the beginning outside al-Jaber airfield while the Iraqis counterattacked allowed them time to move the bulk of their forces and try to withdraw them out of Kuwait. I feel that many of the forces that were caught on that stretch of road north of Kuwait City were those forces that had withdrawn ahead of us as we were moving north. As we moved, we found many things that had been abandoned or moved very recently. We would uncover division command posts where candles were still burning, but no one was there.[327]

U.S. Marine Cpl. Randy Davis: "We went through a bunker complex near the Kuwaiti International Airport. It was a maze. Luckily for us, they had abandoned it. It was a real scary looking place. They could really have messed us up if they'd remained and fought. Thank God they ran." U.S. Marine Lt. Col. William Grubb: "They had so much ammunition and so many

---

326. Cohen et al., *GWAPS: Operations*, pp. 314-315, and *GWAPS: Effects and Effectiveness*, pp. 257-258. A detailed account is given in Swain, *"Lucky War,"* p. 228.

327. Personal interview.

well-sited positions that all they had to do was stay there with their finger on the trigger and they would have killed thousands of us. We were lucky we weren't fighting Iranian fanatics, guys who would rather die at their gun than surrender."

The Fourth Battalion of the 32nd Armored Regiment, a unit of the First Brigade of the Third Armored Division, moved forward at 0720 on 27 February. After 2 kilometers they encountered a mix of T-55s, T-62s, and T-72s: remnants of several Iraqi divisions that were falling back. TOWs and tank rounds dispersed the Iraqis as the First and Third Brigades advanced into Kuwait. Infantry positions were often ill-prepared. Some mortars were camouflaged with little more than a branch from a tree. "You'd look at the guys and say: 'You stupid idiot,'" said Lt. Col. John Kalb, commander of the Fourth Battalion. "There were 40 tanks going 'Boom' and 4 Bradleys launching TOWs. Any place you put that little dot [from the laser] for a sabot round, and that was where it was going to hit." Overwhelming artillery fire was called in on the Iraqi positions and many infantry troops stood up to surrender.

The Iraqis attempted a counterattack on the right flank, but two companies took them on. Kalb: "They didn't know what was going on. They were dead in 12 seconds. It was over that quickly." The battalion moved forward, taking just over 200 prisoners and destroying some 30 APCs and 12 tanks. About 200 Iraqis were killed.[328]

The fate of the Iraqi troops who fled Kuwait City was less pleasant than that of those who surrendered. Apparently obeying orders from Baghdad to retreat, tens of thousands of soldiers piled into trucks and stolen civilian cars and drove out of the city, forming a huge column of vehicles. The road they took runs straight and flat for a while, then turns into a slight uphill gradient. Coalition aircraft spotted this formation; dropped mines in front of and behind it to block any further movements; and directed heavy fire against it. The leading vehicles were hit about three-quarters of the way up the gradient, blocking the rest of the column. Adding its firepower to that of the airplanes, the First (Tiger) Brigade of the U.S. Second Armored Division engaged this column with direct and indirect fire on the evening of 26 February. Thousands of vehicles were destroyed and burned, and, by some accounts, thousands of troops were killed. But reports from the Tiger Brigade indicate that few Iraqis died. According to these reports, most troops fled into the desert after the first air strikes, leaving only empty vehicles to be destroyed. Tony Clifton's eyewitness account:

---

328. Personal interviews, except Corporal Davis's account, which is from Military History Magazine, *Desert Storm*, p. 148; and Colonel Kalb's account, which is from Steve Vogel, "The Tip of the Spear," *Army Times: Desert Storm After-action Review* (13 January 1992): 13, 38.

A vast traffic jam of more than a mile of vehicles, perhaps 2,000 or more. . . . Allied jets had repeatedly bombed the blocked vehicles. As we drove slowly through the wreckage, our armored personnel carrier's tracks splashed through great pools of bloody water. We passed dead soldiers lying, as if resting, without a mark on them. We found others cut up so badly, a pair of legs in trousers would be 50 yards from the top of the body. Four soldiers had died under a truck where they had sought protection. Others were fanned out in a circle as if a bomb had landed in the middle of their group. . . . Most grotesque of all was the charred corpse of an Iraqi tank crewman, his blackened arms stretched upward in a sort of supplication.

Another, who visited the scene months later:

The paint on every single vehicle had burned completely away, leaving bare metal. It was so bad that this tough British ex-career officer working for the Red Cross down there would nearly cry every time he drove by the mess on his way from Kuwait City to the refugee camp for Bedouins and Palestinians.[329]

By the morning of 28 February the SCUD threat to Israel and Saudi Arabia had essentially ceased to exist; known biological, chemical, and nuclear production facilities had been destroyed; the Iraqi national leadership had lost command and control in the theater of operations; the Republican Guard divisions were combat ineffective and incapable of further coordinated resistance; surviving Iraqi forces were in full retreat towards Basra under heavy Coalition pressure; heavy casualties were being inflicted on those forces that continued to resist; and huge numbers of prisoners of war had been taken.

Table 8.1
Statistics of Coalition advance

Hour[330]	tanks destroyed	divisions destroyed	prisoners taken
24	NA	NA	5,500
38	NA	NA	10,000
41	300	NA	20,000
55	700	21	30,000
79	1,000	29	50,000
100	2,100	40	86,000

329. Tony Clifton's account is from *Newsweek* (11 March 1991). The other account is based on a personal interview.

330. Compiled from multiple official sources, including Central Command briefings and afteraction reports. The number of tanks destroyed may be overestimated.

Table 8.1 shows the escalating statistics of Iraqi losses during the 100 hours of the Coalition's ground offensive. With the achievement of the Coalition's military objectives, offensive operations ceased at 0500 GMT on 28 February. A temporary cessation-of-hostilities protocol was agreed to in military-to-military talks on 3 March at Safwan airfield in southern Iraq, just north of the Kuwaiti border. According to the protocol accepted by both sides at Safwan, the Coalition would continue to occupy the southern part of Iraq until a permanent cease-fire was agreed upon.[331]

BEHIND-THE-SCENES POLITICAL MANEUVERS

The intense political maneuvering that took place just before the beginning of the ground war continued even as Coalition forces advanced into Kuwait and Iraq. Immediately after the initial ground attack, on 24 February, an Iraqi military communique claimed that Coalition forces had suffered heavy casualties, denied that numerous Iraqi POWs had been taken, and claimed that Coalition parachutists had been repulsed in Kuwait City. None of these claims was true. On 25 February, Radio Baghdad claimed that the Coalition attack had been repulsed with heavy Coalition casualties.

In fact counterattacks by Iraqi second-echelon forces against U.S. Marines and Joint Arab Forces advancing into Kuwait were repulsed during 25 February. It is conceivable that the Iraqi leadership decided to give up fighting at that point, since Radio Baghdad announced in the early morning of 26 February that an order to retreat from Kuwait had been given. The Iraqi announcement could have motivated some Coalition nations to call for a cease-fire, but the United States declared that it expected a *personal* declaration by Iraqi President Saddam Hussein announcing the retreat, accepting the restoration of the Emir of Kuwait, and declaring Iraq's willingness to pay war reparations.

The tough U.S. policy risked alienating public opinion in the poorer Arab countries; indeed, one year after the end of hostilities, many Arabs considered the Gulf War to have been the result of a U.S.-Israeli anti-Arab conspiracy; to them the only result of the war was the devastation of two Arab countries.

On 26 February, as the Coalition continued its destruction of the Iraqi army, Saddam Hussein announced an unconditional withdrawal from Kuwait.[332] However, the language he used was somewhat ambiguous, since he reiterated the claim that Kuwait was legally part of Iraq and would cease to be so only after the withdrawal of Iraqi troops.

Coalition political leaders rejected Saddam Hussein's withdrawal speech because it did not explicitly recognize the independence of Kuwait; because it

---

331. Schwarzkopf, *It Doesn't Take a Hero*, p. 488.

332. This was officially communicated to the United Nations, and the time of withdrawal was given as dawn Kuwaiti time, 27 February, that is, around midnight New York time, 26 February. United Nations, *Iraq-Kuwait Conflict*, p. 181.

did not mention that Iraq would pay war reparations; and, most important, because Coalition forces had not observed signs of military retreat—on the contrary, they claimed that Republican Guard divisions were fighting, not withdrawing.

Reinforcing the tough position taken by the United States, the USSR concurred that Iraq would have to accept all 12 U.N. resolutions relating to Kuwait. All five permanent members of the U.N. Security Council (China, France, U.K., United States, USSR) rejected the Iraqi request for a cease-fire, on the ground it had been made *before* Iraq's formal acceptance of all 12 resolutions.

At midnight New York time on 27 February (28 February, 0500 GMT), Coalition forces suspended hostilities, having destroyed 40 Iraqi divisions—essentially all of the Iraqi forces in the war zone—and leaving only 1 or 2 Iraqi divisions relatively intact. At that time the Coalition occupied roughly 30 percent of Iraq, and stated that it would continue to do so until a permanent cease-fire was signed. It demanded from Iraq acceptance of all 12 U.N. resolutions; release of Coalition POWs and any arrested Kuwaiti citizens; maps of minefields; and cessation of SCUD attacks.

There have been subsequent speculations that the Coalition ceased hostilities too soon, because the Iraqi army retained sufficient capability to suppress the civil war that soon broke out and also to do harm among neighboring states. These speculations ignore the political and military objective of the campaign: the liberation of Kuwait. Once that objective had been attained (indeed, exceeded, since part of Iraq had been occupied), the Coalition confronted a choice: either to cease hostilities or to agree on a new set of objectives. In fact, the U.S. congressional resolution authorizing President Bush to use military forces specifically stated that those forces were to be used to achieve implementation of the U.N. resolutions. At the time of cessation of hostilities, Coalition military forces had liberated Kuwait, and Iraq had accepted all 12 U.N. Security Council resolutions. Since total destruction of the Iraqi army and the overthrow of the Iraqi regime were neither avowed Coalition objectives nor mandated by U.N. resolutions, the Coalition was politically obliged to stop its campaign. On the military side, any additional equipment and human losses that might have been inflicted on the one or two intact divisions deployed against the Coalition at the cessation of hostilities would have had little effect on Iraq's postwar fighting power, since there were certainly very significant forces deployed around Baghdad and in the north, and these forces would have remained intact unless the Coalition had attempted to occupy all of Iraq.[333]

It became fashionable in 1994 and 1995 to criticize the Coalition for not having gone on to take Baghdad. These criticisms appear unfounded from

---

333. Swain, *"Lucky War,"* p. 290 and Craft, *An Operational Analysis*, pp. 39-41. For a less favorable analysis of Coalition actions, see Gordon and Trainor, *The Generals' War*, pp. 416-432.

both the political and the military points of view. The Coalition did not have the political will to invade the capital of Iraq and replace its government. As Gen. Khaled bin Sultan put the matter: "There was never any suggestion of marching on Baghdad nor, as far as I know, was the subject ever discussed. Needless to say, any such move was out of the question for the Arab members of the Coalition, and indeed would have been vigorously opposed by Saudi Arabia."[334] In addition, Western political leaders were certainly sensitive to Western public opinion's distaste for casualties, and most likely did not wish to risk incurring casualties once the Coalition's main objective had been achieved.

From a military point of view, Iraqi troops might well have fought hard and inflicted significant casualties on Coalition troops if they had advanced toward Baghdad. The lack of determination of Iraqi soldiers to defend Kuwait was a key factor in allowing the Coalition to win with few casualties of its own; no one can say whether Iraqi troops would have been determined to keep Western soldiers out of Baghdad. Indeed, military planners had concluded that Baghdad "was too far away to hold even if it could be captured, and . . . that its capture would exceed the U.N. charter for the Coalition forces."[335]

General Schwarzkopf gives the following account of his own thoughts on the decision to cease offensive operations: "My gut reaction was that a quick cease-fire would save lives. If we continued to attack through 28 February, more of our troops would get killed, probably not many, but some. What was more, we'd accomplished our mission. . . . Why not end it? Why get somebody else killed tomorrow? That made up my mind."[336]

334. bin Sultan, *Desert Warrior*, p. 426
335. Swain, *"Lucky War,"* p. 87.
336. Schwarzkopf, *It Doesn't Take a Hero*, p. 469.

9

Analysis of the Coalition Victory

Know yourself, know the enemy; your victory will never be endangered.
Know the ground, know the weather, your victory will then be total.

—Sun Tzu

Treaties ensuring the ability of the United States quickly to intervene militarily in the Gulf should future circumstances require it to do so; civil war in Iraq followed by harsh repression; the apparent emergence of an autonomous Kurdish region; the devastation and liberation of Kuwait; increased U.S. influence in the Middle East and on the oil production policies of its states, resulting in the virtual demise of OPEC's power to set oil prices; continued sanctions on Iraq; a de facto reduction of Iraq's sovereignty—these were the key consequences of the war.[337]

Kuwait's citizens greeted Coalition forces enthusiastically as they entered the capital city. Not present when the liberating soldiers arrived were the many Kuwaitis who had fled to Saudi Arabia, Egypt, and other safe havens when Iraq invaded the emirate. But more than enough people were present to put on a great show for Coalition forces. U.S. Marine Brig. Gen. Carlton Fulford:

By the time the sun came up on 26 February and we were on the outskirts of Kuwait City, citizens by the hundreds were coming out toward us, kissing the feet of Marines. Cute little girls were bringing bouquets of flowers. There was just an overwhelming

---

337. The U.N. resolutions imposing strict conditions on Iraq are summarized in United Nations, *Iraq-Kuwait Conflict*, pp. 29-33. The devastation of Kuwait is well described in ibid., pp. 191-193.

feeling of relief that the Iraqis had gone and gratitude for the forces that had liberated their country.

U.S. Marine Col. Richard Hodory:

There were people all over the place, all flying the Kuwaiti flag, shooting rounds in the air. It was total jubilance; they were just happy, hugging us, kissing us, men kissing men, throwing flowers at us.

Young women kissed Coalition soldiers, U.S. and Kuwaiti flags were waved everywhere, people embraced and danced in the street. "It must have been like this in Paris in World War II," said one American soldier, shaking his head in disbelief as he drove through Kuwait City after its liberation. Horns honked, people waved, children begged for bits of military equipment to keep as souvenirs.[338]

Early official accounts of the performance of the Coalition troops in the Gulf War were largely enthusiastic, stressing the results achieved with low casualties because of superior weapon systems, training, and leadership.

However, it soon became fashionable to publish negative evaluations of the Coalition effort, that stressed that certain weapon systems had not worked as well as initially claimed and implied that the persistence of Saddam Hussein as president of Iraq was a failure of Coalition policy.[339]

In reality, the Coalition attained all its political and military objectives (see Chapter 3), on schedule, and with remarkably few casualties on its side, thanks to skillful and adept use of available forces. Iraqi equipment in the theater was reduced from some 3,500 tanks to 850, and from 2,500 artillery pieces to 280.[340] Coalition weapon systems mostly performed as intended and in some cases better than expected. In many cases, failure rates in the field were lower than during training. Modern troop training methods proved their worth.

Coalition military leaders had a very good knowledge of Iraqi capabilities and were able to use that knowledge to concentrate their strengths against Iraqi weaknesses: lack of airpower and an apparent inclination to rely on static defenses. Like any prudent military leader, the Coalition planners assumed a worst-case scenario, in which the Iraqi troops would use all their weapons with determination and effectiveness. But the morale of most Iraqi soldiers proved to be much lower than could have been expected, and in many cases they hardly used the weapons available to them. A key contributor to the erosion of Iraqi morale was the intensive air campaign.

On the negative side, the U.S. logistic system did not function as it should have; airpower did not meet the expectations of extremist proponents who

---

338. All personal interviews.

339. There are many such books. A popular account is U.S. News & World Report, *Triumph Without Victory*; a more reasoned version is Jeffrey Record, *Hollow Victory* (Brassey's, 1993).

340. Cohen et al., *GWAPS: Operations*, p. 317.

thought that it could win the war on its own; some very modern and expensive weapon systems did not perform much better than older and less expensive ones; sea mines laid by Iraq proved to be an effective and inexpensive method to hamper naval operations; and the dissemination of intelligence from the Pentagon to the field did not work well.

THE POLITICAL AND ECONOMICAL CONSEQUENCES

A U.S. soldier:

We hadn't had a shower in like 30 days, and then one night it started raining. So we decided to get out and take a shower in the rain. The next day when we woke up, we were completely black. It was oil. The only thing that wasn't black were these two little holes where our eyes were.

An official of the Federation of Red Cross and Red Crescent Societies:

It's the closest thing I can imagine Hell to be like. Pillars of smoke, the ground just bubbling with fire.[341]

When the war ended, the sky in Kuwait was as dark as night at noon. Few who didn't see the live television pictures can believe the description, yet it was literally true. Clouds of smoke from burning oil wells turned day into night: following orders, and carrying out Iraqi President Saddam Hussein's threats, Iraqi troops, as they fled from Kuwait, set fire to hundreds of oil wells. The resulting fires burned for months. On an overall scale, the damages to Kuwait have been estimated at over $25 billion.[342]

The dual goal of Western powers to liberate Kuwait and to regain control of oil resources is clearly illustrated by the fall in the price of oil, from an average of $33 per barrel in October 1990 to $19 in March 1991 and even through 1992 and 1993. In 1990, spot prices rose from about $29 in early September to just under $40 at the end of the month, dropped in early October, peaked at just over $40 in mid-October, then dropped rapidly to $29 by the end of the month. On 17 January 1991, the day the war started, the spot price dropped by nearly $10 for a short time. Figure 9.1 illustrates the effects on the price of oil of Iraq's invasion of Kuwait and the subsequent campaign to liberate the country. The shortfall in production caused by the shutdown of Iraqi and Kuwaiti production was immediately compensated by production from other OPEC nations, notably Saudi Arabia, which increased its production from 5.4 MBPD before the invasion to 6.0 on 2 August, to 7.5 in September, and to 8.2 in November 1990. Saudi Arabia maintained these high production levels through the beginning of 1992.[343]

341. Personal interviews.
342. United Nations, *Iraq-Kuwait Conflict*, p. 217.
343. United Nations, *Energy Statistics Yearbook*; and OECD, *Economic Outlook*.

On 5 April, the United Nations agreed on conditions for a permanent cease-fire. Iraq was required to destroy its SCUDs, chemical weapons, and biological and nuclear weapons development capabilities at its own expense.[344] The total embargo on arms sales was extended and a fund, to be financed by Iraqi oil revenues, was set up to pay for war damages. Iraq was required to agree to the 1963 version of its borders with Kuwait and to accept a demilitarized border zone patrolled by U.N. forces. These conditions were accepted by Iraq, and the cease-fire officially started at 2130 EST on 12 April, under U.N. Security Council Resolution 687.[345]

Figure 9.1
Oil prices and production, 1990-1991

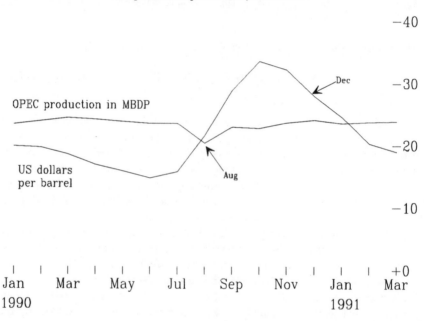

On 15 April, Iraq requested that Iran return 148 planes. Iran claimed that only 22 planes were present on its territory and refused to return them. U.N. inspectors soon arrived in Iraq to start supervising the destruction of its nuclear, chemical, and biological weapons capability. On 17 June, the United Nations agreed that Iraq would have to pay for this work, estimated to cost between $200 and $800 million.

---

344. United Nations, *Iraq-Kuwait Conflict*, p. 267.
345. For a full account of the postwar destruction of Iraq's weapons of mass destruction, and Iraq's continued attempts to hinder this effort by concealing residual capabilities, see ibid., pp. 74-98.

On 20 September, the United States and Kuwait signed a military agreement allowing the United States to preposition heavy military equipment (such as tanks) in the emirate. The United States thus secured the ability to intervene rapidly in the region in the future.

Iraq, which had entered the 1980s as a regional economic superpower, and the 1990s as a regional military superpower, was reduced to military insignificance and saw its economy severely diminished. Its foreign debts were huge, and Western powers appeared determined to earmark a considerable portion of any future oil revenues for payment of war reparations. Jordan also suffered considerable economic loss; the return of several hundred thousand Jordanians who had been working in Kuwait and Saudi Arabia, together with lost trade, accounted for a significant drop in GNP.

At the same time OPEC appeared to have lost any possibility of reducing production to force an increase in oil prices in the near future: Saudi Arabia was producing at high volumes while Kuwait was beginning to resume production. Thus prices remained low despite the fact that Iraq was not exporting. Ironically, Saudi Arabia was in effect producing what had once been Iraq's quota, in order to pay for the cost of the war.

Hence the war achieved its fundamental goal of securing oil supplies and of maintaining stable prices for this essential commodity. Furthermore, through 1992 and 1993, Western powers were exercising a de facto protectorate over countries in the region that possessed over half of the world's identified oil reserves and accounted for nearly one fifth of total oil production.

However, apparently against all odds, Saddam Hussein remained in power at the time this book was written, more than five years after the end of the war. His survival is probably due in part to the fact that all the regional powers fear that his replacement by an unknown figure could result in the dismemberment of Iraq and result in regional instability that might favor Iran. Indeed, all the regional powers support the territorial integrity of Iraq and are wary of the fact that the Iraqi defeat moved the balance of power in the Gulf in favor of Iran.[346]

The crisis triggered by the Iraqi invasion of Kuwait in August 1990 appears at this time to be one of the outstanding politicomilitary events since World War II, yet its importance derives mainly from its timing with respect to the end of the Cold War and the search for a new international order.

The U.N.-sponsored, U.S.-led Coalition assembled against Iraq in response to its invasion of Kuwait came together as a result of the new international climate prevailing after the end of the East-West confrontation. The formation and cohesion of the Coalition was aided by the Western perception of Iraq's actions as unjustified aggression. More important, the invasion of Kuwait directly threatened the West's vital interests, so its response was strengthened by economic as well as political, legal, and domestic factors.

---

346. Gawdat Bahgat, "Regional Peace and Stability in the Gulf," *Security Dialogue*, 26, no. 3 (1995): 317-330.

While the Gulf War can and will teach many lessons to political and military decision makers, as well as to historians, it probably does not provide evidence that the type of collective action waged against Iraq will become the rule in the future.

DECISIVE ADVANTAGES

Two points have been stressed again and again by all the soldiers that we have interviewed: the Iraqi soldiers' lack of will to fight and the key importance of the extensive training carried out by Coalition forces during Operation Desert Shield. In addition, the Coalition enjoyed a decisive advantage in a number of other areas, notably logistics, weapon systems, firepower, and leadership.

Training

Troops spent nearly four months training full-time for the potential outbreak of hostilities. In interview after interview, we heard that during the first exposure to fire, people were more afraid of not doing their job than of death—a striking tribute to the quality of Coalition training.

A special training team, equipped with computer simulation software, deployed to Saudi Arabia to conduct exercises for corps and division commanders. Countless obstacle-breaching exercises were performed by ground forces. Ground-attack aircraft practiced with ground forces. Air forces rehearsed the exact missions they were to fly during the first two days of the planned air campaign. Live fire and live bombing ranges were established in the Saudi desert.[347]

U.S. F-15C pilot Lt. Col. Don Kline:

Towards the end of September, we finally figured out that we couldn't just keep doing combat air patrols. Fighter pilot skills are so time perishable that we thought our abilities were being eroded. We began to do continuation training when we weren't on patrol. It was basic fighter maneuvers. One-on-one, just to hone the skills and get the gs back on your body. From there we went into air combat tactics. If I took a four-plane formation up, it would be two against two, with one pair acting as adversaries.

U.S. F-111 Weapons Systems Officer Capt. Mark Hiebert:

We had the unusual benefit of preparing for this war a number of months before it actually started. We practiced and practiced . . . we had about five months to plan the actual first day of the war. So we had a lot of cross talk with the different services, with the different people who were going to be in the target area. We had a lot of time to build and refine the actual plan of operations for the first couple of days of the war.

---

347. U.S. Department of Defense, *Conduct of the Persian Gulf War*, pp. 106-107; and Cohen et al., *GWAPS: Command and Control*, p. 169.

For five months we planned low-level, precision-guided munitions attacks. By the end of November we knew our tasking, we knew what we were good at.

U.S. Marine Brig. Gen. Carlton Fulford (a colonel during the Gulf War), commander of Task Force Ripper:

We had been assigned the task of developing the concept for the breach since October. We had built what we thought was the best replica of the Iraqi defenses in our training area. We spent almost every waking moment from October through February working on that breaching concept. I had estimated that it would take us about a day to make breaches in the two defensive lines we would face. As we began to get additional equipment and improve our training, we narrowed the estimate. The day before we went into Kuwait, we ran a dress rehearsal for our task force. The rehearsal was an exact replica in terms of distance, time of movement, separation of the two breaches, and so on. The actual execution when we went into combat came within minutes of what we had done on that rehearsal the day before.

Every Marine in my task force could have done his job blindfolded: we had done it so many times, and talked about it, and thought about it, and plotted it. It was just a perfect example of what you can do when you have the opportunity to train effectively for a long period of time.

Captain Yakovleff of the French Foreign Legion:

We'd practiced breaching the front 10 or 20 times. Every company and every platoon had practiced it, by day and by night, on an escarpment behind our positions that was exactly like the front. There was no difference in the type or intensity of the work we did before or during the war. It's true—that's how it works. You have to try for excellence, and you're never good enough and there are always things to improve. When we crossed the line, it was the same world. It was just like in training. It worked well because we had already faced and solved all the problems.

Lt. Col. Terry Tucker:

Through most of the five days that we were fighting, at my level there was virtually no difference with going through a training exercise at the National Training Center. It was exactly the same, including the sounds, the visibility, the smoke and all that kind of stuff. In fact, at times I caught myself thinking that this was just another exercise. The only difference was when I was getting reports of destroyed vehicles and casualties—it was real as opposed to being part of the exercise.

But no amount of training can simulate the tension of actually going into combat for the first time. Lt. Horst Herting of the Third Armored Division:

We just came straight out of Hohenfels, straight to war, so we were very well trained, but when it really came down to it, it wasn't the same, because there was much more control for maneuver and there was strict control for fire: we were very self-conscious about friendly fire. The scale of movements of desert training was larger. There was a lot of confusion during the war.

Chief Warrant Officer-2 Jackely, one of Lieutenant Colonel Tucker's officers:

What we did in the Persian Gulf was nowhere near anything that we've ever trained for. I was concerned about getting shot, but once it came to the point where I was doing my job, you just kind of shut out everything else, and so all I was thinking about was talking to the commanders to tell them what I saw.

Highly realistic simulated training experiences are provided by the U.S. Army (National Training Center), Marines, Navy (Top Gun school), and Air Force (Red Flag exercises). These training measures confounded Iraqi President Saddam Hussein's prediction that his forces would win because "[Iraqi troops] have combat experience, unlike the Americans using military manuals." Indeed Iraqi training appears to have been poor. U.S. F-15 pilot Capt. Dane Powell:

In the Iraqi war there was no high-g maneuvering, simply because the Iraqis were very poor tacticians, very poor pilots. In 90 percent of the engagements we had, they attempted to disengage prior to actual combat, and the actual engagements that we did have, resulted when they made their abort too late. They were inept. In all the engagements that I heard about, at every decision point the Iraqis generally did the very worst thing that they could do. It was to the point where it was ridiculously easy. I would attribute that to lack of training and system knowledge.

U.S. Marine Lt. Col. Cliff Myers:

Iraqi training was not as high as it could have been; it was somewhat deficient. It seems that the top-caliber individuals didn't go to the Republican Guard any longer, nor to the tanks. Perhaps Saddam Hussein was concerned that if there were a coup or any internal strife, he didn't want to have his top-quality people driving tanks around. The best people seemed to be in engineering units. So they didn't start off with the cream of the crop in tanks anyway, and that affected the training.

When a person fights, if you can't look the man the eye and see the fire there, and know that he has that fire burning in his belly, then he's not going to do well. And that's what we found out on the night of 29 January: that our enemy was not 10 feet tall, he was not real well trained, there wasn't a great deal of discipline—and that was early, only fifteen days or so after the air war had started.

U.S. Army Lt. Curtis Palmer:

Trenches were poorly dug, usually not deep enough. They were deficient at basic military skills that go back to Caesar. . . . We drove right on top of some of their bunkers. They could have come out of the ground and hit us. With the dense battlefield, tanks packed in there, friendly fire going every which way, Iraqis popping RPGs, it could have been a catastrophe. We would definitely have had something to deal with. And that's what a well-trained, highly disciplined army would have done."

Lt. Col. Frank Kabelman, commander of the First Combat Engineer Battalion, attached to the U.S. First Marine Division:

If I had put those minefields in place, I think I could have stopped the assault, and I think any other combat engineer would tell you the same thing. Give me six months to build a minefield, and let me cover it with indirect fire, and I bet there would have been a lot more casualties than we received.

U.S. Marine artillery officer Lt. Col. Rob Rivers:

Their equipment was good. It was badly maintained, and they didn't know how to use it properly. Their artillery was not well camouflaged against air attacks. If we had had the same equipment that the Iraqis had, we would have been able to use it more effectively.[348]

On the Coalition side, the root cause of its poor performance in battle damage assessment (BDA) can be directly attributed to inadequate training.[349] BDA consists of analyzing satellite and other imagery to ascertain and disseminate to the field the effects of air strikes.

Morale

At the beginning of the war it was not known which side would have the better morale. Many of the Iraqi troops were thought to be battle-hardened veterans of the Iran-Iraq War. While most of the officers and senior NCOs of the U.S. forces had seen combat, an overwhelming majority of the Coalition troops had never been in combat.

In the course of the land battle it became clear that Coalition morale was far superior to Iraqi morale and that this superiority contributed in no small measure to the Coalition victory. The NATO forces' extensive training on simulated battlefields worked well in building troop confidence, as did amenities such as packages and letters from home, access to telephones, entertainment, and so forth. Relentless bombing and the resultant lack of food and water undermined the morale of frontline Iraqi troops (see Chapter 6, section "Air Strikes Against Dug-In Troops" for a detailed account). Many veterans of the Iran-Iraq War turned out to be older men tired of fighting, rather than hardened veterans.[350] Some Iraqi division commanders abandoned their troops prior to the ground assault.

U.S. Apache pilot Lt. Col. William Bryan:

In the desert you couldn't hide. It should have been extremely dangerous, since some of their anti-aircraft missile systems out-ranged us, but the Iraqis showed little or no desire to fight. They had the equipment, but they didn't have the resolve.

---

348. All personal interviews. For an overall confirmation of these anecdotes, see Cohen et al., *GWAPS: Planning*, pp. 72-73.

349. Cohen et al., *GWAPS: Command and Control*, p. 304, and *GWAPS: Effects and Effectiveness*, p. 34. A very detailed account is given in Mandeles et al., *Managing "Command and Control,"* pp. 101, 103, 105, 110.

350. Cohen et al., *GWAPS: Operations*, p. 320.

U.S. Marine Brig. Gen. Carlton Fulford:

While the air campaign was effective, there were many weapon systems that had been dug in and were not disturbed in any way by air. They could have fought, but the air certainly affected the Iraqi morale. I don't think that the basic Iraqi soldier believed in what he was doing and in why he was there in the first place.

U.S. Marine Lt. Col. William Grubb:

The key factor was that to a man the Iraqi prisoners I talked to said it was stupid to be in Kuwait. They're a fairly well-educated country, with a big middle class; they would tell us that fighting the Iranians was a fairly important thing to do because there were some important economic and political matters on those border disputes. But fighting the United States over Kuwait was idiotic. We don't know how good these guys could have been, because they didn't want to be there; not because they were necessarily scared of us—although 40 days of pounding from the air and naval gunfire had its effect. They thought fighting us for Kuwait was the dumbest thing they'd ever been exposed to, and they were so happy to get a chance to survive that they didn't see any advantage in fighting us. A soldier whose heart is not in the battle just doesn't fight very well. How hard they would have fought us if we had gone to Baghdad is hard to say.[351]

The words of Sergeant Gino Pulizzi of the U.K. Staffordshire Regiment illustrate the morale of Coalition forces:

We really just wanted to get on with it. Just get out there and have a go at the Iraqis. We didn't rate any reports about the Republican Guard. . . . We knew that we were better, man for man, than they would ever be.[352]

Firepower

U.S. Secretary of Defense Richard Cheney and others had stated that the Iraqi army was the fourth largest in the world. These statements are based on a comparison of numbers of men, tanks, and artillery. However, such comparisons can be misleading if they ignore differences in the range, accuracy, and firepower of weapon systems and the ability of soldiers to use the equipment they have.[353] After the fact, it is obvious that the Iraqi army was not the fourth largest in the world, in terms of fighting power.

The large difference in firepower might help to explain the unusually one-sided casualty ratio, which exceeded Coalition expectations: Central Command planners[354] had estimated 12,000 to 15,000 total U.S. casualties

---

351. All from personal interviews, except Colonel Bryan's account, which is adapted from Morse, *Gulf Air War Debrief*, p. 160.

352. Benson, *Rat's Tales*, p. 63.

353. The classic treatment of the importance of firepower is F. W. Lanchester, *Aircraft in Warfare: The Dawn of the Fourth Arm* (Constable, 1916).

354. Personal interview.

(about 5%),[355] with 1,200 to 1,500 dead, which corresponds well with the 18,000 hospital beds provided on the basis of doctrinal rules. U.K. forces planned medical services on the basis of 5% casualties, of which 25% would be killed.[356] (Table 9.3 lists Coalition casualties.)

Logistics

The Coalition logistical lines were never threatened, much less attacked, by Iraqi forces, allowing unimpeded movement of huge quantities of material (see section Chapter 4, section "Logistics").

In contrast, Iraqi logistics were seriously hampered by the Coalition's successful effort to target bridges, railroads, and road traffic (see Chpater 6, section "Air Strikes Against Logistic Support"), to the point where deserters from Iraq's frontline troops reported shortages of food and water. Combat effectiveness was also reduced by shortages of spare parts and ammunition.

Coalition Weapon systems

Modern weapon systems are sophisticated devices, that often incorporate electronic subsystems. One statistic will help in grasping this concept: the U.S. military employs about 30% of its enlisted people in maintenance and repair roles, as opposed to the 17% it classifies as combat forces.

Many Coalition weapon systems relied on built-in microprocessors to achieve their high performance. Powerful computers provided the capabilities of the aerial, ground, and naval surveillance systems. But many logistic and support computer systems failed to perform adequately, due to hardware inadequacy, software problems, and/or lack of trained personnel.[357]

To a great extent, the Coalition benefited from what we can call "intrinsically superior weapon systems." These can harm without being harmed. For example, fighters are designed to be intrinsically superior to bombers and do not suffer serious casualties when attacking unescorted bombers. Aircraft carriers are intrinsically superior to other surface ships, provided they keep their distance. Coalition aircraft proved intrinsically superior to most Iraqi antiaircraft weapons, thanks to the HARM missile and other antiradar measures. The most modern Western tanks and APCs were intrinsically superior to Iraqi tanks, since they could fire and destroy while out of range of Iraqi tank guns.

Much weapon systems reasearch and development is devoted to the search for intrinsic superiority, or to ways of defeating enemy attempts to acquire such superiority. The following highlights some of the key Coalition weapon

---

355. But a higher number of 20,000 is given by Swain, *"Lucky War,"* p. 205.

356. De La Billière, *Storm Command*, p. 118.

357. Cohen et al., *GWAPS: Summary*, pp. 232-233, and *GWAPS: Command and Control*, p. 54 footnote 56, and pp. 74-75.

systems and the ways in which technology allowed them to attain intrinsic superiority. Although communications and control is not, strictly speaking, a weapon system, we start with it, because the Coalitions weapons systems could not have been used effectively without sophisticated command and control systems.

Communications and Control

The Coalition devoted considerable resources to communication and control: overall, the U.S. military employs about 10% of its enlisted personnel in communications and intelligence roles. Essentially all U.S. Air Force tactical command and control systems were deployed, leaving it with no effective reserve.[358] Overall, at the height of operations, the U.S. communications system supported more than 700,000 phone calls and 152,000 messages per day, relying on 130 satellite terminals, 60 voice and 20 message switches.

Nevertheless, the dissemination to ground units of satellite imagery, that was able to show individual vehicles and the details of Iraqi fortified positions, was inadequate.[359]   Air campaign planners developed direct links to intelligence sources in Washington, D.C., bypassing the chain of command. This resulted in confusion and tension regarding responsibility for target selection.[360] Furthermore, a shortage of people, delays in acquiring satellite images due to bad weather, and a larger-than-expected workload contributed to significant delays in battle damage assessment.[361]

Aerial Surveillance

Airborne Warning and Control System (AWACS) planes gave an overview of the air war. Fourteen land-based E-3A Sentries and 30 carrier-based E-2C Hawkeye airborne radar surveillance planes were used to detect any Iraqi air activity and to control the thousands of daily sorties of Coalition aircraft. These planes carried powerful onboard computer systems that kept track of all flights in the covered zone and calculated intercept vectors; since the highest-performance models of these planes could observe activity in a radius of some 500 kilometers, two planes airborne simultaneously would have been able to cover the entire Iraqi airspace. In fact five U.S. AWACS were continuously

---

358. Cohen et al., *GWAPS: Command and Control*, pp. 129-130.

359. Scales, *Certain Victory*, pp. 165, 172; and U.S. General Accounting Office, *Operation Desert Storm*, p. 3.

360. Cohen et al., *GWAPS: Summary*, pp. 131-132, 135. A detailed account is Cohen et al., *GWAPS: Command and Control*, pp. 172-175, 180-185, p. 294 footnote 103, with a summary on 201. See also Mandeles et al., *Managing "Command and Control,"* pp. 21, 108.

361. Cohen et al., *GWAPS: Summary*, p. 140. Cohen et al., and *GWAPS: Command and Control*, p. 294 footnote 104, pp. 300, 302-303; Mandeles et al., *Managing "Command and Control,"* p. 22.

airborne during the war: three operational and one spare in Saudi Arabia, and one in Turkey; missions ran as long as 15 hours. In addition, Saudi Arabia maintained between one and three AWACS aloft, and carrier-based E-2Cs provided surveillance over the Red Sea and Persian Gulf. By using the IFF (Identification Friend or Foe) system carried by Coalition aircraft, the AWACS computer could distinguish between friendly and enemy aircraft.

In addition, two experimental JSTARS ground-surveillance aircraft proved capable of detecting mass vehicle movements, such as the Iraqi attempt to retreat from Kuwait City during the last days of the ground battle. One of these planes was in the air every day, and in total the JSTARS flew 54 sorties. A typical mission lasted 14 hours.

Both AWACS and JSTARS work by using computers to compare successive radar images of the same area. Any moving objects will show up in different places on two images, and the computer identifies and displays only those objects. The size and speed of the objects that can be detected depends on the characteristics of the radar and the available computing power. AWACS was designed to track airplanes, which move fast, but it can sometimes pick out large trucks. JSTARS is a more recent system, so it can pick out smaller objects moving more slowly. JSTARS transmits its data to ground stations via radio link, so that tactical ground commanders can view the images as they are collected; the ground station is mounted on a five-ton truck: six were deployed during the Gulf War. Radar imaging of ground targets (with less sophisticated computer processing) was also provided by high-flying U-2/TR-1 aircraft, and tactical radar reconnaissance was provided by OV-1D planes.

Fighter Aircraft

Coalition planes, guided by AWACS and equipped with highly effective infrared or radar-guided air-air missiles, had a significant technological superiority over Iraqi fighters and, combined with better trained pilots and AWACS controllers, probably constituted intrinsically superior weapon systems. Coalition forces quickly attained total aerial supremacy, preventing Iraqi aerial surveillance of Coalition troop movements; the ability to perform massive troop movements unobserved enabled the outflanking maneuvers of the final Coalition ground assault.

Few air-air encounters took place, and Coalition forces downed 35 fixed-wing aircraft with only one loss. Most of the kills were made by U.S. F-15 Eagles using AIM-7 Sparrow missiles.

Electronic Warfare Aircraft

The EA-6 Prowler, EC-130 Hercules, EF-111 Aardvark, and F-4 Phantom were used to detect and suppress Iraqi radar-controlled air defense systems. In addition to active and passive jamming, HARM antiradiation missiles were used. These weapons lock on to radar emissions and follow them to destroy the source of the emissions, normally an air defense radar. Even if the radar operator shuts off his radar when he detects the approaching missile, the HARM has achieved its effect: the radar has been rendered inoperative. The U.K. version of the HARM, the ALARM, is even more sophisticated, using a parachute to remain aloft until radar emissions are detected and then homing in on their source.

In addition to being accompanied by specialized escort aircraft, most airplanes were equipped with some self-protection system: at a minimum, radar warning receivers, chaff, and flare dispensers. However, most also had jammers and some had radar decoys.

A jammer is an electronic device that disturbs the function of an enemy radar. There are many modes of operation; for example, a strong signal can be emitted in order to fill the radar screen with white noise; or the pulse of the radar can be monitored and signals emitted to create a ghost target: one that does not exist but appears on the radar screen. A simple type of jammer, which can be added to a high-performance fighter such as a Mirage, works as follows. The device passively monitors a series of incoming radar pulses, then uses a mathematical model to predict the times at which future pulses will be received. It emits a pulse of its own just before and after the predicted time. Thus what should be a point on the radar screen becomes a large blob so that the position of the fighter cannot be accurately determined.

Radar decoys are gliders or drones (remotely piloted vehicles) that contain electronic circuits allowing them to simulate the radar signature of a much larger plane. Thus radar screens show the image of a warplane when in fact only the decoy is present, and antiaircraft fire will be directed against the decoy.

F-117 Nighthawk

This bomber uses "stealth" technology to reduce its detectability by radar and make it an intrinsically superior weapon system, at least against the level of defenses deployed by Iraq. Stealth consists both in designing the shape of the plane so that much of the arriving radar energy is reflected away from the source radar, and also in using materials that absorb rather than reflect radar waves (for example, by arranging layers so that signals reflected off inner layers will cancel incoming signals in outer layers). Bombs are carried in an internal bay, and zigzag patterns are used in the landing gear doors.

Other Bombers

The A-6 Intruder, A-7, AV-8 Harrier, B-52 Stratofortress, F-15E, F-16 Falcon, F-18 Hornet, F-111 Aardvark, Jaguar, and Tornado formed the backbone of the Coalition air campaign. Many were equipped with television-guided and laser-guided precision munitions. These bombs and missiles had ranges on the order of tens of kilometers, which means that they could be launched well before anyone at the target could be aware of the attacking plane's presence, thus again resulting in an intrinsically superior weapon system. The precision of these bombs is on the order of meters, meaning that a small target like the door of a hardened shelter can be consistently hit.

Guided Missiles

The highly accurate long-range (over 2,000-kilometer) Tomahawk missile improves the accuracy of its inertial guidance system by using onboard radar to match the contour of the terrain over which it flies with a preprogrammed map in its computer. It has an accuracy on the order of meters, and avoids detection by flying at tens of meters above the ground. Thus it can destroy targets that have no warning of its arrival. It is, however, far more expensive per ton of delivered explosive than a precision-guided bomb.[362]

Satellites

A wide range of optical and radar satellites were used to obtain information on the disposition of Iraqi forces. For example, the contour-following navigation package in the Tomahawk cruise missile was programmed with the help of data acquired from a range of satellites, and map overlays showing actual Iraqi defensive positions were distributed to Coalition ground forces. Satellites were also used to provide early warning of SCUD launches, communication services, and weather data.

In addition, satellites provided navigational aids through the Global Positioning System (GPS). GPS was used by SLAM missiles to perform midcourse corrections, by aircraft, and by land forces. Iraqi commanders reportedly did not expect the sweep through the desert by VII Corps because they did not know that GPS would allow such a coordinated advance to be conducted through the trackless, featureless terrain. GPS proved so useful during initial deployment and training (in fact, it was essential to avoid people's getting lost) that some 4,500 civilian units were acquired by U.S. forces, who did not have enough military units available (about 840 military units were deployed).

Ground Attack Aircraft

At least in the Gulf War, helicopters and airplanes equipped with laser-guided munitions were an intrinsically superior weapon system compared with tanks, whose antiaircraft defenses (mostly machine guns) they could avoid by staying out of range. The A-10 airplane (Thunderbolt or Warthog), and the

---

362. A good discussion is provided by Hallion, *Storm over Iraq*, p. 251.

AH-64 Apache and AH-1 Cobra helicopters represented weapon systems not available to the Iraqis.   Iraqi tanks and fortified positions proved very vulnerable to attack by these aircraft, which carried extremely powerful armor-piercing machine guns in addition to rockets, guided missiles, and bombs. Critical components of both the A-10 and the AH-64 are armored and can survive direct hits by 23 millimeter cannon. The A-10 carries titanium armor for the pilot, engines, and other critical parts, a 4,200 round-per-minute 30 millimeter, one-ton, 6.5-meter-long machine gun that shoots 30-centimeter-long bullets weighing nearly one kilogram and made of depleted uranium (nonradioactive uranium; since they are much heavier than lead bullets, their armor-piercing power is greater), and up to eight tons of bombs and missiles. Over 4,800 Maverick guided missiles were fired by A-10s, accounting for 90% of the Warthog's tank kills.

The Apache carries armor made of modern plastic composites such as Kevlar; in addition to a 30 millimeter cannon, its armament consists of 16 Hellfire laser-guided antitank missiles with a range of 6 kilometers and state-of-the-art infrared vision systems. The Cobra is unarmored and carries a 20 millimeter cannon; the U.S. Army version carries TOW missiles with a range exceeding 3,500 meters; the U.S. Marine version can also carry Hellfire missiles. Both the Apache and the Cobra are extremely narrow aircraft, so as to present a very small target when seen head-on: the two crew members sit one behind the other. While not every Warthog or Cobra was equipped with infrared sensors, A-10s with night capability were on call at all times.

French and U.K. forces also deployed helicopters with antitank guided missiles. Most Coalition Navies deployed helicopters equipped with anti-ship missiles; the most effective was reportedly the U.K. Lynx helicopter firing a Sea Skua missile. In addition, bombers equipped with precision munitions and night-attack capability proved very effective against tanks.

Artillery

Iraq possessed a formidable conventional artillery force, estimated at over 3,000 pieces before the war.   Using rocket-assisted shells, this kind of conventional artillery can attain ranges around 35 kilometers, with rates of fire around 4-6 shells per minute.   However, besides having the same kind of conventional artillery, Coalition forces had the multiple launch rocket system (MLRS), which can shoot 12 rockets in one minute at ranges over 35 kilometers. Radar tracking is used to correct firing parameters, thus ensuring very high accuracy. Each rocket carries about 150 kilograms of munitions, typically 600 antitank/antipersonnel bomblets (grenades) that are dispersed over a wide area. Thus a single MLRS rocket has about the same firepower as several conventional cannon rounds, and in one minute the MLRS system can deliver more firepower than eight conventional artillery pieces. Accounts from Coalition troops who were within a couple of kilometers of incoming MLRS fire suggest that its effect is far more devastating than that of conventional cannon.

Today the precision of cannon fire is limited only by the artilleryman's knowledge of his own position and the enemy's position, together with an estimate of variable factors such as air density and wind. Coalition Global Positioning System (GPS) equipment (based on reception of satellite transmissions) provided very precise information to troops concerning their own position; aerial observation (with manned aircraft or unmanned drones) and computer-aided analysis of incoming artillery radar tracks provided precise determination of Iraqi artillery positions; computer-aided analysis and drone observation of outgoing artillery radar tracks provided accurate correction for variable factors. The combination of these techniques provided an accuracy of artillery fire that far exceeded the Iraqi capabilities. Superior accuracy combined with the vastly superior firepower of the MLRS gave the Coalition qualitatively superior artillery, thus negating Iraq's numerical superiority.

To this land-based artillery we can add the 18 406 millimeter guns of the battleships USS *Missouri* and *Wisconsin*, which relied on radar and drone aircraft to ensure precise placement of the one-ton shells they fired.

U.S. forces employed a total of six Pioneer unmanned aerial vehicles (UAV or RPV or drone) units: three Marine, two Navy, one Army. Each unit consisted of about five vehicles. French forces also deployed drones. One U.S. UAV was airborne at all times during the war, and 522 missions totaling 1,641 hours were flown. One UAV was lost to Iraqi fire and 11 for other reasons; 11 more were damaged. In addition, the U.S. Marines deployed 20 Pointer drones with far less sophisticated capabilities, and some 60 Exdrones, whose performance is between that of the Pioneer and the Pointer.[363] Other drones were used for classified purposes and no details have been released.

Tanks

Coalition forces used a variety of tanks. The primary ones were the U.S.-made M1 and M60, the British-made Challenger, and the French-made AMX-30. These tanks were equipped with high-technology, long-range, low-visibility target acquisition systems (based on thermal imaging: infrared sensors), laser range finders, and computerized fire-control systems, giving them the ability to destroy enemy tanks while remaining out of the range of Iraqi fire. In addition, Coalition tanks were protected by modern reactive and/or Chobham armor. Reactive armor is normal armor plating covered with a layer of explosives; the explosives detonate when struck by an enemy shell and deflect its charge; this armor is particularly effective in protecting against shaped charges (HEAT) but not against sabots, which are high-velocity metal arrows. Chobham armor consists of a secret composite of steel, porcelain, and

---

363. See David Fowell and J. R. Wilson, "UAVs Win Plaudits in The Storm," *International Defense Review* (October 1991).

plastic, and is supposed to be effective against all types of munitions. No M1s were penetrated by Iraqi projectiles (but some may have been damaged by friendly fire).

Iraq's best main battle tank, the USSR-made T-72, weighed 45 tons, had a top speed of 60 kilometers per hour (km/h), and a gun range of 1,500 meters. By comparison the U.S.-made M1 was rated at 63 tons, 72 km/h, and an over 2,000-meter range; and the British-made Challenger, 68 tons and 56 km/h. M1 ammunition proved capable of killing tanks located behind dirt embankments and other defensive emplacements. There is no reason to doubt the anecdotal reports of Iraqi tank crews being surprised when neighboring tanks were hit by rounds from undetected Coalition tanks. One Iraqi tank commander, the only survivor of his crew, thought his tank had been hit by a rocket from an airplane or a helicopter. He wouldn't believe that he had been hit by a round from an M1: he had seen no tanks on the horizon. As an example of the superiority of the Coalition equipment, consider that in one engagement the Second Brigade of the U.S. First Armored Division destroyed 100 Iraqi tanks and 30 APCs in 45 minutes.

It is worth stressing the superiority of tanks equipped with laser range finders and fire-control computers. Without an electronic range finder, the gunner must use optical devices based on grids or superposition of images to estimate the range. A precise estimate of range is essential for accuracy, since shells fall towards the ground as they fly toward the target, and will not reach it unless the gun is given the right elevation. Without a computer, the gunner must estimate a correction for wind; for changes in the geometry of the cannon's barrel as it heats after repeated firing; and, even more difficult, for the relative motion of a nonstationary target. In contrast, a fire-control computer automatically corrects for all these factors, computing elevation and traverse as a function of range, wind, barrel temperature, motion of the tank, and observed relative motion of the target. While the trigonometry required to solve the moving target problem is elementary, solutions cannot be found within practical times without a computer.

Also, a Western APC equipped with a modern antitank guided missile could destroy a T-72 tank while remaining out of range of the tank's gun. For example, the U.S. TOW missile had a range in excess of 3,500 meters and could penetrate the T-72's armor. Thus, although the APC's armor could not resist the fire from a tank, a properly manned APC could destroy the tank before coming within range of the tank's gun, which made it an intrinsically superior weapon system.

Iraqi Weapon Systems

Iraqi weapon systems were older, less sophisticated, and generally no match for those of the Coalition. While the Iraqis had abundant artillery, tanks, and ground-based antiaircraft defenses, none of these proved effective against the more modern Coalition weapons and countermeasures. Only two Iraqi weapon systems proved difficult to locate and destroy: mobile SCUD missiles and bottom-influence mines. In addition, the Coalition was concerned by Iraq's chemical, biological, and nuclear capabilities.[364]

Mobile SCUD Missiles

While highly inaccurate and susceptible to interception by the Patriot missile, the SCUD weapon system was nevertheless the only one in Iraqi hands that posed unexpected difficulties for the Coalition. By modern standards it is obsolete because of its lack of accuracy and the ease with which it can be detected by radar. However, the mobile version (truck-mounted launcher) proved easy to hide and deploy. This missile had about the same use as the World War II German V-2: both were aimed at civilians to produce an essentially political effect, with limited results.

The longest-range variant of the Iraqi SCUDs could deliver warheads of about 250 kilograms at distances of around 600 kilometers, with accuracies measured in kilometers. The liquid-fueled SCUD is a purely ballistic missile, that is, it has no in-flight guidance. The inaccuracy of the SCUD was such that it was useless against a point target (such as a military command post): over 30,000 SCUDs would have had to be launched in order to achieve a 50% probability of destroying a hardened command post, and over 3,000 to attain the same probability against a soft post (protected only by sandbags). The SCUD was not even of much use against airfields: some 40 launches would have been required to achieve a 50% chance of one or more hits on a runway.

Iraq constructed its long-range version of the SCUD (called the al-Husayn) by cutting the original missile, adding a new section to increase its fuel capacity, and reducing the weight of the warhead. Taken together, these changes increased not only the missile's range, but also its speed as it descended toward the target and its tendency to wobble as it was buffeted by the atmosphere. The resulting aerodynamic forces were large enough to cause many SCUDs to break up in flight, actually increasing their effectiveness, because the Patriot antimissile defense was confronted with multiple targets for each SCUD launched.

Bottom-influence Mines

These are devices that sit on the ocean floor in shallow waters, and detonate when they sense the magnetic field disturbance caused by a steel hull or when they detect the propeller noise of a large ship. Devices of this type were hard to find and caused significant damage to the USS *Princeton*.

---

364. For an overall review of Iraq's weapons of mass destruction, see United Nations, *Iraq-Kuwait Conflict*, pp. 74-98, 771-790.

In general, the extensive use of mines by Iraq forced the Coalition to devote considerable resources to mine clearance, slowed the advance of Coalition warships near the Kuwaiti coast, and was one of the factors that argued against actually attempting an amphibious landing. Without a concentrated mine-clearing effort, the ships required for an amphibious assault needed to remain some 100 kilometers away from the coast.

Chemical Warfare Capability

Many of the soldiers we have interviewed were quite concerned about the risk of chemical attack: although they were equipped with protective equipment (including suits that use activated charcoal to absorb any lethal gas in the air) and trained in its use, the fear of the unknown effects of this weapon persisted.

Worse from the Coalition's point of view, a well-designed chemical warhead reaching a city would be deadly indeed, dispersing lethal agents over an area a couple of hundred meters wide and a couple of kilometers long.[365] After the war a U.N. inspection team discovered 16 SCUD warheads, each containing 200 kilograms of nerve gas and equipped with barometric fuses, and another 13 empty warheads.[366] While these devices were crude, they were usable and had a good chance of working as intended.[367]

U.N. inspectors also found nearly 7,000 bombs, 13,000 artillery shells, and 6,500 rocket warheads filled with mustard and nerve gas at sites that had been heavily damaged by Coalition air attacks (plus another 6,000 empty rocket chemical warheads). Some 500 tons of chemical agents (80 tons of nerve gas) and nearly 3,000 tons of chemicals that could be used to produce weapons were found after the war.[368] These figures can be compared with the 32,000 tons of chemical agents available at the time to the United States and the 40,000 tons available to the USSR.

In addition, Iraq had produced biological weapons consisting of toxins such as anthrax and botulinum, but these were not used.[369] Many U.S. troops had been vaccinated against anthrax and botulinum as a precaution.

It is likely that Iraq did not use chemical or biological weapons for fear of military or political retaliation. Gen. Wafic al Samarrai, who was head of

---

365. Theodore Postol, *The Prospects for Successful Air-Defense Against Chemically-Armed Tactical Ballistic Missile Attacks on Urban Areas*, Defense and Arms Control Study Program Working Paper (Center for International Studies, Massachusetts Institute of Technology, March 1991).

366. United Nations, *Iraqi-Kuwait Conflict*, p. 656.

367. Personal interview with Dr. Johan Santesson, head of the U.N. inspection team.

368. United Nations, *Iraq-Kuwait Conflict*, p. 656. A detailed account of Iraq's chemical program is at pp. 345-361, 363-366, 416-421, 441-456, 492-504, 572-586, 604-623, 644-659, 699-717, 758-763, 810-821.

369. Ibid., pp. 94, 781-786, 818.

Iraqi military intelligence and defected after the war, stated in a 1991 interview with the British Broadcasting Corporation: "Chemical SCUDS were not used because of fear of retaliation by Israel and the Coaltion." Iraqi troops appear to have lacked adequate protection against chemical weapons, in particular full body suits. It was public knowledge that the United States had substantial offensive chemical warfare capability. General Schwarzkopf states, relating a telephone conversation: "Powell said he was pressing the White House to inform Tarik Aziz that we would use our unconventional weapons if the Iraqis use chemicals on us. Powell believed that Secretary of State Baker would deliver this message to the Iraqi foreign minister."[370]

In fact, what Baker said to Tarik Aziz in Geneva on 9 January 1991 was "If . . . chemical or biological weapons are used against our forces . . . our objective would not be only the liberation of Kuwait, but also the toppling of the present regime."[371] It is possible that field commanders may have feared being judged as war criminals if they ordered the use of chemical weapons, because use of such weapons is banned by the Geneva Conventions on warfare.

In late 1996, a U.S. presidential panel investigating postwar illness among veterans announced that several thousand U.S. soldiers may have been exposed to toxic substances when ammunition dumps containing chemical weapons were blown up after the war.[372] Subsequent studies reached contradictory conclusions regarding the causes of the postwar illness.[373]

Nuclear Weapons Capability

The material required to make an atomic bomb (called "fissile material") can be either the uranium isotope with atomic weight 235 (U-235) or plutonium. U-235 is found in concentrations of less than 1% in the uranium ore mined from the earth and must be concentrated to produce fissile material: this process requires large machines and is time-consuming. For example, about 1,000 centrifuges are required to produce the material for one bomb annually. Plutonium is not found in nature and is produced from uranium within nuclear reactors; its chemical separation from uranium is difficult and dangerous. However, possession of fissile material is not enough to produce a bomb. The material will not undergo fission until a sufficient quantity is concentrated into a very small volume (this is called "attaining critical mass"). The details of how to do this are secret, but it is well known that U-235 must be highly

370. Schwarzkopf, *It Doesn't Take a Hero*, p. 389.

371. According to a transcript released by the Iraqi News Agency (INA) in January 1992.

372. For up-to-date information on this and related topics, see U.S. Department of Defense Persian Gulf War Illness Senior Level Oversight Panel, *Persian Gulf War Illness Investigation Team Information* (http://www.dtic.dla.mil/gulflink).

373. Constance Holden, ed., "Evidence for Gulf War Syndrome?" *Science* (17 January 1997): 313.

compressed to attain fission: the compression is usually achieved by surrounding an appropriately shaped mass of U-235 with conventional explosives. Unclassified literature states that about 35 kilograms of U-235 are required to make a bomb.[374] Very fast electronic circuits can be used to trigger the conventional explosives. Devices that can be used to construct these circuits were seized on their way to Iraq by U.K. customs inspectors on 28 March 1990.

Extensive U.N. inspections after the war revealed that Iraq had a well-developed clandestine program to develop nuclear weapons. At the time of the war Iraq possessed 68 reactor fuel assemblies enriched to 80% U-235 and containing about 11 kilograms of U-235; 10 assemblies at 36% concentration with just over 1 kilo; and additional plates at 93% with less than 0.5 kilo. In addition, about 35 kilos of U-235 concentrated to 93% were present in irradiated fuel (irradiated fuel is highly radioactive, and thus difficult and dangerous to work with—it can be used to produce an atomic bomb, but less easily than nonirradiated fuel). Finally, Iraq had about 6 grams of plutonium which it had produced clandestinely.[375]

International Atomic Energy Agency (IAEA) inspectors also found two sites with facilities designed to concentrate U-235, using both the electromagnetic isotope separation method and the centrifuge method, and about 400 tons of natural uranium; the production capacity of each site was estimated at 15 kilograms per year once in operation.[376] Last but not least, the inspectors discovered equipment and plans related to warhead development and assembly.

The IAEA removed the nuclear material from Iraq. In addition, it noted that most of the buildings that had housed the clandestine nuclear weapons program had been destroyed by Coalition bombing. IAEA inspectors supervised the destruction of the electromagnetic and centrifuge separation equipment and rendered inoperable "hot cells" used to manipulate radioactive material.[377]

Leadership

Coalition leadership was competent or better than competent, at both the political and military levels. U.S. President Bush and his advisers and allies were able to construct and maintain the Coalition's political consensus and military forces. Coalition military commanders cooperated with each other

---

374. Cohen et al., *GWAPS: Effects and Effectiveness*, p. 315 footnote 110. Other sources suggest that 15 kilograms is sufficient: Philip A. Abelson, "Need for Enhanced Nuclear Safeguards," *Science* (18 March 1994): 1543.

375. United Nations, *Iraq-Kuwait Conflict*, pp. 367-368.

376. Cohen et al., *GWAPS: Effects and Effectiveness*, p. 315.

377. United Nations, *Iraq-Kuwait Conflict*, pp. 94, 367-369, 456-458, 505-507, 535-538, 587-591, 596-599, 605-607, 641-644, 659-661, 685-691, 718-719, 746-754, 756-771.

and appropriately used the available forces (but did not exhibit any special genius[378]). From our study of the primary sources,[379] we conclude that U.S. Lt. Gen. Chuck Horner provided the strategic vision for the air campaign and U.S. Brig. Gen. Buster Glosson and his team worked out the necessary tactics and implemented it. The Third Army (U.S. Lt. Gen. John Yeosock), despite its administrative accomplishments, was unable to establish good two-way communications between Schwarzkopf and XVIII and VII Corps, resulting in a lack of common understanding regarding the nature and purpose of the air campaign and the timing of the VII Corps attack on the Republican Guard. Schwarzkopf understood and projected upward to Washington and downward to his troops a clear vision of the campaign, and consistently stuck to it. However, he lost control at the end of the war because he relied on Yeosock to relay information to and from his operating corps (XVIII and VII), an arrangement that proved unworkable. His bursts of rage at times appear to have been out of place.[380] U.S. Maj. Gen. Gus Pagonis used ingenuity and improvisation to minimize the constraints imposed by logistical capabilities.[381] U.S. Gen. Colin Powell ensured that political leaders set appropriate military objectives and committed adequate forces to attain them, thus avoiding the errors of the Vietnam War. Saudi Lt. Gen. Khalid bin Sultan maintained good working relations between the Arab members of the Coalition and U.S. forces.

In contrast to the overall competence of the Coalition leaders, Iraqi leadership appears to have made a number of misjudgements, of which the most important are not understanding that control of oil is a vital Western interest for which these countries will fight; underestimating the enmity of Syria, Egypt, and Iran and overestimating Arab and Muslim solidarity; overestimating Soviet support; alienating the Western peace movement by violent anti-Israeli and anti-Western rhetoric, calls for terrorist actions, SCUD attacks on cities, TV shows of brutalized POWs, and oil spills; annexing all of Kuwait rather than just the northern portion; and underestimating Western military capabilities, especially technology, air power, and the morale of Coalition troops.[382]

In the military sphere, Iraq failed to exploit the strong defensive position offered by Kuwait City, which could have obliged Coalition troops to engage

---

378. Cohen et al., *GWAPS: Command and Control*, p. 329.

379. bin Sultan, *Desert Warrior*; Cohen et al., *GWAPS*; De La Billière, *Storm Command*; Gen. William G. Pagonis, *Moving Mountains: Lessons in Leadership and Logistics from the Gulf War* (Harvard Business School Press, 1992); Gen. Colin L. Powell, *My American Journey* (Ballantine, 1995); Scales, *Certain Victory*; Schwarzkpof, *It Doesn't Take a Hero*; Swain, *"Lucky War."*

380. Swain, *"Lucky War,"* pp. 340-341.

381. For a less favorable view and a critical analysis of logistics operations, see Charles R. Shrader, "Gulf War Logistics," *Parameters* (Winter 1995-1996): 142-148.

382. Regarding morale and airpower, see the quotations from Iraqi President Saddam Hussein in Cohen et al., *GWAPS: Planning*, pp. 61, 65, and the analysis on 72.

in house-to-house fighting, possibly incurring heavy casualties. It failed to realize that the Coalition relied heavily on satellite-based communications that could easily be jammed or otherwise disrupted. A strong signal broadcast from an earth station will automatically be relayed by a satellite transponder, thus denying use of the channel to other users. There are of course many counterjamming measures, including the physical destruction of the jamming transmitter, but these measure consume resources that could be used elsewhere. Considering the limited capability Iraq had to disrupt Coalition operations, development of methods to disrupt satellite communications could have been worthwhile from a military point of view.

It also failed to attack Saudi Arabia's ports in order to disrupt the Coalition's logistic infrastructure at its weakest choke point. Huge quantities of supplies were moved through a few ports. While Iraq had very limited capabilities to attack the ports, at least it could have attempted to do so, for example by commando attacks by land or sea, or by attempting to lay mines secretly on key access lanes.

THE AIR CAMPAIGN

Looking at events from its own point of view, the U.S. Air Force stated: "Airpower found, fixed, fought, and finished the Iraqi military." This is an exaggeration.[383]   Although airpower did have a decisive effect, the fact remains that the Iraqis were forced out of Kuwait only by a combined-arms ground assault that relied on air, naval, and ground forces; and that succeeded thanks to factors such as deception, psychological operations, surprise, technological superiority, good logistics, and training. The U.S. Air Force statement seems to reflect the fundamental outlook underlying the theory of airpower enunciated by Gen. Giulio Douhet, that airpower substitutes for land and sea power.[384]

Douhet believed that by bombing factories, airpower would have the decisive effect of depriving the foe's armed forces of weapons and supplies essential to their operation: a logistic strategy. Moreover, he believed that air raiders could also give victory through the political effect of bombing cities.

In World War II the United States and the UK invested sufficient resources in bomber fleets that they could test Douhet's theories in an air war against Germany. In bombing cities at night, the British applied the political strategy, while the American daylight raids aimed at economic targets. The U.K. bombing of cities and the damage incidental to the U.S. bombing caused some 300,000 civilian deaths and 780,000 wounded. But, instead of being cowed into submission, the German people maintained a stoic resistance to the end.

---

383. Cohen et al., *GWAPS: Effects and Effectivness*, p. 104.
384. Giulio Douhet, *The Command of the Air* (Coward-McCann, 1942).

Thus casualties and destruction at this level failed to have the expected political effect.[385]

The final concentration of the U.S. bombing on rail transport and synthetic oil production virtually disarmed the German forces by drying up their fuel supplies. Yet by that time the depleted German forces were so overmatched by their adversaries that no amount of fuel nor abundance of weapons could have made them capable of effective resistance. So, although a decisive effect had not been achieved, many continued to argue that the bombing of industrial targets showed promise.

But these discussions made it easy to overlook the fact that airpower had always had another key role. Whereas Douhet had looked upon airpower as essentially a substitute for land and naval forces, soldiers and sailors had viewed the airplane as a complement to their existing weapon systems.

That the belligerents built over 200,000 aircraft during World War I illustrates how valuable the soldiers and sailors had found the airplane. Aircraft owed their importance and their immediate and emphatic acceptance to the complementary relationship between the airplane and the infantry and artillery that then dominated the ground forces. Indeed, the machine gun had made horse cavalry almost invariably too vulnerable to carry out its traditional strategic functions of reconnaissance, pursuit, and the raiding of supply lines, depots, and road movements. Almost immediately, air forces gained enough maturity to fill these roles by carrying observers, cameras, bombs, and guns and by attacking beyond artillery range. Thus airplanes admirably filled the functions of the horse cavalry.

Moreover, the experience of World War I showed that the differences between ground and air forces made them perfectly complementary. In both attack and defense the tactics used in ground warfare depended on the concept of an inviolable line bristling with firepower. But aircraft could act as skirmishers in finding and assailing the weakness of a convoy of wagons or trucks, a column of troops exposed on a road, or inadequately camouflaged depots, headquarters, and artillery positions. Their hit-and-run tactics made the planes difficult targets, and their machine guns and small bombs made them formidable.

The complementary tactical relation of the air forces supplying the skirmishers and the ground forces supplying the line troops carried over into strategy: the land forces gained and held ground while the air forces necessarily relied on the brief incursions of traditional raiding strategy.

Indeed, the appreciation of the complementary relation—that is, mutually supplying one another's lack—between ground forces and cavalry of the air flourished during World War II. The combatants equipped themselves with huge numbers of fighters for defense and a multitude of attack, dive, and fighter bombers to serve as cavalry of the air in tactical cooperation with

---

385. U.S. Strategic Bombing Survey, quoted in Maj. Gen. J.F.C. Fuller, *The Conduct of War: 1789-1961* (Eyre and Spottiswoode, 1961), pp. 282-298.

ground forces and in the strategic missions of pursuit, reconnaissance, and attack on enemy troop movements.

Meanwhile, navies had seen that air power at sea could contribute much more than vastly superior reconnaissance. So the fleets of the principal naval powers (U.K., United States, and Japan) equipped themselves with aircraft carriers, and had enough of them to have equal importance with battleships in European waters and largely to supersede them as capital ships in the Pacific.

World War II also saw the emergence of air transport, enabling airpower's high speed and ability to fly over such obstacles as the mountains and jungles of New Guinea to make a complementary logistical contribution corresponding to those in tactics and strategy.

Thus the implicit theory of airpower as a complementary arm began nearly 80 years before Desert Storm and has received continuous validation since. Its history confirms the theory that an attempt to control any land or sea without combining airpower with land or sea power would almost surely fail when pitted against an adversary that made adequate use of complementary airpower.

Table 9.1
Summary of the air campaign

Objective[386]	Sorties[387]	Strikes[388]
Ground forces	33,560	22,790
Airfields and radars	3,748	3,968
Military industries	825	1,943
Command and control	1,547	1,697
SCUDs	1,599	1,459
SAMs	5,161	1,367
Roads and railroads	945	1,168
Oil facilities	431	539
Electricity	175	345
Other	3,155	6,033
TOTAL	51,146	41,309

Recently, this theory of airpower was promulgated in the form of the U.S. AirLand doctrine for ground combat, and had yet another demonstration of its

---

386. Cohen et al., *GWAPS: Statistical Compendium*, Table 63, p. 227, and Table 177, p. 418. The category NBC has been combined with Military Industries; and Government Control with C3 (shown as command and control).

387. Planned (in the ATO), but not neccessarily flown.

388. A strike is defined as the delivery of a weapon against a specific target. There might be more than one strike in a sortie.

effectiveness in the Gulf War. Here airpower had a decisive effect on the success of the combined-arms ground assault that relied on air, naval, and ground forces and succeeded thanks to sound strategy, deception, surprise, superiority in weapons, training, leadership, and successful management of logistics. The air campaign was extremely successful, and it was instrumental in bringing about the rapid and decisive Iraqi defeat.[389]

But in the Gulf War, as in previous wars, airpower proved unable to win the war on its own: this is due to the fundamental fact that airplanes, limited to a raiding strategy, cannot implement a persisting strategy by occupying territory. Indeed, the fact that airpower showed its limitations despite the very favorable conditions it operated under in the Gulf War is evidence that those limitations are inherent.[390]

Chapter 6 contains assessments of the effectiveness of air power on different types of targets. Table 9.1 shows the number of planned attacks (sorties) and the number of actual attacks (strikes) for different types of targets, sorted by number of strikes.

While the United States contributed the bulk of the airpower, other nations had a significant presence. On the basis of total sorties actually flown, the United States contributed 85%, Saudi Arabia 6%, the UK 5%, France 2%, other Arab countries 1%, Canada 1%, and Italy 0.2%.[391] Table 9.2 shows the relative contributions of different types of U.S. aircraft.

U.S. forces dropped some 9,000 precision-guided bombs (5,400 tons) and 210,000 conventional bombs (about 65,000 tons).[392] It must not be inferred from these figures that the bulk of the bombing was totally imprecise or "random." With modern computer-assisted sights that partially compensate for wind, conventional bombs can be quite accurate, even if not as accurate as guided bombs. The lower accuracy of conventional bombs does not imply that targets against which they are used will not be destroyed: more bombs are used in order to compensate for the lower accuracy. For example, 2 precision-guided munitions suffice to attain a 99% probability of hitting a given target, whereas 15 conventional bombs are required to attain the same probability.

The U.S. F-111Fs dropped over 3,300 tons of precision munitions and the U.S. F-117s, 2,000 tons. Thus some 100 planes delivered the bulk of the laser-guided weapons that proved so devastatingly accurate. (The laser-guidance pod for the F-15E was still under development and not available when hostilities started; about half of the F-15Es received their pods during the second week of the air campaign. French Jaguars, Saudi A-5s, U.K. Buccaneers, and U.S. Navy A-6s also had laser designators and could deliver laser-guided munitions or designate targets; U.K. Tornados received laser-guidance pods during the fourth week of the war; U.S. OV-10 and certain

---

389. Cohen et al., *GWAPS: Effects and Effectiveness*, p. 26.
390. Ibid., pp. 15, 104.
391. Cohen et al., *GWAPS: Statistical Compendium*, Table 64, p. 232.
392. Cohen et al., *GWAPS: Statistical Compendium*, Table 191, p. 553.

other observation aircraft carried laser designators, as did ground forces.) B-52s dropped about one-third of the conventional bombs. Nearly half the U.S.-delivered precision-guided bombs were 228-kilo GBU-12 laser-guided weapons, that proved very effective against tanks. In addition, some 5,300 Maverick missiles were fired, mostly from A-10 aircraft; about one-third of the Mavericks were TV-guided, the remainder infrared.[393]

Table 9.2

Summary of U.S. air campaign: Numbers of aircraft and sorties flown, by type of aircraft

Aircraft						

Aircraft	U.S. Air Force		U.S. Navy		U.S. Marines	
F-16	244	13,087				
KC-135	184	9,559				
A-10	144	8,084				
F-15C	96	5,685				
F-4	49	2,687				
F-111F	64	2,423				
F-15E	48	2,172				
B-52	66	1,741				
KC-10	22	1,465				
F-117	42	1,299				
EF-111	18	1,105				
F-111E	18	458				
E-3	11	379				
F/A-18			89	4,449	84	4,936
F-14			109	4,005		
A-6			96	4,824	20	795
E-2C			29	1,183		
EA-6			27	1,126	12	504
AV-8					84	3,359
Total	1,006	50,144	350	15,587	200	9,594

Number of sorties[394]

393. Ibid., Table 191, p. 553.
394. Cohen et al., *GWAPS: Summary,* Table 6, p. 199, and *GWAPS: Statistical Compendium* Table 5, p. 27, and Table 81, p. 316 (these sources give somewhat inconsistent numbers); KC-135 and KC-10 numbers from *GWAPS: Planning*, Table 9, p. 34.

Total bombing intensity by U.S. forces was comparable with that of World War II.[395] Aerial operations were relentless, averaging about 2,800 sorties per day, of which about 1,600 were combat sorties, with an average of about 1 loss per day (of which 0.84 was a combat loss). The tempo of operations tired pilots, a majority of whom used stimulants and sedatives to keep awake and to go to sleep.[396]

Of the 46 planes lost, 38 were lost in combat. Breakdown of losses by nation and type shows 27 U.S. (6 A-10/OA-10, 3 F-16, 5 AV-8, 3 A-6, 2 F/A-18, 2 F-15E, 2 OV-10, 1-EF 111, 1 F-14, 1 AC-130, 1 F-4G), 7 UK (all Tornado GR.1), 2 Saudi (1 F-5, 1 Tornado GR.1), 1 Kuwaiti (A-4), and 1 Italian (Tornado GR.1).[397] Three U.S. helicopters were lost in combat, including one Apache AH-64 and one Marine Cobra AH-1, and 14 crashed for noncombat reasons.

Before the war started, credible estimates of air losses were around 1% of sorties on the first day, declining to perhaps 0.2%.[398] Actual losses (even if measured as percent of bombing sorties) were far lower, attesting to the effectiveness of Coalition efforts to suppress air defenses. Excluding the Tornados, loss rates for all types of aircraft are comparable. From a statistical point of view, the observed losses are not inconsistent with the hypothesis that all bomber-type aircraft (except Tornados) had equal chances of being downed. Thus the actual data don't provide any evidence that the stealth F-117 bomber was less likely to be shot down than the conventional F-111F.[399] (But the F-111F required support planes to ensure its safety, while the F-117 could fly alone.)

THE WAR AS A WHOLE

Iraq has not released any casualty data, and Coalition forces either did not keep or have not released counts of Iraqi dead and wounded, so our estimates for Iraqi forces are extremely tentative. In fact it is unlikely that there will ever be a reliable, definitive calculation of Iraqi casualties.

There have been numerous conflicting estimates of Iraqi casualties; the large differences between estimates from various sources are due to the lack of data: many of the estimates are little more than informed guesses. Immediately after the conflict, the U.S. Defense Intelligence Agency estimated 100,000 Iraqi military deaths, plus or minus 50%.[400] The editors of U.S. News & World

395. U.S. General Accounting Office, *Operation Desert Storm: Evaluation of the Air War*, p. 2.

396. Cohen et al., *GWAPS: Summary*, p. 178, and *GWAPS: Support*, p. 230.

397. Cohen et al., *GWAPS: Statistical Compendium*, Table 203, p. 641.

398. Cohen et al., *GWAPS: Effects and Effectiveness*, Table 9, p. 116.

399. Excluding the Tornados, the bomber loss rate was roughly .05 percent per sortie. This gives a 55 percent probability of 0 losses in 1,299 sorties for the F-117s and 32 percent in 2,423 sorties for the F-111Fs.

400. Heidenreich, "The Gulf War: How Many Iraqis Died," p. 109.

Report, arguing that perhaps as few as 200,000 Iraqi soldiers were actually present in the theater of operations at the start of the ground war, and that dead-and-wounded rates were unlikely to be outside the 5% to 10% range, go on to argue that the air campaign caused few casualties, and conclude that total Iraqi military deaths were in the range from 8,000 to 18,000.[401]

Richard Heidenreich relies heavily on the assumption that Iraqi dead-to-wounded ratios would not exceed the historical average of 1 to 3, and on the fact that there were at most 2,000 wounded among the Iraqi prisoners of war, to conclude that Iraqi casualties during the ground war were in the range of 1,500 to 9,500 dead and 3,000 to 26,500 wounded.[402] But there is no reason to believe that Iraqi dead-to-wounded ratios should not be higher than those of the Coalition (which were 1 to 3): Iraqi soldiers did not wear flak jackets, their medical evacuation facilities were in no way comparable with those of the Coalition, and their damage control procedures for armored vehicles were probably not as sophisticated as those of the Coalition (for example, keeping ammunition in blastproof compartments). In fact, publicly available data suggest that the Iraqi dead-to-wounded ratio was 1 to 1 for the air campaign,[403] and it likely was higher for the ground campaign.

John Mueller uses dubious arthimetic to conclude that no more than 1,000 Iraqi soldiers died during the ground fighting,[404] an astonishing contention considering that the battle of Medina Ridge (see Chapter 8, section "Breakthrough") by itself may have resulted in approximately that many Iraqi dead, and that several other well-documented engagements likely resulted in hundreds of dead. It is estimated that over 2,000 Iraqi tanks and over 500 APCs were destroyed during the ground war, implying at least 10,000 casualties, of whom an unknown proportion would have died, either immediately or because of lack of medical care. To this one must add casualties among dismounted infantry and artillery.[405]

But in fact all such computations are of dubious validity, being based on numerous unverifiable assumptions with respect to numbers of men and casualty rates. Just over 85,000 Iraqis were taken prisoner, and some 15,000 were left in good fighting order at the end of hostilities. If there were 220,000

---

401. U.S. News & World Report, *Triumph Without Victory*, pp. 403-409.

402. Heidenreich, "The Gulf War: How Many Iraqis Died," pp. 110, 111, 123-124.

403. Losses reported for the air campaign by captured officers for four divisions and two brigades are about 5 percent killed and 5 percent wounded. See Gordon and Trainor, *The Generals' War*, p. 352.

404. Mueller, "The Perfect Enemy," p. 90.

405. Heidenreich, "The Gulf War: How Many Iraqis Died," p. 120, estimates total casualties for destroyed tanks and APCs at 14,000, and for destroyed artillery at 12,000, but assumes that there were no casualties among infantry, which is not compatible with available anecdotal evidence. However, it can be argued that there were few casualties among artillerymen, who apparently tended to desert their guns when they came under attack from airplanes or counterartillery.

Iraqi soldiers in the theater of operations at the start of the ground war, then some 120,000 soldiers are not accounted for; they may have been killed, may have deserted, or may have been dispersed during the fighting and found their way home by their own means. Fewer than 2,000 Iraqi prisoners suffered from battle wounds; thus there is an inexplicable lack of identified wounded soldiers. Either total casualties were very low or most of the casualties were deaths: we simply don't know.

It is telling that low estimates of Iraqi casualties have been provided only by non-combatants. Those who were there either are silent on the matter or explicitly or implicitly refer to very significant numbers of dead. Colonel Swain, who reviewed masses of after-action reports (some classified), refers to "hecatombs."[406] It does not seem appropriate to second-guess those who were there and who actually saw what happened.

Anecdotal evidence from ground troops indicates that Iraqi deaths may have been as high as 50% among units that actually engaged in intensive fighting during the ground war.[407] If we estimate that two-thirds of the Republican Guards fought, as did one-third of the men along the front lines and around Kuwait City, then 35,000 deaths does not seem an unlikely figure.[408] But in fact there is no firm evidence that would allow ruling out the hypothesis that 100,000 Iraqis died during the ground campaign. In the absence of reliable data, and taking into account estimates of casualties during the air campaign (see Chapter 8, section "The Opposing Forces"), we can only conclude that a total between 30,000 and 150,000 Iraqi soldiers were killed or wounded, with somewhere between 10,000 and 100,000 dead, about 50,000 being a probable best estimate.[409]

---

406. Swain, *"Lucky War,"* p. 291.

407. See, e.g., De La Billière, *Storm Command*, p. 297; Scales, *Certain Victory*, p. 291; and Benson, *Rat's Tales*, p. 138. Some gruesome media accounts exist, but were never broadcast or published: see Taylor, *War and the Media*, pp. 253-256. The 1991 British Broadcasting Corporation documentary on the Gulf War contained graphic images and interviews. Abu Fatima, Iraqi soldier: "Dead soldiers were everywhere"; Capt. Sebastian Willis Fleming, U.K. First Armored Division: "[When we reached the Highway of Death] that's when it came across how much carnage was there"; Sgt. John Scaglione, U.S. First Armored Division: "We took very few prisoners at [the battle of] Medina Ridge. I saw three. In the desert you can see for miles. Most of the people I saw were dead."

408. An estimate of 14,000 to 34,000 deaths in the ground war is given by Cohen et al., *GWAPS: Effects and Effectiveness*, p. 262.

409. This is consistent with the assumptions used by the U.S. Census Bureau, an organization widely respected for its statistical skills—Hobbs, *Population Estimates for Iraq*—and is not inconsistent with the thoughtful discussion by Freedman and Karsh, *The Gulf Conflict*, p. 408, who estimate 35,000 Iraqi dead. It is perhaps not coincidental that two statisticians (Hill and Hobbs) who have examined the available data reach similar conclusions.

Reliance on statistical techniques can hide the grim reality of what a "casualty" really is. The following account by a U.K. soldier reminds us of what war really means.

We drove through [an Iraqi position] and there were lots of human remains. It looked like an infantry company's position where they had obviously come under air attack, thought it was over, and all got out to go back to their secondary position; and while they were all out in the open, in came another attack which cut them to pieces. There were arms, legs, torsos, heads, bits of torso all over the place. Probably about 150 men.

The mother of a U.K. soldier, just after having been told her son was dead:

I went a bit mad. I jumped up off the chair, and he [the officer bringing the bad news] tried to grab me, and I said get off, and pushed him out of the way. I think I kicked him as well, but I'm not sure. I ran off round to my friend's house, banged the door open and ran round screaming, he's dead, he's dead![410]

Many more such scenes no doubt took place in Iraq.

U.S. forces captured 63,948 POWs (including 1,492 civilians who became intermingled with Iraqi troops); Joint Arab Forces, 16,921; French forces, 869; and U.K. forces, 5,005. Of the prisoners captured by the United States, nearly 14,000 refused to be repatriated after the conflict and remained in Saudi Arabia. Starting in September 1992, these people were resettled in the United States, Sweden, and other countries, under the auspices of international humanitarian agencies.[411]

The comparison with Coalition casualties is striking. U.S. forces lost only 15 tanks in combat; no M1s were pierced by enemy rounds. Table 9.3 shows human losses by nation.

Several of the U.S. casualties in action were women: 4 were killed, 16 wounded, and 2 taken prisoner;[412] all female casualties were the result of indirect causes, such as SCUD attack, mines, or helicopter crash. About 66 Coalition fliers were downed in combat; the entire 14-man crew of an AC-130H Specter gunship was killed when it was shot down during the battle for Ras al-Khafji. Two Italian aircrew and one Kuwaiti pilot were taken prisoner, as were 9 Saudi troops. All 45 POWs were released by Iraq at the end of hostilities.

Coalition casualties were astoundingly low. Consider, by way of comparison, that during the course of the war, 138 U.S. and 23 U.K. soldiers died from noncombat causes (for example, accidents or heart attacks) and nearly 3,000 U.S. soldiers suffered noncombat injuries. An additional 84

---

410. Benson, *Rat's Tales*, pp. 131, 136.
411. United Nations, *Iraq-Kuwait Conflict*, p. 64.
412. Cohen et al., *GWAPS: Support*, Table 11, p. 129 (which is not consistent with the figures on p. 126).

U.S. personnel died during the course of Operation Desert Shield—the prewar deployment. The air noncombat loss rate was about 1 in 10,000, while the chances of a combat plane being shot down were about 1 in 2,000 sorties.

Comparisons with dangers on the U.S. home front are illuminating. During the 6 weeks of the war, in the United States some 2,700 people were murdered and some 12,000 raped or sexually assaulted. To put it another way, the chance of a Coalition soldier being killed during the ground attack, or of a Coalition combat plane being downed during a sortie, was one-third that of an infant dying in the United States of Sudden Infant Death Syndrome (1.5 in 1,000 live births), five times the risk of a woman in the United States dying during childbirth (0.9 in 10,000 live births), or one-tenth those of an infant dying within one year of birth.

Table 9.3
Coalition casualties, by nation

Nation[413]	Killed in action	Wounded in action	Taken prisoner
U. S. air action	33	34	16
U. S. ground action	84	338	5
U. S. SCUD hit	28	98	0
U. S. total[414]	145	470	21
Saudi Arabia	38	175	9
UK	24	13	12
Egypt[415]	11	84	0
UAE	5	21	0
Syria	3	0	0
France	2	25	0
Kuwait	1	7	1
Italy	0	0	2
Total	229	795	45

413. Compiled from a variety of official sources that are not mutually consistent. Even the detailed breakdowns for U.S. forces differ in different official reports.

414. Cohen et al., GWAPS: Support, Table 11, p. 129, in conjunction with GWAPS: Statistical Compendium, Table 203, p. 641. But GWAPS: Statistical Compendium, Table 208, p. 658, reports only 134 U.S. killed-in-action.

415. Data from bin Sultan, Desert Warrior, p. 420, which confirms some Western sources. But Egyptian Ministry of Defense, Al Kitab Harab Tahrir Kuwait, states that there were no Egyptian losses.

Risk of death for pilots was much higher, since each typically flew many sorties; for example, the risk of death for an A-10 pilot was around 1 in 100. On the last day of the war, an A-10 pilot was about to start his next mission:

As we're on our way out the door [to the planes], I overhear that there's a hog [A-10 Warthog] coming in with battle damage. He's been hit by an infrared SAM in the tail, and he's flying with no hydraulics. The control tower asks if we would mind flying Combat Air Patrol over the airfield while he comes in, so we take off. We are overhead when he crosses the end of the runway as he is about to land. He is lined up and everything looks good. All of a sudden the aircraft hits the ground very hard, all three landing gears collapse and shear out from under him. The aircraft bounces about 15 meters into the air. Then it rolls into the wind, to the right. The flight leader starts yelling into the radio, and someone on the ground yells for him to bail out. It is too late though: he is probably unconscious from the hard landing. The plane rolls and hits nose first. He didn't have a chance—the aircraft instantly goes up into a ball of flame. . . . We land, park our jets, and go through a debrief. Not more than two words are said. The next day the war is over, and we have won a big victory. Some have paid a higher price than others.[416]

A single SCUD missile falling on the U.S. base in Dhahran accounted for 28 dead, 13% of the total. Friendly fire accounted for 118 casualties (35 U.S. dead, 72 wounded; 9 U.K. dead; 2 Saudi dead), about 22% of the Coalition's killed-in-action (by comparison, friendly fire supposedly accounted for less than 3% of U.S. dead in World War II).

Most friendly-fire casualties were caused by ground-ground fire.[417] Of the 35 U.S. soldiers killed by friendly fire, 24 were killed by ground fire and 11 by air strikes. About three-fourths of the 35 U.S. Army tanks and APCs damaged in combat were hit by friendly fire; of these, 2 APCs were hit from the air (by an Apache helicopter) and the other 33 vehicles were damaged by ground fire. Both the air-ground and the ground-ground incidents underscore the fact that attackers have no reliable means to identify the exact nature of distant ground targets that cannot be seen visually and are spotted by sensitive infrared sensors.

The United States identified some 19 separate ground-ground incidents among its forces and 9 air attacks on friendly forces. The main air-ground incidents were: an A-10 strike on U.S. Marines during Iraq's probing attack during the night of 29 January; an A-6 attack on a U.S. Marine convoy returning from an artillery raid on 2 February; a U.S. Apache helicopter attack on U.S. forces mistaken for an advancing Iraqi column on 17 February; a U.S. air strike on Joint Arab Forces on 24 February; an A-10 attack on U.K. troops during the ground assault on 26 February. The worst ground-ground incident occurred on 27 February, resulting in 6 U.S. deaths.

---

416. U.S. Department of Defense, *Conduct of the Persian Gulf War*, p. 243.
417. Hallion, *Storm over Iraq*, p. 247.

Coalition munitions were involved in other incidents that might be considered friendly fire.   For example, U.S. and French troops suffered casualties either from previously unexploded Coalition bomblets that were strewn about an abandoned Iraqi position in as-Salman or perhaps from an Iraqi mine.

We recount here two friendly fire incidents: one air-ground and one ground-ground. The 17 February incident resulted in the death of two soldiers and ended the career of Lt. Col. Ralph Hayles, commander of the Apache battalion attached to the First Infantry Division.

At 0015 local time on 17 February (a moonless night), division headquarters called for an air raid against Iraqi forces advancing south. Strong winds blew sand into the air, reducing visibility to zero. Considering the poor flying conditions, Hayles—who, in the tradition of General Patton and others, liked to lead his men from the front—decided to fly himself, accompanied by two other helicopters. "I had never flown in weather that bad," he said later, "... and I wouldn't order my people out in that without me." At 0056 hours the Apaches detected two vehicles at a range of 3000 meters. Hayles reported that he had spotted two vehicles about a kilometer north of the Coalition lines.   "Can you engage those two vehicles?" asked the ground commander. "Roger, I can shoot those easy," replied Hayles. "Go ahead, take them out." At 0100 hours a Hellfire missile struck the first APC, a Bradley; the second, an M113, was hit a minute later; four soldiers were inside each vehicle. "It exploded like the inside of a volcano," said one survivor.   Flames shot high in the air and ammunition in the vehicles continued to explode for several minutes.

Hayles was dismissed from command largely on the grounds that commanders should not personally fire on the enemy: "We don't pay generals and battalion commanders to be in direct-fire situations," said division commander Maj. Gen. Thomas G. Rhame. Hayles might have fared better in the French Foreign Legion, whose officers are taught: "In the Legion you don't say, *forward*; you say, *follow me*." His reputation for aggressiveness might have contributed to his dismissal, but as he put it: "There isn't much difference between a hotdog and a great pilot. A totally sane person doesn't take off in a sandstorm in a helicopter loaded down with missiles."

One of the ground-ground friendly fire incidents occurred around 1900 hours on 26 February:

Scouts from the Fourth Battalion of the 32nd Armored Regiment, part of the First Brigade of the U.S. Third Armored Division, spotted Iraqi ground troops, then a T-72 tank. TOWs launched from one of the scout Bradleys destroyed the enemy tank, but a second Bradley was hit from behind with 25-mm rounds. (It has not been determined where these U.S. rounds came from.) Soldiers ran out of the vehicle and collapsed on the ground. Another Bradley came up to give assistance; it was commanded by Lt. James Barker.   The commander of the stricken vehicle, Staff Sgt. Christopher Stephens, was dead. Sgt. Donald Goodwin had an open chest wound. Sgt. Adrian Stokes had severe wounds and was still stuck in the Bradley. Pvt. Frank Bradish had lost part of his right hand but, together with Pvt. John McClure, he went back to the vehicle to pull out Stokes. Despite the injury to his hand, Bradish radioed for help, then pried open a flare canister with his teeth and fired several flares to signal their position. Barker called for mortar fire to hold off advancing Iraqi troops, and an M1 tank commanded by Sgt. First Class Craig Kendall came up to help defend the Bradleys. By then medics had arrived. Stokes died and Bradish went into shock. Barker, Bradish, and McClure received Silver Stars.[418]

U.S. ground-attack planes and helicopters were very effective against Iraqi armor. About 144 A-10 Warthogs and 277 AH-64 Apaches were used in Operation Desert Storm. The A-10s destroyed nearly 1,000 Iraqi tanks, and the Apaches, over 500.[419] No official data are available for the 145 AH-1S Cobras, but ground units who had Cobra support speak highly of the effectiveness of TOWs launched from this helicopter (the Marine AH-1W version, of which 75 were deployed, can also launch Hellfire laser-guided missiles). One Apache and one OA-10 were lost during the ground attack.

At the end of hostilities Iraq was left with no navy; very limited air forces; and a greatly reduced number of tanks, armored vehicles, and artillery. Subsequent U.N. inspections ensured the destruction of nonconventional weapons capability and the partly completed very-long-range supercannon.

MILITARY LESSONS

Great caution must be applied when drawing conclusions for the future from the events of the Gulf War. Iraqi tactics, training, and morale were so poor that Desert Storm hardly provided a convincing test of how Coalition forces would have performed against a more competent adversary. The terrain and weather were very favorable to aerial operations, and it cannot be concluded that airpower would be as decisive in other circumstances. U.S. A-10 pilot Capt. Todd Sheehy:

This was what we call a reduced-threat war, as opposed to what we thought might happen in Europe—a high threat from a lot of radar-guided missiles. We had always trained to fly in at low altitude, shoot our standoff Maverick missiles, and get back out. We weren't going to carry a lot of free-fall ordnance, we were going to use forward-firing standoff ordnance, and that's what the Maverick was designed for.

What we did in Iraq and Kuwait was very different: it was a reduced-threat war. Much like World War II, because there were no radar-guided missiles. Here in Iraq

---

418. The 7 February incident is described in Robert Johnson and Caleb Solomon, "'Friendly Fire' Ends the Soaring Career of American Colonel" and "Chilling Tapes Show How Soldiers Died in 'Friendly Fire'," *Wall Street Journal Europe* (12 September and 7 November 1991). The 26 February incident is in Steve Vogel, "The Tip of the Spear," p. 13.

419. Again, these numbers need to be taken with caution. Anecdotal evidence from ground troops who encountered destroyed tanks and APCs as they advanced supports the claim that A-10s killed many armored vehicles during the air campaign. The numbers for the A-10 and Apache are not in any way comparable, since the A-10s flew throughout the entire war, while the Apaches were used intensively only during the ground attack.

they had the equipment: very formidable Soviet stuff. But the problem for the Iraqis was, and this is my personal conjecture, maybe a bit of lack of motivation in a lot of their forces (not the Republican Guards but a lot of the others). And secondly somebody put together a tremendous air campaign to go right after those threats with jamming aircraft and stealth aircraft and aircraft that can deliver precision-guided munitions and create an environment where a lot of those radar operators knew: "If I turn on my radar, I'm going to get some kind of HARM in my bunker with me. So I'm not going to turn on my radar for very long." And that gave us an environment that we were a little bit freer to use high altitudes in. So the real threat was AAA, particularly 57mm. Those were everywhere.

So just like World War II we used high-altitude dive bombing. The main difference is that our delivery systems are more accurate. The inertial navigation gives us a wind correction—it's not a computer-controlled bombing system like the F-16 or F-15, but it improves our accuracy compared to pure visual systems.[420]

Official reports speak highly of the performance of the most modern weapon systems, but anecdotes from troops are not always consistent with the official view. Older weapon systems are more familiar, and work-arounds to bugs and glitches are well known. Any complex device will develop some unexpected behavior over time, and operators must learn to compensate for it. When a new system is introduced, its operators need time to get used to it. The following conclusions can be drawn from the available unclassified data.

Initiative

Initiative, defined as the ability to threaten or assail an opponent who cannot counter-threaten or assail, is an invaluable advantage. As U.S. Marine Col. James Fulk stated:

We maneuvered very quickly and did not allow the Iraqis to react against what we were doing. Our philosophy was "Don't wait, act." A key factor was the thought process of taking quick, decisive action that allowed us to exploit Iraqi weaknesses. Our soldiers could make decisions on the spot because they understood what we were trying to do. I think the Iraqis had a centralized command system, which resulted in very slow decisions being taken. They were very good soldiers as long as you were in front of them and did what they expected, but they didn't know what to do when you maneuvered on them and did the unexpected.[421]

As a corollary, the ability to innovate and improvise is essential. For example, no one had planned to use F-111s flying above 3,000 meters and dropping laser-guided bombs to destroy tanks at night. Yet this tactic was highly effective, accounting for nearly 1,000 tanks and APCs.[422] Another

---

420. Personal interview.

421. Personal interview.

422. Like all other data of this nature, this figure needs to be interpreted with caution. Because of the difficulty of identifying targets from the air, the 1,000 might include some self-propelled artillery that could be mistaken for a tank or APC.

example was the unexpected impossibility of exactly planning rendezvouses with tanker aircraft: this was solved by placing tankers in particular flight patterns and allowing planes to fly up to them.[423] In peacetime soldiers should learn, not how to wage war but how to *learn* how to wage war.[424] "Military organizations that cannot cope with the unexpected lose wars."[425]

Airpower

Although airpower cannot win a war on its own (see section "Decisive Advantages" above), its importance in contributing to victory cannot be overestimated.

Ground forces, including heavy armor, can be devastated by specialized ground-attack aircraft using visually, infrared, and laser-guided missiles, unless they are protected by friendly air forces. The first large-scale use of antitank helicopters proved their effectiveness. Long-range standoff missiles and guided bombs demonstrated their value. Extreme accuracy can be achieved by using appropriate technology, such as inertial navigation coupled with contour-following radar, detection of a laser reflection, infrared imaging of the target, and electronically enhanced visual imaging of the target.

Therefore, air supremacy needs to be acquired by any and all means, including AWACS, superior fighters and air-air missiles, attacks on enemy airports, and evasion or suppression of antiaircraft defenses by means such as stealth, chaff, jammers, flares, ground-hugging flight, and antiradar missiles. These means proved highly successful in evading or suppressing radar-guided air defense.

As a corollary, the fact is inescapable that today's ships, including carrier task forces, are vulnerable to attack by radar-evading planes. Current ships rely on powerful radars (airborne or on the ship itself) to detect incoming aircraft and to direct defensive fire from ship-based missiles or airborne interceptor aircraft. Stealth planes might approach ships undetected, and damage or destroy them with precision-guided bombs or standoff self-guided missiles (such as the radar-guided Exocet). In addition, antiradar missiles might prove to be as effective against ship-based radar as they proved against land-based radar.[426]

The importance of defeating air supremacy cannot be overestimated. Means include mobility, dispersal and camouflage, weapon systems that can strike

---

423. Cohen et al., *GWAPS: Command and Control*, pp. 213-214.

424. Ibid., p. 4.

425. Ibid., p. 330.

426. Hallion, *Storm over Iraq*, p. 265, provides a good discussion of the relatively poor performance during Desert Storm of carriers as a means of projecting airpower ashore. Norman Friedman, *Desert Victory* (United States Naval Institute, 1992), pp. 239, 241, defends the opposing view.

while remaining out of range of enemy defenses, and optical-guidance-system countermeasures.

Mobile missile launchers are difficult to track down and destroy. Relatively simple measures can be taken to reduce a missile's susceptibility to interception by an antimissile missile. Thus many nations could acquire the capability of launching at least conventional warheads against cities.

The success of the U.S. Tomahawk cruise missile, which relies on ground-hugging flight to evade detection and interception, might motivate less-developed nations to develop their own crude versions of this weapon. Commercially available technology for small airplanes, satellite-based navigation, and a small computer could no doubt be combined to create a weapon whose threat would at least equal that of the SCUD. It would appear feasible to equip such a weapon with primitive stealth technology and chemical weapons capability.

Optical-guidance-system countermeasures could consist of aerosol clouds (smoke screens) composed of particles designed specifically to block infrared radiation.[427] An airport covered by a large infrared-opaque cloud could not be targeted by standoff laser-guided munitions (because the lasers emit in the infrared portion of the spectrum). Other countermeasures might take the form of missiles that home in on the laser designator, much as antiradar missiles home in on radar stations.

Future developments in optically guided short-range surface-air missiles should permit ground forces to defend themselves against ground-attack aircraft. If an Apache can detect and hit a vehicle at 3,000 meters with a Hellfire missile, there is no reason why the APCs of the future should not carry equivalent sensors and missiles capable of targeting and destroying the helicopter. Indeed, the unmoving earth provides an inherently superior aiming platform, and ground-based systems can be heavier and enjoy larger power supplies and ammunition reserves. While the Iraqis had no defense against the Warthogs and the Apaches, it would be a mistake to assume that future armies will not be able to shoot down such low-flying aircraft, or at least to reduce their effectiveness by forcing them to maneuver to evade visually, infrared, or laser-guided surface-air missiles.

Furthermore, countermeasures to antiradar missiles could be developed. Obvious countermeasures include the dispersal of radar antennas; dynamic switching between multiple antennas; and launching of defensive decoys, perhaps coupled with frequency switching.

Sea Power

Control of the seas remains a fundamental requirement for successful military operations far away from home bases. Although unprecedented

---

427. Iraqis did use smoke to some extent: Cohen et al., *GWAPS: Weapons, Tactics, and Training*, p. 329.

resources were devoted to moving men and material by air, in the end 95% of the Coalition's cargo was moved by sea. The number of ships available to carry weapon systems and supplies constrained the timing of deployment; for example, VII Corp's Third Armored Division did not arrive in the theater until 12 February.[428]

As a corollary, antiship weapons (including aircraft and helicopters) are essential. Furthermore, modern mines deployed in the sea are hard to detect and can slow down naval operations in shallow coastal waters. Mining of ports might remain an effective method of hampering logistical operations.

High-Technology Weapons

High-technology weapons work in battlefield conditions. As a corollary, because high-technology weapons depend largely on sophisticated hardware and software, nations that dominate these industries (notably the United States and its Western European allies) would appear to have a natural advantage in weapon systems technology.

The importance of alternative sensor systems was confirmed. Thermal sights often worked well when visual sights did not. Single-sensor radar-based air-defense systems were easily blinded by countermeasures. However, Coalition sensors did not always permit targets to be acquired. Weather conditions at times degraded sensor systems and affected operations.[429] A blind army has no chance. It is essential to see and know what is happening on the battlefield. No weapon system can be effective if the location of its potential targets cannot be identified. The ability to detect and destroy distant targets creates the need for systems able to distinguish friend from foe (for ground forces as well as air forces).

Training

Training that relies on high-technology to realistically simulate a battlefield works well in preparing troops for battle. Highly trained and motivated professional soldiers (volunteers) are best suited to control modern, sophisticated, high-technology weapon systems in actual combat conditions. Part-time volunteers (reserve forces) are well suited to provide logistical and other noncombat support.

Antimissile Missiles

The technical feasibility of antimissile missiles was not proven by the Patriot's performance in the Gulf War (see Chapter 6, section "Patriot Against SCUD"). Countermeasures could degrade the effectiveness of radar-based

---

428. Swain, *"Lucky War,"* p. 105.
429. U.S. General Accounting Office, *Operation Desert Storm*, p. 3.

missile defenses. They could consist of multiple warheads released outside the interception range (something the SCUD did when it broke up in flight—a design flaw that some computer experts might call a feature), of active radar decoys released in flight, of jamming technology, of chaff release, of low radar-reflectivity coating on the missile to reduce its detectability (a simple example of stealth technology).[430]

Navigation Systems

The satellite-based Global Positioning System (GPS) is far superior to traditional methods of determining position. In order to deny precise position coordinates to enemy forces, the United States normally introduces random error into the unencrypted data broadcast by GPS satellites. Military receivers receive accurate encrypted data. This mode of operation is called selective availability (SA); it causes positions determined by commercial receivers to be in error by up to 100 meters (the accuracy of military receivers is classified, but it is reportedly on the order of 1 meter). Selective availability was turned off during the Gulf War, since most of the receivers available to the Coalition forces were in fact commercial models.

Iraqi forces apparently were not able to exploit the military capabilities of accurate GPS receivers. In future conflicts, it can be expected that GPS will be used by both sides and that SA would be defeated by applying the "differential" principle,[431] where one fixed GPS station whose position is known with great accuracy transmits corrections for the SA-induced errors to a mobile station. These receivers, which are commercially available, as are services broadcasting differential corrections, achieve accuracies on the order of 2 meters.[432]

Alternatively, it is possible that one or both sides could develop and deploy jammers that would impede the operation of the GPS receivers (for example, by broadcasting high-strength spurious positioning data).

Women Soldiers

In addition to proving the worth of high-technology weapon systems, the Gulf War once again proved that women can be valuable soldiers. On the basis of experience in this war, the United States has decided to allow female

---

430. Theodore Postol, "Lessons of the Gulf War Experience with Patriot"; "Policy Issues for Theater Missile Defenses in a Shrinking Budget," paper prepared for the U.S. House of Representatives (29 October 1991); and "Lessons for SDI from the Gulf War Patriot Experience: A Technical Perspective," testimony before the U.S. House Armed Services Committee (16 April 1991).

431. Bill Brogdon, "Corrected Fixes," *Ocean Navigator* (January-February 1992).

432. For example, RDS-DGPS is such a service offered by the Swiss Telecom PTT in conjunction with the Swiss Federal Office of Topography.

pilots to fly combat missions, and perhaps someday women will even drive tanks through enemy lines.

Indeed, the performance of the U.S. women was so impressive that the United Arab Emirates (UAE) started recruiting and training female soldiers—something supposedly unthinkable in a conservative Arab state. Uniforms were designed to comply with Islamic customs, hiding hair and body curves. After five months of training under experienced U.S. instructors (all female), the performance of the UAE women surprised the Arab officers. While the initial plan was to use the women in noncombat roles, as in the United States, new ideas are emerging. "Why not a pilot or a missile operator?" asked one UAE officer. "Why not indeed?" answered the U.S. chief instructor. She continued, "We underestimated them. There is nothing these women can't do. Nothing at all."[433]

QUESTIONS FOR FUTURE RESEARCHERS

We make no claim that this book is a definitive account of events and we outline in this section some questions that could be topics for future research.

1. War has been likened to chaotic systems.[434] Did the Coalition use appropriate nonlinear feedback mechanisms to control the war, or were traditional linear mechanisms prevalent?

2. Did AirLand really work as planned? The details of AirLand tactics were not thoroughly tested during the Gulf War because of the vast inferiority of Iraqi forces in training, morale, and weapon systems technology. For example, the A-10 Warthog ground-attack airplane was able to conduct its missions at medium-level altitudes, above the range of most antiaircraft artillery; this was not part of the NATO AirLand scenario for a war in Europe.

To the extent that the AirLand doctrine depends on synchronization,[435] Desert Storm cannot be viewed as a successful instance of its application. In fact, it proved impossible to synchronize the movements of VII Corps with those of other forces, resulting in significant deviation from the plan of destroying the Republican Guard before it retreated north. If the timing of deep attacks proved difficult to synchronize in such favorable circumstances, what would have happened against determined resistance in less favorable terrain? Does Desert Storm merely confirm the age-old lesson that ground operations are difficult to conduct according to any preconceived plan?

3. Is the crushing effectiveness of the aerial forces during Desert Storm a fleeting phenomenon or a permanent change in the art of war? If countermeasures to precision-guided munitions can be developed, will the effectiveness of air forces be reduced to what it was during earlier conflicts?

---

433. Geraldine Brooks, "Thanks to Saddam, Women Warriors Join Arab Emirate's Army," *Wall Street Journal Europe* (8 August 1991).

434. Roger Beaumont, *War, Chaos, and History* (Praeger, 1994).

435. U.S. Department of Defense, *Conduct of the Persian Gulf War*, p. 330.

A deeper analysis of the events of the Gulf War suggests that we cannot yet know whether aerial supremacy will result in a sustained change in land warfare, as it did in naval warfare during World War II. The vast differences in technological sophistication, training, and morale of the two sides during the Gulf War make it difficult to extrapolate the Coalition's success to future conflicts against better-prepared forces. Furthermore, the weather and terrain favored intensive use of airpower; an important factor that should not be underestimated.

Defenses against air forces can be passive or active. Passive defenses include dispersing ground forces and camouflaging them. It is precisely these measures that caused Western military leaders to express skepticism about the effectiveness of a Western air-based intervention in the Yugoslav civil war that raged through 1992 and 1993.

Active defenses can be deployed on the ground or in the air. As we know, Coalition countermeasures rendered Iraqi radar-guided ground defenses ineffective. As noted above, counter-countermeasures may or may not prove effective in the future. Also, potential future optically guided ground defenses may prove harder to defeat.

Turning to defenses deployed in the air, Iraq made no serious attempt to defend its airspace with its own air forces. As with ground forces, air forces can dominate an area if they are numerically superior, qualitatively superior, and/or have the advantage of position. The Coalition had an overwhelming advantage in all areas.

Qualitative superiority of fighter aircraft depends on the airframe's speed and maneuverability, the quality of the avionics, the quality of the air-air missiles deployed, and, above all, the quality of the pilots. Coalition fighters orbited in position at high altitude, ready to swoop down on any Iraqi airplanes that challenged Coalition bombers. But they relied on AWACS to detect Iraqi forces and direct them toward the enemy. Thus, AWACS appears to be an integral element of aerial supremacy. No anti-AWACS weapons are known to exist at this time, but one can envisage such a weapon: a long-range radar-homing missile. Indeed, one can imagine two versions: one easily detectable by radar, meant to force the AWACS to make evasive maneuvers or shut down its radar (thus reducing its effectiveness); and one based on stealth technology, meant to destroy the AWACS before it is detected.

Traditionally, the defensive has dominated contests between similar weapon systems. The Iraqi air force was so inferior from all points to view to the Coalition air force that no conclusions can be drawn regarding a conflict between similar air forces. Planes like the A-10 and the F-111 would have been very vulnerable to attack by fighters, while planes like the F/A-18 and F-16 could presumably have held their own, if necessary by jettisoning their bomb loads when threatened.

4. Is stealth technology really as effective as claimed? There is no question that the stealth F-117 Nighthawk bombers were undetectable by Iraqi radars

and that, as a consequence, they did not require supporting electronic countermeasure planes as conventional bombers did. All operational details regarding the F-117 are classified. However, it appears that achieving a low radar signature imposes certain restrictions on flight patterns. Using laser-guided weapons imposes certain visibility conditions. Thus the F-117 was limited by the weather. Nearly 19% of strikes were adversely affected by weather.[436] In other climates, low cloud ceilings would have occurred more often, perhaps severely curtailing F-117 operations.[437] In fact, the F-117 was the only U.S. combat aircraft (apart from the B-52) that conducted significantly less than one sortie per day. The F-117s averaged less than 0.75 sortie per day; the F-111F, a plane with comparable strike capabilities, 0.90 (see Table 9.2).

Was the F-117 cost-effective compared with the conventional F-111F, whose loss rates were comparable to those of the F-117 within statistical limits? While it is always better to have more and better weapons, military budgets are, like most other budgets, finite. Thus, in order to obtain optimal performance for a given level of expenditure, planners need to evaluate the effectiveness of different types of weapon systems in light of their cost.[438]

5. Is the very advanced AH-64 Apache helicopter really much more effective than the most modern version of the older AH-1 Cobra (the AH-1W, deployed by U.S. Marines)?

6. Will combat airframes become more specialized or more general-purpose? There appears to be a trend toward developing airframes that can be configured either as fighters or as bombers. Single-purpose airframes used in the Gulf War include the A-6 (first flight in 1960), F-111 (1964), F-14 (1970), and A-10 (1972); dual-purpose airframes include the F-15 (1972), F-16 (1974), Tornado (1974), and F/A-18 (1978). The very modern and very specialized F-117 is an exception to this trend, as is the very flexible AV-8 (which is based on an airframe first flown in 1964, but this plane is hard to compare with others, given its fundamentally different design).

7. What is the most cost-effective combination of antiarmor forces? The Coalition deployed vast antitank forces, and all were effective. But future analysis might show that some were more cost-effective than others. The bulk of Iraqi tanks were destroyed by one of the following types of forces: laser-guided bombs released from medium altitude by long-range aircraft (F-111, F-15E); infrared homing missiles (Mavericks) fired from ground-attack fixed-wing planes (primarily A-10, although the AV-8, F-16, and F/A-18 were also effective against tanks); laser- or optically guided missiles fired from ground-attack helicopters (AH-1, AH-64); optically-guided missiles (TOWs) fired from APCs; HEAT or sabot rounds fired from tanks.

---

436. Cohen et al., *GWAPS: Summary*, p. 225; *GWAPS: Operations*, pp. 134, 144, 152, and 163.

437. Cohen et al., *GWAPS: Summary*, p. 173.

438. U.S. General Acounting Office, *Operation Desert Storm*, p. 4.

The APC was originally conceived as a means for moving infantry through areas subject to indirect artillery fire: the armor protects the people from shrapnel. It also has another role: a platform to carry a heavy machine gun and its ammunition, for use against enemy infantry. During the Gulf War, the APC played a third role: a platform to carry and fire antitank missiles.

Will improvements in tank armor (such as Chobham armor) make shaped-charge munitions less effective, thus reducing the helicopter's and the APC's role as antitank weapon systems? Will direct-fire artillery pieces resume their role as antitank weapons?

Results from the Gulf War suggest that if total aerial supremacy can be achieved, fixed-wing airplanes are the most effective antitank platforms: their greater range, speed, and payload allowed fixed-wing aircraft such as the F-111, F-15E, and A-10 to be used against armor earlier and with greater geographical coverage than helicopters. The potential of the A-10 is truly frightening. Theoretically a single 2-plane mission (2 sorties) could, under optimal conditions, virtually destroy an entire tank battalion; 20 sorties could account for an armored division.

Today's antiaircraft artillery (AAA) would appear totally ineffective against both fixed-wing and rotary-wing antiarmor platforms: the TOW missile deployed on Cobras has a range exceeding 4 kilometers, the Hellfire on Apaches has a range of over 6 kilometers, and the Maverick carried on the A-10 a range of over 20; compare this with the maximum 3.5 to 4 kilometer range of the best light AAA (40mm cannon) or the 1-2 kilometer range of the machine guns mounted on tanks and APCs (the M163 Vulcan and the ZSU-23-4 Shilka have a range of about 1.6 kilometers in antiaircraft mode). Even detecting the attack aircraft poses a serious problem to ground forces, given the range and the aircraft's ability to hide and loiter behind ground cover or in clouds.

Radar-guided missiles do reduce the effectiveness of ground-attack aircraft, but countermeasures such as antiradar missiles, jamming, and chaff are too effective to make radar-guided SAMs a credible defense. The situation in 1991 was very different from that of 1973, when Israeli air forces suffered serious losses from adroit Egyptian and Syrian use of a combination of SAMs and AAA. The main differences appear to be much improved antiradar countermeasures and optically guided standoff weapons such as the Maverick, TOW, and Hellfire. Would optically guided antiaircraft missiles be more effective than radar-guided SAMs?

Would other platforms be more effective in the absence of aerial supremacy? In this context, the extreme opposite of the airplane is the foot soldier, but the Gulf War provides no data to discount his effectiveness. Many soldiers who fought in the Gulf have told us that Iraqi soldiers hidden in trenches and foxholes and equipped with light antitank weapons could have caused serious damage to Coalition armor, if they had chosen to fight.

8. Will tanks and armor become obsolete? Can precision-guided long-range antitank weapons (particularly missiles) be perfected to such an extent that effective protective armor on tanks will become impractically heavy? This is not the case today, but such a future cannot be excluded, even though the best Western armor (Chobham) appears to be extremely effective against the shaped charges carried by missiles.

It is worth stressing the considerable progress made by antitank missiles since 1973, when Israeli tanks were able to seriously degrade the effectiveness of Egyptian optically guided missiles by using machine-gun fire to force the missile operator to take cover, thus causing the missile to become unguided. The effective range of modern vehicle-mounted antitank weapons far exceeds the range of the machine guns mounted on tanks, thereby rendering the 1973 missile countermeasure ineffective.

9. Is there a trend towards capital-intensive armed forces? Throughout the course of history, the trade-off between capital and labor in armed forces has varied, just as it has in industry. Medieval armies composed of heavily armed knights were capital-intensive, whereas the massed infantry of Napoleon's time was relatively labor-intensive.

The performance of high-technology tanks, attack helicopters, and airplanes during the Gulf War suggests that the most effective combat forces of the future might consist primarily of expensive equipment operated by highly trained soldiers.

10. How effective would the Coalition forces have been in less favorable terrain and/or climate? Many of the Coalition weapon systems depended on clear lines of sight to attain optimal performance. Would low cloud covers, fog, and natural obstructions such as trees and hills have significantly degraded their performance? What about a jungle?

Glossary

A-10	Warthog or Thunderbolt. A U.S. ground-attack fixed-wing airplane.
A-6	Intruder. The main type of bomber deployed on U.S. aircraft carriers.
AAA	Antiaircraft artillery.
Aardvark	*See* F-111.
acquire	In military jargon, to determine the position of a target.
AH-1	Cobra. A U.S. ground-attack helicopter.
AH-64	Apache. The most modern U.S. ground-attack helicopter.
AIM-7	Sparrow. A radar-guided air-air missile.
AIM-9	Sidewinder. An infrared-guided air-air missile.
airframe	The wings and fuselage of an aircraft.
Apache	*See* AH-64.
APC	Armored personnel carrier. A lightly-armored vehicle designed to carry troops while protecting them from the shrapnel of indirect artillery fire. Most such modern vehicles carry machine guns and/or antitank missiles, and are properly called IFVs.
APFSDS	*See* sabot.

APV	Armored personnel vehicle. *See* APC.
army	When referring to a unit of organization, the term denotes one or more corps.
ATO	Air tasking order. The list of all flights in the theater of operations.
AV-8	Harrier. A jet capable of vertical takeoffs and landings. Used by British forces in the Falklands War and U.S. Marines in the Gulf War.
avionics	Electronic equipment in an airplane; for example, radar and navigational equipment.
AWACS	Airborne Warning and Control System, an airplane equipped with powerful radar and computer systems so that it can track friendly and hostile aircraft, and direct intercept fighters against threats.
B-52	A very large long-range U.S. strategic bomber.
barrel	A unit of measurement for oil, equal to 42 U.S. gallons, 158.99 liters. There are about 7.3 barrels in a metric ton, at an average density of 0.86.
battalion	A subunit of a regiment, from 500 to 1,200 persons in Western forces (40 to 60 tanks for armored battalions).
battleship	A large warship, carrying the biggest guns and the heaviest armor. Flourished 1875 to 1945.
BDA	Battle damage assessment. Evaluation of the effects of air strikes.
berm	A dirt wall. Used as a linear fortification or to surround a tank or other vehicle.
BMP	A Soviet IFV.
box	In U.S. Air Force jargon, a small, well-delimited area on the ground containing potential targets and assigned to one or more bomber or ground-attack aircraft.
Bradley	A U.S. IFV.
brigade	A subunit of a division. Size is quite variable (from 3,000 to 5,000 persons in U.S. forces), and there are typically three brigades in a division. The commander is typically a brigadier general. *See also* regiment.
BTR	A Soviet IFV.

Buccaneer	An older attack and reconnaissance plane used as a laser designator by U.K. forces during the Gulf War.
captain	*See* officer.
casualty	A person who is killed, wounded, or taken prisoner.
chaff	Strips of radar-reflecting material released by aircraft in order to create a cloud that blinds radar.
chain gun	A type of machine gun, typically mounted on APCs.
Chobham armor	A secret composite of steel, ceramic, plastic, and, in the latest versions, depleted uranium. The alternating layers of material, their shape, and the angle at which the armor is mounted on a tank provide enhanced protection, compared with steel armor against sabot rounds, and greatly enhanced protection against HEAT rounds.
cluster bomb	A canister that releases many grenade-size submunitions, each of which explodes into deadly high-speed fragments.
Cobra	*See* AH-1.
colonel	*See* officer.
company	A subunit of a battalion. Typically from 100 to 200 persons for Western forces, commanded by a captain. The equivalent for artillery units is a battery, and for U.S. cavalry units, a troop.
corporal	A non-commissioned grade higher than private and lower than sergeant.
corps	A group of divisions.
cruise missile	A long-range missile that flies close to the ground to avoid detection.
CWO	Chief warrant officer. *See* Warrant officer.
daisy cutter	A very large bomb.
designation	In military jargon, to indicate a target, as in "laser designation."
destroyer	A warship intermediate in size between a frigate and a battleship.

direct	When referring to artillery fire, a situation in which the guns are visually aimed directly at the target, in the same way as a rifle is aimed. *See also* indirect.
division	A large body of personnel and equipment that can fight on its own, having its own artillery, etc. About 22,000 persons for NATO armies, about 12,000 men for Iraq. Typically commanded by a major general.
EA-6	The electronic warfare version of the A-6.
Eagle	*See* F-15.
envelopment	Reaching and assaulting the enemy's rear, normally through a turning movement.
Exocet	A French-made antiship missile, that had a proven success record.
F-111	Aardvark. A heavy, long-range bomber.
F-117	Nighthawk. A U.S. bomber that uses stealth technology to evade radar observation.
F-14	Tomcat. A long-range interceptor (fighter) deployed on U.S. aircraft carriers.
F-15	Eagle. The C and D versions are modern high-performance primary interceptors (fighters). The E model is a very new bomber.
F-16	Falcon. A small, flexible fighter/bomber.
F-4	Phantom. A relatively old fighter, primarily used in the Wild Weasel configuration to fire HARM missiles during the Gulf War.
F/A-18	Hornet. A fighter/bomber deployed by U.S. Marines and on U.S. aircraft carriers.
Falcon	*See* F-16.
flare	A device released by airplanes that burns in order to create a heat source to confuse infrared-guided missiles.
frigate	A relatively small warship.
fuel-air bomb	A device that relies on a mixture of air and flammable fluids for its explosive effect.

g	A unit of acceleration equal to that imparted by the earth's gravity (9.8 m/sec^2). In air force jargon, an expression for high-acceleration manuevers, as in "pulling g's", or "high g's."
GCC	Gulf Cooperation Council, an alliance of monarchies in the Gulf area: Bahrain, Kuwait, Oman, Qatar, Saudi Arabia, and the United Arab Emirates.
general	A high-ranking officer commanding a brigade or more. U.S. army general ranks are (from lowest to highest): Brigadier General, Major General, Lieutenant General, General.
GI	Jargon for a U.S. soldier (from Government Issue).
GMT	Greenwich Mean Time. The time zone of London, U.K.. Used by the military.
GNP	Gross National Product. A commonly used measure of a nation's total production of goods and services.
GPS	Global Positioning System. A navigational system consisting of receivers that process data transmitted by satellites in order to provide longitude, latitude, and altitude.
hardened	In military jargon, reinforced. For example, a shelter designed to resist blasts from bombs exploding nearby; or a thick steel casing for bombs designed to penetrate concrete walls.
HARM	High-speed anti-radiation missile. A missile that tracks and follows radar emissions to their source. Used to destroy or silence radar-controlled surface-air missile sites and aerial surveillance radars.
Harrier	*See* AV-8.
HEAT	High-explosive antitank round. A projectile that uses a shaped charge to penetrate armor, in contrast to a sabot, which relies on kinetic energy. Antitank rockets and missiles typically have HEAT warheads, but cannon on tanks can also fire HEAT rounds.
Hellfire	A U.S. laser-guided antitank missile carried by Army Apache and Marine Cobra helicopters.
HET	Heavy equipment transporter. A large truck used to move tanks.

Hornet	*See* F/A-18.
Humvee	A light all-terrain wheeled vehicle, somewhat equivalent to the old jeep.
IFV	Infantry Fighting Vehicle. An APC that carries significant offensive weapons, such as machine guns and antitank missiles.
indirect	When referring to artillery fire, a situation in which the guns are aimed at a target that cannot be seen. Fire is controlled by forward observers or aircraft. *See also* direct.
inertial guidance	A navigation system based on gyroscopes that precisely measure the acceleration of an airplane or missile in three dimensions. Given these data, a computer can determine the position of the airplane or missile with respect to its starting point and guide it to its final destination.
infrared	Light of a wavelength that cannot be seen by the human eye. Warm and hot objects emit infrared light.
Intruder	*See* A-6.
IV	Intravenous. Medical jargon for treatment based on replacement of lost bodily fluids.
Jaguar	A French/U.K.-made heavy bomber.
jamming	Use of electronically generated signals to confuse radar detection and missile guidance systems.
JSTARS	An advanced U.S. radar surveillance plane, capable of detecting moving ground vehicles.
kilo	Kilogram.
kilogram	One thousand grams, that is, about 2.2 pounds.
kilometer	One thousand meters, that is, about 0.62 miles.
laser designation	*See* designation.
laser-guided	A bomb or missile equipped with a seeker head and fins so that it can home in on the reflection of a laser beam.
LAI	Light armored infantry. U.S. Marine units equipped with antitank missiles and LAVs.
LAV	Light armored vehicle. A U.S. Marine IFV.

lieutenant	*See* officer.
liter	One thousandth of a cubic meter, that is, about 0.26 U.S. gallons.
lock	In military jargon, to obtain a constant fix on a target, usually by keeping it constantly illuminated by radar.
M1	The most modern U.S. main battle tank.
M113	A U.S. armored personnel carrier.
M16	The personal weapon (automatic rifle) carried by U.S. soldiers.
M60	An older model of U.S. main battle tank.
major	*See* officer.
Maverick	A precision-guided missile, often used by A-10 aircraft against armored vehicles. Different versions exist, with TV or infrared guidance.
MBPD	Million barrels per day, a unit of oil production.
MH-53	Pave Low. A helicopter often used by U.S. special forces.
MICLIC	Mine clearing line charge, a device used to clear obstacle systems, including minefields. It consists of a rocket that is fired to unreel a chain of explosives, the "line charge."
MiG	A Soviet fighter maker.
millimeter	One thousandth of a meter, that is, about 0.04 inches.
Mirage	A French-made fighter.
MLRS	Multiple launch rocket system, an artillery weapon based on missiles.
mm	Millimeter.
MRE	Meal ready to eat: U.S. forces' field rations, generally considered to lack culinary excellence.

NATO	North Atlantic Treaty Organization. A military alliance comprising the United States, Canada, and most Western European countries. Members at the time of the Gulf War included Belgium, Canada, Denmark, France, Germany, Greece, Iceland, Italy, Luxembourg, Netherlands, Norway, Portugal, Spain, U.K., United States, Turkey.
NBC	Nuclear, biological, chemical.
NBC suits	Special clothing and masks worn to protect against biological and chemical agents. Also effective against fallout from nuclear weapons.
NCO	Non-commissioned officer, such as a sergeant or a corporal.
Nighthawk	*See* F-117.
officer	A commander of a military unit, holding a commission from the commander-in-chief. U.S. Army, Marine, or Air Force ranks below general are (from lowest to highest): First or Second Lieutenant, Captain, Major, Lieutenant Colonel, Colonel.
OPEC	Organization of Petroleum Exporting Countries. A group of producing nations, dominated by the Middle Eastern countries, that attempts to limit production and control world oil prices. Members are: Algeria, Indonesia, Iran, Iraq, Kuwait, Libya, Nigeria, Saudi Arabia, United Arab Emirates, Venezuela.
OV-10	A U.S. observation and reconaissance airplane.
Patriot	A U.S. antiaircraft missile system, used to defend against SCUD missiles during the Gulf War.
Pave Tack	A laser-designation system used on the F-111 bomber.
Pesh Merga	Kurdish guerrillas.
Phantom	*See* F-4.
pickle	In U.S. Air Force jargon, the act of pulling the trigger to release a bomb.
platoon	A subunit of a company. Typically from 20 to 40 persons for Western forces, commanded by a lieutenant.

POW	Prisoner of war. A soldier who surrenders or is captured in combat.
precision-guided	A bomb or missile that has a very high accuracy because it is TV- or laser-guided.
private	An enlisted soldier of the lowest rank.
recon	Military jargon for reconnaissance.
regiment	Same as a brigade in most modern armies. Sometimes a subunit of a brigade; typically somewhat over 1,000 men commanded by a colonel.
revetted	Dug in and protected by a dirt wall or revetment.
RPG	Rocket propelled grenade, a light antitank weapon.
RPV	Remotely piloted vehicle, same as UAV.
sabot	Common designation for an antitank round consisting of a thin, heavy metal lance that relies on its high speed and kinetic energy to penetrate armor, in contrast to a HEAT round, which relies on explosive. The correct designation for this type of round is armor-piercing fin stabilized discarding sabot (APFSDS). Properly speaking, the sabot is a light shell surrounding the lance; it falls away when the round exits the gun barrel. The purpose of the sabot is to increase the diameter of the round so that it fills the barrel. Cannon on tanks can fire sabot or HEAT rounds.
Sagger	A Soviet-made antitank missile.
SAM	Surface-to-air missile, an antiaircraft weapon.
SCUD	The NATO designation of the Soviet SS-1 missile, a weapon designed in the 1950s to carry nuclear warheads, and later sold with conventional warheads to less-developed countries.
section	A subunit of a platoon.
sergeant	See NCO.
Shia	Heretical Muslims who believe that only Ali, Mohammed's son-in-law, and his descendants, could lead Islam.
Shiite	The adjective for Shia.

Sidewinder	*See* AIM-9.
Silkworm	A Chinese-made antiship missile.
SLAM	Standoff land-attack missile. An air-launched missile that uses inertial guidance, GPS, and TV-guidance to achieve very high accuracy. It has a range of over 80 kilometers, allowing the launching aircraft to remain out of range of any anti-aircraft systems deployed around the target area.
sortie	An individual aircraft flight, from takeoff to landing.
Soviet	pertaining to the USSR.
Sparrow	*See* AIM-7.
squad	A subunit of a platoon, typically 10 to 12 persons in U.S. forces.
squadron	In U.S. cavalry units, a battalion-sized unit.
stealth	Technology used to reduce the radar signature of aircraft or missiles. Techniques include shaping that reflects radar waves away from their source and the use of radar-absorbent or -transparent materials.
strike	The delivery of a weapon against a specific target. There can be more than one strike in a sortie.
Sunni	Orthodox Muslims who recognize the legitimacy of the Caliphs that succeeded Mohammed.
Sunnite	The adjective for Sunni.
T-55	A Soviet-made main battle tank.
T-64	A Soviet-made main battle tank.
T-72	The most capable Soviet-made main battle tank available to Iraq.
tanker	An airplane capable of refueling other airplanes in flight.
thermal sights	Devices capable of detecting light of a wavelength that cannot be seen by the human eye. Thermal sights detect a different wavelength than infrared sights.
Thunderbolt	*See* A-10.
Tomahawk	A U.S. cruise missile.

Tornado	A European plane. Two versions exist: a bomber and a long-range interceptor (fighter).
TOW	An antitank missile that carries a HEAT warhead. The initials stand for tube-launched, optically wire-guided.
track	In military jargon, any tracked vehicle; for example, an APC.
troop	In U.S. cavalry units, a company-sized unit.
turning	Going around an enemy's flank, in order to reach and assault the enemy's rear.
TV-guided	A bomb or missile equipped with a television camera in its nose and fins so that it can be visually guided to its target.
UAE	United Arab Emirates.
UAV	Unmanned aerial vehicle, also called RPV. A drone aircraft that carries a television camera and other sensors, and is used to observe the battlefield and direct artillery fire.
U.K.	United Kingdom of Great Britain and Northern Ireland.
U.N.	United Nations.
United States	United States of America.
USSR	Union of Soviet Socialist Republics. A now-defunct state which was dominated by Russia and controlled by the Communist Party.
Warrant officer	An officer, usually a specialist, holding a so-called warrant rather than a commission. A higher rank is chief warrant officer; the U.S. Army recognizes four ranks: CWO-1, CWO-2, CWO-3, and CWO-4.
Warsaw Pact	During the Cold War, an alliance among the USSR and its allies in Eastern Europe. The main potential military threat to NATO.
Warthog	*See* A-10.
West	When not used in a specific sense, the economic community formed by the United States and its close allies: Canada, Western Europe, and Japan.
Wild Weasel	*See* F-4.

Selected Bibliography

BOOKS AND SPECIAL REPORTS: PRIMARY SOURCES

48 TFW. *Operation Desert Storm*. Taif, Saudi Arabia, undated.

Austrian Landesverteidigungsakademie, Zentral-dokumentation. *Sonderheft: Der Golfkrieg 1991*. Vienna, 1 December 1992.

Bengio, Ofra. *Saddam Speaks on the Gulf Crisis*. Dayan Center for Middle Eastern and African Studies, Tel Aviv University, 1992.

Benson, Nicholas. *Rat's Tales: The Staffordshire Regiment at War in the Gulf*. Brassey's, 1993.

bin Sultan, HRH Gen. Khaled. *Desert Warrior: A Personal View of the Gulf War by the Joint Forces Commander*. HarperCollins, 1995.

Cohen, Eliot A., et al. *Gulf War Air Power Survey*. U.S. Department of the Air Force, 1993.

Conrad, Scott W. *Moving the Force: Desert Storm and Beyond*. Institute for National Strategic Studies, National Defense University, 1994.

Craft, Douglas W. *An Operational Analysis of the Persian Gulf War*. U.S. Army War College, Carlisle Barracks, 1992.

De La Billière, Gen. Sir Peter. *Storm Command: A Personal Account of the Gulf War*. HarperCollins, 1993.

Egyptian Ministry of Defense. *Al Kitab Harab Tahrir Kuwait* (Report on the War to Liberate Kuwait). 1992.

Hine, Air Chief Marshal Sir Patrick. "Despatch." *The London Gazette*. 28 June 1991, second supplement.

Hobbs, Frank. *Population Estimates for Iraq*. Center for International Research, U.S. Bureau of the Census, January 1991.

International Labour Organization. *Migration*. 1992.

Iraq. *Annual Abstract of Statistics*. 1988.

Kamiya, Maj. Jason K. *A History of the 24th Mechanized Infantry Division Combat Team during Operation Desert Storm*. 24th Infantry Division (Mechanized) Public Affairs Office, 1992.

Kuwait. *Annual Statistical Abstract*. 1989.

Marshman, Lt. Col. Stephen J. *Lessons from the Desert*. U.S. Army War College, Carlisle Barracks, 1993.

McNab, Andy. *Bravo Two Zero*. Corgi, 1994.

OECD. *Economic Outlook*. 1990-1991.

OECD. *Energy Statistics*. 1987-1988.

OECD. *Main Economic Indicators*. 1990-1991.

Pagonis, Gen. William G. *Moving Mountains: Lessons in Leadership and Logistics from the Gulf War*. Harvard Business School Press, 1992.

Peters, John and John Nichol. *Tornado Down*. Michael Joseph, 1992.

Powell, Gen. Colin L. *My American Journey*. Ballantine, 1995.

Primakov, Yevgeni. *Missione a Baghdad*. Ponte alle Grazie, 1991.

Rivista Italiana Difesa. *Guerra nel Golfo: L'Impegno Italiano*. 1 January 1992, supplement.

Saudi Arabia. *Statistical Yearbook*. 1987-1989.

Saudi Arabian Ministry of Defense. *Al-Difaa* (Defense Magazine). 1991, 1992.

Saudi Press Agency. *Asdah al-Moukef al-Saudi Khilal Ahadath al-Kalij al-Arabi* (The Saudi Position During the Events in the Arabian Gulf). 1991.

Scales, Brig. Gen. Robert H., Jr. *Certain Victory: The U.S. Army in the Gulf War*. U.S. Army, 1993.

Schwarzkopf, Norman H. *It Doesn't Take a Hero: The Autobiograpy*. Bantam Books, 1992.

Service d'Information et de Relations Publiques des Armées. *Armées d'Aujourdhui*, no. 161 (June-July 1991).

Service d'Information et de Relations Publiques des Armées. *Terre Magazine*, no. 22-23 (March-April 1991).

Sifry, Micah L. and Christofer Cerf. *The Gulf War Reader*. Times Books, 1991.

Swain, Col. Richard M. *"Lucky War": Third Army in Desert Storm*. U.S. Army Command and General Staff College, 1994.

U.K. Secretary of State for Defence. *Statement on the Defence Estimates*. July 1991.

United Nations. *Energy Statistics Yearbook*. 1980-1990.

United Nations. *Monthly Bulletin of Statistics*. 1990-1991.

United Nations. *National Account Statistics*. 1985-1988.

United Nations. *The United Nations and the Iraq-Kuwait Conflict 1990-1996*. 1996.

U.S. Air Force. *Air Force Performance in Desert Storm*. April 1991.

U.S. Air Force. Briefing by Gen. Tony McPeak. Washington, D.C., 15 March 1991.

U.S. Air Force. *Fact Sheet: Airpower in Operation Desert Storm*. March 1991.

U.S. Army VII Corps. *The Desert Jayhawk: Opertion Desert Shield/Storm*. 1991.

U.S. Central Command. Briefings during operation Desert Storm. Riyadh, January-March 1991.

U.S. Department of Defense. Briefings during operation Desert Shield, Washington, D.C., August 1990-January 1991.

U.S. Department of Defense. Briefings during operation Desert Storm, Washington, D.C., January-March 1991.

U.S. Department of Defense. *Conduct of the Persian Gulf Conflict: An Interim Report to Congress*. July 1991.

U.S. Department of Defense. *Conduct of the Persian Gulf War: Final Report to Congress*. April 1992.

U.S. Department of Defense Persian Gulf War Illness Senior Level Oversight Panel. *Persian Gulf War Illness Investigation Team Information*. http://www.dtic.dla.mil/gulflink.

U.S. Department of the Air Force. *Reaching Globally, Reaching Powerfully: The United States Air Forces in the Gulf War.* September 1991.

U.S. Department of the Air Force. *White Paper: Air Force Performance in Desert Storm.* April 1991.

U.S. Department of the Navy. *The United States Navy in "Desert Shield"/"Desert Storm."* 15 May 1991.

U.S. General Accounting Office. *Operation Desert Storm: Evaluation of the Air War.* 2 July 1996.

U.S. Marine First Air Naval Gunfire Liaison Company. *After Action Report for the Battle of Khafji 29 January-1 February 1991.*

U.S. Marine First Air Naval Gunfire Liaison Company. *Command Chronology for the Period 1 January Through 31 January 1991.*

U.S. Marine First Air Naval Gunfire Liaison Company. *First Anglico After Action Report, Liberation of Kuwait, 21 February to 1 March 1991.*

U.S. Senate Committee on Foreign Relations. *Chemical Weapons Use in Kurdistan: Iraq's Final Offensive.* 1988.

BOOKS AND SPECIAL REPORTS: SECONDARY SOURCES AND REFERENCE WORKS

Abdel-Malek, Anouar. *Il Pensiero Politico Arabo Contemporaneo.* Editori Riuniti, 1973.

Abu-Hakima, Ahmad Mustafa. *The Modern History of Kuwait.* Luzac, 1983.

al-Khalil, Samir. *Irak: La Machine Infernale.* Jean-Claude Lattes, 1991.

al-Khalil, Samir. *Republic of Fear: Saddam's Iraq.* Hutchinson Radius, 1991.

al-Marayati, Abid A. *A Diplomatic History of Modern Iraq.* Robert Speller and Sons, 1961.

Atkinson, Rick. *Crusade: The Untold Story of the Persian Gulf War.* Houghton Mifflin, 1993.

Balta, Paul. *Iran-Irak: Une Guerre de 5000 Ans.* Anthropos, 1987.

Bausani, Alessandro. *Il Corano.* Bibilioteca Universale Rizzoli, 1988.

Bausani, Alessandro. *Islam.* Garzanti, 1980.

Beaumont, Roger. *War, Chaos, and History.* Praeger, 1994.

Berque, Jacques. *Gli Arabi.* Piccola Biblioteca Einaudi, 1978.

Blackwell, James. *Thunder in the Desert: The Strategy and Tactics of the Persian Gulf War.* Bantam Books, 1991.

Blair, Col. Arthur. *At War in the Gulf: A Chronology.* Texas A&M University Press, 1992.

Boyne, Walter, et al. *Weapons of Desert Storm.* Publications International, 1991.

Brown, Ben and David Shukman. *All Necessary Means: Inside the Gulf War.* BBC, 1991.

Bulloch, Johan and Harvey Morris. *Saddam's War: The Origins of the Kuwaiti Crisis and the International Response.* Faber, 1991.

Chubin, Shahram and Charles Tripp. *Iran and Iraq at War.* I.B. Tauris, 1988.

Clausewitz, Carl von. *On War.* Barnes and Noble, 1966; abridged version, Penguin, 1982.

Cooley, John K. *Payback: America's Long War in the Middle East.* Brassey's, 1991.

Corm, Georges. *Le Proche-Orient Eclaté 1956-1991.* Gallimard, 1991.

David, Peter. *Triumph in the Desert.* Random House, 1991.

Douhet, Giulio. *The Command of the Air.* Coward-McCann, 1942.

Dunnigan, James F. and Austin Bay. *From Shield to Storm: High-Tech Weapons, Military Strategy, and Coalition Warfare in the Persian Gulf.* William Morrow, 1992.

Dupuy, Trevor N., et al. *How to Defeat Saddam Hussein.* Warner Books, 1991.

Elliott, Kimberly, Gary Hufbauer, and Jeffrey Scott. *Economic Sanctions Reconsidered.* Institute for International Economics, 1990.

Ferrard, Stephane. *Les Armes de la Guerre du Golf.* Presses de la Cité, 1991.

Freedman, Lawrence, and Efraim Karsh. *The Gulf Conflict 1990-1992: Diplomacy and War in the New World Order.* Princeton University Press, 1993.

Friedman, Norman. *Desert Victory: The War for Kuwait.* United States Naval Institute, 1992.

Fuller, Maj. Gen. J.F.C. *The Conduct of War: 1789-1961.* Eyre and Spottiswoode, 1961.

Game Designers Workshop. *Desert Shield Fact Book.* Game Designers Workshop, 1991.

Ghareeb, Edmund. *The Kurdish Question in Iraq.* Syracuse University Press, 1981.

Gordon, Michael R., and Gen. Bernand E. Trainor. *The Generals' War: The Inside Story of the Conflict in the Gulf.* Little, Brown, 1995.

Graz, Liesl. *L'Irak au Present.* Editions des Trois Continents, 1979.

Graz, Liesl. *Le Golfe des Turbulences.* L'Harmattan, 1991.

Gresh, Alain, and Dominique Vidal. *Golfe: Clefs pour une Guerre Annoncee.* Le Monde Editions, 1991.

Gunston, Bill, and Mike Spick. *Modern Air Combat.* Salamander Books, 1983.

Gunston, Bill and Mike Spick. *Modern Fighting Helicopters.* Salamander Books, 1986.

Hallion, Richard P. *Storm over Iraq.* Smithsonian Institution Press, 1992.

Heikal, Mohamed. *Illusions of Triumph: An Arab View of the Gulf War.* HarperCollins, 1993.

Helms, Christine M. *Iraq: Eastern Flank of the Arab World.* The Brookings Institution, 1984.

Henderson, Simon. *Instant Empire: Saddam Hussein's Ambition for Iraq.* Mercury House, 1991.

Hilsman, Roger. *George Bush vs. Saddam Hussein: Military Success! Political Failure?* Presidio Press, 1992.

Hiro, Dilip. *Desert Shield to Desert Storm: The Second Gulf War.* Paladin, 1991.

Hiro, Dilip. *The Longest War: The Iran-Iraq Military Conflict.* Paladin Grafton Books, 1990.

Hitti, Philip K. *History of the Arabs.* Macmillan, 1964.

Hussein, Saddam. *Iraqi Policies in Perspective.* Translation and Foreign Languages Publishing House, Baghdad, 1981.

Ishow, Habib. *Le Koweit: Evolution Politique, Economique et Sociale.* L'Harmattan, 1991.

Johnson, Lt. Col. Douglas V., Stephen C. Pelletiere, and Leif R. Rosenberger. *Iraqi Power and U.S. Security in the Middle East.* U.S. Army War College, 1990.

Jones, Archer. *The Art of War in the Western World.* Oxford University Press, 1989.

Jones, Archer. *Elements of Military Strategy: An Historical Approach.* Praeger, 1996.

Karsh, Efraim, ed. *The Iran-Iraq War: Impact and Implications.* St. Martin's Press, 1989.

Karsh, Efraim and Inari Rautsi. *Saddam Hussein: A Political Biography.* Futura, 1991.

Keegan, John. *The Face of Battle*. Penguin Books, 1978.

Khadduri, Majid. *The Gulf War: The Origins and Implications of the Iraq-Iran Conflict*. Oxford University Press, 1988.

Khadduri, Majid. *Republican Iraq: A Study in Iraqi Politics since the Revolution of 1958*. Oxford University Press, 1969.

Khadduri, Majid. *Socialist Iraq: A Study in Iraqi Politics since 1968*. The Middle East Institute, 1978.

La Découverte. *L'Etat du Monde 1991*. La Découverte, 1990.

Lanchester, F. W. *Aircraft in Warfare: The Dawn of the Fourth Arm*. Constable, 1916.

Langendorf, Jean-Jacques. *Le Bouclier et la Tempête: Aspects militaires de la guerre du Golf*. Georg, 1995.

Lauterpacht, E., et al. *The Kuwait Crisis—Basic Documents (1991)*. Cambridge Grotius, 1991.

Liddell Hart, B. H. *History of the Second World War*. Pan Books, 1973.

Longrigg, Stephen H. *Iraq 1900 to 1950: A Political, Social and Economic History*. Oxford University Press, 1953.

Maalouf, Amin. *The Crusades Through Arab Eyes*. Schocken Books, 1984.

Mandeles, Mark D., Thomas C. Hone, and Sanford S. Terry. *Managing "Command and Control" in the Persian Gulf War*. Praeger, 1996.

Mansfield, Peter. *Kuwait: Vanguard of the Gulf*. Hutchinson, 1990.

Marr, Phebe. *The Modern History of Iraq*. Longman, 1985.

Mazarr, Michael J., Don M. Snider, and James A. Blackwell, Jr. *Desert Storm: The Gulf War and What We Learned*. Westview Press, 1993.

Micheletti, Eric and Yves Debay. *Operation Desert Shield*. Windrow and Greene, 1991.

Middlebrook, Martin. *Task Force: The Falklands War, 1982*. Penguin, 1987.

Military History Magazine. *Desert Storm*. Empire Press, 1991.

Miller, David and Christoper F. Foss. *Modern Land Combat*. Salamander Books, 1987.

Miller, Judith and Laurie Mylroie. *Saddam Hussein and the Crisis in the Gulf*. Times Books, 1990.

Morrison, David E. *Television and the Gulf War*. John Libbey, 1992.

Morse, Stan, ed. *Gulf Air War Debrief*. Aerospace Publishing, 1991.

Mowlana, Hamid, George Gerbner, and Herbert I. Schiller, eds. *Triumph of the Image: The Media's War in the Persian Gulf—a Global Perspective*. Westview Press, 1992.

Nonneman, Gerd. *Iraq, the Gulf States and the War: A Changing Relationship 1980-1986*. Ithaca Press, 1986.

Nye, Joseph S., Jr., and Roger K. Smith, eds. *After the Storm: Lessons from the Gulf War*. Aspen Institute and Madison Books, 1992.

Palmer, Michael. *L'Etat des Media*. La Découverte-Mediaspouvoirs-CFPJ, 1991.

Patai, Raphael. *The Arab Mind*. Charles Scribner's Sons, 1983.

Postol, Theodore. "Lessons for SDI from the Gulf War Patriot Experience: A Technical Perspective." Testimony before the U.S. House Armed Services Committee, 16 April 1991.

Postol, Theodore. "Policy Issues for Theater Missile Defenses in a Shrinking Budget." Paper prepared for the U.S. House of Representatives, 29 October 1991.

Postol, Theodore. *The Prospects for Successful Air-Defense Against Chemically-Armed Tactical Ballistic Missile Attacks on Urban Areas*. Defense and Arms

Control Study Program Working Paper. Center for International Studies, Massachusetts Institute of Technology, March 1991.

Record, Jeffrey. *Hollow Victory: A Contrary View of the Gulf War*, Brassey's, 1993.

Ridgeway, James, et al. *The March to War*. Four Walls Eight Windows, 1991.

Rodinson, Maxime. *Gli Arabi*. Sansoni, 1980.

Rossi, Pierre. *L'Irak des Révoltés*. Le Seuil, 1962.

Runciman, Steven. *A History of the Crusades*. Penguin, 1980.

Saint-Prot, Charles. *Saddam Hussein: Un "Gaullisme" Arabe?* Albin Michel, 1987.

Salinger, Pierre and Eric Laurent. *Guerre du Golfe: Le Dossier Secret*. Olivier Orban, 1991. Also available in English as *Secret Dossier: The Hidden Agenda behind the Gulf War*. Penguin Books, 1991.

Sasson, Jean. *The Rape of Kuwait*. Knightsbridge, 1990.

Schofield, Richard. *Kuwait and Iraq: Historical Claims and Territorial Disputes*. Royal Institute of International Affairs, 1991.

Sciolino, Elaine. *The Outlaw State: Saddam Hussein's Quest for Power and the Gulf Crisis*. Wiley, 1991.

Summers, Col. Harry G. *On Strategy II: A Critical Analysis of the Gulf War*. Dell Publishing, 1992.

Survival Magazine. *The Gulf War. Survival*, 33, no. 3 (May/June 1991).

Taylor, Philip M. *War and the Media: Propaganda and Persuasion in the Gulf War*. Manchester University Press, 1992.

Timmerman, Kenneth R. *The Death Lobby: How the West Armed Iraq*. Houghton Mifflin, 1991.

Toynbee, Arnold. *A Study of History*. Weathervane, 1972.

Tzu, Sun. *The Art of War*. Translated by Samuel B. Griffith. Oxford University Press, 1963.

U.S. News & World Report. *Triumph without Victory: The Unreported History of the Persian Gulf War*. Times Books, 1992.

Vernier, Bernard. *L'Irak d'Aujourd'hui*. Armand Colin, 1963.

VSD. *La Guerre du Golfe*. VSD, 1991.

Watson, Bruce W., et al. *Military Lessons of the Gulf War*. Greenhill Books, 1991.

Wolton, Dominique. *War Game: L'Information et la Guerre*. Flammarion, 1991.

Woodrow, Alain. *Information Manipulation*. Du Felin, 1991.

Woodward, Bob. *The Commanders*. Simon and Schuster, 1991.

Yant, Martin. *Desert Mirage: The True Story of the Gulf War*. Prometheus Books, 1991.

ARTICLES

Axelgard, Frederick W. "A New Iraq? The Gulf War and Implications for U.S. Policy." *The Washington Papers*, 133 (The Center for Strategic and International Studies, 1988).

Bahgat, Gawdat. "Regional Peace and Stability in the Gulf." *Security Dialogue*, 26, no. 3 (1995): 317-330.

Balaj, Barbara S. "France and The Gulf War." *Mediterranean Quarterly* (Summer, 1993): 96-116.

Brooks, Geraldine. "Thanks to Saddam, Women Warriors Join Arab Emirate's Army." *Wall Street Journal Europe* (8 August 1991): 1.

Chubin, Shahram. "Reflections on the Gulf War." *Survival* (July-August 1986).

Cigar, Norman. "Iraq's Strategic Mindset and the Gulf War: Blueprint for Defeat." *Journal of Strategic Studies* (January 1992).

Dannreuther, Roland. "The Gulf Conflict: A Political and Strategic Analysis." *Adelphi Papers*, no. 264 (Winter 1991-1992).

Donini, Pier Giovanni. "Formazione e Sviluppo del Kuwait." *Politica Internazionale* (Istituto per le Relazioni tra l'Italia e i Paesi dell'Africa, America Latina e Medio Oriente, November-December 1990).

Evron, Yair. "Gulf Crisis and War: Regional Rules of the Game and Policy and Theoretical Implications." *Security Studies*, 4, no. 1 (Autumn 1994): 115-154.

Fowell, David and J. R. Wilson. "UAVs Win Plaudits in The Storm." *International Defense Review* (October 1991).

Freedman, Lawrence and Efraim Karsh. "How Kuwait Was Won: Strategy in the Gulf War." *International Security*, 16, no. 2, (Fall 1991): 5-41.

Gallois, Pierre M. "Le Paradox de la Mère des Batailles." *Stratégique: La Guerre du Golf*, no. 51-52 (March/April 1991).

Gallois, Pierre M. "Rivalry in the Gulf or the Birth of a Crisis." *Geopolitique*, no. 32 (Winter 1990-1991): 58-61.

Gertz, Nurith. "Routine and Normality as Objects of Desire: Israel and the 1991 Gulf War." *Israeli Affairs*, 1, no. 4 (Summer, 1995): 128-149.

Ghebali, Victor-Yves. "Le Conseil de Securité Face au Conflict Irak-Koweit." *Le Trimestre du Monde* (4th quarter 1990).

Guazzone, Laura. "Italy and the Gulf Crisis: European and Domestic Dimensions." *The International Spectator*, 26, no. 4 (October-December 1991): 57-74.

Harris, John L. Editorial in *Peace Review: The International Quarterly of World Peace* (Winter/Spring 1991).

Heidenreich, John G. "The Gulf War: How Many Iraqis Died." *Foreign Policy*, no. 90 (Spring 1993).

Henry, Paul-Marc, "The Middle East: the Crossroads of History." *Geopolitique*, no. 32 (International Institute of Geopolitics, Winter 1990-1991).

Hoveyda, Fereydoun. "Deciphering the Persian Gulf Crisis: Toward an Understanding of the Arab Mindset." *Geopolitique*, no. 32 (International Institute of Geopolitics, Winter 1990-1991).

Howorth, Jolyon. "United Kingdom Defence Policy and the Gulf War." *The Gulf Crisis, Contemporary European Affairs*, 4, no. 1 (1991): 149-161.

Huntington, Samuel. "The Clash of Civilizations." *Foreign Affairs*, 72, no. 3 (1993).

Johnson, Robert, and Caleb Solomon. "'Friendly Fire' Ends the Soaring Career of American Colonel" and "Chilling Tapes Show How Soldiers Died in 'Friendly Fire'." *Wall Street Journal Europe* (12 September and 7 November 1991).

Idemudia, Taiwo. "OPEC and the International Oil Markets." *OPEC Review* (Summer 1989).

Ishow, Habib. "The Reasons Behind the Invasion of Kuwait." *Geopolitique*, no. 32 (International Institute of Geopolitics, Winter 1990-1991).

Karabell, Zachary. "Backfire: U.S. Policy toward Iraq, 1988-2 August 1990." *Middle East Journal*, 49, no. 1 (Winter 1995).

Karsh, Efraim and Inari Rautsi. "Why Saddam Hussein Invaded Kuwait." *Survival*, 33, no. 1 (January-February 1992): 18-30.

Kincade, William H. "On the Brink in the Gulf. Part 1: Onset of the 'Classic' 1990 Crisis." *Security Studies*, 2, no. 2 (Winter 1992). "Part 2: The Route to War." *Security Studies*, 2, no. 15 (1992).

Kindsvatter, Lt. Col. Peter S. "VII Corps in the Gulf War." *Military Review*, (January, February, and June 1992). Articles respectively subtitled "Deployment and Preparation for Desert Storm," "Ground Offensive," and "Post-Cease-Fire Operations."

Kriegel, Annie.   "The Ambiguities of Soviet Policy."   *Geopolitique*, no. 32 (International Institute of Geopolitics, Winter 1990-1991).

"Kuwait Quits Smoking." *Science* (13 March 1992): 1357.

Marshall, Eliot. "Fatal Error: How Patriot Overlooked a SCUD." *Science* (13 March 1992): 1347.

Masters, C. D., D. H. Root, and E. D. Attanasi. "Resource Constraints in Petroleum Production Potential." *Science* (12 July 1991): 146.

Maull, Hanns W.   "Energy and Resources: The Strategic Dimension."   *Adelphi Papers*, no. 244 (Autumn 1989): 500-518.

Mortimer, Edward J. "New Fault-lines: Is a North-South Confrontation Inevitable in Security Terms?" *Adelphi Papers,* no. 266 (Winter 1991-1992): 74-86.

Mueller, John. "The Perfect Enemy: Assessing the Gulf War." *Security Studies*, 5, no. 1 (Autumn 1995): 77.

Newhouse, John.   "The Diplomatic Round: Misreadings."   *The New Yorker* (18 February 1991).

Noja, Sergio.   "I Due Livelli del Nazionalismo Arabo."   *Politica Internazionale* (Istituto per le Relazioni tra l'Italia e i Paesi dell'Africa, America Latina e Medio Oriente, November-December 1990).

Norman, Colin. "Iraq's Bomb Program: A Smoking Gun Emerges." *Science* (1 November 1991): 664.

Nosenko, Vladimir. "Iraq's Aggression against Kuwait in the Context of North-South Relations." *Mediterranean Quarterly*, 3, no. 2 (Spring 1992): 96-108.

Pearl, Daniel. "Hiding and Seeking: Iraq's Best Planes Are Mainly in Iran." *Wall Street Journal Europe* (30 April 1998): 1.

Postol, Theodore. "Lessons of the Gulf War Experience with Patriot." *International Security*, 16, no. 3 (Winter 1991-1992): 119-171.

Reifenberg, Anne. "Bloody but Unbowed, Iraq Is Weathering U.N. Trade Sanctions." *Wall Street Journal Europe* (3 October 1996): 1.

Salamé, Ghassan. "Bush and the Gulf Crisis." *Geopolitique*, no. 32 (International Institute of Geopolitics, Winter 1990-1991).

Salinger, Pierre. "The United States, the United Nations, and the Gulf War." *Middle East Journal*, 49, no. 4 (Autumn 1995): 595-613.

Shrader, Charles R. "Gulf War Logistics." *Parameters* (Winter 1995-1996): 142-148.

Skelly, Robert A. Letter in *Science* (24 January 1992): 382.

Terzian, Pierre, "The Gulf Crisis from the Point of View of Oil." *Geopolitique*, no. 32 (International Institute of Geopolitics, Winter 1990-1991).

van Bruinessen, Martin. "The Kurds Between Iran and Iraq." *Middle East Report*, no. 141 (1986).

"Viral Tall Tale." *Science* (24 January 1992).

Weitzman, Bruce M.   "The Inter-Arab System and the Gulf War: Continuity and Change."   *Occasional Papers*, Series 2, no. 1 (Carter Center of Emory University, 1992).

NEWSPAPERS

Al Anouar (Tunisia)
Al Chaab (Algeria)
Arab News (Saudi Arabia)

Corriere della Sera (Italy)
El Moujahid (Algeria)
France Soir (France)
International Herald Tribune (Europe)
Le Figaro (France)
Le Monde (France)
Liberation (France)
L'Opinion (Morocco)
New York Times (United States)
Repubblica (Italy)
Sunday Times (U.K.)
The Times (U.K.)
Wall Street Journal Europe (Europe)
Washington Post (United States)

MAGAZINES

Espresso (Italy)
Le Monde Diplomatique (France)
Newsweek (United States)
Panorama (Italy)
Science (United States)
Time (United States)

Index

About the Authors

ALBERTO BIN holds a Ph.D. from the Institut des Hautes Etudes Internationales in Geneva, Switzerland. He is the Deputy Director of the Mediterranean Academy of Diplomatic Studies, University of Malta, and holder of the Chair of Mediterranean Diplomacy and Relations. He is also Visiting Professor at the Department of Political Studies, University of Catania. His research interests include Italian foreign policy, and issues of security and cooperation in the Mediterranean and Middle East.

RICHARD HILL holds a Ph.D. in Statistics from Harvard University and a B.S. degree in Mathematics from the Massachusetts Institute of Technology. He has worked for the National Bureau of Economic Research and other organizations as a statistician and an economic analyst, and has taught at Webster University in Geneva, Switzerland. He has visited the Middle East several times.

ARCHER JONES is Professor Emeritus at North Dakota State University. He also served as Director of the Institute for Regional Studies which sponsored research and served as the University's press. He is author of numerous articles on military and economic history, and he jointly authored three award-winning Civil War books. His books include *Elements of Military Strategy: An Historical Approach* (Praeger Publishers, 1996) and *The Art of War in the Western World* (1989).

ISBN 0-275-96319-5

HARDCOVER BAR CODE